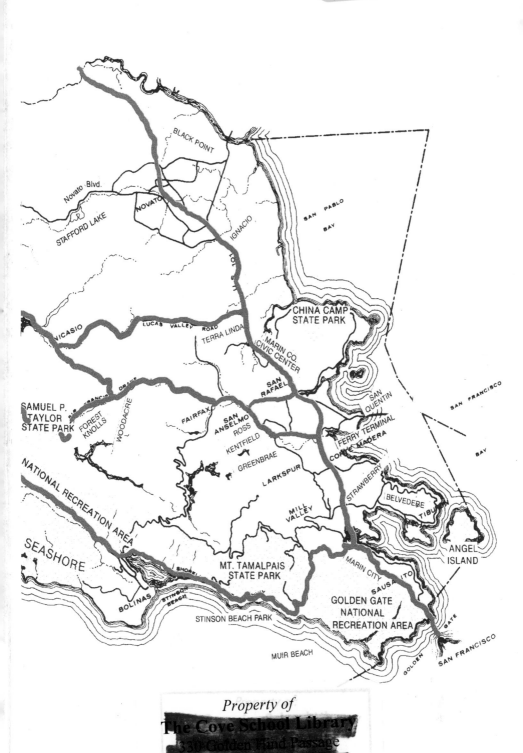

Making the Most of Marin

A California Guide

This Book was Donated
by

Patricia Arrigoni
Author

to Support the Education of Students
in Marin County

Making the Most of Marin

A California Guide

Third Edition, Revised 2001

by Patricia Arrigoni

TRAVEL PUBLISHERS INTERNATIONAL

To Peter

Who encouraged me to write it over one more time . . .

First Printing, 1981
Second printing, completely revised, 1990
Third printing, 1991
Fourth printing, 1994
Fifth printing, completely revised, 2001

Published by Travel Publishers International
P.O. Box 1030, Fairfax, California 94978

www.travelpublishers.com

Library of Congress Cataloging-in-Publication Data

Arrigoni, Patricia
   Making the Most of Marin: A California Guide/by Patricia Arrigoni
     p. cm.
   Includes bibliographical references.
   ISBN 0-9625468-7-9
   1. Marin County (California)—Description and travel—guidebooks.
   2. Marin County (California)—History, Local. I. Title

Library of Congress Control Number: 00-091459
Printed in the United States of America

Book Design by Janet Bollow
Cover Design by Janet Bollow
Edited by Carroll Dana
Horse Trail Map by Connie Berto

Cover photographs   *Front cover (counter clockwise):* The Golden Gate Bridge at night (photo by Bob David, Golden Gate Bridge, Highway and Transportation District); the rugged Pacific coast; Bolinas Mesa overlooking Duxbury Reef in the Point Reyes National Seashore; Larkspur Ferry Terminal; Sailing on the Seadrift Lagoon, Stinson Beach. *Spine:* California poppies, the state flower. *Back cover:* Wendy Schirripa and Mary Liz Rooney hug a redwood tree at Muir Woods National Monument; Sunset at Stinson Beach.

Frontispiece photographs   *Page ii:* Larkspur Ferry Terminal with Mount Tamalpais in the background. *Page iv:* Point Reyes Beach, Point Reyes National Seashore.

All photos in this book have been taken by the author unless otherwise acknowledged.

Contents

Introduction

M arin County has been the vacation playland of San Francisco residents since ferryboats first brought visitors across the bay to its pristine shores in the second half of the nineteenth century. When the summer fog poured through the Golden Gate and settled over the city, San Franciscans headed north to the warm sunny hills and valleys of Marin. From the ferry landings at Sausalito and Tiburon, they boarded trains or stagecoaches and headed for Mill Valley to hike on the trails of Mt. Tamalpais, or ride "the crookedest railroad in the world" to the mountain's summit and then glide down to Muir Woods to gaze at the towering redwoods. The heartier souls would go to tent camps at Stinson Beach, or to summer cottages in the San Geronimo Valley. Young people enjoyed the Rose Bowl dances in Larkspur or the Portuguese festivals in Sausalito. Lured by the natural beauty of the county, many of these San Franciscans eventually made their home here.

Marin had originally been settled in the early 1800s by Spanish padres, who established a mission in San Rafael and set about converting the local Coast Miwok Indians. Large Mexican land grants divided up the rest of the land. Life on these ranchos was leisurely and comfortable. The pace quickened with the arrival of the railroad and ferries. Then, in 1906, refugees from the big San Francisco earthquake and fire began moving into Marin, increasing its population by sixty percent. Towns sprang up overnight. The Arrigoni family was part of

Old steam engine Number 498 (without its large diamond spark-attesting smoke stack), on top Mt. Tamalpais in the early 1900s. Note cable car. (Photo courtesy of Nancy Skinner)

this migration, arriving in 1907. My husband's grandfather, Dante Divita, settled in Manor (now Fairfax), where his descendants remain to this day.

With the opening of the Golden Gate Bridge in 1937, a new rush to Marin began. Tied now to the city, Marin grew into a suburban community. The new residents (an affluent, educated group with a high percentage of professional people and artists) shared with the early settlers an appreciation for the beauty of their county and a desire to preserve it. As Marin's population increased, adamant conservationists fought against exploitation of the land, with great success—the Pacific coastline is unspoiled, protected by thousands of acres of parkland. Virgin redwood forests remain; West Marin is still rural, and open space borders developed areas.

Today, Marin County is one of the most beautiful places to live or visit in the world. Millions of people come each year, attracted by the picturesque villages, extensive parkland, and also by a curiosity about the casual (and often over-publicized) lifestyle of Marinites.

Making the Most of Marin is an insider's guide to the pleasures of our county—to the well-known places: the beaches, seaside villages, redwood forests, and the mountain; but also to little-known spots even residents may have missed: an earthquake trail, China Camp State Park, old forts and bunkers in the Headlands, historic Victorian homes, and unique shops and restaurants. There are also historical sketches of Marin towns, based on extensive research and on interviews with descendants of Marin's pioneer families.

This updated third edition (and fifth printing) of *Making the Most of Marin* is illustrated with photographs taken by the author, and some rare historical pictures of Marin shot in the nineteenth and early part of the twentieth centuries. This edition contains several brand new chapters: Chapter 13, Dog Parks; Chapter 14, Sports: Golf, Tennis, Fishing; and Chapter 18, Marin County Public Schools. Scattered throughout are new short biographies on twenty Marin residents who have contributed in a large way toward making Marin County the most strikingly beautiful and intellectually challenging county in California.

For current hours, admission fees and other information, call the phone numbers included or look up details on the internet as listed. All telephone numbers in Marin have a 415 area code.

Golden Gate Bridge

A Miracle of Engineering

The magnificent Golden Gate Bridge linking San Francisco and Marin County is an international symbol of the entire Bay Area and is one of the most visited attractions in the world. Its art deco design is one of essential simplicity, the graceful lines of a single suspended span running between two well-proportioned post-braced towers. Known poetically as the "Span of Gold," the bridge is actually painted a vivid orange-vermilion color called "International Orange."

Visitors gazing at its brilliant color and splendid artistic sweep can little guess at the swirl of controversy that preceded its construction. The Golden Gate Bridge District, consisting of San Francisco and five northern California counties, was formed in 1923 by the California legislature for the purpose of financing the building of the bridge by selling bonds totaling $35 million. For six years the District was dragged through various courts in an effort to prevent construction.

The Citizens Committee Against the Golden Gate Bridge Bonds argued that the bridge was physically and financially impossible, that it was an outrage, a wildcat scheme. Opponents screamed that a bridge would mar San Francisco's beautiful natural harbor entrance and destroy Sausalito's splendid isolation. Further, they argued that enemy bombing or gunfire could destroy the bridge and bottle up the harbor. Many wor-

◀ *Looking at Marin from on top of the South Tower of the Golden Gate Bridge.*

ried about an earthquake. Others called it an economic crime, claiming that Marin was so sparsely settled it would not support sufficient traffic to allow a toll bridge to meet its financial obligations.

Despite all the controversy, the District moved ahead. On August 15, 1929, Joseph B. Strauss of Strauss Engineering of Chicago was hired as chief engineer. Strauss recommended a single suspension bridge, which he felt would be effective in resisting irregular and turbulent wind forces as well as earthquake movements. His theory proved correct and the bridge has withstood severe storms; winds blowing 50 miles-per-hour have swayed the bridge laterally 4.9 feet, and vertically up to 2 feet, without damage. On December 1, 1951, a record wind was recorded of 69 miles-per-hour.

Actual designing of the bridge took place in Chicago. Irving F. Marrow, a consulting architect, is credited with the details of the architectural design which allows motorists to enjoy the spectacular views while driving across the bridge. Clifford E. Paine, the engineer in charge of the designing staff, interpreted Strauss's ideas and, while keeping a low profile, ensured the success of the project.

Construction began January 5, 1933, with a groundbreaking ceremony at Crissy Field adjacent to the bridge site in San Francisco. Even the United States fleet participated in the celebrations. Citizens cheered the opening up of thousands of jobs during the heart of the Depression.The bridge progressed steadily across the expanse for the next four years. Before it was completed, however, eleven men had lost their lives, ten in a single accident when the stripping scaffold of a painting contractor gave way and fell, destroying 2,100 feet of safety net. Other nets saved the lives of nineteen men, who formed a group called the "Halfway to Hell Club" in commemoration of their miraculous survival of close calls.

The completed bridge was truly a miracle of structural design. Its total length, including approach structures, is 8,981 feet; its width is 90 feet between cables and can accommodate six lanes of traffic. The height of the towers is 746 feet, and the clearance above high tide is 220 feet.

Crowds gather for the 50th birthday of the Golden Gate Bridge,
May 24, 1987.

On May 27, 1937, a huge celebration was held to open the "Span of Gold." Pedestrians crossed the bridge that day; vehicular traffic began the next day and has continued ever since except for the bridge's 50th birthday party held May 24, 1987.

Estimates of 250,000 people jammed the bridge for a historic dawn walk causing the span to temporarily flatten out. Another 500,000 celebrators were in the Presidio and Toll Plaza area as well as north of the bridge attempting to join the Bridge Walk.

Over one million joined in the general festivities which included concerts, a cavalcade of antique cars, a Golden Regatta parade of vintage boats, a fly-over of old airplanes, and finally a spectacular fireworks display with a 4,000 foot long (fireworks) waterfall suspended between bridge towers.

The finale to the bridge's party was the permanent lighting of the two 746-foot towers. This subtle lighting of the Golden Gate Bridge and the bright lights spanning the Bay Bridge have added a glittering new dimension to the San Francisco Bay scene at night.

PROFILE: ## Carney Campion

The popular General Manager for the Golden Gate Bridge, Highway and Transportation District, Carney J. Campion, began work on December 1, 1975, as District Secretary, then moved on to become the eighth General Manager in December 1984. He served in that position for twenty-three years until his retirement in 1998.

Under his leadership, the bridge was painted and repaired on a continuing basis and now is being completely retrofitted for earthquake safety. This is a monumental job costing 217.6 million dollars and will run through four phases until the year 2004.

On May 24, 1987, Carney directed the Bridge's 50th birthday party which was attended by over one million people. Around 250,000 actually walked on the bridge and enjoyed the Golden Regatta of vintage boats sailing in the bay below and the fly-over antique airplanes. An antique car parade, concerts and a huge fireworks display completed the spectacular celebration.

Carney, originally from Santa Rosa, California, lives with his wife, Kathryn Campion, in San Rafael. They have six children and ten grandchildren, and both are active in many Marin organizations.

When not working for the Bridge, Carney administered and officiated Amateur Athletic Union Swimming, traveling twice to Kuwait and once to India to work with coaches and officials in upgrading competitive swimming programs. He is also involved with the Society of California Pioneers and the Marin Forum.

In connection with his job at the bridge, he was a member of the American Public Transit Association, California Transit Association and past president of the Board of Directors of the International Bridge, Tunnel and Turnpike Association.

Most people see the Golden Gate Bridge from their cars on the mile-and-a-half drive across the bridge to Marin. There is no toll driving north on Highway 101; when you return to San Francisco going south, there is a toll. But if you feel adventurous, you can walk, jog, or bicycle across the bridge. It is a unique experience.

The east sidewalk, facing San Francisco, is open all daylight hours; the west side is open only for bicycles on weekends and holidays. There is no toll for walking or bicycling across the bridge. Bicycles must be walked around the towers. Be sure to bring a sweater, for the winds are usually strong and the air chilly, especially when the fog rolls in.

You may park your car on the east side of the San Francisco Toll Plaza where there are meters. A pedestrian and vehicle

Golden Gate Bridge under construction. View from Crissy Field, October 1936. (Photo by Chas. Hiller. From the Archives of the Golden Gate Bridge, Highway & Transportation District.)

underpass runs under the Toll Plaza to the administration building of the Golden Gate Bridge, Highway and Transportation District where you may pick up bus and ferry schedules in addition to other information on the bridge.

Begin your walk at the small park on the east side of the Toll Plaza. A statue of Joseph B. Strauss, Chief Engineer of the bridge, is situated amid benches and flower gardens. Restrooms, a gift shop and cafe (all with wheelchair access) adjoin the park. You may notice brick walkways decorated with people's names. Ninety-thousand bricks were sold for $30 to $75 each with 15% of the proceeds going to Friends of the Golden Gate Bridge to help pay off the 50th birthday party debt.

Historic Fort Point is just below the bridge and can be reached by driving or hiking down. Constructed from 1853 to 1861, the fort at one time housed 600 soldiers; its cannons could fire 65-pound balls for a distance of two miles. The water that swirls below is a popular, though dangerous, surfing and fishing area. The fort is open daily from 10:00 to 5:00 p.m. Wear something warm for your visit. (You will see that the rangers are usually dressed in heavy parkas and gloves.) Phone for information on Fort Point at 556-0505 or 921-8193 to reach the Historical Society of the Presidio and Fort Point.

FORT POINT
556-0505
or
921-8193

As you start across the bridge, look down for a bird's-eye view of old Fort Point. The first, or south, sixty-five-story bridge tower houses a service elevator that goes to the top. At the tower's base is a plaque dedicated to the engineers and directors of the District in celebration of the bridge's "Silver Anniversary" in 1962. The tower also houses airplane beacon lights and foghorns.

There used to be an old-fashioned emergency telephone with a receiver and crank for ringing a bell, but now the District has installed twelve call boxes for people needing help, eight on the east side and four on the west side. When you pick up the receiver, it connects directly to the sergeant's office. About mid-span are two foghorns, called diaphones, which guide ships safely through the main channel.

Golden Gate Bridge under construction. View from San Francisco anchorage looking toward Marin, February 16, 1935. (From the Archives of the Golden Gate Bridge, Highway and Transportation District)

The view is breathtaking. Below are the rushing waters of San Francisco Bay dotted with sailboats, motor yachts, heavy tankers and cruise ships. Beyond is the panorama of the San Francisco skyline, the Bay Bridge, Treasure Island, Alcatraz, the cities of the East Bay, the Marin shoreline and Headlands, and Angel Island.

The second or north tower marks the entrance to Marin County. Lime Point, a lighthouse whose construction in 1900 helped usher in the new century, is just below this tower. It has fully-automatic lights and foghorns. A little to the north are the perpendicular rocks called the Needles.

As you gaze across the waters of San Francisco Bay, you may wonder if Sir Francis Drake, the intrepid English pirate, navigator and explorer, did indeed find this secret harbor over four hundred years ago in 1579. On March 8, 1975, a replica of his ship, the *Golden Hinde,* sailed under the bridge after a long and hazardous trip from Plymouth, England. The *Golden Hinde II* was greeted on that memorable afternoon by hundreds of private yachts and sailboats, San Francisco fireboats spraying arcs of water, dignitaries from all over the Bay Area, and thousands of cheering people hanging out of the windows of tall office buildings and standing along the shore.

In 1775, the Spanish packet *San Carlos,* under the command of Lieutenant Juan Manuel de Ayala, was recorded as the first European vessel to sail into the bay. On August 5, Ayala anchored off an area he called "Little Willows," or in Spanish, "Saucelito." Ayala left the next day to explore and survey the waters and became well acquainted with the coast Indians. He remained almost six weeks and made the first map of the area.

San Francisco Bay was originally a coastal valley developed by the Sacramento and San Joaquin rivers, which joined in what is now the Delta west of Stockton, passed through the Carquinez Straits, and flowed out to the Pacific Ocean. A gradually sinking coastline allowed ocean water to flood the valley, thus forming the bay.

In 1769, when the overland explorer Gaspar de Portola first gazed at the waters of San Francisco Bay, they covered 700 square miles, including the northern San Pablo Bay. The area has shrunk to about 400 square miles, but a strong Bay Conservation and Development Commission has been formed to protect what is left. The volume of water that flows in and ebbs out four times a day with the tides averages 1,250,000 acre feet.

At the end of the bridge you will arrive at Juan Manuel de Ayala Vista Point, a Roadside Ecological Viewing Area with a parking lot, restrooms, telephones, and, of course, spectacular views of the "City by the Bay." A plaque honoring the 400-year anniversary of Sir Francis Drake's landing in Marin is attached to a cross section of a huge coast redwood tree.

(If you are driving south on Highway 101 and would like to visit Vista Point before crossing the Golden Gate Bridge, exit at the Golden Gate National Recreational Area, drive a short distance, then turn right at the sign to "Forts Baker, Barry and Cronkhite." Instead of driving straight up the hill, turn left and proceed down to the parking lot. A pedestrian underpass leads to the observation area at Vista Point.)

Look away from San Francisco, and you will see the magnificent Headlands to the west, the piers of Fort Baker below, a winding road leading to the town of Sausalito, and Highway 101 disappearing into a rainbow tunnel. You are in Marin.

The Marin Headlands 2

Hidden Beaches, Sweeping Vistas

The Marin Headlands loom above the Golden Gate—fifteen square miles of coastal hills, valleys, steep cliffs and uninhabited shoreline. This area, once a strategic part of the United States coastal defense system, is now the heart of the Golden Gate National Recreation Area, a 76,000 acre national park located in both Marin and San Francisco. From the Headlands there are spectacular panoramic views of the ocean, the Golden Gate Bridge, and the dazzling city of San Francisco.

Visitors can explore the remains of the military bunkers that housed large coastal guns set up in defense of the Golden Gate from 1870 on, a period covering the Spanish-American War, World War I, and World War II. Old installations of brick and batteries of granite and concrete give silent evidence of the world of yesterday when a harbor could be defended by shooting a gun.

Now cracks appear, weeds grow, iron rusts, and cement crumbles. The land has returned to peaceful purposes, saved from urban sprawl by the powerful military which mercifully kept its wildness intact.

How miraculous to find this sprawling open space adjacent to a city the size of San Francisco, a place where wildflowers carpet the hills in a rainbow of color each spring. Here you will find orange poppies, blue and yellow lupine, red Indian paint-

---

◀ *The Golden Gate Bridge as seen from the Presidio Yacht Harbor in Sausalito.*

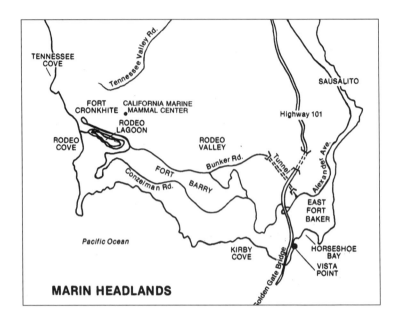

brush, and white flowering poison hemlock with tiny dots of red on the stems. Here also you can enjoy the pungent smell of eucalyptus mixed with the fragrance of sage. Wildlife is abundant and you may spy a doe with her tiny, spotted fawn grazing peacefully in the evening light, a family of raccoons, or an occasional fox.

Overhead a red-winged blackbird flies slowly by, silhouetted against a setting sun. A Steller's jay screeches, and the sea gulls cry out as they swoop down on currents of wind along the cliffs.

Below, the waves race upward against the shore while white foamy water crashes over jagged rocks. The tide turns, the water recedes, and a tiny beach appears, inaccessible to all but the curlews, cormorants, and sanderlings racing on tiny legs along the edge of the water. When the fog rolls in, the sharp line of the ridge disappears and all is silent except for the wind, the crashing of the surf, and a lonely warning from a distant foghorn.

Whether it is misty or clear, take time to visit the Marin Headlands and explore the old gun batteries once so important to the defense of the bay.

From Highway 101 northbound, take the Alexander Avenue exit. Bear right toward Sausalito. Take the first left turn to the one-way tunnel, following Golden Gate National Recreation Area/Marin Headlands signs. Southbound on U.S. 101, take the last Sausalito exit, then bear right toward "Sausalito." After crossing under the freeway, follow Golden Gate National Recreation Area/Marin Headlands signs toward a long one-way tunnel. Just before entering the tunnel, make a sharp right turn and follow that road down into Fort Baker to visit that historic area first. You will see a sign that says "Fort Baker" and "Discovery Museum."

Fort Baker was built on part of a Mexican land grant awarded to William A. Richardson, an English seaman, in 1838. It was called *Rancho Saucelito* and covered 19,000 acres. In 1886, the government purchased a large portion and developed the Lime Point Military Reservation on San Francisco Bay.

From this Fort Baker was carved out. Begun in 1897 as a harbor defense, the fort was named for a Civil War hero, Colonel Edward Dickinson Baker. Baker, a friend of Abraham Lincoln, fell in the Battle of Ball's Bluff, Virginia, in 1861. He fought with Lincoln in the bloody Black Hawk War in 1832, and in the Mexican War with General Zachary Taylor in 1845.

Five gun emplacements at Fort Baker house Endicott cannons, rifle-barreled, armor-piercing guns capable of shooting accurately for a range of twelve miles.

A sign at the entrance to the old fort reads, "Fort Baker, Golden Gate National Recreation Area." There is also the Coast Guard Station Golden Gate nearby. When the fort was active in coastal defense, hundreds of men were stationed there.

The heart of the base is the picturesque parade ground surrounded by several two-story white houses. At one time the military used the base as a headquarters for a much larger series of Army forts. During World War II, Fort Baker had a military hospital. A chapel was built in addition to a baseball diamond, tennis courts and a gym.

In the southeast part of the base is the private Presidio Yacht Harbor and Horseshoe Bay, a good area for fishing. This is an excellent place to view the Golden Gate Bridge from another angle as it looms overhead.

Fort Baker is currently being transferred from the U.S. Army to the National Park Service as the Defense Department no longer needs the post. The transfer of the 335 acre site (plus 183 acres in the bay) to the Golden Gate National Recreation Area is scheduled to be completed by 2001, at which time the National Park Service plans to open a conference and retreat center.

The new facilities will include the restoration and conversion of many of the fort's 46 historic buldings and 32 nonhistoric buildings. The plan also recommends constructing two new buildings on the fort's central parade ground and adding 25,000 square feet to the Bay Area Discovery Museum. A 70-slip marina will be replaced with overnight moorings for 60 boats; a building now used as a yacht club will be turned into a museum and education center with a cafe. The plan also calls for Coast Guard facilities to be enlarged to include a classroom and dormitory, hiking, biking and equestrian trails to be improved, and the beach at Horseshoe Bay to be restored. Old batteries and other fortification structures will be preserved and other areas will be rehabilitated such as the pier, walkways, road and tennis courts. A visitors center will be created and the endangered mission blue butterfly habitat restored. For more information check the fort's website: www.nps.gov/goga.

FORT BAKER
www.nps.gov/goga

The Discovery Museum, for children ages one to ten, their families and caregivers, occupies eight historic buildings at East Fort Baker. Run by a non-profit organization, the museum offers hands-on programs in the arts, humanities, science and technology plus field trips, permanent and changing exhibitions, a birthday party room, media center, carousel and cafe.

Children can discover how to work in clay; they may paint and paste and even bind books. All the exhibits in the different halls are beautifully presented. For example, in the San Francisco Bay Hall there are replicas of the Point Bonita Lighthouse, a Discovery Boat, the Ports of San Francisco and Oakland, Fisherman's Wharf, and a salt marsh with a bridge. A gift shop offers educational books, toys, art supplies and science kits. For information: 487-4398 or www.badm.org.

DISCOVERY MUSEUM 487-4398 or www.badm.org.

After exploring Fort Baker, go on to historic Forts Barry and Cronkhite in the ocean-facing portion of the headlands by taking Bunker Road back to the one-way tunnel. The half-mile tunnel was built in 1918 (enlarged in the 1930s) and was used to haul guns to Fort Barry. Also named for an army hero, General William F. Barry, this strategic coastal defense base had battery emplacements for fifty guns.

In 1937, eighty-two acres north of Fort Barry were acquired for a third fort named for General Albert Cronkhite. Sixteen-inch guns capable of firing thirty-two miles were installed.

After World War II, missile installations for the Nike-Ajax and Nike-Hercules were built in the Headlands. When these too became obsolete, they were removed, and the bases were gradually phased out. They all became part of the Golden Gate National Recreation Area in 1972.

At the entrance to the tunnel signs read: "5 minutes red light—Bicycles in tunnel when light flashing. Speed 25 MPH. Push button to activate. No hiking—clearance, 14'4"." The tunnel was completely restored between March 1989 and April 1995. Five million dollars were spent in repairs and the two new bicycle lanes were added, each going one-way.

Enter when the light turns green, drive through the tunnel, and follow Bunker Road to Rodeo Lagoon. The Marin Headlands Visitor Center is located in the Fort Barry Chapel, once used by the military for religious services. The chapel, constructed in 1941, is located at the intersection of Bunker and Field roads.

This serves as an educational and informational center as well as gift shop with books, posters, sweatshirts and cards. Historical displays include replicas of a World War II barracks, the Point Bonita Lighthouse, dairy ranches in Marin, the Vaqueros, and information about the Coast Miwok Indians. Nature

displays are of hillsides in the Headlands with their plants, ponds and beaches, and the lagoons are shown in all seasons. Information on hiking, camping, special walks and exhibits is available at the Visitor Center. For further specifics, including information on the lighthouse, call 331-1540.

HEADLANDS
VISITOR CENTER
331-1540.

The major Coast Trail runs through the Headlands and all the way north to the Point Reyes National Seashore. It is recommended only for reasonably experienced hikers as it is quite steep in parts. Numerous other trails offer hikes for every level of experience.

Point Bonita Lighthouse, first built in 1855, is a half-mile hike from the lighthouse parking lot located up Field Road. You may park in a small lot at the trail head marked by a large sign. The original top of the lighthouse came in an unassembled "kit" from Paris and was erected in 1855 on a hill near its current location. The top "Gold Rush" section was moved to its present site and put on a base in 1877.

In 1993 the lighthouse was closed to repair the trail along the cliff which had badly eroded. It took $100,000 and three years to rebuild the trail. Fiberglass bridges were flown in by Coast Guard helicopters. The work included restoring the lighthouse brick tile floor, new metal wall plates and a new catwalk around the lens housing. A steep metal stairway leading up to the 1000-watt light was rebuilt using original hand-made screws. The lens had been built in Paris by Fresnel in the 1850s and shipped to California around Cape Horn. In 1981 the last light keeper left and the facility was fully automated.

You may also hike to Kirby Cove from Battery Spencer, off Conzelman Road. The distance is .9 mile, and you will be rewarded by a nice beach with a dramatic view of the Golden Gate Bridge and a good fishing area. The water here, averaging 55 degrees with strong currents, is too cold and too dangerous for swimming. Privies, including facilities for wheelchairs, are located just past the parking lot.

◀ *The 1877 Point Bonita Lighthouse located in the Marin Headlands along the rugged Pacific Coast.*

A wooden bridge spans the tip of Rodeo Lagoon leading to Rodeo Beach, Rodeo Cove, and the Pacific Ocean. Dogs need to be on leashes on the Lagoon side of Rodeo Beach to protect the habitat of the endangered tidewater goby. This beach is a good spot for watching the surf but the strong currents, steep drop-off, and rip tides make it hazardous for swimming.

To the south is Bird Island. From spring through fall, you may see large birds with six-and- one-half foot wingspans and summer plumage of dark brown feathers gliding gracefully over the waves, then diving with accelerated speed into the ocean. These birds are brown pelicans. Many observers feel the brown pelican resembles a prehistoric bird and, indeed, it is considered a rare and endangered species. DDT had weakened the eggs laid by the females, causing shells to crack and be destroyed before the chicks were ready to hatch. With DDT now illegal in the U.S., the breeding success is beginning to increase. The birds nest in the Channel Islands off Santa Barbara and Baja California.

A pair of binoculars will help you get a good look at the Heermann's gulls, western gulls, and other sea birds found

Bird Island sits just off Rodeo Beach at Fort Cronkhite.

around Bird Island. Cormorants build round nests here of dried seaweed.

Several organizations are located in the Marin Headlands. The Headlands Institute, a member of the Yosemite National Institute, conducts educational programs "directed toward the improvement of environmental perceptions and ethics." The institute is set up for field studies, seminars and conferences. There are summer camps, teacher training, Elderhostel and corporate programs. Call 332-5771.

HEADLANDS
INSTITUTE
332-5771

The YMCA Point Bonita Outdoor and Conference Center, up Field Road, provides housing and food services to groups of over twenty people. Arrangements may be made for a regular school class to stay at the Center and be taught by its own teacher. Field studies with school groups are also conducted.

The facilities—concrete barracks built for the Nike Missile Site, then remodeled for use by the National Guard—are also popular for church retreats, adult special interest group meetings, and outdoor education. The Center provides multi-purpose meeting rooms for 25 to 150 people, full-service dining and catering, dormitory-style lodging for up to 150 people, recreational areas and a campfire amphitheater. For general information, 331-9622, (800) 332-9622.

YMCA POINT
BONITA OUTDOOR
AND CONFERENCE
CENTER
331-9622,
(800) 332-9622

The Headlands Center for the Arts occupies eleven historic former military buildings, providing a laboratory for creativity for artists from Marin and other areas. Events sponsored by the organization include talks, performances and readings. They also produce a variety of publications. An Artist-in-Residence program provides studio space and stipends to nine Bay Area artists and twenty artists from around the country and abroad who live and work at the Center for up to five months annually. Studio space may also be rented for up to three years. Call 331-2787 for information.

HEADLANDS
CENTER FOR
THE ARTS
331-2787

The Marine Mammal Center is located in an old Nike missile site at Fort Cronkhite. This unique institution, founded in 1975 by Paul Maxwell, Lloyd Smalley and myself, is federally and state licensed to rehabilitate sick and injured marine mammals. It also conducts research, and provides a data bank of information. The Center services an area covering 1,000 miles of coastline. Volunteers pick up orphaned and injured marine mammals and nurse them back to health.

Visitors may see a seal lion being nursed for respiration problems, an undernourished baby elephant seal or an abandoned harbor seal pup being fed. In June 1997, the first otter pup, brought in from Carmel, joined the Center. The mammals are kept an average of six months before being released back to their native habitat. The Center has an admirable 60 to 70 percent survival rate and can accommodate up to 750 marine mammals in one year.

In 1989 the Marine Mammal Center was named one of the eighteen national winners of the President's Volunteer Action Award. A silver medal from President George Bush was presented at the White House to then executive director, Peigin Barrett, and publicist Mary Jane Schramm on April 11.

Also in 1989, Marine Mammal Center professional staff members went to Alaska to establish protocol and train volunteers for the care of oiled otters after the *Exxon Valdez* oil spill. Closer to home, when sea lions appeared by the hundreds at Pier 39 in San Francisco, the Marine Mammal Center set up a sea lion natural history program at the pier.

In 1990, Humphrey, the errant 40 ton humpback whale, reappeared in San Francisco Bay and was stranded in mud flats near 3 Com (Candlestick) Park. Members managed to free him and guide him back to the ocean for the second time.

The 1990s saw new labs constructed, the Interpretive Center and store opened on Pier 39, a new feed room constructed, portable X-rays added to diagnostic equipment and a holding facility opened in Monterey Bay.

MARIN MARINE
MAMMAL CENTER
289-SEAL,
289-7325 or
www.tmmc.org

The Marine Mammal Center is open from 10 a.m. to 4:00 p.m. daily. There is no admission fee. For information, 289-SEAL, 289-7325 or www.tmmc.org.

Overnight visitors in the Headlands can make arrangements to spend the night in the Marin Headlands Hostel in Fort Barry. It may be reached by turning uphill on Field Road off Bunker Road and following the well-marked directions. Guests here observe the international hostel customs which include no alco-

The Golden Gate Hostel at Fort Barry.

hol or pets, and smoking outside only. Guests must be willing to contribute to clean-up in the morning.

Facilities include two historic 1907 buildings with space for 103 guests, dormitory-style bedrooms, family rooms and couples' rooms, hot showers, country kitchens, dining room, common room, fireplace, laundry and outside bike storage.

Reservations must be made and paid for in advance. The address is: Building 941, Fort Barry, Sausalito, California 94965. Phone 331-2777 or 1-800-909-4776, ext. 62.

For the most spectacular views of the Golden Gate and the bridge, take Conzelman Road (Sausalito exit off Highway 101), a long scenic road which twists up the face of the Headlands. You will usually see a variety of cameras set up along here as this is an extraordinary place to shoot photographs. There are old military bunkers to explore and benches where you can rest. The road becomes one-way at the top, then continues down to Rodeo Lagoon.

GOLDEN GATE HOSTEL, FORT BARRY Building 941, Fort Barry, Sausalito, California 94965. Phone 331-2777 or 1-800-909-4776, ext. 62.

PROFILE: **Peigin Catherine Barrett**

Executive Director and CEO of the Marine Mammal Center, 1982-1996

Peigin Barrett was a part of the Marine Mammal Center at Fort Cronkhite almost from the beginning. From 1977 to 1981 she volunteered her time while still working for Harcourt, Brace and Jovanovich Publishers in San Francisco. In 1982 she became the Center's Executive Director. Her qualifications included a BA from the College of New Rochelle (New York), a Masters in Public Administration from Golden Gate University, (San Francisco, California), and four years of on-the-job training. She led the Center from its small, grassroots non-profit infancy to national and international stature.

Peigin's enthusiasm, linked with her vision of where the Marine Mammal Center could go, plus a willingness to work two other jobs so she could be at the Center forty to fifty hours a week at little or no pay, eventually spelled success.

It was a long, difficult road, but membership climbed from 1200 to 35,000; volunteers rose from 50 to 800, and revenues rose from $159,000 to $2,750,000.

Peigin established formal education programs, satellite rescue operations and internationally recognized scientific studies. New pens and pools were built as were modern labs, a marine mammal library, fish prep and formula rooms, and a pup intensive care unit. All were built by volunteers and funded with donations. Rescue vehicles were solicited and used to pick up distressed and injured marine mammals for a thousand miles along the California coast.

In 1992 a successful store and interpretive center was opened at Pier 39 in San Francisco to educate the thousands of visitors coming to see the live sea lions on the adjoining docks.

In 1989 Peigin Barrett and a volunteer leader accepted the President's Volunteer Action Award on behalf of the Center presented by President George Bush at formal White House ceremonies. This came after the 1985 Chevron Conservation Award, one of the oldest and most prestigious conservation awards in the United States. In 1993 Barrett received the DAISY Award from the San Francisco Bay Girl Scouts Council and in 1995, the Beryl H. Buck Award for Achievement by the Marin Community Foundation.

There were many more awards, but the true legacy Peigin Barrett left when she stepped down from her executive position at the Marine Mammal Center was a well-run, well-funded organization responsible for saving thousands of seals, sea lions, elephant seals, otters and even a few whales.

Besides the scientific research which has come out of the Center, Peigin has raised the level of understanding of marine wildlife for the children and adults of Marin. Her influence in the conservation and care of these animals will remain as long as the Marine Mammal Center survives.

An old military building at Fort Baker.

Farther north in the Headlands are Gerbode and Rodeo Valleys, which were once slated to become a city of 30,000 people. To be called "Marincello," the city would have housed thousands of people in as small a space as possible by the generous use of high-rises. Today you may park your car where the gates of Marincello once proudly marked the road which led through Tennessee Valley to Rodeo Valley and the site for the new city. (Exit Highway 101 at Stinson Beach sign, which puts you on Shoreline Highway 1. Turn left on Tennessee Valley Road.)

It is a level one-and-a-half-mile hike from the Tennessee Valley parking area to the lovely beach at Tennessee Cove; or you may hike the Bobcat and Miwok Trails which both lead to Rodeo Valley.

Thomas Frouge, who owned a gigantic construction company in the East, picked this site to build his dream city. The proximity to San Francisco, plus the spectacular views, assured the project's success. Never mind the heavy winds and daily fog. With the financial backing of the Gulf Oil Corporation, Frouge hired architects and lawyers who drew up the plans and contracts. When all was ready, a huge public relations campaign was launched.

The developer rented space in an industrial building in Sausalito where he installed a model of the proposed city. Members of the Marin County Board of Supervisors and Planning Commission, city councilmen, and other VIPs were invited to a steak dinner and tour of the model. Like Peter Pan, one could view the miniature Marincello from above by crossing a specially-constructed bridge.

Frouge gave his visitors glowing facts and figures based on the premise that population studies proved that many thousands of new residents would be moving into Marin in a specified number of years. He contended that his city would be the best way to plan for this influx. The Board of Supervisors approved Frouge's plan.

Many conservationists in Marin circulated petitions against the hasty approval, and the city of Sausalito filed a lawsuit. But what really brought construction to a halt was a three-year legal battle beginning in 1967 between the Gulf Oil Corporation and Frouge. Then in January 1969 Frouge unexpectedly died, and the project died with him.

The Nature Conservancy bought the land from Gulf Oil in 1972, preserving it for a park, and it is now part of the Golden Gate National Recreation Area. So what was to have been a model city of thousands of inhabitants is preserved forever as a lovely open area of valleys, rolling hills, streams, and a quiet lagoon—a place of peace and natural beauty for all to enjoy.

Sausalito   3
Riviera of the West

Travelers visiting Sausalito for the first time often recognize the similarities to the exquisite French/Italian Riviera. Like Portofino on the Italian Mediterranean, Sausalito rises from the blue waters of Richardson Bay, an exclusive hillside community tucked in among oak, willow, and eucalyptus trees, with commanding views of glamorous yacht harbors and graceful sailboats. Flourishing gardens with rhododendrons, begonia, wisteria, honeysuckle, and magnolia grow in profusion all over the hills.

Sausalito affords even more impressive vistas than the Riviera, including the long, graceful Bay Bridge which may be seen in a glow of shimmering sun, or floating in mist or fog. And there is the magnificent skyline of San Francisco, shining white during the day and diamond-like at night.

Visitors to Sausalito find no end to the pleasures in this little town. Shoppers delight in discovering the perfect gift among the international array of import stores, jewelry shops, art galleries, gift boutiques, and designer clothing establishments. History buffs can explore the old landmarks. A wide variety of excellent restaurants offer seafood and Italian, French, Mexican and Japanese food among others.

The most exciting way to arrive in Sausalito, short of your own forty-eight foot yacht, is by one of the Golden Gate Transit

◀ *Plaza Vina del Mar in Sausalito. The elephants are from the 1915 San Francisco Panama Pacific International Exposition.*

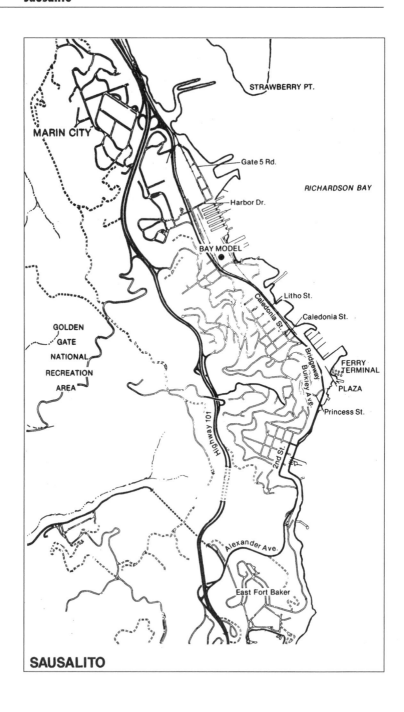

STRAWBERRY PT.

MARIN CITY

Gate 5 Rd.

RICHARDSON BAY

Harbor Dr.

BAY MODEL

Litho St.

Caledonia St.

Caledonia St.

GOLDEN
GATE
NATIONAL
RECREATION
AREA

Bridgeway

Bulkley Ave.

FERRY
TERMINAL

PLAZA

Princess St.

Highway 101

2nd St.

Alexander Ave.

East Fort Baker

SAUSALITO

District ferryboats from San Francisco (455-2000), or the Blue and Gold Ferry (773-1188). The ride itself is pure pleasure. Standing on deck with the wind in your hair, you can watch the city recede and the Marin hills gradually become a towering presence. If you prefer, you can stay below and have a drink and snack at the bar, relax, and look out the windows to watch the boats on the bay.

GOLDEN GATE TRANSIT DISTRICT 455-2000

BLUE AND GOLD FERRY 773-1188

By automobile, driving north on Highway 101 just after leaving the Golden Gate Bridge, exit at Alexander Avenue; driving south, take the Sausalito/Marin City exit. Parking in town is tight and strictly policed, so be careful to watch your time. It is probably easier to use one of the large city-owned parking lots.

The principal street, which follows the shoreline, is Bridgeway, named because it shows you the way to the Golden Gate Bridge which opened in 1937. Prior to that, it was called "Water Street." The south end of Bridgeway runs into Richardson and Second Street in an area that is known as Sausalito Old Town. A creek fed by hillside springs once flowed into the bay along what is now Main Street and provided fresh water for ships. It still runs underground today going out into the cove.

Around 1836 Mexican ships referred to the area as *El Puerto De Los Balleneros*, or "Whalers' Cove." It was a popular anchorage for several reasons: sailors claimed that the water found here stayed fresher for a longer period than any other found along the West Coast; the anchorage was sufficiently deep; the area was protected from westerly winds by Table Mountain to the northwest (now called Mt. Tamalpais), and wood was readily available.

In 1838 Captain William A. Richardson was awarded the 19,000-acre Mexican land grant called *Rancho Saucelito*, which in Spanish meant "little willow," and in 1841 he built an adobe house at what is now Pine and Bonita Streets. As captain of the port, he acted as pilot to guide ships into the cove. He also owned the water supply, the source of wood, and collected all the Mexican anchorage fees. It was a time of flourishing activity. Mexican schooners, Russian brigs, British man-of-war ships, and United States naval vessels anchored at Sausalito.

A traffic jam develops in the 1920s as cars line up for the auto ferry. Notice the trains on the right. (Courtesy of the Sausalito Historical Society)

In 1868, Samuel R. Throckmorton, administrator of Richardson's land, sold 1,200 acres to the Sausalito Land and Ferry Company. That section of town was subdivided (including around 125 building lots which were in the bay), shares of stock were sold, and a steamer was chartered to ferry people back and forth to San Francisco. Hotels and homes were built, and by 1875 the narrow-gauge North Pacific Coast Railroad was serving the town. A wharf and shops were built in the area where the ferries dock today, on land donated by the Sausalito Land and Ferry Company.

Sausalito was on her way. By 1855 she had a new ferryboat, eight hotels, and a population of 1,500. The first issue of the *Sausalito News,* published February 12, 1885, reported that there were "two restaurants, three blacksmith shops, two news agencies, one barber shop, one bakery, two boat houses, seven general merchandise houses and a very fair representation of saloons." The town had become a melting pot of English, Irish, Portuguese, Greeks, Norwegians, Germans, and Americans.

In 1887 the name of the town, which was being misspelled, was changed to it present spelling by the United States Post

Office, and in 1893, Sausalito voted to become an incorporated town. Civic improvements such as wooden sidewalks, sewers, and street lights were initiated. By 1900, however, gambling interests had taken over, leaving the town wide open for all kinds of corruption. At least twenty-five saloons and as many poolrooms were in operation. The poolrooms were actually bookie joints which had been outlawed in San Francisco. Undesirable crowds flocked aboard the ferryboats on racing days and, reportedly, a "decent woman" had trouble getting past Water Street (Bridgeway). The area downtown smelled of stale beer, while the streets were full of mud. This situation lasted for about ten years until a reform political ticket was voted in.

As the railroad grew, Sausalito became a major ferry and rail terminal. It was here that all the Marin commuters left the suburban trains and boarded boats headed for San Francisco. The completion of the Golden Gate Bridge in 1937 caused land values to soar in Marin although Sausalito was bypassed by the new highway. San Franciscans could now reach the county in ten to fifteen minutes.

By early 1941 the ferries had closed down and the trains stopped running since they could no longer compete with the bridge. Ferries used for public transportation would not be seen again in Sausalito until 1970 when the Golden Gate Bridge, Highway and Transportation District resumed this service.

During the Second World War, Sausalito became a shipbuilding center. The Maritime Commission condemned over two hundred acres of waterfront on North Bridgeway, filled a marsh, rerouted the street and opened a shipyard, Marinship. It was operated by the W.A. Bechtel Corporation and eventually employed 70,000 workers. The ferries were temporarily put back into use for the shipyard workers, who built fifteen Liberty ships and seventy-eight tankers. A total of ninety-three ships were launched. When the war ended, hundreds of new Sausalito residents were left without work.

In the 1950s a community of houseboats was gradually established on Richardson Bay. These boats were occupied by artists, poets, and writers. Many were home-built creations of fascinating designs and materials which included wood from the deserted buildings of Marinship. Others were old ferry-boats remodeled and divided into living sections. Sausalito became known as an artists' and writers' retreat. Over the years, much of the floating boat community has become legitimate by complying with local codes such as electrical, water and sewer hookups.

During the late 1970s many handsome new houseboats designed by architects and built by professional carpenters were added to the community and occupied by doctors, lawyers, and other professionals. The socio-economics of the area changed as these people also learned to enjoy the shimmer of the sun on the water, the sight of a blue heron or other shore-birds feeding nearby, and the feel of a gentle rocking with the waves and tide.

To begin your tour of Old Sausalito, walk south along Bridgeway to Second Street and Main, where the fresh water creek once flowed into the bay. This area is called Hurricane Gulch because wind and fog whip through here regularly. The actual name was bestowed on the area around 1884 or 1886 when the Sausalito Bay Land Company was trying to promote the sale of land here with a summer picnic. The wind came up and blew the tablecloths, cutlery and glasses right off the tables.

Hurricane Gulch is the location of a restaurant at 201 Bridgeway. (The boardwalk running along the water is an extension of that street.) The building, constructed in 1893, was originally a German beer garden called *Walhalla,* which is the German spelling for *Valhalla,* a Scandinavian term meaning an abode where the soul of those who have fallen in battle are received by the god Odin. In this building, rooms were provided upstairs as a haven for seafaring men. Water running down the hillside was piped through the building of the *Walhalla* and out the back into the casks and barrels of waiting boats. Sailors were supplied with liquor while they waited.

During Prohibition, the *Walhalla* became a center for bootlegging and was raided periodically by federal agents. When Marinship opened during World War II, the old building provided badly needed sleeping quarters. In 1948 Sally Stanford, a

Sausalito children looking down at Central School in 1901. (Courtesy of the Sausalito Historical Society)

former bootlegger and "lady of the house" in San Francisco, bought the *Walhalla,* changed the name to *Valhalla,* and made it into a successful restaurant, decorating it with Victorian furniture, Tiffany lamps, and art nouveau pieces. Miss Stanford became involved in town politics and ran for city council six times before being elected in 1972. She served as mayor in 1976-77, and vice-mayor in 1979. Over the years she gained the respect of elected officials county wide, and in 1979, a street called "Stanford Way" was named in honor of the grande dame of Marin politics. Sally Stanford passed away February 4, 1982, at the age of 78.

From the restaurant at Hurricane Gulch follow the boardwalk past four wooden houses and you will arrive at the house where Jack London was reported to have lived. While the Sausalito Historical Society has never been able to officially cor-

roborate London's presence there, it is promoted as local lore. The house is situated on the curve of Richardson and Bridgeway, where London was supposed to have watched ferries ply the waters of San Francisco Bay. Some residents think this was his inspiration for the novel *Sea Wolf,* published in 1904.

This whole area was once threatened by a wall of buildings when a developer applied for a use permit to cover ten lots with apartments built right out over the water. Outraged citizens managed to stop the construction and save the waterfront for the public.

Along stretches of open waterfront, as you walk north on Bridgeway, you can see San Francisco, the Bay Bridge, Alcatraz, Angel Island, and Belvedere Island. Benches have been placed along here, while below the street level, a concrete walkway (covered by water at high tide) has been provided for fishermen.

Across Bridgeway is Tiffany Beach Park which runs parallel to the street. It was named for former city clerk William Zobel Tiffany, who served the town for twenty-six years between 1913 and 1939. When he retired, his daughter Zelda continued in his job until 1944. The park features a garden and benches.

Proceeding along the waterfront, you will see a bronze sea lion statue just off shore. It was designed in the 1950s by the artist Al Sybrian, who liked to sketch the sea lions playing on the rocks in this area. The sea lions and brown pelicans can still be seen here, especially during the herring runs in the bay in January.

Sybrian's first sculpture, donated in 1955, stood four feet high and was made of concrete and haydite. It lasted eight years before cracking under the pressure of tides and floating debris. Because of its enormous popularity, funds were raised to replace the sea lion in bronze. The new sculpture was completed and placed here in 1966.

Up the hill from Bridgeway you will notice, almost hidden now among the trees, a large concrete and stonework retaining wall. It was built by newspaper mogul William Randolph Hearst, who planned to build a grand castle on the site. Hearst lived in a Queen Anne-style home called "Sea Point" located a little above and south of the wall foundation; at this time, he was the owner of the Piedmont Land and Cattle Company. In 1890 Hearst donated band instruments, uniforms, and a cart for the local Sea Point Chapter of the Native Sons of the Golden West to wheel through the streets of Sausalito during parades. This $1,000 contraption, with flag tassels of pure gold, is often on display at the Sausalito Historical Museum.

Around 1919 Hearst tore down Sea Point. Old-time Sausalito residents remember that he had been invited to leave town by a delegation of husbands and fathers of the Hill. It seems William Hearst had a special lady friend he had installed at Sea Point, a striking blond whose presence offended the local matrons. The town board of trustees, as the city council was called in those days, was more generous. On July 21, 1921, they wrote Hearst a letter requesting he return to Sausalito and build on his home site. Hearst built his castle at San Simeon instead.

After passing Hearst's retaining wall, the next building you will see as you walk north is the old San Francisco Yacht Club at 558 Bridgeway which now houses a restaurant. Constructed in 1897, the old building also was used at various times as a town meeting place, a bait and tackle shop, and an artist's studio. It was the second yacht club built on the site. The first burned in 1878, and divers have brought up fascinating artifacts from the original building, many of which are on display at the Sausalito Historical Society.

Shoppers may begin in earnest at this point. There are a variety of shops, the Venice Gourmet (an excellent deli), several restaurants and art galleries. Princess Street marks the end of the sidewalk overlooking the water. Princess Street was named for the first ferry that came to Sausalito in 1868 and which made two trips daily to Meiggs Wharf in San Francisco.

The original landing site was a submarine net depot during World War II. It is now Yee Tock Chee Park, a tiny area containing several benches and a concrete platform for fishing. Look for a plaque with the inscription: "Yee Tock Chee Park." In loving memory of Willie Chee, November 1, 1891 – March 2, 1975.

Yee Tock Chee was born in Canton, educated in China, and went to work in a Hong Kong shipyard at age sixteen. After a long steamer ride and a month in the old immigration center on Angel Island, he arrived in Sausalito in 1912. He went to work for Wing Low Ming in a tiny grocery store delivering groceries in a two-wheeled horse cart. In 1919 he bought the business and is remembered with affection for carrying half of Sausalito on his books during the lean Depression years. He also loaned ferryboat fares to commuters short of cash and performed innumerable favors to his customers throughout World War II. The family store, the Marin Fruit and Grocery, remained in business for eighty-three years until 1997.

As you continue along Bridgeway you will pass more shops, then a short street called El Portal adjacent to the Plaza Vina del Mar. This park, dating from 1904, was originally called Depot Park, but in 1960 was renamed Plaza Vina del Mar in honor of Sausalito's sister city in Chile. Its unique elephants and fountain were salvaged from the 1915 San Francisco-Panama Pacific International Exposition by the fountain's designer, architect William B. Faville, a Sausalito resident. It is a "Point of Historical Interest" for the State of California.

The elephants, which originally held 100-foot flagpoles of Oregon pine, were designed by architects McKim, Mead and White of New York. In 1977, citizens of Sausalito donated nearly $16,000 to have the fountain completely refurbished by a skilled Italian craftsman, Eugene Mariani, of the Western Art and Stone Company of Brisbane. The water of the fountain is turned on at 8:00 a.m. daily, a lovely, quiet time to visit.

There is also a drinking fountain at the western tip of the park which was dedicated in 1912 to Jacques Thomas. Thomas, a former Sausalito mayor, was instrumental in having the park, then part of the shoreline, filled in and donated to the city by the North Shore Railroad. Just across Bridgeway from the park are steps leading uphill to Bulkley Ave.

At 801 Bridgeway is the elegant remodeled Casa Madrona Hotel which was built in 1885 as the private residence of William Gront Barrett, a wealthy Vermont-born lumber baron. The original house contained marble fireplaces, stained glass windows, brass chandeliers and elaborate wrought iron grillwork. In 1910 it was turned into a hotel and has been greatly enlarged.

Owner John Mays, who purchased the property in 1976, refurbished the old section of the hotel and added a 16-room addition so that the building now runs from Bulkley Avenue down to Bridgeway and obscures the old building. In 1998 Mays purchased the Village Fair next door to expand his hotel. The shops are now closed and the expanded hotel is scheduled to open in 2001.

The part of Sausalito just described, which includes the ferry landing, park, downtown Bridgeway, up Princess Street on both sides and up to the Alta Mira Hotel on Bulkley Avenue, is part of Sausalito's Historic District. A three year effort finally resulted in recognition by the Secretary of the Department of Interior in Washington, D.C., in 1980, and protects the area for all time. Plans for remodeling any of the buildings in the Historic District must be submitted to various boards.

"The Pirate," a houseboat in Sausalito once owned by actor Sterling Hayden, was built in 1880.

On Anchor Street, off Bridgeway just beyond the plaza, is Gabrielson Park, where a two-ton, twenty-two-foot metal sculpture by Chilean artist Sergio Castillo is on display. On a sunny day, a carpet of sunbathing bodies will cover the entire park. Past Anchor on Bridgeway are public restrooms and telephones. In March 1999 an anchor and plaque were dedicated to honor historic pioneer William Richardson by three historical groups.

The century-old Ice House, now at the corner of Bridgeway and Bay, was donated to Sausalito by resident Michael Rex in June 1997. In March 1999 the building was moved to its present site and in August 1999 opened as a historical visitor's center by the Sausalito Historical Society. Hours are Tuesday through Sunday from 11:30 a.m. to 4:00 p.m.

Four-tenths of a mile farther, at Litho and Caledonia Streets, the city offices, library and the Sausalito Historical Society are located in the old 1927 Sausalito Central School building. The school was remodeled and dedicated as the civic center in March 1975.

At the east end of Litho Street, along the waters of Richardson Bay, is the Earl F. Dunphy Park, dedicated in 1972 to a former mayor of Sausalito who is credited with four decades of dedicated public service. The two-acre Dunphy Park was the culmination of a long conservation battle in the 1960s. Developers bought underwater lots totaling thirty-five acres off the waterfront and drew up plans to build a large development complex. Sausalito passed a bond issue to buy and establish the park in 1970, stopping this development. In 1971, volunteers were organized to plant a lawn and trees on an area of mudflats. Today there is a white gazebo and a flagpole with the dedication: "Two Centuries of Freedom, Erected by the People of Sausalito, July 4, 1976."

Facilities at the park include benches, a picnic area, volleyball court, preschool children's playground, and a bocci ball court. There are also a small sandy beach, large grassy area, and good views of the water, houseboats, sailboats, water birds and the wonderful fresh smell of sea air.

The Bolinar Plaza, dedicated in 1994, is just beyond the foot of Napa Street on Bridgeway. The plaza displays a sixteen-foot stainless steel sculpture by John Libberton depicting three sails plus a low wall forming a semicircle. Bolinar in Portuguese means "close to the wind." The plaza was a joint project of the Sausalito Friends of the Festival and the Sausalito Foundation.

Continue north to Easterby, turn right onto Marinship Way to drive to where the United States Army Corps of Engineers built a hydraulic scale-model of the entire San Francisco Bay and Delta in a building two acres in size. The model's purpose was to "test the physical effects of human activities on Bay and Delta waters... and to help measure the effects of drought, floods, dredging, shoreline development and freshwater diversions to cities and farms."

Originally built in the 1950s, the Bay Model was completely restored. An extensive visitor center was added complete with an introductory video, model overlooks, phone pads explaining various parts of the model, and interactive exhibits about the ocean, bay, local environment and the Corps of Engineers. Ranger-guided tours are available by reservation and self-guided audio tours are available in English, Spanish, German, Japanese and Russian. In July 2000, all research ended using the Bay Model, as engineers decided it would be much cheaper to work with computers. The model remains open to the public. Call 332-3871 or 332-3870 for recorded information which will also give you the hours. New: www.spn.usace.army.mil/bmvc. There is no admission charge.

BAY MODEL
332-3871 or
332-3870
www.spn.usace.ar
my.mil/bmvc.

The Sausalito Historical Society set up an exhibit on a 2500 square foot section of the Bay and Delta Model dedicated to Sausalito's "Marinship," a 210-acre shipyard which produced 93 ships (Liberty ships, oilers and tankers) in just three years during World War II. It is a tribute to the World War II civilian war effort. Artifacts from the USNS Mission Santa Ynez, a tanker built in Marinship, are included in the exhibit.

Anchored at the U.S. Army Corps of Engineers' dock adjacent to the Bay Model is the last of 225 steam schooners, the *Wapama,* sitting on a barge. She was built in 1915 in Oregon and was being restored under the direction of the National Maritime Museum of San Francisco. In 1996 the National Park Service targeted the old ship for demolition but a group called "Save the *Wapama* " campaigned for the ship to be turned into a

Sausalito around 1880. Caledonia Street runs from the foreground toward Hannon's Hill near Napa Street. The railroad trestle crosses Richardson Bay in the background. In the middle (left) *is the old white adobe home of William Richardson.* (Courtesy of the Sausalito Historical Society)

museum. The National Maritime Historical Society donated $50,000 in 1998 for restoration and volunteers began working replacing duckboards, chipping away old deck insulation and applying new paint and varnish. Much more will be needed to stabilize the vessel, millions to actually restore it. In September 2000, the National Park Service announced that the *Wapama* would be moved to Kaiser Shipyard Number 3, Richmond; the U. S. Army Corp of Engineers decided that they needed the docking space at the Bay Model returned for their own use.

From Marinship Way to Harbor Drive, turn right and proceed past the old Marinship building (now called the Industrial Center), then turn left on Gate 5 Road. During World War II, workers entered the shipyard here through guarded gates. It is now the area of the houseboat colony which numbers around five-hundred boats from Gate 5 Road to the north end of Sausalito.

The famous Heath Ceramics is located at 400 Gate 5 Road. Heath manufactures ceramic tableware, decorative gift items, and architectural tiles. There are many bargains at their "Second Shop," which is open from 10:00 a.m. to 5:00 p.m. seven days a week except for holidays. Call 332-3732 for group tours.

HEATH CERAMICS
332-3732

Back to the center of town above Bridgeway, the hills of Sausalito rise over six hundred feet and are covered with spacious old homes, hotels and churches which contrast dramatically with the modern houses. To see some of this area walk up the steps across from Vina del Mar Plaza to Bulkley Avenue. Start at the First Presbyterian Church at 100 Bulkley, built in a shingle style with all-redwood interior. It dates from 1909 and was designed by the architect Ernest Coxhead. Next, stop by the famous Alta Mira Hotel at 125 Bulkley. Rebuilt in 1926 after a fire, the hotel is best-known for its Sunday brunch, served on a spacious deck overlooking the bay.

Another prime attraction of old Sausalito is the Christ Episcopal Church, built in 1882 and located at Santa Rosa and San Carlos Avenues. It is a shingle-style American Gothic design

The ferryboat "Tamalpais," crosses San Francisco Bay around the turn of the century. (Courtesy of Nancy Skinner)

PROFILE: **Phil Frank**

Phil Frank, an author and cartoonist, is a dedicated member of the Sausalito Historical Society. His famous comic strip, "Farley," appears in the *San Francisco Chronicle* and the *Sunday San Francisco Examiner.* The following shows his love affair with his adopted home of Sausalito.

"I was a Midwest visitor to the Bay Area in 1971, a free-lance artist on a late-night search for gasoline when I wandered down Mount Tamalpais and took the exit marked Sausalito. At the stop sign my car's headlights lit up the ghost-like apparition in the blackness of an ancient land-locked ferryboat looming in the fog. I parked my car beside its collapsing bow and stood staring, slack-jawed, up at the behemoth. When I saw a person emerge from the darkness I said, 'What is this? Where am I?' The bemused local says, 'This is Sausalito, man! You're at the houseboats!' and wandered off down a rickety gangplank into a floating village.

"Two years later I returned to California, to Sausalito and those apparitions in the fog. In 1972 my soon-to-be wife Susan and I bought a once glorious houseboat built about 1900 that was in its marine death throes, sinking into the mudflats of the San Francisco Bay waters. We refloated it, restored it and for 13 years called it and the houseboats of Sausalito our home. While Sausalito is where the residents of the houseboat community school their children, buy their groceries and have their workshops, their floating homes are in reality just outside Sausalito, beyond a mythical line in the mud, in county waters.

"It is a curious stew, indeed—the City of Sausalito, with its expensive hillside homes, has always had a love-hate relationship with its waterfront and the denizens that inhabit it. Our curiosity about the turn-of-the-century houseboat we purchased led us to the Sausalito Historical Society and 25 years of local involvement. The town has a fascinating history which visitors can get a taste of at the Icehouse Visitors Center at Bridgeway and Bay.

"Today the busy and elegant ferryboat system that preceded the bridges is now history. The trains of the Northwestern Pacific are gone, as are the fleet of Italian fishing boats and the Portuguese boatbuilders.

"But things change. After 15 years we sold the houseboat and moved to land and suddenly we were looking down at the waterfront. Since we'd also spent many years looking up at the hills, the scene we saw was a bit different.

"Since the 1950s Sausalito's downtown has been a tourist mecca that feeds the needs of families and groups that arrive by car, tour bus and ferryboat (ferry service returned in the 1970s). They come mostly for a few hours, and more commonly these days, for an overnight stay. There are import shops, jewelry stores, ice cream parlors, restaurants, clothiers and eateries. Residents still come downtown to bank and to patronize the restaurants and bars, but the bulk of the resident-serving businesses and city services moved to another part of town years ago.

"So Sausalito is, in many ways, two towns—one being the residential areas that climb the steep hillsides above Bridgeway, its resident-supporting businesses, and waterfront businesses and offices. The other is the downtown with its historic buildings, charming little park and shops aimed primarily at the visitor.

"The residents have accepted the situation, much as the residents of Carmel, Monterey and other attractive seaside towns have. It's a beautiful town with stunning views and a proximity to San Francisco that makes it a handy visitor attraction. Because it is surrounded by former military forts (now the Golden Gate National Recreation Area on two sides), the approach road to the Golden Gate Bridge, and on its eastern side by the waters of Richardson Bay, it will always remain a small town—a special place that residents and visitors love to visit or come home to."

with an especially graceful bell tower and stained glass windows that date from the 1880s, memorial gifts of early Sausalito families. The center windows, installed in 1945, were designed by architect Arnold Constable.

Of special interest, also, is the Sausalito Woman's Club, 120 Central Avenue at San Carlos, designed by Julia Morgan and built in 1917. Morgan also designed a woman's club in Berkeley, buildings at the University of California at Berkeley, and the castle at San Simeon for William Randolph Hearst. The Sausalito Woman's Club is a brown-shingled, split-level building with an all-redwood interior and French windows. It was Sausalito's first official landmark. Today it has a perfectly manicured lawn, brown picket fence, and brick walkways in front.

A fifteen-foot granite bench, affording a gorgeous view of Angel Island and the bay, can be found at Bulkley and Harrison avenues. It is called "Daniel O'Connell's Seat" in memory of the unofficial poet laureate of Sausalito and was installed by fellow members of the San Francisco Bohemian Club in 1901. In the walkway, there is a handsome three-leaf shamrock mosaic, added to celebrate O'Connell's Irish birth. A dedication reads:

In Memory of Daniel O'Connell, Poet, 1849-1899.

Sausalito houseboat community. ▶

Southern Marin   4

From Bay to Mountain

MARIN CITY

A s you leave Sausalito and the Marin Headlands and drive
north on Highway 101, you will see Marin City on your
left. The town evolved as a housing community for workers at Marinship shipyards during World War II. Now the old
prefabricated community has been rebuilt into a small city of
handsome apartments and single-family homes.

In 1996 a new development called "Marin City, USA" opened,
the result of nearly sixteen years of planning for 200,000 square
feet of retail space and 340 new housing units. The project, when
completed, is estimated to cost between seventy-five million and
one-hundred million dollars.

The consortium who put it all together included the BRIDGE
Housing Corporation of San Francisco (Bay Area Residential
Investment and Development), a non-profit organization whose
goals are to build high quality housing at exceptionally afford-
able prices; The Martin Group, an Emeryville developer; The
Marin City Community Development Corporation; The Marin
City Project organized to train residents for permanent employ-
ment; The Marin City Redevelopment Agency; the Security
Pacific Bank; the Marin City Community Services District; the
County of Marin; and the Marin Community Foundation,

◄ *The historic Lyford Tower on Paradise Drive in Tiburon. In July 2000, a
bronze plaque was attached to the tower honoring Eugenia Marans and
Louise Teather. These two women saved the tower in 1976 when it was
threatened by development when they managed to get it listed on the
National Register of Historical Places.*   **47**

which put money in the purchase of land from the Tamalpais High School District and other land acquisition, funded quite a lot of the early planning, paid for a portion of the new highway interchange and overpass, and contributed much to the building of the affordable housing.

The 47-acre site in the heart of the old city where a flea market was once held has now been developed into retail stores and offices. Of the 340 housing units, 85 will be townhouses and 255 apartments.

Also included in Marin City, USA, are a child care facility and community service buildings. Six hundred new permanent jobs have opened up, of which 45% were filled by Marin City residents as well as 45% of the construction jobs.

Other plans, some now complete, include parks, playgrounds, a new library (already open), inter-city bus terminal, additional child care centers, two churches (the First Missionary Baptist and Village Baptist), community activity space and wetlands habitat.

An enlarged Fire and Sheriff's Department public safety building was authorized by the Marin County Board of Supervisors in March 1998 and was estimated to cost $1.5 million. It was to be paid for with $625,000 in Gateway Center redevelopment money earmarked for the new facility and $905,000 to be financed over thirty years. Money generated from sales tax revenue from the Gateway Center would cover the $90,000 annual debt payments. The new facilities, consisting of a firehouse and sheriff's office, opened in June 2000. Also included were a commercial kitchen for the firemen and a community meeting room. The total project was estimated to have a cost over two million dollars.

The architects for the new city included James Guthrie Associates, Michael Willis Associates, Architectural Dimensions and The SWA Group. The contractors were Devcon and Roberts Ohbayashi.

When you stop in to see the new shopping center, take a few minutes to drive up Donohue Drive into the hills where there are some beautifully built apartment houses and spectacular views of Richardson Bay and the sailboats anchored in Sausalito.

MILL VALLEY

Nestled in the southeastern slopes of Mt. Tamalpais, Mill Valley has the charming look of a European mountain village. The town's public buildings and half-timbered shops are built among tall, stately redwood trees. Homes are hidden along the wooded slopes of the lower mountain.

The beauty and uniqueness of the town has always attracted brilliant and talented people. Mill Valley's population includes many famous artists, writers, composers, and performers. Most residents take an active interest in their local government and have fought to keep the private, small-town flavor.

Mill Valley is located in the first Mexican land grant in Marin. Awarded to John Reed by Governor Figueroa in 1834 (some early records show his name as "Juan Read"), *Rancho Corte de Madera del Presidio* was an area that provided "cut wood

John Reed's sawmill in Old Mill Park, Mill Valley.

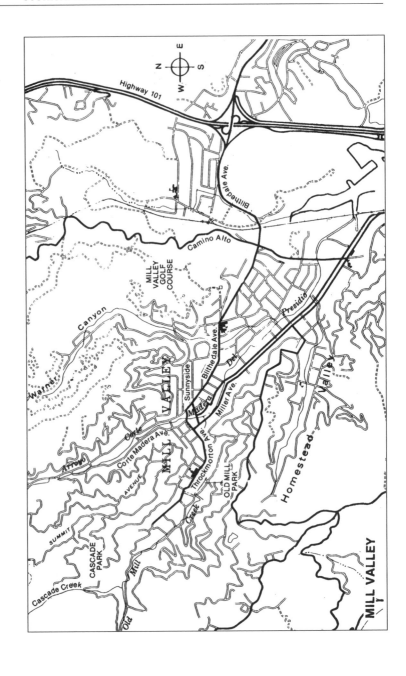

for the Presidio." The grant was 8,878.82 acres and included what is now the Strawberry, Tiburon, Belvedere, and Corinthian peninsulas, as well as parts of Mill Valley, Corte Madera and Larkspur.

John Thomas Reed was born in Dublin, Ireland, in 1805, but left when he was fifteen years old on his uncle's ship to seek his fortune. Their voyage took them to Acapulco, Mexico, then on to California, where they arrived in 1826. Reed turned twenty-one while visiting Los Angeles.

Traveling north, he took a liking to Sausalito and applied unsuccessfully for a grant of the *Rancho Saucelito*. He then moved on to Cotati in Sonoma County. Disaster overtook him there—Indians destroyed his crops and drove him off his land. From Sonoma he went to the mission in San Rafael where he became *mayordomo*, the manager.

Returning to Sausalito in 1832, he lived in a wooden house near Old Town and established the first ferry on San Francisco Bay, a small boat that ran across the water irregularly to Yerba Buena, or what was later San Francisco.

Having applied for several land grants over the years, Reed finally became the recipient of the *Corte de Madera del Presidio* adjoining *Rancho Saucelito*. Here he erected the first sawmill in the county in 1836, planted orchards, put up fencing, and raised imported cattle. He married Hilaria Sanchez, daughter of the commander of the San Francisco Presidio, Don Jose Sanchez. They were married only eight years before Reed died of a "fever" at the early age of thirty-eight. He apparently had a sunstroke, and the friends who started bleeding him as a cure could not stem the flow of blood.

In 1856, Samuel Reading Throckmorton, a real estate dealer from San Francisco, bought *Rancho Saucelito* from Captain William Richardson. The land encompassed 19,000 acres to the west of the *Corte de Madera del Presidio* Creek. A court decision in the late 1860s declared that it also included the site of the sawmill. The two grants were actually divided by a creek that flowed through what is now midtown Mill Valley and continued up Blithedale Canyon.

A 512-acre unclaimed pocket of land in the canyon, between the two grants, was homesteaded in 1873 by Dr. John Cushing, who built what became the fashionable and widely-known Blithedale Resort Hotel.

Captain Richardson's affairs in *Rancho Saucelito* had been in disarray when Throckmorton took them on. Throckmorton never was successful in clearing the major debts, and when he died in 1883, his daughter Susanna was forced to give up 3,790 acres to clear a $100,000 mortgage. The city of Mill Valley was eventually built on this land.

The Tamalpais Land and Water Company was formed to build the new town. Joseph Green Eastland, president of a development company, hired an engineer to survey the prospective town and persuaded the North Pacific Coast Railroad to run a spur line into the area. Train service began in 1890 and continued until 1941.

A successful auction for lots was held in May 1890 at a big picnic near the old sawmill site, where 3,000 prospective buyers purchased 200 acres of land. In 1892 the name of the town was changed to "Eastland" in honor of its most prominent citizen. The depot had a signboard with the new name placed over the old one, but residents still referred to their town as Mill Valley.

The town began as an area of summer homes for wealthy San Franciscans wanting to escape the summer fog. It grew in popularity in 1896 when a railroad was built to take sightseers up to the top of Mt. Tamalpais. Several resort hotels were constructed for the visitors who came from all over the world. (See Chapter 6 about the "Crookedest Railroad in the World.")

On September 1, 1900, the residents voted to incorporate and to reestablish the name of Mill Valley. A story persists to this day that on election day, pro-incorporation forces hired a man named Dan Slinky who, for $50 and a flask of whiskey, jumped off the 5:15 p.m. Marin-bound ferry *San Rafael.* This delayed commuters until the polls closed, assuring a victory for incorporation forces. Four years later, the post office dropped the name "Eastland" altogether.

As Mill Valley prospered, a few stores were built in the downtown area and the plank sidewalks were replaced with concrete. In 1906, refugees from the San Francisco earthquake and fire settled in Mill Valley, then called the "Switzerland of America." Population figures before the fire indicated there were around 900 residents. By 1910, the number had jumped to 2,891, and a library was built on Lovell Avenue.

One of Mill Valley's traditions is the Dipsea Foot Race, founded by athletes of the San Francisco Olympic Club in 1905. The race is 6.8 miles over tortuous terrain, starting in Mill Valley, continuing over Mt. Tamalpais to Stinson Beach, and originally ending at the Dipsea Inn. The Inn was located on a sandspit between Stinson Beach and the town of Bolinas. The race now ends in downtown Stinson Beach.

Rain dampened the first race, held November 19, 1905, so the following year it was moved up to October. Since then it has been moved up several times and is currently held in June because of fire hazards in late summer.

To get to Mill Valley, exit Highway 101 at the Mill Valley turnoff which is "Tiburon Boulevard-East Blithedale Avenue." Follow East Blithedale Avenue to the center of Mill Valley, a distance of 1.8 miles. Just before the Camino Alto intersection you will pass the Blithedale Plaza Shopping Center on the right.

The center of downtown Mill Valley is called Lytton Square, named for Lytton Barber, the city's first casualty of World War I. He died in Fort Lewis, Washington, a victim of the flu epidemic that struck the country in 1917–18.

Lytton Square is not a real square in the traditional sense, but a widening of Throckmorton Avenue, bordered on one side by half-timbered shops and the other by the old Northwestern Pacific Railroad depot, now the Depot Bookstore and Cafe. Next to the old depot is a tiny plaza made of red bricks with a round brick planter box and benches. It is dedicated to Richard Haitt, who designed houses in the area. The plaque reads, "In Appreciation of His Services and His Love for Mill Valley." In the center of Lytton Square are a stand of towering redwoods and beds of flowers.

A particular Mill Valley tradition is the Mill Valley Market in the heart of town at Throckmorton and Corte Madera avenues. One of the finest markets anywhere, it boasts exclusive gourmet

The old train depot in Mill Valley is now a bookstore and cafe.

supplies, an outstanding deli, fine wines and liquors, fresh fruit, vegetables, and meat.

Be sure to visit El Paseo (which means "ornamental passageway"), a narrow old-world Spanish street between Throckmorton and Sunnyside avenues near the Sequoia Theater. This street contains a cluster of shops, offices, studios, and a restaurant. The buildings are constructed of old adobe bricks imported from Mexico, hand-hewn lumber, railroad ties and spikes from the old mountain railroad, and handmade tiles.

The dream of Mill Valley residents Edna and Henry Foster, El Paseo took eight years to build because of delays caused by World War II. The designer, Gus Costigan, was off fighting in the African and Italian campaigns. Edna's interest in Spanish missions and her idea of a complex where artists and craftsmen could live, work and display their wares, led to the final design. The complex features arcades, tile roofs, outside stairways, balconies, patios and built-in seats. The narrow, uneven, sunken street of red brick winds under a heavy-beamed roof where ivy grows abundantly. Located near the Throckmorton entrance is a tiny shrine to St. Francis, showing the saint surrounded by five white doves made of colored tile and abalone shell.

There are several interesting buildings in Mill Valley. At number One Blithedale Avenue stands the beautiful Mill Valley Outdoor Art Club, designed by famous architect Bernard Maybeck and built in 1904. In 1979, it received the protection of a listing on the National Register of Historic Places and designation as a California State Historical Landmark.

Across the street is the round Catholic Church of Our Lady of Mt. Carmel, built in 1968 to replace the original. The twelve-sided sanctuary of brick and stone holds 900 worshippers. The church also features a 134-foot copper spire and gold leaf cross.

In keeping with the decor of the town is the old European-style architecture of the city hall and firehouse, built in 1936 at 26 Corte Madera Avenue. The building consists of red brick, half-timbers over stucco with a steep-pitched shingle roof, mullioned windows, and a tower topped by a weather vane. The police station and part of the fire department have now moved to larger quarters in the eastern part of town.

The old railroad depot, built in 1925, stands on the corner of Miller Avenue and Throckmorton (87 Throckmorton). The building was bought by the city in 1954 along with the railroad right-of-way. It now houses the Mill Valley Depot Bookstore and Cafe where you can buy coffee and deli-type foods in addition to books, magazines, and newspapers. (The original depot was located where the crosswalk from Sunnyside to Miller is today.)

MILL VALLEY
PUBLIC LIBRARY
375 Throckmorton
Telephone:
389-4292

Of special interest is the award-winning Mill Valley Public Library at 375 Throckmorton, which overlooks a picturesque flowing creek in Old Mill Park. The original building, completed in 1966, was designed by architect Donn Emmons of Wurster, Bernardi and Emmons. It is built of concrete with exposed aggregate. A steep roof with a wide overhang, covered with flat shingle-like clay tiles, plus four dormer windows, make an attractive street facade.

The library was renovated and expanded with a 9,000 square foot wing in 1998. The renovation was designed by William Turnbull in a style which closely resembles the original design. The space contains adult fiction, meeting rooms and a new children's room.

PROFILE: **Mimi Farina**

Sing Sing Prison may be a long way from Marin, but there is a definite connection in the person of Mimi Farina, founder of Bread and Roses, located in Corte Madera. Mimi had accompanied her sister, Joan Baez, to the famous penitentiary in New York to hear Baez, B.B. King and others entertain the inmates at a Thanksgiving show. "This was the first time I realized how much live entertainment affects people," Farina recalls. "The guards and prisoners alike became human. Something clicked for me on that occasion and I discovered that music has a healing quality. It is something everyone wants. It is uplifting."

Mimi, a singer herself, started her organization in 1974 ... "with a couple of girlfriends who could type. We called up institutions and asked if they would like some free entertainment. These were people shut in with no future."

The name they picked for their new organization came from a slogan on a banner carried by women in a 1912 Massachusetts textile strike. The strike was the result of women and children being burned in a fire. The slogan read, "Give us bread, but give us roses too!" Today Bread and Roses has 500 volunteers who perform in 400 shows a year. "Think of it this way," Mimi explains proudly. "You'll find Bread and Roses somewhere bringing live entertainment to people shut in every day of the year! We go to 73 institutions, but there are 100 more on the waiting list."

Bread and Roses offers a wide range of performers, including rock and roll, classical piano, a harp player, belly and ballet dancers, and even a bird act. They perform free at convalescent homes, hospitals, prisons, homeless shelters, drug and alcohol rehabilitation centers, AIDS wards, psychiatric facilities and other places around the nine Bay Area counties where people are shut in. "The new trends now," Mimi says, "are toward more performances for youth and multicultural audiences. We are also performing at the cultural center in Marin City."

Bread and Roses had long suffered from inadequate space at their headquarters in Mill Valley, so in 1998 they moved into a larger office building in Corte Madera. This was done as part of a five year plan. In 1999 and 2000 they celebrated their 25th Anniversary. Mimi was excited about the milestone, feeling it showed the organization had "stability and longevity." Over its 25-year history, Bread and Roses produced 10,000 performances for more than 200,000 institutionalized individuals.

Future plans for Bread and Roses include setting up a long-term endowment program. Also on their wish list is publishing a book of photos taken of stars while they were performing for Bread and Roses as a legacy of the first 25 years. Some will be of celebrities such as Peter Coyote, Michael Feinstein, Jerry Garcia, Arlo Guthrie, B.B. King, Joan Baez, the Kingston Trio, Eartha Kitt, Kris Kristofferson, the Mills Brothers, Van Morrison, Peter, Paul and Mary, Bonnie Raitt, Rob Reiner, Pete Seeger, Paul Simon, the Smothers Brothers, Lily Tomlin, Robin Williams, Neil Young and others and will include Mimi herself.

To the right of the main entrance is a sculpture group of grey and black granite designed by the late Richard O'Hanlon, a Mill Valley resident and professor emeritus of art at the University of California at Berkeley. A bench, also of his design, is on the left; it was given to the library in memory of the writer Nathan Asch by Asch's wife, a Mill Valley resident.

When you enter the library, a sweeping view through large windows across the width of the building to the deck and redwood trees beyond gives an open feeling and sense of being outside. Windows in the new addition offer extraordinary views of the meandering creek below. The deck is suspended ten feet above the ground, becoming part of the park.

The furniture throughout was custom-designed and built by Arthur Carpenter in collaboration with the architect. Carpenter's shop, Espenet, is near Bolinas. Except for the chairs, the library furniture is fine hand-rubbed walnut with an oil finish.

Downstairs is the History Room, dedicated in June 1977 and greatly expanded in the 1998 addition, in honor of Lucretia Hanson Little, official city historian and retired deputy city clerk, who died later that year. The Mill Valley Historical Society provides docents and helps collect historical materials. A collection of books, photographs and memorabilia on California, Marin, and Mill Valley history lines the walls.

Old Mill Park below the library on Cascade Drive contains the original site of John Reed's mill, California Historical Landmark Number 207. A reconstruction of the old structure is beside the creek: nine large timbers laid across side beams which supported the floor of the mill and a roof. A replica of the Mt. Tam gravity train car sits opposite the old mill. The park, open from sunrise to sunset, also provides a children's playground, barbecues, picnic tables, and restrooms.

Old Mill Park is the site of the Mill Valley Fall Arts Festival, held annually in September. The festival features fine arts and crafts of ceramics, glass works, jewelry, leather, fabrics, woodwork, and sculpture. Varied entertainment is provided for the two days of the fair.

Continue up curvy Throckmorton Avenue to Cascade Park at the north end of Cascade Drive. The "cascade" is a waterfall dropping thirty feet over a rock channel in a canyon of redwoods and other trees. A small tributary, the East Fork, joins the stream below the falls. The combined stream then flows under Cascade Drive and joins Old Mill Creek. About a hundred yards downstream is the "Three Wells" area, actually three natural pools.

At Cascade Park there are hiking trails, but no restrooms or picnic areas. The park is open from sunrise to sunset, and no parking is allowed in the area from 11:00 p.m. to 6:00 a.m. Call the Parks and Recreation Department at 383-1370 for more information.

In 1938, Mill Valley bought out a private golf course and opened it to the public. This lovely nine-hole course, the first public course in Marin, is open seven days a week and is located at 280 Buena Vista Avenue. (Turn off Blithedale Avenue at Carmelita, then right on Buena Vista.) It features a proshop, provides lessons, club sales and repairs.

MILL VALLEY PARKS AND RECREATION DEPARTMENT 383-1370

MILL VALLEY GOLF COURSE 388-9982

STRAWBERRY PENINSULA

On the east side of Highway 101, opposite Mill Valley, is the Strawberry Peninsula. To get there, turn onto Tiburon Boulevard, then make a right turn at the first stoplight onto Frontage Road. The red tile roofs of the Town and Country Village are visible from the freeway. This popular shopping center includes a supermarket, gas station, several restaurants, pharmacy, exclusive clothing shops, and dozens of specialty stores.

To visit the 146-acre Golden Gate Baptist Theological Seminary, continue on Frontage Road to Seminary Drive and turn left. On your right will be Belloc's Lagoon, a salt water marsh which provides an excellent spot for watching migratory birds. There is a parking area to the right and an asphalt path that runs along the edge of the marsh. Hilary Belloc and his wife once owned the adjacent de Silva Island, which is the home for many deer, raccoons, and a variety of birds. In 1980 a great blue heron rookery was built.

Stay to your right on Seminary Drive for half a mile, then turn left on Hodges Drive. Golden Gate Baptist Theological Seminary was organized in 1944 in Berkeley and is one of six seminaries sponsored by the Southern Baptist Convention.

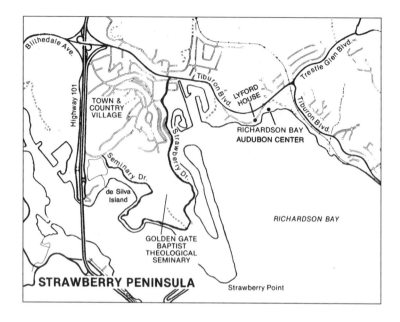

STRAWBERRY PENINSULA

This site on the Strawberry Peninsula was considered for permanent world headquarters of the United Nations before New York City was finally selected. The Southern Baptist Convention bought the property in 1954 and engaged John Carl Warnecke, a prominent San Francisco architect, to design the buildings. Classes began in 1959, and today there are students here from all over the world.

Visits by the public are encouraged. You may take a scenic drive through the peaceful campus and enjoy views of Richardson Bay and Mt. Tamalpais. As you wind up and around, you can see Belvedere and Sausalito along with San Francisco and the Oakland Bay Bridge. For more information on the Golden Gate Seminary call 388-8080 or 380-1300.

GOLDEN GATE
SEMINARY
388-8080 or
380-1300

To tour the Strawberry Peninsula, continue on Seminary Drive which joins Strawberry Drive in a circle that will bring you out to Tiburon Boulevard, a drive of about two-and-a-half miles. This land once belonged to Hilarita Reed, who inherited 1,467 acres from her mother, Ylaria Sanchez Reed de Garcia. She received 446 acres in Strawberry and 1,021 acres at *Punta de Tiburon*. Hilarita married Dr. Benjamin Franklin Lyford in 1872.

Four years later, they visited the Centennial Exposition in Philadelphia where they viewed all the latest inventions from the Industrial Revolution to get ideas for the house they were planning. Two years later, they built a three-story Victorian home with a tower at Harbor Cove.

Behind the Lyford mansion, the North Pacific Coast Railroad operated a line along the eastern shore of the Strawberry Peninsula. The trains ran from Sausalito to San Rafael, and the Lyford family was allowed to ride free in exchange for the right-of-way. Dr. Lyford is remembered not only for the development of his wife's property and his "Eagle Dairy" of Jersey cows, but for his unique embalming experiments which caused many a lifted eyebrow.

In 1957 the Lyford mansion was barged across the waters of Richardson Bay to the headquarters of the Richardson Bay Audubon Center and Sanctuary operated by the National Audubon Society. The house was donated by Sam Neider and $25,000 for restoration work was given by Mrs. Donald Dickey in memory of her husband, a well-known ornithologist.

To learn more about Audubon, look up the Website: www.audubon.org. To learn about specific classes at the Richardson Bay Audubon Center, call 388-2524.

TIBURON PENINSULA

RICHARDSON BAY AUDUBON CENTER, 388-2524 www.audubon.org.

As you come out of Strawberry, turn right on Tiburon Boulevard, which winds along the shoreline toward the town of Tiburon. At the first traffic light, opposite the Cove Shopping Center, is Greenwood Cove Drive. To visit the Richardson Bay Wildlife Sanctuary, turn right from Tiburon Boulevard and follow Greenwood Cove Drive (which becomes Greenwood Beach Road).

Richardson Bay Audubon Center and Sanctuary

About half a mile down Greenwood Beach Road are nearly nine hundred acres of rich tidelands saved from development by the efforts of many local conservationists. The tidelands are part of the Richardson Bay Audubon Center and Sanctuary, which provide shelter for flocks of migrating waterfowl. This area is closed to boating from October to March for the protection of the birds.

The Richardson Bay Sanctuary is a major destination for birds on the Pacific Flyway. During the winter, there are high densities of water birds, including some 80 species, and thousands of water fowl and shorebirds. Other birds stop over while flying to Central and South America.

The grounds, which encompass an eleven acre education center, are open all year, Wednesday through Sunday, except holidays, 9:00 a.m. to 5:00 p.m. Public programs such as bay shore studies and field trips are conducted on Sundays. There are also classes taught on water birds such as ducks, shorebirds, herons, pelicans, grebes, cormorants, gulls and terns. Still other classes teach beginners about bird watching and about birds around the Bay Area.

You can pick up information and trail maps in a store called the "Book Nest." There is also an education center which has displays on endangered species and outdoor native plants and gardens.

Beyond the education center at 376 Greenwood Beach Road is the Lyford House, painted yellow with white trim. The charming old mansion was moved onto the present site after the land was donated by Rosa Rodriques da Fonte Verrall. "Rosie" was known as the "Goat Lady" who kept a small herd of goats that kept the grass down. She had received the land as a gift from John Paul Reed. Open 1:00 p.m. to 4:00 p.m. on Sundays, November through the end of April. (388-2524)

LYFORD HOUSE
388-2524

Dr. Lyford, an embalming surgeon during the Civil War, was one of the first persons to ever use color on corpses. In his 1871 embalming patent Lyford included instruction to "color the lips, cheeks and other part of the face to life." This was far in advance of the techniques of the time. In 1870, the *San Francisco Evening Bulletin* reported that a woman Lyford embalmed was still lifelike (and unburied) two-and-one-half years later.

Benches outside the mansion were dedicated to Carol Sealy Livermore in 1960, and to Rosa da Fonte Verall on her eightieth birthday, August 8, 1963. Immediately inside the Lyford House is an elegant, curved African mahogany staircase. Furnished rooms include a living room, study, library, bedroom and child's room.

You can climb up the nearly-straight eighteen steps to the tower of the Lyford House and look toward San Francisco through an old E. Krauss telescope from Paris. The view all around is spectacular.

Blackie's Pasture and the Richardson Bay Path

As you continue northeast on Greenwood Beach Road to Tiburon Boulevard, you will notice a large open field that is known as Blackie's Pasture. Blackie was an old sway-backed horse who grazed here for over a quarter of a century until his death February 26, 1966.

Before that Blackie had quite a career. He was a cavalry horse at the San Francisco Presidio, then belonged to the National Park Service where he was used to patrol at Yosemite National Park in the summer. Blackie was finally pastured in Tiburon where he lived to age forty. Children would come down and feed him carrots and sugar and show him a lot of love.

Blackie was so popular that a group of residents took up a collection and had a life-size statue of the horse placed in the field in 1995. The project was headed by Larry Smith, former Mayor of Tiburon and Jim Mitchell, a former member of the Belvedere Planning Commission. Under the umbrella of the Tiburon Peninsula Foundation, of which Smith was President and Mitchell, Vice-President, they commissioned sculptor Albert Guibarra of Burlingame to design a statue of Blackie to be cast out of bronze sheets. Most of the money for the sculpture, $30,000, came from a bequest which was designated for the good of the community, left by Gordon Strawbridge, the first mayor of Tiburon.

Blackie, the old, beloved horse.

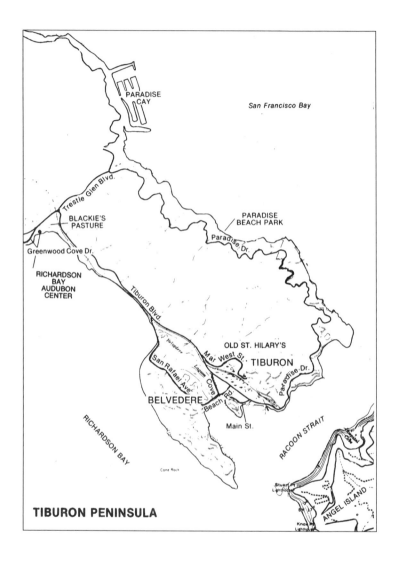

San Francisco Bay

PARADISE CAY

Trestle Glen Blvd.

BLACKIE'S PASTURE

PARADISE BEACH PARK

Paradise Dr.

Greenwood Cove Dr.

RICHARDSON BAY AUDUBON CENTER

Tiburon Blvd.

Belvedere

OLD ST. HILARY'S

Mar West St.

San Rafael Ave.

Lagoon

Cove Rd.

TIBURON

Paradise Dr.

BELVEDERE

Beach Rd.

Main St.

RICHARDSON BAY

Cone Rock

RACOON STRAIT

Stuart Pt. Lighthouse

ANGEL ISLAND

Knox Lighthouse

TIBURON PENINSULA

Another $80,000 in grants came from the Metropolitan Transportation Commission to build two parking lots in the pasture, one paved and one gravel.

The Tiburon Peninsula Foundation is now working on a Tiburon Historical Trail with the Landmarks Society, who will provide photos and text for some planned interpretive boards.

There will be archival pictures (and text) taken from the same location as the new boards, allowing a "yesterday" and "today" comparison. The trail will go between the Donahue Railroad-Ferry Depot and Blackie's Pasture.

Turn right on Tiburon Boulevard and continue down the peninsula. The road narrows and takes a sharp right turn around Blackie's Pasture. On your left is Trestle Glen Boulevard, where an old wooden railroad trestle once crossed Tiburon Boulevard. Trestle Glen Boulevard leads northeast to Paradise Drive, which winds along the east side of the Tiburon Peninsula facing San Francisco Bay.

Following the shoreline toward downtown Tiburon is the fifty-five-acre Richardson Bay Lineal Park. The McKegney Green sports field, used mainly for soccer, is named in memory of George McKegney, a popular member of the Tiburon Parks and Recreation Commission. It is just a short distance from the pasture where ample free parking is available.

From Blackie's Pasture, a two-mile blacktop path, used for bicycles, jogging, walking, and skating, runs all the way into Tiburon along what was once the railroad right-of-way. Bicyclists and others may continue from downtown Tiburon by ferry to Angel Island.

Old St. Hilary's Historic Preserve

About two miles past Blackie's Pasture, watch for a sign on the right which announces a historical landmark. Turn left on Beach Road (stoplight), cross Mar West Street where the street name changes to Esperanza, and drive a mile or so to Old St. Hilary's Church. Here you will have a striking panoramic view of downtown Tiburon, Belvedere, and San Francisco.

Old St. Hilary's is an example of "Carpenter's Gothic," defined as a simplified interpretation of Gothic Revival architecture by a carpenter using available materials. This Catholic mission church, built of redwood and Douglas fir, held services for residents of the area from 1888 to 1954. In 1959, Old St. Hilary's was acquired by the Belvedere-Tiburon Landmarks

Old St. Hilary's, Tiburon.

Society, which maintains the building and wildflower preserve. It is used for lectures, concerts, ceremonies and is a favorite place for weddings.

Inside the church the woodwork is redwood while the ceiling is Douglas fir. Wooden knobs on the walls mark the former Stations of the Cross. There are also round-end pews, chandeliers, replicas of the original oil lamps and an original window donated by Dr. and Mrs. Benjamin Lyford depicting St. Hilary, patron saint of scholars. A Spanish copper cross from Sante Fe is on the back wall.

To preserve the unique wildflowers of the area, in the 1960s three-and-a-half acres were added to the original half-acre lot donated by Dr. and Mrs. Lyford for the church. Two-hundred-and-seventeen plant species have been identified on the site, including the black jewel flower (*streptanthus niger*), a member of the mustard family found growing only on serpentine rock on the southern end of the Tiburon Peninsula. There are also several endangered flowers: the Tiburon paintbush (*Castilleja neglecta*); the Tiburon buckwheat (*Eriogonum caninum*); and the Marin dwarf flax (*Hesperolinon congestum*).

Some flowers bloom all year long, but most blossom in April and May. Spring flowers include biscuit root, blue dicks, gold fields, tidy tips, and California placella. From May to July there are many species of lilies blooming, while summer and fall plants include common buckwheat, tar weed, and Bigelow's sneezeweed.

In the fall, members of the grass families are on display, such as grass of Parnassus and Pacific hairgrass. These grow on the lower portion of the preserve where there are natural springs.

You may climb down the steps from the church to the lower section and walk along the path called the Old Alemany Road. Benches are built into a stone wall. You may also walk the trails over the hill.

The preserve includes the John Thomas Howell Botanical Garden, the Caroline S. Livermore Vista Point, and Dakin Lane, a pedestrian link between streets named in honor of a family of Landmarks Society benefactors. Old St. Hilary's is open from April through October on Wednesdays and Sundays from 1:00 p.m. to 4:00 p.m. Group tours may be arranged all year by calling the Landmarks Society at 435-1853.

LANDMARKS
SOCIETY
435-1853.

Tiburon

"Tiburon" is the Carib Indian word for shark which was adopted by the Spanish explorers. It first appeared on the Ayala maps of San Francisco Bay, 1776, as *Punta de Tiburon* or "shark point." The small town grew up around a railroad complex built at Point Tiburon in 1884 by Peter Donahue, owner of the San Francisco and North Pacific Coast Railroad. Donahue extended the line from San Rafael to Tiburon in order to compete for the fastest ferry service between San Francisco and Marin. The boats were designed to carry train cars and passengers in thirty minutes one-way. Commuter fares were just fifteen cents (twenty-five cents round trip). A roundhouse, shops, depot, train sheds, wharf, and ferry slip served the trains and ferryboats. This area is now occupied by the library, town hall, and retail and condominium development. In June 2000 the new 1.2-acre Zelinsky Park was dedicated to honor Fred and Juanita Zelinsky, who donated land for the Town Hall and library. The park is located behind the Town Hall.

At 1920 Paradise Drive in the shoreline park along Racoon Straits is the gray, two-story landmark building which was the Railroad-Ferry Depot. In 1997-98 the building was restored to its original historic dimensions and a museum installed. The work, a project of the Belvedere-Tiburon Landmarks Society, was done by Michael Stasse, a contractor experienced in historic restoration, with the pro bono advice of structural engineers Peter Culley and Robert Van Blaricom, both residents of Tiburon. The architect, Thomas Everett Brown, is a Belvedere resident and past president of the Landmarks Society. The depot is on the National Register of Historic Places and is significant because of its unique use as both a depot and station master's house. It originally sat on a pier, but after a storm in 1920, Northwestern Pacific decided to move the building to dry

The train yard in Tiburon in the 1950s. (Photo courtesy of Bob Molton)

land where it is located today. In 1999, when restoration was completed, the Society received the prestigious Governor's Award for Historic Preservation for that year.

Installation of the railroad-ferry history museum is in progress in the depot known locally as the Donahue Building. The ground floor will house working models of the Tiburon yard and waterport circa 1900 and the upstairs will be a house museum representing the station master's quarters circa 1920. Historic photographs and paintings of Point Tiburon and the railroad-ferry system are on exhibit. The depot museum is open April through October, Sunday and Wednesday afternoons, from 1:00 p.m. to 4:00 p.m.

In its early days, Tiburon's Main Street was a tough waterfront area of stores, hotels, a post office, and several rowdy taverns from which came stories of bootlegging during Prohibition. Fire swept through these commercial waterfront buildings three times, and each time they were rebuilt.

The progressive Dr. Lyford saw an opportunity for real estate development at Point Tiburon and in 1890 subdivided an area which he called "Lyford's Hygeia," after the goddess of health, with impressive stone towers and an arch at the entrance. The waterside tower still stands at 2036 Paradise Drive, preserved through the efforts of the Town of Tiburon's Heritage Commission and donations from many individuals. It is listed on the National Register of Historical Places.

Early industries of the Tiburon/Belvedere area were drying and packing Alaska cod, working the oyster beds, stripping and burning old ships for salvage, powder and brick works, boat yards, and dairy ranches. A Navy coaling station base on the east side contributed to Tiburon's salty population.

Ferryboats lasted until 1909, when travelers were rerouted to Sausalito. Until 1934, a small boat, the *Marin,* hauled passengers to Sausalito, where they boarded the larger ferries to San Francisco. Freight shipping continued until 1967 on the Northwestern Pacific Railroad, or NWP, created by mergers of five lines in 1907.

As you near downtown Tiburon, the Boardwalk shopping complex is on the right. The shopping center and this portion of Tiburon were constructed on landfill in the 1950s.

Tiburon stayed small until after World War II, when the town experienced a great burst of population. After the Boardwalk was built, basic business shifted away from Main Street. The old grocery, butcher shop, garage, and post office disappeared, opening up the area for dress shops, gift stores, art galleries, restaurants and bars.

In 1955, as Tiburon was changing from a railroad to a suburban/tourist town, a campaign was launched by volunteers to repaint faded facades of the buildings on Main Street. On the appointed weekend, September 24-25, men, women, and teenagers painted, bagpipes played, and tables were set up in the street to provide the hundred or so volunteers with food, coffee, beer and wine. They called it the "paint-up party."

Today, Main Street in Tiburon is a colorful collection of shops and restaurants, some designed to look like stores in the California gold country a century ago. You can easily spend a whole day browsing through the fascinating shops, or eating and drinking on an outdoor deck. On Main Street there are also several excellent restaurants and bars. A "must" for visitors is to enjoy lunch on Sam's dock while watching the endless panorama of graceful sailboats gliding by. There is always a refreshing breeze, the smell of the sea, the sounds of the waves lapping against the shore, and the call of the gulls.

Where Main Street turns and becomes Ark Row, you will find the entrance to the Corinthian Yacht Club. Walk in a few steps and you will immediately see a forest of boat masts and white sails with the spectacular skyline of San Francisco in the background. The clubhouse itself is a graceful old white wooden building on the water's edge.

Founded in 1886, the Corinthian sponsors several races, including the Buckner Ocean Race and the Midwinter Regatta. The major event of the year is the "Pageantry of the Blessing of the Pleasure Craft" on San Francisco Bay, held on the opening day of yachting season in the spring. As Main Street curves around to the right, the "Village Ark Row Shops" begins. This block was added to Main Street in 1957. Two of the shops are in old remodeled arks in which people used to live. They are iden-

Elephant Rock off Paradise Drive, Tiburon.

tified by blue and white plaques. Others are remodeled cottages, and still others are brand-new buildings.

Tiburon Vintners is on the corner leading to the arks in an old wooden building built as a rooming house. Inside, notice the tongue-and-groove ceiling and the wooden floor. The Vintners is open daily and offers free tasting. Wines are from the Windsor Vineyards of Sonoma County which produce premium California quality wines. They are sold only here and at the winery, though some may be purchased by mail order. Additional wines are bottled under the Rodney Strong label and are sold throughout the United States. In 1998, according to the "California Wine Winners" which keeps track of eight big wine tasting competitions, Windsor Vinyards came in number one in California

Continuing along Ark Row you can find imported clothes, antiques, flowers, an art gallery, toys, books, crafts and antiques. If you look up as you walk along here, you will see handsome modern homes on what is Corinthian Island, now linked to the peninsula. Main Street ends at Beach Road.

PROFILE: **Beverly Bastian**

Beverly Wright Bastian of Belvedere has been a volunteer for 52 years and is the founder and mainstay of the Belvedere-Tiburon Landmarks Society. Old St. Hilary's, the China Cabin, the Railroad-Ferry Depot and a new project, the historic Brick Kiln site, are all evidence of her dedication to the saving of important historical buildings. Of course, there have been many people working on these projects and donating money, but Beverly has always been a driving force to see the job through to completion.

The Wright family came to California in the 1860s. During World War I, Beverly's father, while in the Navy, met her mother in New York City where she was an American Red Cross Volunteer Hostess. They were married and Beverly was born in 1919. The family returned to California and lived in Contra Costa County.

Beverly is a graduate of the University of Pacific with a B.A. in English Literature. She met her husband, Robert Bastian, a political cartoonist, in school, and they were married after he returned from Marine Corps duty in the Pacific. They bought a lot in 1946 on Belvedere Island for $1500. She remembers her first house in Belvedere cost only $9000.

After their three children were born, the family moved to a larger home; Beverly became involved in school work and earned an M.A. in Early Childhood Education. She established six non-profit nursery schools: Belvedere, Marin City at St. Andrews Church, Tamalpais in Mill Valley, Strawberry, Hawthorne in Tiburon and the Marin Child Development Center. She also was a consultant for reorganizing the Ross Valley Nursery School, and starting two nursery schools in Northern Marin. All of the schools were cooperatively owned by the parents but professionally staffed. She was the Executive Director of all the schools for 25 years and designed and constructed new schools in Mill Valley and Strawberry.

Vera Schultz, the first woman elected to the Marin County Board of Supervisors, nominated Beverly to the Family Service Agency Board where she served for eight years. During that time it was established as a nationally accredited agency.

Beverly's work with the Belvedere-Tiburon Landmarks Society as Projects Director has covered forty years. Purchasing the land adjacent to Old St. Hilary's, which is a wildflower preserve, took ten years. They bought it parcel by parcel. China Cabin took eight years and cost $600,000.

The Donahue Depot, the only structure left of the extensive Railroad-Ferry Terminal, was donated by Southern Pacific Railroad, along with the Shoreline Park, to Tiburon for a history museum. It took a decade to negotiate a 99-year lease with the town, after which the society restored the building and started installation of Railroad-Ferry exhibits.

Fifteen years ago a friend, Helen Newman, who was on the first Planning Commission of Tiburon and worked on saving Richardson Bay, talked to Beverly about bequeathing the Newman home and an acre of garden at 841 Tiburon Boulevard to the Landmarks Society. (She left a will to this effect.) The historic site is being converted into a community art and garden center which will include the restored 1870 cottage, terraced gardens and a new studio complex for art classes. It will take a few years of construction before it is open to the public.

Beverly Bastian has been honored over the years for all her volunteer work. She is the only Peninsula resident to be named "Citizen of the Year" by both the cities of Belvedere and Tiburon. In 1980 she received the Jefferson Award, given by the American Institute for Public Service, "In recognition of outstanding public service" in the San Francisco Bay Area.

In 1992 the University of the Pacific gave her the "Distinguished Alumni Award for Public Service." Other awards have come from the Marin Conservation Council, Family Service Agency of Marin, Marin Child Development Center, and the Conference of California Historical Societies. In addition, the Belvedere-Tiburon Landmarks Society's award stated: "In grateful recognition of the Catalyst, the Master Mind, the Guiding Spirit in our conservation program."

On November 19, 1979, the Tiburon Town Council approved a master plan submitted by Southern Pacific Railroad to develop thirty-eight acres of downtown Tiburon that once were railroad yards. Included in this plan was a shoreline park connecting the ferry landing to the Donahue Depot and Elephant Rock Pier.

The master plan was completed in the 1980s, changing forever the sleepy railroad town that was once Tiburon. One-hundred-and-fifty-five condominiums are now located in buildings three stories high with natural wood shingles and steep red roofs. Most look out over the water with views of San Francisco.

The park is a bright green strip of grass adjacent to the rock wall built along the bay. People can rest on benches and enjoy the view. Elephant Rock, with its 70-foot pier extending into Racoon Straits, was completely rebuilt in 1999 after being damaged by a heavy storm three years earlier. The platform which encircles the rock was built in memory of an 11 year old boy, Robert "Bunkie" Keener of San Rafael, who drowned when fishing here on October 1, 1960. Residents wanted a safe place where children could fish, and now children who have fished there since 1961 have grown up and are returning with their children to fish.

Part of the Tiburon master plan included 25,000 square feet of commercial space which was built between the housing units and the road. A lagoon with a jet of water was added, along with a bridge connecting the shopping areas. The sidewalks are an attractive red brick.

Tiburon was thrust into the world spotlight when its favorite son, 22 year old Jonny Moseley, won the gold medal for freestyle moguls in the 1998 Olympics in Nagano, Japan. Moseley went on in the same year to win the World Cup title, having won five contests during the winter, and was honored as the nation's Number One Skier for 1998. He was also awarded the Beck International Award, given by the U.S. Ski and Snowboard Association every year to the outstanding competitor of the previous season.

Belvedere

Belvedere Island, linked by former sandspits that are now San Rafael Avenue and Beach Road, has some of the most elegant homes in the Bay Area, many with waterfront docks and almost all with spectacular views. To get there, turn right off Tiburon Boulevard onto San Rafael Avenue or Beach Road. Perhaps the best way to see the island is to follow the lovely, landscaped San Rafael Avenue until it ends at Beach Road.

Belvedere, like Tiburon, was part of the original *Rancho de Madera del Presidio* Mexican land grant awarded to John Thomas Reed, but his heirs, like all Californians, had to go to a U.S. court to prove the claim after the gold rush. The "island" had been taken over by a man named Israel Kashow, a blond-haired giant of a man who stood six feet, three inches tall and weighed 250 pounds. Kashow, who married four times and sired seven children, was described as tough, stubborn, and short-tempered. He once fired a mixed dose of birdshot and salt at uninvited visitors who went swimming in the cove in front of his house. The swimmers sued but did not gain much by their efforts; the judge gave them one dollar.

From 1855 to 1885, Kashow and his family lived on what he called Kashow's Island. Along with the problem of transportation, his thirty-year residency kept the land from premature development. In 1868, James C. Bolton, the Reed family's attorney, received this land in payment for his successful court case against Kashow; this was eventually sold to Thomas B. Valentine. Valentine organized the Belvedere Land Company with five San Francisco businessmen as partners. They subdivided the island in 1890. In 1896, Belvedere's few residents voted thirty-three to twenty-four to incorporate.

Valentine also owned Corinthian Island but did not include the "little hill" in the Belvedere Land Company properties. When the city was incorporated, the boundary line divided the unoccupied island, with the half overlooking Tiburon's Main Street remaining in county jurisdiction and the half overlooking

Belvedere Cove included in the new city. In 1907, Valentine's widow sold the island to the Kelley Brothers, Tiburon businessmen who formed the Corinthian Land Company. They took the name from the yacht club which had been leasing the south point. The Corinthian Yacht Club bought their site when the island was subdivided for residential development. Belvedere and Corinthian Island were now connected by a drawbridge over a channel nine-feet deep which provided passage from the bay to the extensive lagoon.

The four-story Belvedere Hotel was built on Belvedere Cove, where Kashow's house used to stand. On this same spot today, at 98 Beach Road, is the San Francisco Yacht Club, the oldest yacht club west of the Mississippi. The club started originally in San Francisco in 1855 and was incorporated in 1869. Club members moved to Sausalito at the turn of the century, and then to Belvedere in 1927 to escape the heavy ferry traffic.

The City of Belvedere has worked for the past several years to provide an open view of the San Francisco skyline from Beach Road. One of the structures that had to be moved to accomplish this was the "China Cabin," which was being used as part of a private home. When the "China Cabin" was slated for demolition, the Landmarks Society intervened, which resulted in Belvedere deeding the structure to the Society and leasing the cove site where it is now located.

The "China Cabin" was the elegant social saloon on the *S.S. China,* a wooden sidewheel steamer commissioned by the Pacific Mail Steamship Company. Designed by W.H. Webb, an American naval architect, the *China* was built in 1866 in New York and came to its homeport, San Francisco, via the Strait of Magellan. It sailed between California and the Far East until 1879.

Today, visitors can view the cabin which includes the saloon and staterooms of the ship's surgeon and chief engineer. All have been beautifully restored. The interior is white and gold with an oak floor trimmed in walnut. There are cut glass windows, and brass and crystal replicas of oil burning chandeliers. The Landmarks Society of Belvedere-Tiburon spent eight years and $600,000 to restore the glittering gilded China Cabin. Although

China Cabin

the decoration inside consists of only three ounces of 22 carat gold, the cost of the gold leaf application was $50,000.

The China Cabin at 52 Beach Road is open April through October, Wednesdays and Sundays from 1:00 p.m. to 4:00 p.m. There is no admission charge, but donations are welcome. It is also open all year by appointment and is available for private social events. Call the Landmarks Society, 435-1853.

LANDMARKS
SOCIETY
435-1853

Paradise Drive

Paradise Drive winds its way from the town of Tiburon around the peninsula and ends back at Highway 101. As you follow Paradise Drive from town, you will pass large gates on your right with signs identifying the Romberg Tiburon Center for Environmental Studies (RTC), San Francisco State University (SFSU). Further down the road, again on the right, you will find the second entrance to RTC as well as the center's Bay Conference Center.

Bay and ocean-related activities have been going on at this site for over one-hundred years, beginning with a cod fishery and including a U.S. Navy Coaling Station, Nautical School, Navy Net Depot, and Oceanographic Center. San Francisco State University established the Romberg Tiburon Center for Environmental Studies, which is a marine and estuarine educational and research facility, in 1978. The facility occupies 25 acres overlooking San Pablo Bay and includes research laboratories, classrooms, administration offices, a conference center and a guest center for visiting scientists and conference attendees.

Research being conducted at the Center is diverse and includes the fields of marine biology, marine physiology, biological oceanography and physical oceanography. RTC scientists are concerned with problems in San Francisco Bay such as introduced species, bay productivity and the effects of the physical aspects of the bay on organisms that live there. Research at RTC is not limited to San Francisco Bay. Many of the scientists conduct research in other regions of the world, including Monterey Bay, the Atlantic Coast, the Equatorial Pacific and Antarctica.

Education through research and classroom instruction has been part of the Romberg Tiburon Center since it was first established. With its close proximity to salt marshes, the rocky intertidal areas, sandy beaches and open waters, RTC is a perfect setting for active field study. Each semester, undergraduate and graduate courses are taught in marine plants and animals, wetland ecology and management, biology of the algae, ecology of estuaries and lagoons, biological oceanography, general oceanography and remote sensing of coastal zones. Education facilities include outdoor and indoor research laboratories, culture rooms and research vessels. Many graduate students conduct thesis research at RTC. Courses are also offered each summer to SFSU students and the public through SFSU's College of Extended Learning.

In 1993, the Romberg Center acquired a 38-foot motor yacht which has been re-engineered for oceanographic use. The *R/V Questuary* is well-suited for work in the San Francisco Bay. The vessel is used by RTC scientists and students as well as by other local institutions, federal and state agencies and commercial environmental consulting groups.

BAY CONFERENCE
CENTER
338-3543

The Bay Conference Center is located in the old Naval Officer's Club which was used during World War II and the Korean War. The remodeled facilities include a 150-seat main hall, lounge area with fireplace, two meeting rooms, picnic areas and parking. Call 338-3543 for more information.

Paradise Beach County Park, just beyond the Bay Conference Center, is a curvy 3.2 miles from downtown Tiburon. Surplus land from original government property was used to establish this nineteen-acre beachfront park, plus the open space area called the Tiburon Uplands Nature Reserve, consisting of twenty-four acres of steep hillside.

Paradise Park has a beach and a long fishing pier where people fish for striped bass, steelhead, rockfish, salmon, jack smelt, sea perch, sturgeon and sharks. Picnic facilities and restrooms are available. There is a fee to enter.

Before arriving back at the freeway, you will pass Paradise Cay, a water-oriented community with houses built out over the water; Marin Country Day School, a private elementary school; and the Ring Mountain Preserve managed by the Nature Conservancy. One-hundred-seventeen acres were acquired to establish the preserve in 1981-82, and another 260 acres in 1984. Besides rare plant species, the area is interesting for the mysterious markings on ridge outcroppings made by Native Americans nearly 2,000 years ago. The significance of these petroglyphs is unknown.

Continuing on Paradise Drive toward Highway 101, you will see the San Clemente Park on your left which contains a picnic area, playground, baseball field, basketball and sand volleyball courts. Beyond, you will pass the Paradise Shopping Center.

Another to way to see this side of the Tiburon peninsula is by riding the ferryboat from Larkspur to San Francisco. Bring binoculars and a map to help orient yourself. There will be some excellent views of Alcatraz, Paradise Drive, Paradise Park, and the east side of Angel Island. It is a splendid, scenic ride.

Angel Island State Park

Angel Island has a colorful history, from its early ranching days to its use as a site for sophisticated Nike missiles. In between, the island has served as a temporary holding site for World War II POW's, a quarantine station, an embarkation area for soldiers on their way to war, a discharge point for servicemen returning home, and, like Ellis Island off New York, an immigration center which has National Landmark Status.

The island was discovered by either Sir Francis Drake in 1579, or Don Juan Manuel de Ayala (pronounced I-ya-la) in 1775, depending on with whom you discuss this lively issue. Since Drake's journal was lost, the honor appears to go to Ayala, who sailed through the Golden Gate on the Spanish naval vessel *San Carlos*.

This Spanish lieutenant is credited with naming the island *Isla de los Angeles*, which has been translated and shortened to Angel Island. Ayala's men explored the island between August 13 and September 7, exchanging presents with local Indians of the Coast Miwok tribes whose ancestors had been making hunting, fishing and gathering visits there for over 2,000 years. Ayala was also the first to survey and chart San Francisco Bay.

Angel Island was awarded as a land grant to Antonio Maria Osio by the Mexican governor, Juan Alvarado, on June 11, 1839. Osio used the land for ranching. He built a small house for his

◀ *Trudy Arrigoni and her daughter Samantha Rose, prepare to board the Angel Island Ferry.*

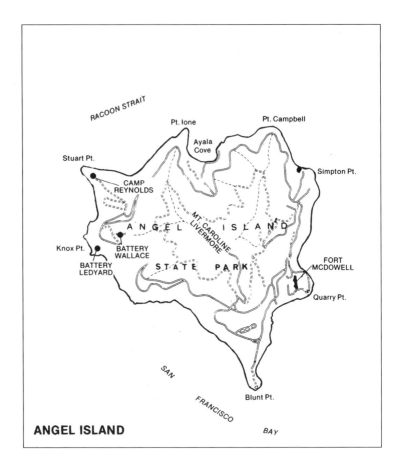

ANGEL ISLAND

mayordomo, erected a dam to create a reservoir to provide water for cattle, built three other houses, and cultivated part of the land. Osio had the bad luck to be on the losing side of America's war with Mexico, however, and the entire island was taken from him in a decision by the United States Supreme Court in 1859. Osio returned to Mexico and the military moved in. Nothing is left to show evidence of his occupation. There are some scattered shell middens, the remains of hunting and gathering discards—a trash heap.

You can see plenty of evidence of the military installations that were built on Angel Island in the next hundred years.

Camp Reynolds (West Garrison) was established in 1863; Fort McDowell (East Garrison) was erected from 1910 to 1912; Point Simpton (North Garrison) was an immigration station from 1910 until a fire forced it to close in 1940. Fort McDowell took over this station, renamed it North Garrison, and set up a holding facility for POWs detained during the Second World War. An asphalt helicopter landing pad on top of the 781-foot summit was built in 1955, as well as missile control radar facilities. A Nike missile site was installed above Point Blunt at the same time. The site was closed in 1962. In the 1980s the helicopter pad was removed and the space was allowed to revegetate.

Angel Island is especially beautiful to visit in the spring when wildflowers seem to blossom everywhere. Park rangers recommend April, May, June, September, and October as the best months to visit—the weather is warmest and there is less likely to be fog.

Getting to the island is half the fun. If you don't have a private sailboat or yacht, you can board a boat of the Blue and Gold Fleet which run trips to the island from Fisherman's Wharf Pier 41 in San Francisco weekends year-round and daily May through October, 773-1188. The Angel Island-Tiburon Ferry leaves from downtown Tiburon weekends year-round and daily May-September, 435-2131. A sign on Main Street in Tiburon identifies the pier where the ferries dock and the trip takes only ten to fifteen minutes. The Vallejo Bay Link Ferry runs trips to Angel Island on weekends only from April through Labor Day, (707) 643-3779. Finally, the Alameda-Oakland Ferry service operates weekends May through October, (510) 522-3300.

Private boats may dock in Ayala Cove in one of the 48 slips that can accommodate boats from 20 feet to 50 feet. Three end ties are available for longer vessels. On a weekend, more than one-hundred boats may be tied up at the Angel Island docks. A small fee is charged per day and the boats must leave by sunset. Boats may also anchor around the island or tie up to the twenty buoys in Ayala Cove and stay for up to five days for a small overnight fee. This is a favorite rendezvous spot for Bay Area yachtsmen, and on any sunny weekend, summer or winter, there are sure to be boats rafted-up and quiet parties in progress.

BLUE AND GOLD FLEET
773-1188
www.blueandgold-fleet.com

ANGEL ISLAND-TIBURON FERRY
435-2131

VALLEJO BAY LINK FERRY
(707) 643-3779

ALAMEDA-OAKLAND FERRY
(510) 522-3300

Passengers embark for Angel Island on the ferryboat from Tiburon.

On the island there are fascinating places to explore either by foot, bicycle, tram, or sea kayak. The open-air TramTour travels the island's five-mile perimeter road, taking passengers on an audio-enhanced tour of the island's Civil War Camp Reynolds, World War I and World War II installations at Fort McDowell, and the immigration station at China Cove. The tour takes an hour. Kayak tours may be reserved on most weekends during the summer and early fall, and mountain bikes plus tandems may be rented. The Cove Cafe is open for lunch or a catered picnic near the docking area.

Walking onto the island at Ayala Cove, visitors will find picnic and barbecue facilities, restrooms, grassy areas for sunbathing, and beaches. Swimming is not recommended because there is no lifeguard on duty. The Park Ranger Station is located in this area, and the Angel Island Association sells brochures and books. First aid is available.

Overnight camping is allowed on the island on nine environmental campsites which supply tables, food lockers, running water, BBQ's, picnic tables and pit toilets. The camps are set up for backpackers and require two miles of hiking. People usually bring their own tents. No dogs are allowed, and wood gathering or wood fires are not allowed; so bring charcoal or a stove. Reservations may be made through Reserve America at (800) 444-PARK.

RESERVE AMERICA
(800) 444-PARK

Angel Island is 740 acres, or 100 acres larger than a square mile. There are thirteen miles of hiking trails, and Perimeter Road, five miles long, circumnavigates the island. Some parts of this road are blacktop, while others are dirt and gravel. Following the road makes a fine half-hour bicycle ride or a hike of about two and a half hours. Rangers recommend you stay on the trails to avoid poison oak and ticks.

Ayala Cove was once known as "Hospital Cove" because a quarantine hospital was operated here by the United States Public Health Service. It was established before the turn of the century, and the last quarantine case went through in 1936. During this period, all ships coming into San Francisco had to stop here so that sailors, mariners, travelers, and immigrants alike could be inspected for the diseases so rampant at this time.

While the ships were docked at Hospital Cove, they were fumigated. An American ship named the *Omaha*, which was drydocked here, ran hoses containing sulfur dioxide into the ships to kill rats. If the cargo prevented this type of fumigation, sulfur dioxide pots were put aboard instead. The rodents were kept from escaping onto the island by cup-shaped barriers which were attached to the lines running to the dock.

Built in 1930, the Ranger Station at Ayala Cove was once the bachelor officers' quarters. Outside there is a large metal bell which was used in the fog to warn ships of the danger of rocks. In the Visitor's Center, located in the Ranger Station, you can view a model of the island in a plastic dome-shaped case. This is a good place to orient yourself and decide what you would like to see on the island. There are also displays of the island's history. Ayala Cove, the displays tell you, was originally named "Racoon Cove" in 1849 for the British sloop-of-war *Racoon*, which visited here for repairs in 1814. (You cross Racoon Straits to reach the island from Tiburon.) The area became Hospital Cove in 1900, and Ayala Cove in 1969. There are other displays titled "Quarantine Station," "Island Outpost," and "Island Flora," plus information on the Immigration Station, Fort McDowell, Native American culture and Spanish history.

Also in the Visitor's Center is a Southampton light beacon lens. Manufactured in Paris in 1836, it was put into operation with a gaslight in an early lighthouse. You can see a Lyle gun, in the shape of a small cannon, which was used by lifeboat stations to fire a line aboard distressed ships.

Hiking or bicycling around the island counterclockwise on Perimeter Road will enable you to view most of the old military facilities in a chronological order. To reach Perimeter Road, take the road leading south from Park Headquarters for about a quarter of a mile. When you reach Perimeter Road, turn right.

Just west of Ayala Cove is Point Ione; to the south is Point Stuart, site of a lighthouse built in 1915. Farther south are the abandoned buildings of Camp Reynolds, built during the Civil War and named to honor Major General John Fulton Reynolds, who was killed at Gettysburg on July 1, 1863. This base was renamed West Garrison when it became part of Fort McDowell.

Still standing at Camp Reynolds today are an old hospital, a mule barn, a church/schoolhouse, and a row of faded yellow

Correne Testa and Gina Burrafato picnic on Angel Island.

TramTours on Angel Island.

wooden officers' houses built side by side running down the hill. They constitute the largest remaining assemblage of wooden Civil War era buildings in the United States.

Near the water's edge is a three-story quartermaster storehouse built in 1908, which was once used to store ammunition. Beyond this is a small beach and the remains of an old dock, now a bird sanctuary. Exotic century plants grow near the water. Strange species of trees and plants can be found all over the island, attesting to its former international population. The purplish *Echium fastuosum* called "The Pride of Madeira" started on the north side and has naturalized itself on the island. The eucalyptus trees were planted for windbreaks in the 1880s.

After exploring Camp Reynolds, hike back uphill to the dirt road that runs off to the right past the white painted chapel. Follow it back to Perimeter Road and stay to your right.

Farther south are Battery Wallace and Battery Ledyard, established around the turn of the century for harbor defense. The artillery installations here, and another at Battery Drew a short distance to the east, were all made obsolete by the airplane. Above the concrete gun emplacements at Battery Ledyard is an overlook with spreading vistas of Marin, the Golden Gate Bridge, San Francisco, and Alcatraz Island.

Point Knox, named for an army engineer who participated in the original island survey, is southwest of Battery Ledyard. It is the site of one of the last of Marin's lighthouses, which began operation in 1886 as a fog signal. A mechanical striker would hit a huge bell and the sound would warn ships away from the island. In 1900 the fog station was converted into a lighthouse, though its mechanical bell was retained.

Many keepers have watched over the bell, including several women. Juliet Nichols is remembered for pounding the bell manually for over 20 hours and 35 minutes in 1906 when the mechanical striking mechanism failed. She became deaf because of her sense of duty.

The lighthouse was used until 1960 when new facilities were built in Point Blunt. In 1963, the Point Knox lighthouse was deliberately burned because it was considered unsafe. A memorial bell, set in cement, marks the spot where the lighthouse stood, but the very steep trail that leads down to it is not recommended by the rangers.

Just beyond this trail is a road leading to Perles Beach, a beautiful, wide, sandy area but not well-protected from the wind. The south side of the island tends to be cooler, with more fog than the north and east. Again, swimming is not recommended because there are no lifeguards. A little farther on is a trail on the left, one of several that lead up to the summit of Mt. Caroline Livermore, named for a Marin conservationist who worked hard to turn Angel Island into a park. It takes about an hour to climb to the top if you take time to observe plants and birds. If you are in a hurry and jog, you can probably make it up in half an hour.

Continuing south and east around the island, you pass a grove of eucalyptus trees once known as "Alcatraz Garden." Gangs of prisoners from Alcatraz were brought here to cultivate vegetables which were used in the prison kitchen. The practice was discontinued because the security risk was too great.

At the southern end of the island you can get a good view of Alcatraz—the flip side of the view from San Francisco. The buildings on the island seem to blend into the San Francisco skyline. The Bay Bridge is also visible, as are Yerba Buena and Treasure Island.

To your left as you continue around the island is an old rock quarry, and along the shoreline, beaches are hidden among the coves. Then on your left is the fenced Nike missile site. The site was built in 1955, along with many others throughout the country for the protection of the United States. The missiles stored inside could be launched to seek out and destroy enemy airplanes, but they were never fired. All that is visible now is flat blacktop, cracked and choked with weeds. It is occasionally used by the rangers for storage. The area, closed to the public, is surrounded by fences. The road takes a deep dip here, and cyclists are warned to walk their bikes.

You will arrive shortly at Point Blunt in the southeast tip of the island. No signs identify the area, but you will see the Coast Guard light facility. It is off-limits to the public. This area was a popular nineteenth-century dueling ground and the site of an equally popular whorehouse. Captain William Waterman of Fairfield (Solano County) lived in a seventeen room house built here by the Pacific Mail Steamship Company. His job with the Steamship Company remains a mystery, although it might have been to inspect the fresh water stored in the hulls of the company's ships. As Waterman was well-respected, Antonio Osio decided to hire him as foreman for his ranch. This was in the late 1850s when squatters were attempting to establish sheep and cattle on the island. Captain Waterman lived on the island six years and the herds of Osio's cattle multiplied under his superior management.

When Osio was forced to give up his land grant, Waterman left also, and Quarry Point workers moved into his house. They were followed by a discharged soldier named Rafferty, who was followed in turn by the whorehouse. It remained in operation until 1867 when the house finally burned, some four years after the United States took over the island. A seven-acre Coast Guard station at Point Blunt now maintains the light facility and fog signal made fully automatic in the 1970s.

Walking north of Point Blunt, you may be startled as you round the corner and see in the distance the "thousand-man barracks," a huge, four-story building with broken windows. This faded yellow building and other structures in the area

PROFILE: Elizabeth Cooper Terwilliger

Elizabeth Cooper Terwilliger (or "Mrs. T," as she is fondly called) has been the Pied Piper of Marin County for close to fifty years, leading school children, their parents, teachers and friends to view and experience the wonders of nature up close. Her hikes have led eager followers to the top of Angel Island, through protected salt water marshes, along the Pacific Ocean, and into stunningly beautiful monarch butterfly groves. Her canoe trips have carried passengers down creeks, estuaries, lagoons and lakes.

Mrs. T's enthusiasm in pointing out "Mr. Crow" and "Mr. Raven" has been transmitted to children and adults alike who have learned the difference between those two birds and others by following her waving arms and wiggling fingers. Even President Ronald Reagan was taught that in 1984 when Elizabeth was honored with the Volunteer Action Award at a ceremony in Washington, D.C.

For years Elizabeth drove a van filled with stuffed birds and animals to show children what these critters looked like close up. Often when there was an accidental killing of a small animal or bird, usually by a moving vehicle, that specimen would end up in Mrs. T's freezer in her house in Mill Valley. The specimen would be taken out for field trips or visits to schools, then returned to the freezer to be used for years.

Elizabeth Terwilliger was trained as an R.N. at the Stanford University School of Nursing. Born in Hawaii in 1909, the daughter of the physician on the Aiea Sugar Plantation in Oahu, she graduated from Punahou and the University of Hawaii. Then she earned a Master's Degree from Columbia University in New York City before coming west for her nurse's training. She married a doctor, the late Calvin Terwilliger, and moved to Marin. They were married fifty years and their two grown children live in California and Idaho.

Upon arriving in Marin, Elizabeth Terwilliger quickly became interested in conservation causes and joined with Caroline Livermore and others to found the Marin Audubon Society to try to save Richardson Bay from big real estate development. They succeeded and the Richardson Bay Audubon Center and Sanctuary in Tiburon is one of the premier bird wildlife refuges in the United States.

Even before that, when she and Calvin were living in Sausalito after World War II, she found a vacant lot and persuaded the Sausalito City Council to purchase it and build a children's playground.

Thousands of children have followed the beloved Mrs. T around Marin, turning her into a legend. In 1975 the Terwilliger Nature Education Center was established in her honor. It emphasized teaching children in the style she created, a multi-sensory environmental technique. The Center later merged with the California Center for Wildlife to become WildCare, which is located on Albert Park Lane in San Rafael. Over 700 volunteers have been trained as naturalists to teach children in Mrs. T's unique educational manner. Volunteer Terwilliger Nature Guides and salaried naturalists reach 45,000 children annually in the Bay Area, while millions of children have also seen the five films based on her teachings titled "Tripping with Terwilliger" which are now on video.

Mrs. Terwilliger has been active in creating bicycle paths, nature trails, salt water marshes, a monarch butterfly preserve at Muir Beach, playgrounds and open space. She also started a very successful Outdoor Education Program for fifth graders in Marin. Later she wrote a book, a collection of her newspaper articles on nature written for the *Marin Independent Journal* titled *Sights and Sounds of the Season*. First published in 1976, the book, beautifully illustrated by Barbara Polach, has had three printings.

Elizabeth Terwilliger was honored by the *San Francisco Examiner* in 1972 as one of the Bay Area's "Ten Most Distinguished Citizens." In 1986 she received the Chevron Conservation Award in Washington, D.C. In 1988 *Newsweek* named her as one of 1988's American Heroes. She has also received two honorary doctorate degrees from universities, and she and her Terwilliger Nature Guides received President Bush's "Points of Light" Award in 1991. She has been inducted into the Marin County's Women's Hall of Fame and in 1994 received the Girl Scout's Daisy Award for outstanding achievement.

Although Elizabeth now lives in senior housing she continues to get out and around in Marin. She says, "As long as you are learning you are living. The more you look, the more you see how little you know and how much more there is to learn." We in Marin are grateful that Elizabeth Terwilliger spent her life teaching us and imparting her joy in nature, a priceless gift which has enriched all our lives.

The old guard house at Fort McDowell, East Garrison, is now a museum open to the public.

were part of the original Fort McDowell, or East Garrison. The fort was established around 1900 as a tent camp for soldiers returning from the Spanish-American War. Buildings were put up from 1910 to 1912. Today there is a visitors' center in the old guard house that tells about the island's history and ecology.

Below on the right is a quiet sheltered cove, a popular anchorage for boats. It is tranquil on this side of the island. The silence, disturbed only by the singing of birds and waves lapping at the shoreline of beautiful, warm Quarry Beach, makes it hard to envision this as the site of a base where 20,000 to 80,000 men passed through yearly in the hectic days of World War II.

You can see the remains of what was a busy military base: the huge barracks; other large buildings that housed a PX, gym and mess hall (these old buildings are now closed to visitors); a baseball diamond overgrown with weeds and wild lilies; and an abandoned tennis court. Concrete barbecues and picnic tables are available here for group picnics.

On your left as you continue is "Officer's Row," a group of concrete houses with red tile roofs built around 1910. The two-story houses are a faded army mustard color. All have a front porch with white columns, plus a small attic room with dormer windows facing out to the water. As you continue walking north, you pass an administration building, a chapel, and the three-story East Garrison hospital, built in 1910, which held seventy beds. A sign tells you that "Veterans were treated here for tropical diseases contracted in such places as the Philippines after the Spanish-American War and Panama during canal construction."

Eighty years of memories are here, and in the silence you become aware of the ghosts—the soldiers in pain, or perhaps others elated at returning home from the war. After World War I, 87,000 men were returned to civilian status here. And in 1945, a sixty-foot-high-sign fully illuminated read, "WELCOME HOME—WELL DONE." Located on the south slope, it was the first thing the American GIs saw when they returned from World War II. East Garrison was closed down a year later.

From this side of Angel Island you can look across to the East Bay—Richmond, Oakland, Berkeley, and the Berkeley Hills. As you round the end of the island, you can see Belvedere Island, Tiburon, San Pablo Bay, the San Rafael-Richmond Bridge, and on a clear day, the hills of Sonoma and Napa counties.

As you continue following the road, you will arrive at a sign that says "North Garrison." A modern firehouse painted gray stands next to the park maintenance yard. The buildings of old Point Simpton, tucked below the road adjacent to Winslow Cove, are now closed to the public.

Point Simpton began operation in 1910 as an immigration station for Asians and Europeans. Mainly, immigrants from the Far East passed through here in search of a better life. More than 175,000 Chinese people were detained on Angel Island between 1910-1940. Because of the "Chinese Exclusion Act" in effect in the United States between 1881 and 1943, the Chinese were held under lock and key, humiliated and roughly interrogated under prison-like conditions. Some made it into the United States. Many were sent home. Poems and writings that the Chinese carved on the walls of their barracks remind us of their agony, which for some lasted years. During World War I, some German and Italian aliens were held here also.

In 1940, fire destroyed the main buildings and the immigration center closed. All operations were moved to San Francisco.

During World War II, the area was turned into a detention center for a few prisoners of the war (the first Japanese POWs were held here) and "enemy aliens"—Germans, Italians, and Japanese who happened to be on ships in the area at the outbreak of the war, or people who, for some other reason, were detained by the United States government. After the war, the area was abandoned.

At the northernmost point of the island is Point Campbell. There are no buildings of interest, but you can enjoy the view. From here it is a half mile back to Ayala Cove where the ferryboat waits to return you to the mainland.

ANGEL ISLAND
ASSOCIATION
435-3522

ANGEL ISLAND
STATE PARK OFFICE
AT AYALA COVE:
435-5390
or
435-1915
Fax:
(925) 426-3075
E-mail:
goplay@angelis-
land.com

Nearly 200,000 people come to the island annually, and the rangers have set up a volunteer program to help prepare for these visitors. Scouts and adult volunteers may join the Angel Island Service Projects by calling the Ranger Office at 435-1915. A volunteer organization called the Angel Island Association is also open for membership. Call 435-3522. For more information on Angel Island, the internet address is: www.angelisland.org.

To reach the Angel Island State Park Office at Ayala Cove: 435-5390; recorded information: 435-1915. Fax: (925) 426-3075; E-mail: goplay@angelisland.com. Angel Island is open from 8:00 a.m. to sunset, every day, year-round. TramTours, bike

A ferryboat arrives at Ayala Cove, Angel Island.

rentals and the Cove Cafe operate seasonally: March and November on weekends; Wednesday through Sunday in April; daily from May through October. For information on TramTours, catered open-air events, and weddings in the Post Chapel at Fort McDowell, call 897-0715. For Sea Trek Ocean Kayaking: 488-1000.

TRAMTOURS, CATERED OPEN-AIR EVENTS, AND WEDDINGS IN THE POST CHAPEL AT FORT MCDOWELL, 897-0715

SEA TREK OCEAN KAYAKING: 488-1000.

Ayala Cove, Angel Island

Mt. Tamalpais and Muir Woods   6

Alpine Trails, Stately Redwoods

M t. Tamalpais is the principal landmark in Marin, as its velvet green slopes and rigid peaks can be viewed from just about everywhere in the southern and central parts of the county. Although the mountain's highest point is just under 2,600 feet, its rise from the sea is so abrupt that it gives a lofty majestic appearance.

Many names for the mountain appeared on early maps. In the 1800s it was known as Table Mountain or Table Butte, Bay Mountain, and Tamales. "Tamal" may have been the Miwok Indian name for "west," or "coast" while "pais" meant "hill," according to the *Bodega Miwok Dictionary* by Catherine A. Callaghan (University of California Publications, 1970).

If you are looking from the south and east, the mountain takes on the appearance of a "sleeping maiden," an image that was transposed into literature over the years: in Neil Compton Wilson's poem, "The Legend of Tamalpais," in 1911 and in another poem, George Caldwell's "The Maid of Tamalpais," in 1919. One early mountain play written by Dan Totheroh and first performed in 1921 was titled "Tamalpa"; it created a romantic myth about an Indian princess whose mother was a famous witch with the power of casting plague spells on other tribes. When the witch learned that Piayutuma, a member of a valley tribe, was to be given the secret of healing by the Great Spirit,

◀ *Entrance to Muir Woods National Monument.*

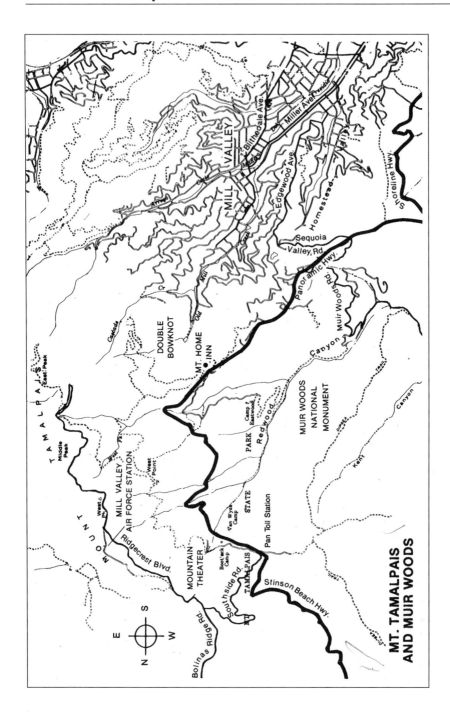

MT. TAMALPAIS
AND MUIR WOODS

she sent her daughter Tamalpa to thwart him.While the maiden succeeded, she fell in love with the young brave. She was accidentally killed by her mother, and her body brought back to a bier at the top of the mountain. So when you see the sleeping maiden, you are actually viewing the beautiful Tamalpa.

Mt. Tamalpais is so loved by the people of Marin that great efforts have been made over the years to preserve its pristine beauty by establishing parks, a monument, and large areas of watershed. During the 1920s, private development threatened to spread over the entire mountain.Through the efforts of the Tamalpais Conservation Club and others, a bill was passed in the state legislature in 1930 appropriating 892 acres for a park. Now there are 6,000 acres in the State Park and the Golden Gate National Recreation Area lands which run from the Golden Gate Bridge to the Point Reyes peninsula.

About thirty miles of trails wind through the park boundaries, and 200-mile-long trail networks include Muir Woods, the watershed lands, and the Golden Gate National Recreation Area. The mountain provides camping and picnic areas, five clear blue lakes excellent for fishing, and an abundance of wildlife.

Mt. Tamalpais also has an interesting geological formation. Rocks 100 to 150 million years old have been found consisting of serpentine, chert, graywacke (sandstone), shale, greenstone, quartz-tourmaline, and limestone. This is called the Franciscan Formation and matches the geology of other regions of the California coast ranges, except that the ridges of Mt. Tamalpais tend to run in a northwest-southeast direction. The rocks and minerals are found in a scrambled or jumbled condition due to the grinding against one another of the North American plate and the Pacific plate along the San Andreas Fault.

It is the magic of the mountain, however, that attracts people who love to hike, camp, or picnic. Virgin redwood forests grow in the lower regions of the fog zone, while higher up, hikers may enjoy the sun shining above the fog in the chaparral plant community. Always, there are spectacular views of the endless blue sea.

The Crookedest Railroad in the World

The first road up the mountain, called the Eldridge Grade, was built in 1884. Visitors could ride a stagecoach eleven miles from the Rafael Hotel to the summit. Then, in 1896, the phenomenal Mill Valley and Tamalpais Scenic Railway began hauling passengers up to the top of the mountain from downtown Mill Valley. The "Crookedest Railroad in the World" was 8.19 miles long, had 281 curves, and featured the famous Double Bowknot, a track that paralleled itself five times as it gained elevation.

The Tavern of Tamalpais was built 220 feet below the 2,436-foot summit. It was a first-class hotel with rooms, meals, liquid refreshments, and a wide veranda with a 150-degree view of the ocean, Marin, the bay, and San Francisco. Advertisements at the time declared that patrons of the Tavern could view "eighty cities and towns and twenty California counties."

The railway cars that took people up the mountain were actually backed up the tracks and eased back down by steam locomotives attached to the downhill side for safety. Most of these Shay and Heisler engines were painted a deep maroon with black trim and were kept clean and highly polished.

A line was added to the railroad in 1907 which took passengers by gravity cars into Muir Woods, and the name was changed to the Mt. Tamalpais and Muir Woods Railway. William Kent, an early pioneer and congressman from Marin, had purchased that property, then known as Redwood Canyon, which was covered with giant virgin coast redwood trees. The problem was that it could be reached only by a narrow stagecoach road. Kent promised to build a hotel if the railroad would extend a new spur into the area. He kept his promise and spent $150,000 to construct the Muir Woods Inn. It burned in 1913 and was rebuilt farther down the canyon.

The gravity cars used on the new spur sped passengers ten to twelve miles per hour around the seemingly endless curves down the mountain and through the woods. Invented by the railroad's master mechanic, Bill Thomas, each car held thirty passengers and would coast silently down from the 1,800-foot double bowknot for approximately six-and-a-half miles.

The number of passengers using the Mt. Tamalpais and Muir Woods Railway topped 102,000 in 1915. The trains were

The Tavern of Tamalpais and a gravity car on the Mt. Tamalpais and Muir Woods Railway around 1920. Dance Hall is on the left. (Photo courtesy of Nancy Skinner)

also used to haul people up to the mountain top for Easter sunrise services and to attend the mountain plays. Visitors from San Francisco could enjoy a full day's outing by catching a ferryboat from the Ferry Building to Sausalito, taking a train to Mill Valley, then heading up the mountain on the Mt. Tamalpais Railway. Lunch at the top could consist of a tasty picnic or an elegant meal purchased at the Tavern of Tamalpais.

In the afternoon the adventurous visitors might take an open-air gravity car down into Muir Woods, a veritable roller coaster ride with the cars flying along the tracks, around curves, and through tall redwood groves. A peaceful walk among the trees, a quiet drink at the inn, then a return trip by train and ferry to San Francisco completed the day.

Fires on the mountain in 1913, 1923 (when the tavern burned), and 1929 brought disaster to the railroad. Showing great heroics, crews of the railroad raced raging fires downhill through black smoke and waves of intense heat, managing to save all lives, though paint on the train cars blistered.

The Great Depression and construction of a scenic road to the top of the mountain for automobiles spelled the final end of the Mt. Tamalpais and Muir Woods Railway. It was abandoned in the summer of 1930, but remained a fond memory in the hearts of the thousands of adventurers who rode her rails.

MUIR WOODS

Redwood Canyon, which William Kent purchased in 1905 for $45,000, was threatened by the North Coast Water Company, which wanted to cut the trees and flood the area for a reservoir. To block this move, Kent tried to give the land to both the county and state but was turned down. Condemnation proceedings were moving along rapidly and the situation was desperate. The trees would soon be cut, a dam built with the profits of the lumber, and the canyon flooded. Since the area was too small to qualify for a federal park, that, too, was a dead end.

Then someone remembered a little-known law that stated if a parcel of land was extremely valuable, it could be given to the United States as a monument. It was under this statute that Kent's Redwood Canyon was presented to the government. The 295-acre gift was accepted by President Theodore Roosevelt on January 9, 1908, as the Muir Woods National Monument, thus ensuring protection for the redwood forest.

When the deed was transferred, Kent wrote to the Secretary of the Interior:

This property is well worthy of being considered a monument, and has surpassing scenic interest. The tract, containing 295 acres, is all heavily wooded with virgin timber, chiefly with redwood and Douglas fir. In the opinion of experts it is a wilderness park such as is accessible to no other great city in the world and should be preserved forever for public use and enjoyment. After having traveled over a large part of the open country in the United States, I consider this tract with its

John Muir (with the beard) and the Newton Family at their cabin in Muir Woods around 1910. (Photo courtesy of Nancy Skinner)   ▶

beautiful trees, ferns, wild flowers and shrubs, as the most attractive. In tendering it I request it be known as Muir Woods in honor of John Muir.

Kent then went on to offer financial help for maintenance and policing of the woods for the next ten years.

John Muir, upon learning that the gift was to be named in his honor, stated:

This is the best tree-lover's monument that could be found in all the forests of the world. You have done me great honor and I am proud of it . . . Savings these woods from the axe and saw, from the money changers and water changers (dam builders) is in many ways the most notable service to God and man I have heard of since my forest wandering began.

Marinites take years to explore their beloved "Mount Tam," but if your time is limited, try at least to visit Muir Woods; it is truly one of the wonders of the world. Each year 1.6 million tourists from all over the world visit this natural wonder which has grown to 560 acres. It is now part of the Golden Gate National Recreation Area and is surrounded by Mount Tamalpais State Park.

Man feels very small, indeed, contemplating these soaring giant redwood trees which were living when Columbus discovered our continent in 1492, and when Sir Francis Drake landed on the shores of Marin in 1579. One can touch the redwood trunks and feel a kinship with generations past, and a link to the future. These trees can live 1,000 years and will probably still be alive when our children's grandchildren are born.

The species of redwood found in the Muir Woods National Monument is *Sequoia sempervirens,* or coast redwood, cousin to the *Sequoiadendron giganteum* that grow in the Sierra Nevada Mountains and may live 2,200 years. A University of California Berkeley study of 400 samples drilled in 1979 revealed that the trees in Muir Woods are from 500 to 800 years old. Rangers, whose talks are scheduled year-round, state there are other trees in the park that are 800 to 1,000 years old.

The redwoods are as tall as 260 feet. One Douglas fir in the park, dedicated to the memory of William Kent, is an incredible

220 feet. (It was 253 feet but the top fell off a few years ago.) The diameters of the coast redwoods at other state and national parks in California have been recorded over 16 feet; the largest here is 13 feet.

At the entrance of Muir Woods is a visitors' center with exhibits and an array of interpretive and educational merchandise including books, postcards, posters and maps. The Muir Woods Park Brochure is available in Italian, German, Spanish, French and Japanese. A self-guided nature tour guide is also available. The visitors center is open from 9:00 a.m. to 4:30 p.m..

Inside the park there are six miles of trails within the woods. You can take an easy walk along Redwood Creek, past the Bohemian Grove and the Cathedral Grove, or you can be more ambitious and go up the slopes of the mountain. In addition to the redwood and Douglas fir, you will see California bay, tan oak, live oak, madrone, buck eye, and California nutmeg trees.

Mary Liz Rooney and Wendy Schirripa in front of the Visitor Center at Muir Woods National Monument.

Wildflowers, ferns, and mushrooms grow in the shaded glades, and you might see black-tail deer, raccoons, chipmunks, woodpeckers, and a variety of birds: sparrows, towhees, hummingbirds, and warblers. But the most important sight will be the awe-inspiring beauty of the tall trees themselves. People tend to whisper in Muir Woods as though they are seeing and touching the very mystery of life.

To get to Muir Woods, leave Highway 101 at the Stinson Beach exit. Go half a mile to a stoplight and turn left on Highway 1, which is also Shoreline Highway. Continue two and one-half miles to the junction of the Panoramic Highway, turn right, drive seven-tenths of a mile, then turn left on the Muir Woods road.

The monument is open daily including holidays from 8:00 a.m. to sunset. (During winter the Monument closes at 5:00 p.m., and in the summer, 8:00 p.m.) At the gift shop visitors can buy redwood souvenirs such as clocks, planters, nut dishes, cable cars, and live redwood burls—gnarled knots cut from the side of the trees which, when put in water, sprout lacy, green redwood branches. Large burls can be polished to a rich dark red color and used for furniture such as tabletops. Slides, books and film are also available. Open 9:00 a.m. to 5:00 p.m.

A small fee is charged for admission to the monument. No pets are allowed. Parking areas and restrooms are located outside the entrance. No picnicking or camping; bicycles or horses are allowed only on fire roads. Vehicles over 35 feet are prohibited and there is no public transportation. For more information call the Ranger Station at 388-2596; for a recording, 388-2595. On the net: http://www.nps.gov.muwo.

RANGER STATION
388-2596;
For a recording:
388-2595.
On the net:
www.nps.gov.muwo

MT. TAMALPAIS STATE PARK

To visit the rest of the mountain, return to Panoramic Highway and turn north—or left. On the way up the mountain, the road passes Camp Alice Eastwood Road and then the Boot Jack Picnic Area, which has tables, stoves, drinking water, and restrooms.

State park headquarters are at the Pantoll Ranger Station, about four miles from the Muir Woods Road-Panoramic Highway intersection. Here you may obtain a brochure with a map of the hiking trails plus information about camping along the Coast Trail and at Pantoll. A parking toll at East Peak, Bootjack and Pantoll was levied in 1989.

The Alice Eastwood Group Camp is open year-round and handles up to seventy-five people. Accommodations include two camp sites: Camp A handles 50 people; Camp B handles 25 people. Each site furnishes tables, drinking water and pit toilets. Because of fire hazards, only self-contained gas-burning stoves may be used in this camp. No trailers or motor homes are allowed.

Pantoll Campground has 14 walk-in sites, first-come, first-served. The historic Steep Ravine Cabins and Campground overlooking the Pacific Ocean must be reserved 10 days in advance. The cabins are very rustic and sleep up to five. They contain wood stoves and pit toilets. (800) 444-7275.

MT. TAMALPAIS STATE PARK RESERVATIONS: (800) 444-7252

Other maps may be purchased that show the trails in more detail. The Erickson Trail Map notes the picnic areas at Laurel Dell, Potrero Meadows, and Rifle camp. Another map for hikers is Jerry Olmsted's "A Rambler's Guide to the Trails of Mt. Tamalpais and the Marin Headlands."

Hikers can stop at the West Point Inn and enjoy coffee, tea, or lemonade on its wide veranda. Build in 1904, the inn is located at the east end of the old stage road that connected with Stinson Beach and Bolinas. That road is now used by hikers. The inn was also a stop on the old mountain railroad for passengers on their way to the summit or to the connecting stage to Willow Camp.

MT. TAMALPAIS STATE PARK HEADQUARTERS 388-2070.

No dogs are allowed on the state park trails or fire roads. For more information phone the Mt. Tamalpais State Park Headquarters at 388-2070.

The Mountain Theater

To reach the Mountain Theater, turn right on Pantoll Road across from park headquarters. The road is open the same hours as the park, generally half-an-hour before sunrise to half-an-hour after sunset.

Up the road one and one-half miles you will reach Ridgecrest Boulevard and the popular picnic area, Rock Spring Meadow. Turn right on Ridgecrest and you will immediately arrive at the Mountain Theater.

This 3750 seat amphitheater is worth taking the time to explore. Here, 2,000 feet above sea level, are incredible views of Richardson and San Francisco Bays, Angel Island, Alcatraz Island, the Oakland Bay Bridge, the Berkeley Hills, and Mt. Diablo beyond.

This entire area was donated by William Kent in 1915 and named for Sidney B. Cushing, president of the Mt. Tamalpais and Muir Woods Railway. In the 1930s, the Civilian Conservation Corps built the seats out of serpentine hauled down from the West Peak. Since 1913, visitors have enjoyed the annual Mountain Play and other dramatic productions, religious services, concerts, weddings, and picnics in the theater.

A park policy which limits seating to 3750 also limits major events of 500 people or more to no more than six such events in May and June. In effect, this means only the Mountain Play can be staged at the Mountain Theater.

Candy Ireton sits in the Mountain Theater on top of Mt. Tamalpais.

Mill Valley Air Force Station (Now Removed)

A mile beyond the theater was the former Mill Valley Air Force Station, now removed, which once operated the huge white radar domes. They look somewhat like a pair of large golf balls sitting on top of the summit. The radar equipment is now under the jurisdiction of the Federal Aviation Agency.

Site facilities on top of the mountain once included a dining room, base exchange, motor pool, housing, and recreational facilities—even a tennis court, swimming pool, bowling alley and movie theater. The facility was closed in 1983 and torn down in 1996.

East Peak

Continue one and eight-tenths miles to the East Peak where the Tavern of Tamalpais used to stand. The road passes through thick manzanita. A Visitors Center and restrooms are near the parking lot. There are also plans to build a Gravity Car Barn here with exhibits, including a replica of a gravity car that used to run down the mountain to Muir Woods.

You will probably meet members of the Mount Tamalpais Interpretive Association, a volunteer group who act as docents to rangers by leading hikes on weekends, Wednesday evenings and on moonlit evenings, staffing the Visitors Center and leading the astronomy program. Call 258-2410 for a recording of upcoming hikes and other information, or check their website: www.mtia.net.

VISITORS CENTER
258-2410
Website:
www.mtia.net.

You can hike up to a fire lookout at the top of the mountain to an altitude of 2,571 feet by way of a short but steep, rocky trail. On a clear day you can see Mt. St. Helena to the north, the Sierra Nevada in the east, and Mt. Hamilton to the south. Mt. Diablo is also to the east behind the Berkeley Hills. Below, you may notice people practicing mountain climbing on the rock outcrops.

For unsurpassed views of the Pacific Ocean, the bay, San Francisco, and the East Bay, follow the asphalt Verna Dunshee

Memorial Trail, dedicated in June 1973. Looking south from Sunrise Point, you can gaze down onto the area of the Double Bow Knot and see the enormous slide area on which the railroad had a stop called the Mesa Station.

As you follow the trail around the mountain, you can identify the towns in Marin (binoculars will help here); first, the picturesque towns of Sausalito, Tiburon, and Belvedere, with houses built on the hills and sailboat masts ringing the shoreline. Closer to the mountain base are Mill Valley and Corte Madera, then Greenbrae with its boardwalk stretching out into the tidelands of the bay; adjacent to Greenbrae is the Larkspur Ferry Terminal and a huge shopping center. To the northeast is the sprawling city of San Rafael. As you continue around, you may glimpse Kentfield, Ross, San Anselmo, Fairfax, and the rural countryside to the west. These towns would run into each other but for the ridges of open space separating one from another.

To the northeast you can also view Phoenix Lake; north of that are Lagunitas and Bon Tempe lakes, plus a small slice of

Porch on Tavern of Tamalpais on summit of Mt. Tamalpais around the turn of the 20th century. (Photo courtesy of Nancy Skinner)

the upper end of Lake Alpine. Mt. Barnabe, Mt. Vision, and Black Mountain are in the distance to the west.

Hikers can choose from many varied and incredibly beautiful trails from Pantoll Ranger Station, Rock Spring, Mountain Home, Phoenix Lake, or the Lake Lagunitas picnic area using the Olmsted map.

Hiking is so popular on Mt. Tamalpais that three hiking clubs with hundreds of members hike year-round and sponsor other activities on the mountain. The California Alpine Club, founded in 1913, has a property at 730 Panoramic Highway. Besides its use by members, this lodge is available for parties, weddings and overnight stays in private rooms and dormitories. Call 388-9940.

CALIFORNIA ALPINE CLUB 388-9940

The West Point Inn, built in 1904, was a place passengers on the railway stopped for refreshments before boarding a stage coach to West Marin. Today the inn is known for its monthly pancake breakfasts and for serving coffee, tea and lemonade to hikers. It also rents out private rooms and small cabins to the public Tuesday through Saturday nights.

You must hike or bicycle for two miles to reach the West Point Inn from Pantoll Station and there is no electricity, so bring your own flashlight in addition to food and a sleeping bag. No smoking or candles are allowed due to fire hazards. Everyone helps with cleanup. Call 646-0702 for current rates. (No weddings are allowed.)

WEST POINT INN 646-0702

The Tourist Club, a branch of the California Nature Friends, built a romantic looking lodge on Mt. Tam in 1914 with painted flowers and gingerbread eaves. It has overnight rooms available for members only, but sponsors four festivals annually (including the "October Fest") which are open to the public. The address is 30 Ridge Lane, Mill Valley. Call 388-9987 for information.

TOURIST CLUB 388-9987

One of the most delightful loops on the mountain begins from Rock Spring. From the parking lot, hike on the Cataract Trail around the knoll on the left. A trail, the Simmons and re-routed Bernstein, takes off to the right. Bear left past the water tank and concrete trough and follow Cataract Creek down through some of the most captivating forest and meadow areas

PROFILE: **Karin Alstrom Urquhart**

Karin Urquhart is one of those rare individuals who has been able to successfully combine the positions of wife and mother with a full-time job while also being a community activist. Karin and her husband, Don Urquhart, an electrical engineer and retired computer teacher at College of Marin, have seven grown children and fourteen grandchildren. In the midst of raising this ever expanding family, Karin found time to serve as the elected President of the Marin Conservation League in 1976-78. She then became its executive director between the years 1980 and 1995. Her fifteen year legacy is one of being able to work well with diverse groups in effective, productive ways. Over the years she projected a steadying influence, earning respect from all sides of the community. Karin Urquhart was known as a person who could be approached with problems, a person who would listen and who could be trusted.

Karin Alstrom Urquhart was born in Oakland in 1935 and moved to Marin at age 13 in 1948. She attended Tamalpais High School, then transferred to Drake and was a member of that new school's first graduating class. From there she went on to San Francisco State. In 1956 Karin married Don Urquhart, who had attended Tamalpais High School, the College of Marin and the University of California at Berkeley. They have enjoyed a long, happy marriage.

In addition to being a conservationist, Karin has a lovely singing voice and artistic talent. She has painted oil and watercolor portraits and landscapes which have been shown in gallery exhibitions and are proudly displayed in many Marin homes. She has also performed as one of the stars in many of former County

Counsel Doug Maloney's musical productions, political satires of Marin politicians and even of the Conservation League itself.

Karin's other accomplishments include chairing the county's Park and Cultural Commission. In addition, she served on the boards of the Marin Agricultural Land Trust, Digital Village Foundation, Marconi Conference Center, Marin Council of Agencies, Marin County Chamber of Commerce, Marin Conservation Corps (Founding Chair), Marin Society of Artists, Environmental Federation of California, People for Open Space, Environmental Forum of Marin and People for Parks and Open Space.

In 1993 she was inducted into the Marin Women's Hall of Fame. In 1995 she was appointed by the Marin County Board of Supervisors to the Board of the Marin Community Foundation which administers the billion dollar Beryl Buck Trust. She was reappointed to that position again in 1999 to serve another four years. Other Board of Supervisors' appointments have included the Marin County Visitors Services Committee, Marin County Waste Management Advisory Committee, and Marin County Parks and Recreation Commission. From 1985 to 2000 she served as a Director of the Marin County Fair.

Karin has received numerous awards, including National Association, Daughters of the American Revolution, Conservation Award; Marin Council of Agencies Executive Director of the Year Award for Excellence in Developing Community Partnerships; Environmental Federation of California Volunteer Award, 1989; and Women Making History, 1983, awarded by United States Senator Barbara Boxer.

Bikers pause near the top of Mt. Tamalpais.

on the mountain. After about a mile-and-a-quarter you will come to the Laurel Dell, an attractive picnic area under fir and laurel trees. You can either stay here for lunch or retrace your steps back up the Cataract Trail to the Mickey O'Brien Trail, renamed in 1948 for one of the earlier old-timers on the mountain. The Mickey O'Brien Trail is about three-quarters of a mile long and climbs slowly along the south side of Barth's Creek through large stands of fir and bay. At Barth's Retreat, you can wander around the little meadow or relax under the trees. Barth's Retreat was named after Emil Barth, a devoted hiker on the mountain from 1886 to his death in 1927.

After a sojourn here, retrace your steps back across the little bridge and turn left immediately onto the Simmons Trail. The trail climbs up the ridge through fine stands of Sergeant cypress and other plants of the chaparral plant community. At the top, take some time to look around to the north and west at the ridges of hills repeating themselves ad infinitum in the distance. Continue hiking down through the chaparral and into the fir forest. Cross Ziesche Creek; follow the creek down awhile, and return to the parking lot. The entire loop is three miles long with 700 feet of elevation gain.

If you are hungry after a day on the mountain, stop at the Mountain Home Inn as you drive back down. Founded in 1912, the inn is located at 810 Panoramic Highway near the Alice Eastwood Camp and offers outdoor dining and rooms to rent.

MOUNTAIN HOME INN
810 Panoramic Highway

From here you can return down the mountain through Mill Valley by taking the Sequoia Valley Road opposite the road into Muir Woods. Just follow the yellow line as Sequoia becomes Edgewood, which becomes Molino. When Molino ends, turn left on Montford, then right on Miller Avenue which will bring you back to Highway 101. The distance is three-and-a-half miles from the Pantoll Station to Miller Avenue.

Or you can continue up over the mountain at Pantoll to Stinson Beach and Bolinas. The distance from the Ridgecrest-Pan Toll Intersection to Highway 1 opposite the entrance road to Bolinas is four miles. This winding narrow road is a slow but lovely drive through wild mountain country with the reward of the beautiful West Marin beaches at the end.

Dining on top of Mount Tamalpais at the Mountain Home Inn are Wendy Schirripa of Medina, Ohio, Mary Liz Rooney of Newport Beach, California, Bettina Foster of Stinson Beach, California, and Patricia Arrigoni of Fairfax, California. (Photo by Brian Wallace.)

Ross Valley and the San Quentin Peninsula

Unique Marin Towns

One hundred years ago, the beautiful Ross Valley was a favorite location for country homes and mansions built by wealthy San Francisco commuters. In the early 1800s, large tracts of timber had covered the valley, but these were soon logged-off and replaced by houses, dairy ranches, gardens, and orchards.

Life moved at a gentler pace then. Visitors staying in elegant hotels swam and bathed in the Corte Madera Slough which wound all the way up the valley. They played tennis, rode horses, danced, and bowled. Fourth of July parades were an ever-popular entertainment. Fine carriages could be seen each evening on all the roads and clustered around railroad stations, waiting to pick up commuters from San Francisco. The Ross Valley women occupied themselves with cultural and charitable activities; the men joined fashionable private hunting clubs and went out to shoot the plentiful game: deer, fox, raccoon, mountain lion, dove, quail, and pheasant.

Today, the Ross Valley, which runs northwest from the town of Corte Madera to Fairfax, remains a fine residential area with several unique small towns and lovely parks.

Generally, the area is divided into Lower Ross Valley and Upper Ross Valley. In the lower valley are the twin towns of Corte Madera and Larkspur (which share some public services),

◄ *The "Twin Cities" (Corte Madera-Larkspur) Annual Fourth of July Parade*

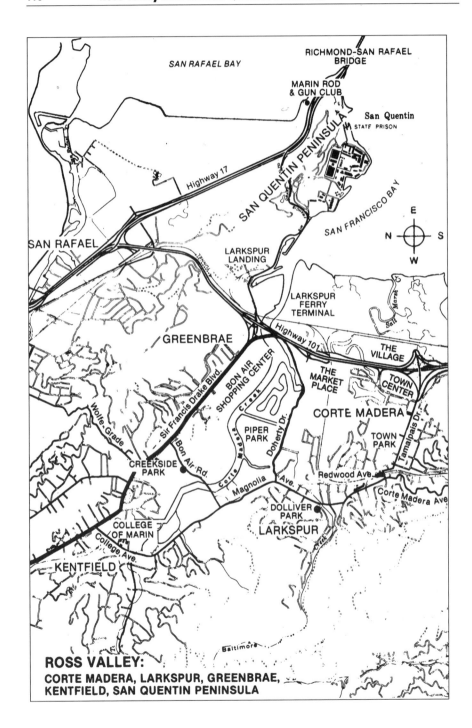

ROSS VALLEY:
CORTE MADERA, LARKSPUR, GREENBRAE,
KENTFIELD, SAN QUENTIN PENINSULA

the San Quentin peninsula, Greenbrae, Kentfield, and the subdivision of Kent Woodlands. Upper Ross Valley includes the towns of Ross, San Anselmo, and Fairfax, and some unincorporated residential areas such as Sleepy Hollow (adjacent to San Anselmo), Oak Manor (Fairfax), and the area west of Fairfax to White's Hill.

From 1875 to 1941 trains ran through the entire valley bringing commuters from the northwest side of Fairfax (known as Manor) to San Anselmo (then called The Junction), through Ross, Kentfield, Larkspur, and Corte Madera to Sausalito, and on to San Francisco by ferryboat. The trip took less time than it does today by automobile on Highway 101 during commute hours.

CORTE MADERA

Corte Madera, named for John Reed's Mexican land grant the *Corte de Madera del Presidio*, actually adjoined the fringes of that territory to the northwest. When Mexico gave California to the United States after the Mexican War in 1848, the area was called *Reed Sobrantes*, meaning "Reed leftovers." Squatters and homesteaders resided on the land until 1885 when Hilarita Reed, John's daughter, was able to reestablish ownership after a legal battle in Washington, D.C. It was then sold to speculators from San Francisco who made settlements with the homesteaders.

Corte Madera's most famous resident was a flamboyant easterner by the name of Frank Morrison Pixley. Educated into the legal profession at Utica College in New York, Pixley rode west in 1848 at the age of twenty-four. After a fruitless year of prospecting gold on the Yuba River, he moved to San Francisco and began a law practice.

In 1853, Pixley married Amelia Van Reynegom, whose family lived on an estate named Owl's Wood, in what was the Chevy Chase area of what is now Corte Madera. John L. Van Reynegom, Amelia's father, who was a sea captain from Philadelphia, had settled on 160 acres of land where he planted an orchard and a vineyard, built a reservoir, and raised cattle. In 1860 and 1862, he applied unsuccessfully for a homestead. After Van Reynegom's death, Pixley bought Owl's Wood from the Reed

PROFILE: **Elaine and William Petrocelli**

Elaine and William Petrocelli own the largest independent bookstore in Marin. Book Passage in Corte Madera not only supplies an outstanding selection of books and magazines, but invites hundreds of talented authors annually who speak and autograph their books in the store.

In addition, this popular bookstore sponsors writing classes, workshops, an annual mystery writers' conference, a children's writers conference, and one of the most important travel writers' conferences in the country. Book sales from the store are often designated to benefit charitable causes such as Hospice, the Marin Abused Women's Center and research on breast cancer. Finally, so that the entire family may become involved, a "Children's' Storytime" is held every Sunday.

Elaine Petrocelli was born in Indianapolis, Indiana, and attended Ohio State where she received a Bachelor's Degree in Education. She worked as a teacher and principal, and after moving to California, was an Associate Director of the Multi Cultural Institute in San Francisco which fought racism in schools in the late 1960s–70s.

In 1975 she opened a general retail bookstore called Lark Creek Books in Larkspur. In 1982 she founded Book Passage in San Francisco as a mail order travel book service, and in 1986 she combined the two businesses and moved them to their present location at 51 Tamal Vista Boulevard. The store has been enormously successful and has been enlarged several times. It is now includes sections of used books and mysteries plus a small restaurant. In 1994 Elaine and Bill Petrocelli even started their own publishing company.

Bill Petrocelli was born in 1938 in Oakland and educated as a lawyer at the University of California Boalt Hall. He is co-owner of Book Passage and has served on the National Board of the American Booksellers' Association for several years, championing the rights of independent bookstores.

Bill writes the store's information newsletter/book catalog, *News and Review*, mailed out to book patrons all over the world. He supervises the store's active Web site, bookpassage.com, and the e-mail newsletter, *Book Passage Fortnightly*.

Elaine is a member of the American Booksellers' Association, International Booksellers, Sister in Crime, Northern California Children's Booksellers Association, Commonwealth Club, and International Women's Forum.

The help that Elaine and Bill have given to aspiring writers has come through the classes they have established at their store. Many of the people who have taken classes have become successful published writers. A recent success story was Book Passage student Sheldon Siegel whose first novel, *Special Circumstances,* brought him a rumored seven-figure sale from Bantam. Siegel has been compared to John Grisham and Tom Clancy and 50,000 copies of his first novel have already been sold. Siegel attended the Book Passage Mystery Writers' Conference and a work class on "How to write a Mystery."

In 1996 Elaine Petrocelli was selected as the outstanding Bookseller in America by the American Booksellers' Association and her photograph appeared on the cover of the book industry magazine, *Publishers Weekly*. She has drawn together a staff that loves to hand-sell an important book that might not be noticed among best sellers.

Elaine and Bill Petrocelli's excellent bookstore has become a center of learning and a meeting place for all of Marin's book lovers, authors and readers alike.

heirs for $2,000 in gold, then put the entire property in his wife's name. By 1885, Pixley had enlarged the estate to 191 acres.

During the years that the family divided their time between San Francisco and Corte Madera, Frank Pixley held many political offices, including state attorney general and state assemblyman. In 1877, at the age of fifty-three, Pixley founded a newspaper called the *San Francisco Argonaut,* which continued to be published until 1958. Famous writers such as Gertrude Atherton, Mark Twain, John Stoddard, and Ambrose Bierce contributed to this very popular newspaper.

After Pixley's death in 1895, a portion of the Corte Madera land was subdivided, and a town grew up around the old railroad depot (in the area that is now the Village Square and Menke Park). Adjacent Larkspur incorporated in 1908 and annexed the portion of Owl's Wood where Pixley's original home stood—much to the outrage of Corte Madera citizens, who did not get around to incorporating until 1916.

Today, the town of Corte Madera extends from San Francisco Bay on the east side of Highway 101 to the Larkspur city limits on the west. Directly off the freeway to the west is the Town Center, built in 1952 on land that once belonged to the Meadowsweet Dairy. It contains several large chain stores and a total of around 60 shops, restaurants and services. In 1986, the shopping center was renovated and expanded to look like a Mediterranean village square. Included in the new design were a series of open-air courtyards, fountains, plazas and covered walkways.

A smaller shopping center located one block west of Highway 101 contains one of the top bookstores in Marin. Take the Lucky/Doherty exit off Highway 101, go straight on Fifer one block, then turn left on Tamal Vista. Just past the Department of Motor Vehicles on the left is "The Market" which contains shops and restaurants.

"Book Passage" at 51 Tamal Vista Boulevard is owned by Elaine and Bill Petrocelli, who claim their store contains the largest travel book section of any bookstore in the United States. They also sell everything from children's books to fine art volumes, mysteries and used books. The store sponsors many authors' events, writing classes, conferences and seminars, making it especially popular with authors.

Across the freeway from Town Center at 1554 Redwood Highway is a high-fashion shopping mall, The Village (Tamalpais/Paradise Drive freeway exit). Anchored by major upscale department stores, The Village contains around 80 specialty and fashion shops. For information, phone the village at 924-8557.

THE VILLAGE
924-8557.

Corte Madera retains a small town flavor, and residents are especially proud of their annual Fourth of July celebrations. The whole town turns out for a spirited parade, with fire trucks ringing their bells, city officials riding in convertibles and waving to the crowd, school bands playing, clowns cavorting, and kids riding bikes decorated in red, white, and blue. An arts and crafts festival and picnic are held in the Town Park.

Take the Corte Madera/Larkspur exit off Highway 101 west onto Tamalpais Drive to arrive at the old Village Square, seventenths of a mile from the turnoff. When you have gone half a mile, you will pass the 22.7 acre Town Park on your right, purchased in 1939 and built on an area of land fill. Built here are the Recreation Center, the Public Safety Building, which contains the police and fire departments, the post office, just behind the Public Safety Building on Pixley, and, beyond the parking lot, the Town Hall at 300 Tamalpais Drive.

Tamalpais Drive turns right and arrives almost immediately at the Village Square and a bus shelter near the site of the old train station. Above the bus stop is the lovely landscaped Menke Park on the corner of Montecito Drive and Redwood Avenue. There are benches and an old brick wall. Tamalpais Drive becomes Redwood Avenue at this point, which then intersects Corte Madera Avenue, and, in a northerly direction (to your right), becomes Magnolia Avenue at the Larkspur city limits. Above the park on Corte Madera Avenue are some interesting shops. To learn more about Corte Madera, look up this website: www.ci.corte-madera@ca.us.

CORTE MADERA
website:
www.ci.corte-
madera@ca.us.

LARKSPUR

Around 1869, William Murray and Patrick King purchased 1,233 acres in the area of Kentfield and Larkspur from the Ross family. The partners divided the property in half, with Murray taking the northern area near Kentfield. King's portion included what is now downtown Larkspur. He built a home at 105 King Street and established a cattle and dairy operation.

The town of Larkspur was actually developed by a man named C.W. Wright, who bought the King Ranch in 1887 for $21,000. He had the land subdivided into lots large enough for a house, with space for some livestock, and he built five Victorian cottages—enough to qualify the "town" for a railroad station. The town was named after a blue flower his English wife misidentified as larkspur instead of lupine.

After the 1906 earthquake and fire, survivors from San Francisco poured into Larkspur, and many stayed permanently. These new residents had an understandable interest in establishing a fire department, and one was organized in 1909. To

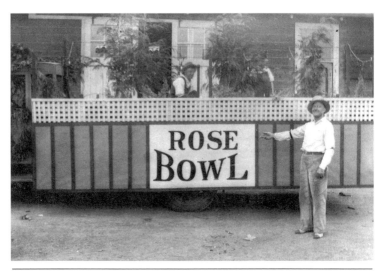

Cap Larsen at the Rose Bowl in Larkspur, 1930. (Courtesy of Betty Krause)

raise money for fire-fighting equipment, they held fund-raising dances at the railroad station park. The dances proved so successful that they were moved to a fancy new location at 476 Cane Street and held on a regular basis. Situated next to a bubbling creek was a half-acre of hardwood dance floors surrounded by rose-covered trellises. These famous Rose Bowl dances drew three to four thousand people weekly from all over the Bay Area from 1913 until 1963. Glowing Chinese lanterns and strings of colored lights made it the ideal spot for romance. Both engagements and anniversaries of couples who had met at the dances were announced by "Cap" Larsen, a secretary of the Larkspur Volunteer Fireman's Association. The highlight of the evening was the famous Rose Bowl "firefall," twenty seconds of falling white sparks cascading down from forty feet in the sky. It was masterminded by Willie Frizzi, who was known as a "one-man electrical company."

For a brief tour of Larkspur, begin at the Lark Creek Inn, 234 Magnolia. This restaurant is located in the old Murphy house built in 1888. The house was thought to be haunted during the 1920s and 1930s, and was occupied by a veterinarian and several hobos who lived in the bottom part during the Depression. In 1938, a gas station, service garage, and automobile sales room were built on the property. Then, in 1971, the house and other structures were remodeled into the restaurant and shops.

Across Magnolia Avenue from the Lark Creek Inn is Madrone Avenue which runs west into Baltimore Canyon, parallel to Larkspur Creek. This creek, also known as Arroyo Holon, was the boundary of the *Corte de Madera del Presidio* Mexican land grant.

Dolliver Park is located on both sides of Madrone, beginning at Magnolia. Ellen Dolliver Jewell, a member of the pioneer San Francisco Dolliver family, gave the north portion of the park to the city of Larkspur in 1923, noting on a plaque that this was "the first redwood grove on the Redwood Highway." You will see redwood trees growing right out of the street.

The property to the south was given by Mr. and Mrs. C. S. Burtchaell (he was the grandson of Thomas Dolliver who owned a leather goods manufacturing company in San Francisco) to honor his grandmother, Ann C. Dolliver. The park includes a children's playground.

At 58 Madrone Avenue is the original Dolliver house, a Victorian-style summer home built in 1888. This was the first house constructed in the new Larkspur township laid out by C.W. Wright. It is listed on the National Register of Historic Places, but is still used as a private residence and is not open to the public.

Madrone Avenue ends about a mile from Magnolia. A trail begins here and follows Larkspur Creek to the old blue-rock quarry and through a dense redwood forest to Dawn Falls. Here, a mile from Madrone, two natural springs join to form the source of Larkspur Creek.

Returning to the business area, continue on Magnolia Avenue through downtown Larkspur, an interesting place to explore since many of the original buildings have been preserved and now house unique shops and restaurants.

At 400 Magnolia you will see the Larkspur City Hall, which was constructed in 1913. It now includes the fire department as well as the library. The building was designed by San Francisco architect Charles O. Claussen in what is known as a Mission Revival style with influences of Italian villa. The Larkspur Heritage Committee has historical photos on display here.

In the middle of town, at 507 Magnolia, is the former Blue Rock Inn. Built in 1895, it was designed in the Queen Anne style and included a short tower. This inn was then known as the Hotel Larkspur and was billed as "A First Class Family Resort." The building survived the 1906 earthquake, but residents of the hotel were startled when bricks from the chimney fell onto the roof and hotel furniture rolled around uncontrollably. They rushed outside for safety only to learn that a neighbor living on Ward Sreet just across the way, August Frizzi, had died of a sudden heart attack during the quake. Frizzi had been known to train boxers in the basement of his yellow house.

In 1910, the hotel was sold to Elizabeth and Serefino Marilli. The new owners remodeled immediately, and on the first story they put a facing of blue basalt rock which had been quarried

A parade in Larkspur in 1910. Frizzi Saloon on the left, Larkspur Hotel on the right. (Courtesy Betty Krause)

on a hill above Paradise Drive. Blue rock pillars were added, and the name of the hotel changed to reflect the new look. Around 12 years later, the Marilli's took in a partner, William Stringa, who had arrived in town as an umbrella salesman.

A historic plaque may be seen farther north in the Larkspur Plaza Shopping Center on Magnolia and Doherty Drive. It states that on or near this Larkspur site were discovered ancient shell mounds and burial grounds of the Miwok Indians. The plaque also makes note of a sawmill landing, a wharf on the salt water which was used by Mexican soldiers in 1816, and a government sawmill which operated here from 1847 to 1850. It goes on to state that the first house in town, built by Jonathan Bickerstaff, was erected near this spot and that the North Pacific Coast Railroad began service in this area in 1875.

The old train station is located just south of here. As you look at the plaque, the two buildings of the train station are directly to your left down the old railroad right-of-way which is now a bicycle path.

Larkspur men prepare to leave for Ft. Lewis Washington and World War I, September 19, 1917. (L. to R) Messrs. Polley, Mert Bain, Walter Frizzi, Henry Foster, Barns, and Rose. In the background on the left is Serefino Marilli, owner of the Blue Rock Inn. (Courtesy of Betty Krause)

The buildings are a light beige stucco with tile roofs and wooden double doors. The smaller building on the left labeled LARKSPUR was the waiting room, while the larger one is where tickets were sold. The original Northwestern Pacific Railroad logos remain on each end of the building on the right. The warehouse beyond was once the location of the station master's house.

Piper Park

As you leave the downtown area, stop at Piper Park to view the old arks along Larkspur Boardwalk One and Two. Before World War II, there were three boardwalks that went all the way up to the Bon Air Bridge. Driving north on Magnolia, turn east (or right) on Doherty Drive. The park is about three blocks away, behind the police station. Pioneer families from the area say that Mr. Doherty lived on the hill above here and was considered the boss of the town.

Piper Park is a 22-acre park on landfill surrounded by the Corte Madera Creek. It has two softball diamonds, a soccer field, cricket field, four tennis courts, volleyball court, and horseshoe pitching area. There is also a fishing dock and 24 picnic tables with six barbecues. Two hundred and fifty people can use this area at one time. Phone 927-5110. Some small fees apply. PIPER PARK
927-5110

To view the old arks, go to the gravel road to the west of the baseball diamond and behind the Henry C. Hall Elementary School, 200 Doherty Drive. There have been arks along the Corte Madera Creek since 1906. At first they were vacation homes, but later were lived in all year. Today, the private residences here are a combination of very old arks and newly-constructed homes.

Marin Community Fields

Also on Doherty Drive, adjacent to Redwood High School, are the Marin Community Fields which opened in September 1987. The facilities include 17 acres of public playing fields providing for softball, baseball, rugby, soccer and a beep ball field for the blind.

This project was a vision of Bob Troppman in the late 1950s. It was brought to reality by Don Wihlborg through his design of the fields. Fred Kritzberg, for whom the amphitheater was named, was the consulting engineer and a great benefactor for the fields.

The driving volunteer force in this project included the Community Fields Association, Henry Moody, Shirley Walker, Bob Troppman, and Dolly Nave from San Rafael who acted as project coordinator. Major donations from business people included Tom Cagwin and David Dorward of Cagwin and Dorward Landscape Contractors; Dan Boyd of Able Fence Co; Alfred Dalecio of Bresnan and Dalecio Construction; the Ghilotti Brothers Contractors (Mario, Dino, Mike, Dick, plus Nick Rado, Jerry Pagna, Frank Palagi and Jerry Elenberger); Maggiora and Ghilotti Contractors (H. J. Babe Ghilotti and his four sons, Greg, Jim, Gary and Glen, plus Ted Lehman); Jim Mahoney of Mahoney Steel; Bruce Mac Phail of McPhail's Inc.; Rich Epidendio of Rich Ready Mix; San

Marin Community Fields, Larkspur, with Mt. Tamalpais in the background.

Marin/Golden State Lumber (Al and Rich Bonfiglio, Glen Nobmann); Bill Dutra and Marv Larsen of San Rafael Rock Quarry; Shamrock Materials (Lee and Eugene Ceccotti, Max Cerini); Tom Bradall of V. Dolan Trucking and Woody Van Lackum of Woodmasters.

The Community Fields Association solicited a grant of $300,000 from the Buck Trust in 1984. A three-to-one match was required after the initial $50,000 for the study. Six hundred thousand dollars was raised in cash from the community and over $900,000 was raised in donated labor, materials and equipment.

In the fall of 1985, the grading and hydroseeding for erosion control was completed in just three weekends with the help of eighteen pieces of equipment and labor provided by the Northern California Landscape Contractors Association. Seven months later, a sand turf plus irrigation and drainage lines were installed. Hydroseeding was done again for the playing surface of the fields. A Thousand-seat amphitheater was built in the spring of 1986. Today the fields are as popular as ever and very heavily used.

North Larkspur

As you continue northwest on Magnolia Avenue, you will pass the old Escalle Vineyards at 771 Magnolia. The area began as a brickyard operated by Claude Callot, a Frenchman, who sent the bricks to San Francisco by barge down the Corte Madera Creek.

Callot's friends, Jean Escalle and his brother Pierre, came from France to help with the brick making. They added some vineyards to the property and began producing an excellent table claret. When Callot died, Jean Escalle married his Irish widow, Ellen. He bought forty more acres and planted Riesling and Zinfandel grapes. Jean and Ellen then opened the Limerick Inn, which served good food and wine in an outdoor setting. A train stopped at the Escalle Station so patrons could eat, drink, and play bocce ball. Additional entertainment was provided by a live band. A special celebration, the Vintage Festival, was held in the fall, and another on Bastille Day.

The old red brick wall of the Limerick Inn can be seen from Magnolia Avenue, although the property is now closed to the public. Above and to the back is the original winery with the name "Jean Escalle" proudly displayed across the front.

Just north of Escalle's is Bon Air Road, which runs northeast to Sir Francis Drake Boulevard past Marin General Hospital.

The hospital grounds were once the site of the elegant Bon Air Hotel, which could brag of the county's first swimming pool, a bowling alley, and a dance pavilion. Stately palm trees still stand in front. Across from the hospital is the twenty-six acre Creekside Park behind Marin Catholic High School. The marsh beside the Corte Madera Creek was purchased by the County of Marin in 1975 as a service area. It includes portions of Larkspur, Greenbrae, and Kentfield along Sir Francis Drake Boulevard. A $750,000 bond issue was passed for the purpose of restoring the marsh, which the Army Corps of Engineers had used as a dumping grounds for spoils when they dredged the adjacent portion of Corte Madera Creek.

The restoration of this salt marsh represents a unique environmental achievement and has received national recognition. Trees and shrubs native to Marin were planted, along with a multitude of wildflowers which bloom here in the spring. A few benches, picnic tables, and winding pathways have been added on dry land. From any vantage point, there is a magnificent view of Mt. Tamalpais. In 1989, the area was refurbished with the planting of additional trees and plants.

The Corte Madera Creek winds out toward the bay, and where it passes under Bon Air Road there is a small bridge. The Bon Air bridge was once a drawbridge that was raised to let barges through. Located nearby was Hill's Boat House where people from the hotel and from other parts of the county came to swim in "warm salt creek water baths."

At 1201 South Eliseo Drive, just south of the bridge, is tiny Hamilton Park. Clarabelle Hamilton, a resident of the nearby Tamalpais Retirement Center, donated this lot in 1975 to provide lasting access to Corte Madera Creek. In an area of doctors' offices, medical clinics, and convalescent homes, this park's lovely blooming flowers and green grass offer a spot of tranquillity. A curving path forms a circle from South Eliseo to a spot overlooking Corte Madera Creek, where on most days, a family of mallards can be seen swimming below. Facilities include benches and picnic tables.

Another small park, also overlooking the Corte Madera Creek, is the Bon Air Landing Park at 557 South Eliseo. It contains two benches and one picnic table plus a pier running into the creek.

North Larkspur, along Magnolia Avenue near the Kentfield border, has more shops and restaurants.

GREENBRAE

The City of Larkspur annexed property on the north side of the Corte Madera Creek known as Greenbrae. This area was part of the *Rancho Punta de Quintin* granted to Captain Juan Bautista Cooper. James Ross purchased the property and started a dairy, running it until his death in 1862. The land was sold a few times and in 1890 the Catholic Church of San Francisco purchased it and subleased it as a dairy farm. The church kept it for the next fifty years.

Greenbrae today contains many apartments, a subdivision of expensive private homes, and the Bon Air Shopping Center adjacent to Sir Francis Drake Boulevard.

THE SAN QUENTIN PENINSULA

This peninsula on the east side of the county juts out into the waters of San Francisco and San Pablo bays. It was named for the courageous Indian warrior Quintin, who was a follower of the Indian chief, Marin. The spelling of the name was changed to "Quentin," and he mysteriously became a saint. In 1968 and 1972, Larkspur annexed property in this area, also once part of the *Rancho Punta de Quintin*. The land grant stretched from Point San Quentin into the Ross Valley.

The Larkspur Ferry Terminal and Larkspur Landing

The Larkspur Ferry Terminal is located on East Sir Francis Drake Boulevard on twenty-five acres at the mouth of the Corte Madera Creek. It is a white, equilateral triangular-shaped steel frame looking somewhat as if it were built out of gigantic Tinker Toys. Designed by San Francisco architect Jacques de Brer, this landmark is visible from both Highway 101 and the water. Its ultramodern triangular design presents a light, airy feeling which is what the Golden Gate Bridge directors wanted, as opposed to a heavy, massive building blocking the view of the bay.

The design was controversial when the structure was built, however, for it failed to include adequate shelter for waiting passengers. Winter rain, cold winds, and fog blew, leaving patrons wet and cold. To solve the problem, the District installed plastic weather protection within the space frame. A section for air at the bottom was left open, and heaters were placed inside.

The Larkspur Ferry Terminal handles thousands of riders a day. It provides a large parking lot and feeder buses for passengers from all over the county who ride both mornings and evenings. Phone 455-2000. To get to the ferry terminal from Highway 101, take the East Sir Francis Drake Boulevard exit.

LARKSPUR FERRY
TERMINAL
455-2000

Ferry Service between Larkspur and San Francisco began in 1976 with gas-turbine ferries built for the District by Campbell Industries in San Diego. These boats, the *Marin, Sonoma* and *San*

Inside the Larkspur ferry terminal.

Francisco, were later modified by installing diesel engines because of skyrocketing fuel costs. Each carries 725 passengers in great luxury with large, comfortable chairs and tables. In 1998 a high-speed ferry called the *Del Norte* was added to the fleet. Coffee and rolls are sold in the morning, and cocktails on the evening run. Cellular telephones are available. In 1999 a public electric vehicle charging station was installed at the ferry terminal so that drivers with electric cars could charge their vehicles while they were at work in San Francisco during the day. Each electric charge provides 70 to 90 miles of driving.

From the parking lot at the ferry terminal, looking south, you can see another ark community called the Greenbrae Boardwalk; beyond is the ninety-five acre Corte Madera Marsh Ecological Reserve. This marsh is rich in feed for shorebirds and you might see an elegant snowy egret with long white plumes stalking the shallow waters. Across from the ferry terminal is Larkspur Landing, an extensive development of offices, apartments, shops, and restaurants, which opened in 1978. This complex was built on the site of the old Hutchinson Quarry, a landmark from 1924. Huge rocks from this quarry were once shipped all over the Bay Area for a variety of projects, including the Bay Bridge ballast, railroad beds, and dikes in the Sacramento delta. In August 2000, a remodel of the shopping center began the job of turning its gray and tan wooden New England styled buildings into a European-like piazza, including cobblestone walkways and a fountain. Across Larkspur Landing Circle are four movie theaters. To learn more about Larkspur look up this website: www.ci.larkspur.ca.us.

To learn more about Larkspur look at this website: www.ci.larkspur.ca.us.

Remillard Brickyard

East of Larkspur Landing is the Remillard Brickyard, a State Historical Landmark. From 1891 to 1915, it supplied 500,000 bricks annually to the Bay Area. Bricks from this yard were used to help rebuild San Francisco after the 1906 earthquake and fire. Today the building has been renovated into office space and contains a restaurant. Some historians believe that the English explorer, Sir Francis Drake, landed near this spot and stayed for a month while he explored the inland area and repaired the *Golden Hinde*. Across Sir Francis Drake Boulevard is Remillard Park, consisting of a jogging path, benches, picnic tables and a large pond. Hikers and picnickers can enjoy watching the ferryboats maneuver in and out of the terminal and windsurfers with their colorful sails skim across the top of the water. A thirty-foot statue of Sir Francis Drake constructed of iron with the figure wearing a golden stainless steel vest and carrying a flag and sword, greets visitors to Remillard Park. The sculpture was created by Dennis Patton and placed here in 1990.

San Quentin Prison

East Sir Francis Drake Boulevard follows the bay around the San Quentin peninsula, and as you round a bend, the mood changes abruptly. Suddenly, there are high chain-link fences topped with strands of barbed wire and a black and white sign announces "Department of Correction, California State Prison, San Quentin." You will pass a black gate with a guard and see a single watchtower atop a hill to your right. Around the next curve, the whole prison spreads out before you. Many of the buildings have been painted a fresh-looking cream color with red and green trim. Small wooden houses are clustered below the fence adjacent to the road.

The main entrance to San Quentin Prison is the last exit before reaching the Richmond-San Rafael Bridge. Turn right and drive down Main Street. The bay is on your left, beyond a row of towering eucalyptus trees and there is a small beach here open to the public. It takes only a couple of minutes to pass through the village of San Quentin, which consists of a few houses, a post office, and the yellow "House"—a resting place for families visiting the prison. At the end of Main Street is the entrance to the infamous prison, scene of riots, murders, prison breaks, and over four hundred state executions.

The first prison was an old brig called the *Waban*, known as the "hell ship," which was anchored off Angel Island, then towed to San Quentin with both men and women prisoners aboard. The state had purchased twenty acres from Benjamin Buckelew for a prison which opened in 1854. During the early years, the prisoners were used to build roads and houses in the county. Conditions inside the prison were described as grim, with prisoners lacking blankets and being forced to sleep in their striped convict suits. On July 22, 1862, 400 convicts escaped, taking Warden John Challis as hostage. This was reportedly the fifth escape in five weeks. Sheriff Valentino Doub gathered a small posse and rode over the trail (on what is now D Street in San Rafael) to Ross Landing (now Kentfield). As the sheriff came down over the ridge, he saw a gun battle going on between the citizens of Corte Madera and some of the convicts who were trying to escape across Corte Madera Creek. In the confusion the warden escaped. Accounts vary as to what happened in the battle that followed, but it is known that a large number of the convicts were recaptured. Some were injured, and a few were killed.

Thirty-five acres of additional land for the prison were purchased in 1864 and two more cellblocks were built. The *1880 History of Marin* describes one of these buildings as being two stories high, forty by twenty feet, and built of poor-quality brick. "In the basement is the dungeon of the prison which contains fourteen cells, seven on each side of the passageway, each cell eleven-and-a-half by six feet, and nine feet high; near the entrance to the dungeon stands the whipping post." Between 1912 and 1922, there were around 1,500 prisoners at San Quentin. The number of prisoners jumped to 5,000 after World War I, with 700 paid guards and other personnel. In 1933, the female prisoners were moved to Tehachapi, and by 1934, the number of male prisoners had increased to 6,400. Escape attempts continued.

Probably no escape has caught the attention and fancy of the public as much as the "Rub-a-Dub-Dub-Marin Yacht Club." The kayak, built in the prison shop, was launched near an unmanned watchtower and soon began taking on water. It was spotted by an unsuspecting guard who offered to call for help. The escapees waved and thanked him politely but refused the offer. Two of the men, William McGirk and John Waller, were recaptured within a year but two different juries, after hearing conflicting stories from guards, refused to convict them of escape. The third, Forrest Tucker, was not captured until 1983 when he was found living in West Palm Beach, Florida, married to a wealthy socialite. He was sent back to San Quentin.

Some attempts at reform have been made within the prison. Since 1975, prisoners have been allowed to marry and may apply for overnight conjugal visits with their wives. Classes have been set up so that convicts can work toward earning a high school diploma or developing special skills. Sports are popular and the inmates also produce a lively newspaper called the *San Quentin News* with coverage of prison events in addition to state and federal court decisions affecting prisoners. Still, racial and other violence continues at the prison. In 1972, then-governor Ronald Reagan announced that San Quentin Prison would be phased out in five years, but nothing came of his plan and the antiquated prison labors on.

SAN QUENTIN PRISON 454-1460

No tours of the prison are allowed, but there is a gift shop just outside the gates. The San Quentin Handicraft Shop carries items made by prisoners such as leather purses, billfolds, belts, candles, carved wooden cable cars and covered wagons, jewelry, jewelry boxes, decorated T-shirts, paintings, and copper pictures. The shop is open from Wednesdays through Sunday from 8:30 a.m. to 2:00 p.m. There is also a museum open to the public inside the gates on the right. Visitors must leave a driver's license to go inside. The prison phone is 454-1460.

Richmond-San Rafael Bridge

East Sir Francis Drake Boulevard ends at the Richmond-San Rafael Bridge, where you can take Highway 580 back to Highway 101, or cross the bridge to Richmond in the East Bay. The two-deck, four-mile bridge (with three quarter-mile bridge approaches) was opened in 1956 after three years of construction. The bridge lacks the open viewing built into the Golden Gate Bridge, and no bicycles or pedestrians are allowed.

The Marin Rod and Gun Club

The Marin Rod and Gun Club is located on fifty-five acres of uplands and tidelands on San Pablo Bay at Point San Quentin, adjacent to the Richmond-San Rafael Bridge. Organized in 1926, the club has active sports people who enjoy fishing for recreation. They are also concerned with the preservation and propagation of fish and wildlife. Over the years, members claim to have fought successfully against commercial net fishing in inland waters and against the commercial fishing of striped bass and abalone. Facilities, which are not open to the public, include a half-mile-long fishing pier built by the C&H Sugar Company in 1924 for loading Marin County water into tankers. This water was taken to the C&H Sugar Refinery at Crockett near the Carquinez Strait. The Marin Rod and Gun Club also has a small boat ramp and several acres of picnic grounds. For membership information, call 456-3123.

THE MARIN ROD
AND GUN CLUB
456-3123.

KENTFIELD

The community of Kentfield is named after the pioneer family who purchased land in the area in 1871. Adaline and Albert Kent, along with their seven-year-old son, William, left Chicago where Albert owned a large meat-packing plant, cattle, and land. The family moved west looking for a better climate for Albert's health. They eventually found an ideal spot in an area then known as Ross Landing, a busy shipping point on the Corte Madera Creek where flat-bottomed schooners and other vessels, ranging from ten to fifty tons, loaded cordwood, bricks and hay. This is the area where the College of Marin is now located, approximately two miles west of Highway 101 on Sir Francis Drake Boulevard.

The Kents bought land from the Murray and Ross families and built a house which is still standing. William was sent east for a college education at Yale. There he met Elizabeth Thacher, the daughter of a Latin professor, and married her in 1890. The young couple first lived in Chicago but moved to California in

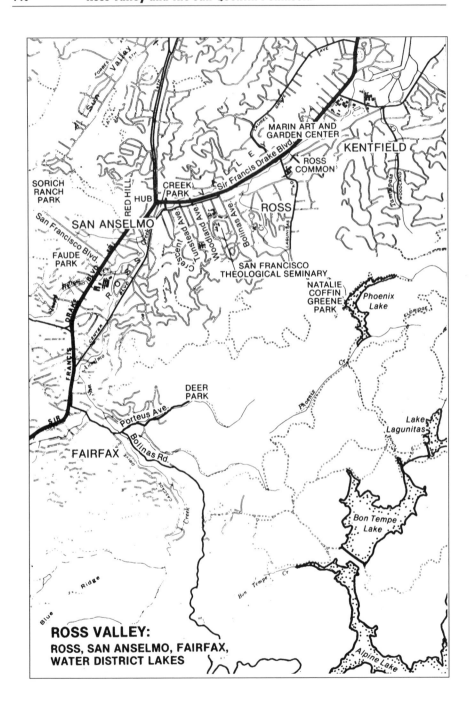

ROSS VALLEY:
ROSS, SAN ANSELMO, FAIRFAX,
WATER DISTRICT LAKES

1906. In 1915, William remodeled the Kent estate to accommodate his seven children. The Kents became active in Marin affairs, especially conservation causes. In 1909, shortly after donating the Muir Woods Monument to the United States, William and his mother Adaline built the Tamalpais Centre for recreation (where the College of Marin gym stands today). Adaline was concerned that the young people of her day have constructive recreational outlets.

The Tamalpais Centre was a huge mission-style building with arches and a tile roof, situated on twenty-nine acres running from Corte Madera Creek to the present College Avenue. The building was so large, in fact, that it was referred to as the Kentfield Stadium, and a small street running along its side was named Stadium Way. It contained a gym, a hardwood dance floor, a kitchen, and a stage with four changes of scenery. Also at the Centre were a racetrack and sports fields. Band concerts provided lively entertainment on Sundays. Dances, plays, luncheons, and Sierra Club meetings were held regularly. A special event was the annual May Day, which continued into the 1930s.

In 1910, William Kent announced his decision to run for Congress on a progressive platform. He was elected to represent California's First District in the Sixty-Second Congress and reelected for two more terms, serving until 1917. He is remembered for authoring legislation to create the National Parks Service, which became effective in 1916. Back in Marin, Kent continued to do major work for conservation. He dreamed of a park on Mt. Tamalpais and donated land to help make this a reality. While her husband pursued his political career, Elizabeth Thacher Kent became involved in the women's suffrage movement. She picketed the White House in 1917 and, when given a choice of going to jail or paying a fine, she said she preferred jail. (William chose to pay her fine.)

Elizabeth was an inspiration to a Kent woman of a later generation, Martye Kent, daughter of William and Elizabeth's son, Thomas, and his wife Anne. Martye made history in April 1969 when she led a fight against the Army Corps of Engineers who had decided to cement Tamalpais Creek, which lies at the entrance to Kent Woodlands, an exclusive subdivision developed by the Kent family.

The project was undertaken in conjunction with the Corps' controversial Corte Madera Creek project, which was designed to prevent flooding by cementing some portions of the creek bank. Tamalpais Creek had not been scheduled for cementing in the proposed plan, nor was public notice adequately provided.

The Corps' action was strongly protested, and forty-three Marin residents and College of Marin students were arrested in a confrontation over tree cutting, but the battle was eventually lost. Martye and the community were forced to watch Tamalpais Creek become a ditch of rippled cement lined by a green plastic-covered cyclone fence.

There were long-term effects. The fight at Tamalpais Creek awakened the aesthetic and political consciousness of the Ross Valley and possibly the nation. An important federally-financed study was conducted and resulted in a published book about nine alternative methods of flood control. In December 1969, a large crowd gathered to plant a sapling maple tree and to dedicate a plaque fastened to a dead tree stump beside the creek. The inscription read:

> *This tree is dedicated to the*
> *Memory of the natural*
> *Tree-lined Corte Madera Creek*
> *And its tributary, Tamalpais Creek,*
> *destroyed in 1969*
> *By the United States Army*
> *Corps of Engineers.*

Members of the Kent family were often in the news, as they continued their tradition of interest in politics and conservation. Until his death in May 1980, Roger Kent, son of William and Elizabeth, was a power in California politics. His brother Sherman had a successful career in U.S. intelligence. Anne Kent (Mrs. Thomas Kent) was a driving force in the effort to preserve Marin County history. A reference room in the Marin County Library was named in her honor after her death in July 1981. It is called the Anne Kent California Room and contains books on California, volumes by California authors, documents, photographs and maps. It also houses the oral history tapes and transcripts of 250 pioneer Marin County families.

Today, the community of Kentfield remains unincorporated, an area mainly of formal, elegant homes enlivened by a college in its midst.

The College of Marin

The College of Marin, which is the heart of Kentfield, began in 1926 as a two-year junior college with eighty-five students. Marinites involved in its formation were Thomas Minto and his real estate/insurance partner, Thomas Kent. To establish the college site, they worked without a commission on the sale of property known as the Butler estate. Ernest E. Wood, principal of Tamalpais High School, used the high school district to

College of Marin, Kentfield.

receive money raised by public subscription to buy the property. When a college district was formed with official sanctions from Sacramento, the land was turned over from the high school district. In support of the new school, the Tamalpais Centre and most of the acreage surrounding it were given in 1927 to the Marin Junior College District with the stipulation that the land would forever be used for educational and recreational purposes. The college used the Tamalpais Centre as an assembly hall. Years later the building was condemned by the local fire department as a hazard and burned in firemen's exercises. The modern gym was built on the property around 1964.

Today, College of Marin has two campuses which each semester have 14,000 students studying in more than 60 degree curriculums and 29 programs offering certificates of achievement in vocational and occupational subjects. Included in this enrollment are 5,000 students each quarter taking non-credit courses, including active older students who in 1974 opened a senior citizen school known as "Emeritus College."

College of Marin also sponsors community classes and a program whereby students are enrolled in "distance learning." This is accomplished by the use of video cassettes, the college website, E-mail, faxes and video teleconferencing, which is a two-way interactive video and audio system. Students at the Kentfield and Indian Valley campuses can view each other on a television screen and converse. College of Marin is famous for its excellent drama productions and has had outstanding stars emerge such as actors Robin Williams, David Dukes and Kathleen Quinlan. The campus is open from 8:30 a.m. to 10:00 p.m., Monday through Friday. Groups may tour the grounds by making arrangements; call 457-8811. Emeritus College: 485-9652. Web page: www.marin.cc.ca.us.

COLLEGE OF MARIN
457-8811.
EMERITUS COLLEGE:
485-9652
WEB PAGE:
www.marin.cc.ca.us

ROSS

The quiet, small town of Ross, just beyond Kentfield, is a place of lovely homes and exclusive estates hidden off shady, tree-lined streets. This area was part of *Rancho Punta de Quintin Canada de San Anselmo* (Quintin Point, Valley of Saint

Carriages gather at the Ross train station to wait for men commuting home from San Francisco, 1895.

Anselm), an 8,877 acre Mexican land grant awarded to Juan B.R. Cooper in 1840. After extensive logging, Cooper sold to Benjamin Buckelew. In 1857, Buckelew sold the land for $50,000 to James Ross, for whom the town is named.

James Ross was born in 1812 in Petty, near Inverness, Scotland. At age seventeen, he left for Tasmania (formerly Van Diemen's Land), an island to the south of Australia, where he met and married Anne S. Grayling in 1839. The couple lived in New South Wales, Australia. In 1849 James Ross joined the rush to California, leaving the family in Australia until he was established in business in 1852. Instead of mining for gold, James opened a wholesale wine business in San Francisco, where he worked until 1857 when he bought Buckelew's land in Marin. Ross rebuilt the Buckelew home at the corner of Redwood Drive and Brookwood Lane and moved there with his wife and three children. The estate included orchards, gardens, and a windmill. (Continued on page 150)

PROFILE: **Peter R. Arrigoni**

Peter R. Arrigoni, a former stockbroker, Marin County Supervisor, Chairman of the Marin Community Foundation and Manager of the Marin Builders Exchange, is a native San Franciscan who has lived most of his life in Marin. His father, Pietro S. Arrigoni, founded a famous restaurant in San Francisco in 1928 called New Joe's, and in his growing up years, Pete Jr. worked there as a bus boy, waiter, bartender and kitchen helper.

He first found prominence in the county as an All-Conference football player the press nicknamed "Pistol Pete" when he attended the College of Marin in 1949-50. Prior to that he had played for St. Ignatius High School in San Francisco, where he was selected All-City. He lived in Marin in Fairfax with his grandfather, Dante Divita, who many years before had left San Francisco for Marin because of the 1906 Earthquake and Fire in San Francisco.

After attending the College of Marin, Arrigoni joined the United States Coast Guard, in which he served in the Pacific from 1952-1955. In 1956 he was drafted by the San Francisco 49ers to play professional football after playing at the University of Arizona in Tucson. At the University he dated an art student and tennis player, Patricia Larry, and they eloped and were married in Nogales, Mexico, in 1956. That same year he was to pitch in the College Baseball World Series in Omaha, Nebraska, and though he went to Omaha with the University of Arizona team, a back injury ended both his baseball and football careers. A back operation for a ruptured disk as well as extensive ther-apy repaired his back, and though he would liked to have played for the 49ers, he decided it would be wiser to retire from contact sports.

He graduated from the University of Arizona with a Bachelor of Science Degree and took a job in San Francisco as a stockbroker with

J. Barth and Company. When that company merged with Dean Witter, he became a Vice-President in sales at their Maritime Plaza office in San Francisco. He stayed in this business for twenty years.

His political career began with an appointment to the Fairfax Parks and Recreation Commission in the early 1960s. During those years he managed to build two tennis courts for the town and provide a comprehensive recreation plan.

He ran for the Fairfax City Council in 1963 and won with the largest vote ever recorded up to that time. While on the City Council he, along with other members, was instrumental in having sidewalks built for the schoolchildren between St. Rita's Church and Oak Manor School, and was responsible for landscaping at the Fairfax Parkade. He served as mayor in 1966-1967.

In 1968 he was drafted by a group of conservationists in Marin, led by Roger Kent and Elizabeth and Al Gatov, to run for the Marin County Board of Supervisors representing the Second District, the Ross Valley. His opponent was the powerful Chairman of the Board, Ernest "Kett" Kettenhofen, who wanted to build a major freeway to West Marin and open that part of the county up to big development. Arrigoni won every single precinct in that election in a landslide victory.

He took office in 1969, a pivotal time when Marin was threatened with huge development plans. Dr. L. Marin Griffin in his 1998 book, *Saving the Marin-Sonoma Coast*, writes:

> Peter Arrigoni turned out to be a knight in political armor. With the support of Kent and the Marin Conservation League, he won two successive elections for a total of eight crucial years, 1968-1976. He was joined on the Board in 1968 by Michael Wornum, a conservationist who replaced another leading conservationist, Peter Behr. Then followed the remarkable but hoped-for political turn-around. On November 3, 1970, the Board withdrew its support of the Marincello Plan, a proposed city of 25,000 people and seven story buildings on the Marin Headlands. Instead, Huey Johnson obtained its two thousand acres for The Nature Conservancy, and it is now part of the Golden Gate National Recreation Area.
>
> In August 1971, by a three-two vote with Arrigoni the new swing vote, the Supervisors repealed the West Marin General Plan which envisioned 150,000 people along Tomales Bay. Then again in 1971 and 1972, with the support of Arrigoni, Arnold Baptiste, and Michael Wornum, the supervisors requested that the state withdraw its Highway 17 plan for coastal Marin County from Highway 101 to Tomales Bay, which

they did. Then in a grand finale in 1971, the supervisors adopted a prece-dent-setting ecological study, "Can the Last Place Last?"—the basis for the Marin Countywide Plan adopted in 1973.

With these profound changes in county policy, the coastal freeways and the new cities were dead, the wildlife of the Bolinas Lagoon and Tomales Bay were safer, and the completion of the National Seashore was more likely.

Next, despite vigorous protests from developers, agricultural zon-ing that allowed only one house for each sixty acres was enacted by Supervisors Arrigoni, Wornum, and Baptiste in March 1972 for the east shore of Tomales Bay, extending to the border of Sonoma County—one-fifth of the county. Prior to this some ranches could be subdivided into two-acre parcels, destroying viable agriculture.

In Arrigoni's second election in 1971 he defeated both Barbara Boxer (who won a seat on the Board of Supervisors after Arrigoni retired, then served in the U.S. Congress and U.S. Senate) and William Filante (later an elected member of the College of Marin Board and the California Assembly).

During his eight years on the Board of Supervisors, Arrigoni served on the Bay Area Air Pollution Control District, 1971-1977 and as Chairman in 1974; Association of Bay Area Governments, 1969-1977; Alternate to the Bay Conservation and Development Commis-sion, 1969-1972; Member, Golden Gate Bridge, Highway and Trans-portation District Board, 1974-1977, (Chairman of the Insurance Committee and member of Finance and Transportation Committee); and representative or alternate to the Local Agency Formation Com-mission, 1969-1977.

Other commissions and boards of which he was a member included the City-County Services Committee; Economic Opportu-nity Council; Community Development Commission; the Housing Authority; Open Space District of which he was Chairman when it was formed; Redevelopment Agency; Transit District and Air Resources Board.

In 1972 a friend, Tony Boitano, decided to sell The Corner Bar, a local watering hole in Fairfax and Arrigoni decided to purchase it. He kept it until 1977 and enjoyed working as a bartender on holidays, a reminder of his days at New Joe's when he was growing up in San Francisco.

Arrigoni decided not to run for re-election after two terms on the Marin County Board of Supervisors and took a job as General Manager with the Marin Builders Exchange in 1977 where he remains today. This organization is a non-profit clearing house and service-oriented business with 960 member firms. The Marin Builders Exchange provides insurance to its members in addition to listing all projects which are ready to go to bid from San Francisco to the Oregon border. Members are contractors, architects, home decorators and other local businesses. The Marin Builders Exchange members have given around $300,000 in scholarship money to Marin students and have established a class at Redwood High School for young people interested in learning the construction trade.

Arrigoni's community activities include Board of Directors, Big Brothers of Marin; Marin County Chairman, National Council on Crime and Delinquency; Board of Directors, Marin Chapter, National Council on Alcoholism; Manager, Little League Baseball Team, Fairfax-Sleepy Hollow Little League; Marin Agricultural Land Trust; and Beryl Buck Institute of Education Board.

In 1987 he was appointed by the Marin County Board of Supervisors to serve as one of their appointments on the Marin Community Foundation Board of Directors which was created to manage the billion dollar Buck Trust. He served for two terms and was Chairman in 1995.

In 1996 he was selected as Outstanding Alumnus from the College of Marin.

Peter and Patricia have two adult children, Robert J. Arrigoni, an energy engineer, and James Arrigoni, a mortgage broker married to Trudy Arrigoni. James and Trudy have a daughter, Samantha Rose Arrigoni.

After his death in 1862, Ross's wife Anne sold off much of the land. She also deeded one and four-tenths acres to the town for a North Pacific Coast Railroad station, now the site of the Ross Post Office with a beautifully landscaped park on the north side. Residents have placed a white stone bench here dedicated to Ross civic leader Benjamin Harrison Dibblee, 1876-1945.

Mrs. Ross also donated another site near the railroad tracks for the valley's first church. This area is now a tiny park at the southwest corner of Sir Francis Drake Boulevard and Lagunitas Road, across the street from the town hall. A plaque reads, "On this spot stood San Anselmo chapel, Protestant Episcopal, the first place of worship in the Ross Valley, built in 1881 on ground given by Mrs. A.S. Ross." As the Episcopalian congregation grew, the tiny chapel became too small and was torn down. Today the second church is called St. John's and is located at the corner of Lagunitas Road and Shady Lane.

Anne Ross sold the family home and 297 acres in 1886, but the lovely old house burned in 1897. She lived in a small home she built across from the Ross train station until her death in 1901.

Ross incorporated in 1908, and at the first meeting of the town council moved to protect the trees in the area by making it illegal to cut them without permission. Soon the streets were paved, street lights installed, concrete bridges built over the creek, and a firehouse constructed. Land for the Ross Commons was sold to the town by Ross's daughter, Annie Ross Worn, in 1911. In 1927, a town hall, new firehouse and police station were built on Sir Francis Drake Boulevard and remain in use today.

Ross is the home of a fine private college-preparatory day school (grades nine through twelve) called The Branson School, which is located on Fernhill Avenue on the old Albert Dibblee estate. Dibblee owned seventy-eight acres of orchards, gardens, rolling grounds and a mansion called Fernhill. It was one of several huge estates established in this area in the late nineteenth century.

The school, at first coeducational and called the Little Gray School, was founded in San Rafael by a group of parents in 1916. In 1920, Miss Katherine Fleming Branson came from the

The Jose Moya del Pino Library in the Octagon House in the Marin Art and Garden Center, Ross.

East Coast to become its first headmistress, and the trustees renamed the school The Katherine Branson School in her honor. Two years later, the school moved to the present Ross campus. In 1972, the trustees founded Mount Tamalpais School for boys on the same campus. In 1985, the school was renamed The Branson School.

Another prominent institution in Ross, also on the site of an old estate, is the Marin Art and Garden Center, located on Sir Francis Drake Boulevard. It is surrounded by an unusual red brick serpentine wall built in memory of Caroline Livermore, one of the original founders. The Center contains facilities for a variety of nonprofit groups that run a children's playground, display arts and crafts, sell antiques, produce theatrical productions, present summer fashion shows, and maintain a unique library. The Center was founded in 1945 with the purchase of ten acres from the estate of A.J. Kittle, a member of the first Ross Town Council. Kittle heirs had decided to sell this land, part of an estate once owned by Annie Ross Worn and her husband

George. The Worns' house, known as "Sunnyside," was remodeled by the Kittles but partially burned in 1931 and was eventually destroyed.

Caroline Livermore, the president of the Marin Conservation League, wanted to save the lovely gardens, which contained a magnificent old magnolia tree and a giant sequoia. She organized a nonprofit group to buy the land and develop the Center's activities. Among the founder groups were the Marin Conservation League, The Garden Society of Marin, the Marin Garden Club, Marin Society of Artists, Ross Valley Players, and the Marin Music Chest.

Affiliate groups who make this such an important center for cultural activities now include the Decorations Guild; Northgate Group, which sponsors outdoor luncheons, table displays and fashion shows; Laurel House Antiques, a consignment shop; Marin Society of Artists who operate the Frances Young Gallery; Pixie Parents, a preschool co-op parents' club, which built and maintains a unique playground; and the historical Jose Moya del Pino Library in the Octagon House.

From 1950 to 1971, the Marin County Fair was held at the Center and is remembered for the beautiful gardens (many of Japanese design), flowers, and displays of original art. This fair is now held at the Marin County Civic Center in San Rafael.

THE ART AND GARDEN CENTER ADMINISTRATIVE OFFICE NUMBER 454-5597.

Events: 454-1301

Website: www.maagc.org

ROSS VALLEY PLAYERS 456-9555

You may visit the Marin Art and Garden Center at 30 Sir Francis Drake Boulevard and Laurel Grove from 9:00 a.m. to 6:00 p.m. For information on renting the grounds for private parties or wedding, call 454-1301. In the Center office you can see an old photo of the Kittle estate.

The Barn, a theater used by the Ross Valley Players, has a seating capacity of 300. There are usually five or six shows, including one musical, produced here yearly. Phone 456-9555 for a recording of current productions.

Luncheons and summer fashion shows held outdoors in the Northgate area can serve up to 500 people. This section of the Art and Garden Center is often used for weddings, as is the Livermore Room.

Across from the Art and Garden Center at Lagunitas Road is the Ross firehouse. In front of it is a large statue of a bear cast in compressed marble dust, designed by the late famous sculptor, Benjamino Bufano. The bear was donated by Jerome and Peggy Flax in 1971.

Cross the bridge on Lagunitas Road and turn left to reach the six-acre Ross Commons Town Park, which is in the center of Ross. The area is used mostly for sports by children attending the adjacent Ross Grammar School. In the summer of 1989, a one-hundred-year-old school house, donated by Richard and Clara Hoertkorn, was relocated to a corner of the Ross Commons. It was restored by the Ross Historical Society.

On Ross Commons and Poplar Avenue just beyond, there are shops—a coffee house, a florist, hairdresser, a butcher shop, grocery and small restaurant.

About a mile from the center of Ross is the Natalie Coffin Greene Park, twenty-five acres beside a winding creek. There are picnic tables, an open stone house and privies. The facilities were originally constructed in the 1930s when the property was owned by the Water District. The land was purchased in 1967 with a donation of $15,000 to the town of Ross from A. Crawford Greene in memory of his wife. To get there, drive west on Lagunitas Road. The park is open from sunrise to sunset. No parking is allowed around the gate at anytime, and no motorcycles, buses, or trailers may enter the park. Pets must be on a leash.

Beyond the park, about a five-minute walk, is Phoenix Lake. This reservoir belongs to the Marin Municipal Water District. All the lakes are stocked by the California Department of Fish and Game.

As you hike up the road, on the right you will pass an old stone kiln built in the shape of a beehive. A little farther on the left is a spillway built in 1986. This long, narrow cement water-run looks like a huge children's water slide in an amusement park. At the bottom the water cascades over some jagged rocks before flowing into a creek. The lake is open for fishing from sunrise to sunset; a valid California fishing license is required. Facilities here include benches and privies. A trail surrounding the lake is popular with hikers and joggers. It takes forty-five minutes to an hour to walk around.

SAN ANSELMO

A fter winding through Ross on tree-shaded, two-lane Sir Francis Drake Boulevard, you will come to the town of San Anselmo. Here the street becomes a four-lane divided boulevard for the short distance to the "Hub," an intersection of five streets with a total of twenty-one lanes of traffic. At this point, Sir Francis Drake Boulevard makes an abrupt left turn and continues northwest to Fairfax. Red Hill Avenue (also called the "Miracle Mile") goes to the east and into San Rafael.

San Anselmo was originally two land grants. The *Rancho Punta de Quintin*, mentioned in connection with the San Quentin peninsula and the town of Ross, ran approximately to the top of Red Hill in San Anselmo; and the *Canada de Herrera* (Valley of the Blacksmith), awarded to Domingo Sais, was in the northern section.

Children picnic in front of the San Anselmo City Hall.

The grandparents of Sais migrated from Mexico to Monterey, California, around 1772. Don Domingo, born in 1805, was a soldier at the Presidio in Yerba Buena (San Francisco) and a member of the militia from 1826 to 1837. From 1837 to 1839 he was an elector and civil authority called a "Regidor." In 1839, he received two leagues of land in Marin County in return for military and public services. This Mexican land grant included 6,658.35 acres of land where north San Anselmo, Fairfax, and part of San Geronimo Valley are located today.

Sais's first house was made of tule rushes and was located in the San Anselmo area known as Landsdale. A finer house of adobe, called La Pavidion, was later built on the south side of Sir Francis Drake Boulevard. Here Sais and his wife, the former Manuella Augustina Miranda, raised seven children. Sais died in 1853. In 1868, a survey was made of the property and the ranch was broken up, with some portions going to the heirs and other parts sold.

In 1881, George and Annie Worn, son-in-law and daughter of Anne and James Ross, subdivided a portion of their *Rancho Punta de Quintin* in the area of San Anselmo they called Sunnyside. Several big portions were sold off, but mortgage problems forced them to sell the land at public auction in 1886. The sale of "villa sites" continued under new ownership.

The railroad arrived in 1875 and officials renamed the growing town "The Junction," as this was the point where the train tracks split for West Marin and continued north to Cazadero in Sonoma County, with a branch line running southeast to San Rafael. The name lasted until 1883 when the original name of San Anselmo was reinstated.

Commute service to San Francisco improved in 1903 when the old narrow-gauge railroad was double-tracked and a new electric railroad was built using an electric third rail for power. It now took only fifty-five minutes, via train and ferry, from San Anselmo to the Ferry Building in San Francisco. Many visitors came to the area, arriving by train to picnic and camp along San Anselmo Creek. Summer homes began to be built, and then a large number of vacationers moved to San Anselmo permanently after the 1906 earthquake and fire in San Francisco.

San Anselmo incorporated in 1907; a volunteer fire department was organized, and a city hall was built in 1911 on land donated by James Tunstead, the former county sheriff. The downtown area that grew up around the city hall, one block west of San Anselmo Avenue, is the heart of San Anselmo today. Access streets include Bolinas Avenue, Ross Avenue, and Tunstead Avenue.

In front of the remodeled city hall is a handsome cast-iron deer that once stood in the gardens of the large Dondero estate in the North Beach section of San Francisco. After the 1906 earthquake and fire, the deer was all that remained of the Dondero home. The family moved to San Anselmo in 1914 and brought this graceful animal sculpture to decorate the front of their new home. When the house was sold in 1963, Daisy Dondero donated the deer to the town of San Anselmo.

The police and fire departments and post office are all located on San Anselmo Avenue. The library is next to the police department but fronts on Tunstead Avenue. San Anselmo's Historical Museum is located in the back of this building and uses the same address as the library, 110 Tunstead Avenue.

San Anselmo has many delightful shops, offering such things as original hand-crafted jewelry, pottery, Native American crafts, many good restaurants, bookstores, vintage clothing, art supplies and miniature furniture for doll houses. An unusual shopping mall is the Courtyard which contains specialty shops and an Italian restaurant. Throughout the town there is a wide variety of antique shops; in fact, San Anselmo is known as the "Antique Capital of Northern California." In the north end of the downtown area, between Sir Francis Drake Boulevard and San Anselmo Creek, is picturesque Creek Park, designed by former San Anselmo planning commissioner Dan Goltz and landscape architect Paul Leffingwell. This park contains two acres of land with grassy knolls, benches, picnic tables, a shady arbor and a redwood grove.

The San Anselmo Community Center is located at 237 Crescent Road in the old seventeen-room Robson-Harrington house. Built in 1910 by lumber magnate Edwin Kleber Wood, the estate was sold in 1922 to Mr. and Mrs. Kernan Robson, who added extensive gardens, orchards, a vineyard, and unusual walls made of bricks. The bricks with melted glaze were salvaged from San Francisco after the 1906 earthquake and fire. Still here, today, are arches, tile fountains, and Italian pottery and ceramic works. The grounds cover two-and-a-half acres with both palm and redwood trees in front, a large lawn area in back, picnic sites, barbecues, and a small plaza with benches, and a large community garden. Below the plaza is a children's playground. The house itself is open only by appointment. Over the years this community center has been used for meetings, classes, conferences, a variety of cultural events, parties and receptions. Phone 453-1602. To get there, turn west on Woodland Avenue off San Anselmo Avenue. Woodland jogs to the right and runs into Crescent before making a left turn. Continue straight on Crescent until you reach number 237.

ROBSON HOUSE
453-1602

The San Francisco Theological Seminary

San Anselmo became an important spot on the map of Northern California when the San Francisco Theological Seminary moved there in 1892. This seminary of the United Presbyterian Church was founded by Dr. William Anderson Scott, who was sent to the booming frontier town of San Francisco to establish a church and a Presbyterian college and seminary. Scott ran into some problems in San Francisco—he was hanged in effigy twice and run out of town for opposing the Committee of Vigilance and for mentioning Jefferson Davis and Abraham Lincoln in the same pastoral prayer.

SAN FRANCISCO
THEOLOGICAL
SEMINARY
258-6500

Scott managed to recover, however, and achieve his goal. The Seminary began classes in San Francisco in 1871. In 1873, Scott's daughter, Louisiana, married Arthur Foster, president of the North Pacific Coast Railroad. Foster later donated nineteen acres in San Anselmo for a new seminary site. In 1891, stonemasons began construction of two buildings out of hand-cut blue stone quarried in San Rafael. Montgomery Hall and Scott Hall still tower today, like medieval castles, above the town of

San Francisco Theological Seminary in San Anselmo.

San Anselmo. The buildings were paid for out of a $250,000 gift from Alexander Montgomery, a San Francisco businessman. When Montgomery died in 1893, he left $50,000 for a crypt to be built for his remains inside a memorial chapel. In 1989 both Montgomery Hall and Scott Hall were damaged by the Loma Prieta earthquake and closed. The Seminary restored the buildings, which were opened in 2000. The cost to renovate and seismecally retrofit the two halls was 10.4 million dollars.

Today the San Francisco Theological Seminary is the second largest Presbyterian seminary in the United States. Students come here from all around the world to receive their training. The twenty-one-acre campus is located at 2 Kensington. To visit, turn west off Sir Francis Drake Boulevard onto Bolinas Avenue, the street that divides San Anselmo from Ross. A self-guided walking tour and free brochure may be obtained in the reception area of the office located on the corner of Kensington and Bolinas. For more information or a guided tour with three weeks advance notice, call 258-6500.

SAN FRANCISCO
THEOLOGICAL
SEMINARY
258-6500.

To learn more about San Anselmo, look up this website: www.sananselmo.com. Following Sir Francis Drake Boulevard to Fairfax look northwest from the Hub and you will see Red Hill, a mound of earth scarred by cracks of red dirt eroding down the sides. There are some duplexes built on this hill which native San Anselmo residents watch with more than casual interest. The whole top of the hill gave way in 1967 after a heavy rainstorm and slid down on four similar apartments. Fortunately, they were unoccupied at the time.

Below the hill, at 892 Sir Francis Drake Boulevard, is the Red Hill Shopping Center, which contains a wide variety of stores, large and small. The four tennis courts at Memorial Park are just northwest of the Red Hill Shopping Center. This nine-acre park contains two Little League baseball fields and a regular baseball field with a 400-foot outfield and bleachers that will seat up to 300 people. There are also a soccer field, which sometimes doubles for a football field, a children's playground, and a few picnic tables.

SAN ANSELMO, WEBSITE: www.sananselmo.com

Outside dining in San Anselmo—Tyler Neely of Nicasio, waitress Breath Thorpe and Lindsey Pancoska of San Anselmo.

The American Legion Log Cabin is located here at 120 Veterans Place. Turn northeast off Sir Francis Drake Boulevard onto San Francisco Boulevard. Go two blocks, then turn right. The Log Cabin was built in 1934 by volunteers for use by the American Legion, Boy Scouts, and other groups. The "Millenium Playground," built in six days by hundreds of volunteers, opened in the summer of 2000 behind the Log Cabin. The project was co-chaired by Merrie Clark and Deborah Cichocki, who found the designer, Robert Leathers of Ithaca, New York, on the internet. Highlights include a dinosaur, wooden maze, and turreted castles. San Anselmo raised $175,000 for the project, considered to be worth over $1 million.

AMERICAN LEGION
LOG CABIN
456-0834

A good hiking area over hilly terrain is Sorich Ranch Park, which can be reached by following San Francisco Boulevard to the end. Here are sixty-three acres of open space, but the facilities are limited to one picnic table.

Another hiking area farther southwest is Faude Park, a fifteen acre parcel of open space donated in 1973 to the town of San Anselmo by C. Frederick Faude, a resident of Marin County for many years. The park may be reached by following Sir Francis Drake Boulevard to the first stop light past Drake High School. Turn right on Broadmoor Avenue and follow it to the end. Turn right on Indian Rock Road and go to the top of the hill, then turn right on Tomahawk Drive for one block to the entrance of the park. Faude park is good for hiking, but there are no facilities available. The land is hilly open space with a scattering of trees and is used mainly by local residents.

Butterfield road leads from Sir Francis Drake Boulevard into Sleepy Hollow, an area of ranch-style homes, many with their own corrals and stables. At the end of Butterfield Road is San Domenico School, a Catholic girls' school on what was once an old dairy ranch, then a golf course.

FAIRFAX

Mr. Alfred Taliaferro sailed to California from Virginia in 1849 to seek gold. He eventually built a home in Fairfax on thirty-one acres of the old Sais Ranch, in the area now known as the Marin Town and Country Club. In 1855, this property was acquired from Taliaferro by his good friend and fellow Virginian, Charles Snowden Fairfax, for whom the town was named. Fairfax, officially Lord Fairfax, Tenth Baron of Cameron, was born in 1829, a member of the State of Virginia Fairfax family. His ancestor, through his mother's side of the family, was Lord Thomas Culpepper. He had received the land in Virginia in 1649 as a royal grant by Charles II, King of England. The land, known as the Northern Neck of Virginia, "bounded by and within the head" of the Potomac and Rappahannock rivers, passed to Thomas, Lord Fairfax, Sixth Baron of Cameron. Thomas's niece, Anne Fairfax, married their next-door neighbor, Lawrence Washington, older brother to George. Lawrence built the family home at Mt. Vernon. (In 1747, George Washington, age 15, had been employed to survey the Fairfax land, more than five million acres.)

Charles Snowden Fairfax moved to California in 1849. Unsuccessful at mining, he entered politics and was elected to the state assembly in 1853, serving as speaker in 1854. In 1855, he married Ada Benham. Their Fairfax home, called Bird's Nest Glen, was situated in a lovely sylvan valley. The family was famous for its Southern hospitality. Entertainment was lavish and bottles of

Fairfax when the train ran through the town around 1920. (Arrigoni Family Collection)

champagne were kept cooling in the creek for refreshment during summer walks.

A famous duel was fought near Fairfax's estate in January 1861. His two friends, Daniel Showalter, a Democrat from Kentucky, and Charles Piercy, a Republican from Illinois, had disagreed politically. The three men ate lunch together before the duel and Fairfax tried to dissuade them, but they persisted. Charles Piercy was killed by a shot from Showalter's rifle. The Kentuckian was indicted for murder by the Marin Grand Jury but fled the county before he could be arrested.

Bill Allen, former President of the Fairfax Historical Society, believes the actual site of the duel was in San Anselmo, He writes, "John Murray, son of William Murray, who settled where Murray Park is today, remembers seeing, as a boy, the combatants leave the Fairfax estate, and walk down the open field toward Landsdale. After the duel was over and all the participants had departed, he visited the spot where the duel was fought. He remembers seeing some of the blood spilled when Piercy was shot. The location according to John was the site of the Landsdale Yolanda School."

Charles Fairfax continued his political career. He was elected to the Marin County Board of Supervisors and also spent five years as clerk of the California Supreme Court. In 1868, he put his affairs in order, including having the title of Bird's Nest Glen cleared, then went east to the Democratic Convention being held in New York. Already suffering from tuberculosis, Lord Charles Snowden Fairfax died at the home of his mother in Baltimore, Maryland, on April 4, 1869. (Although Charles never claimed the title Baron of Cameron, his nephew later went to England, assumed it, and the titled family line continued. They now reside on an estate north of London.)

After Charles's death, the thirty-one acre estate was sold by Ada Fairfax to Mary and Peter Owens. The site was later sold again to George Wright, then to Emma Woodward and in 1905 to Charles and Adele Pastori. Pastori was a well-known chef, and his wife Adele was a former opera singer at La Scala in Milan, Italy, and in England. Her daughter, Tina, claimed that her mother lost her voice singing on the English operatic stage because of the English fogs. Charles and Adele opened an Italian restaurant, providing outstanding cuisine to visitors coming by train from San Francisco.

After Pastori died, the restaurant burned but was rebuilt by Adele. In 1925, the Emporium Stores purchased the property to use as a club for employees. Between 1937 and 1943, it was leased to the Marin Boys School. In 1943, Max Friedman bought it and a year later opened the Marin Town and Country Club for outdoor Saturday night dances much like Larkpur's Rose Bowl, swimming and wading (in seven separate pools), picnicking, and baseball. The club was popular with people throughout the Bay Area and remained open until 1972.

Over the years, the town of Fairfax became well-known for picnics held in the Fairfax Park and the Pavilion, built in 1921, on the site of an ancient Indian mound. To raise money for equipment, members of the volunteer Fire Department brought in big bands to play in the Pavilion in the twenties and thirties. They also sponsored a bang-up Fourth of July picnic.

Funicular runs up Manor Hill off Scenic Road in Fairfax around 1914. (Arrigoni Family Collection)

In the Manor Hill area of Fairfax, a funicular railroad was opened in 1913 to provide access to building lots. It was modeled after funiculars Edward S. Holt had seen in the mountains of Europe. With his partner, Prentis Gray, he organized the Fairfax Incline Railroad Company. The car, built on three levels, held twenty-six passengers for the ride up the 500-foot hillside. To help sell lots adjacent to the funicular, auctions were held with big barbecues, beer drinking, and entertainment. The lots sold for $200 and $400. In 1929, the funicular was declared unsafe and was abandoned in 1930.

Today Fairfax still maintains its small-town atmosphere. Where the old station stood in the middle of town, there is a parking lot with trees, bushes, flowers and benches. On the corner of Broadway Street and Bolinas Avenue stands the Alpine Building, built around 1919 which was opened originally as a grocery store and ice cream parlor. Old photographs remain of early western films being shot in this area by the Essanay Film Manufacturing Company. Many movies featuring Bronco Bill Andersen were made here, and the wild west locations were filmed on Bolinas Road, past Deer Park Villa.

Other studios who used Fairfax included the Keanograph Factory between 1913-1915, the Testa Photo Studio in 1921, and the Navarra Picture Corporation in 1922. An epilogue to this story is that in February 1989, filmmakers George Lucas and Steven Spielberg were back in Fairfax at Deer Park School for five days shooting scenes for a movie starring Harrison Ford and Sean Connery. The film was called "Indiana Jones and the Last Crusade," and was the third in a trilogy which included "Raiders of the Lost Ark" and "Indiana Jones and the Temple of Doom."

The downtown shopping area of Fairfax runs along Sir Francis Drake Boulevard, Broadway Street (which parallels Sir Francis Drake), and southwest on Bolinas Road. Fairfax has many unique shops, selling everything from antiques to fine china. There is also a popular movie theater offering a choice of four films and several bars which traditionally provide live music. Fairfax hosts an outstanding jazz festival in September.

The lovely Fairfax Library, a branch of the Marin County Library system, is located at 2997 Sir Francis Drake Boulevard,

The Fairfax Library.

just northwest of the downtown area. This was the site of the old Buon Gusto Restaurant, originally the "Firenze Villa" owned by P. Recommi. He sold it to a Mr. Andreazzi, owner of a restaurant called Buon Gusto in San Francisco. In 1913, Mr. Andreazzi sold Buon Gusto to the great-grandfather of former Fairfax Police Chief Chuck Grasso. The restaurant was purchased in 1922 by Fiori Giannini, whose family ran it for another forty-four years. His daughter, Eleanor McArdle Jean, sold the property to the county in 1976 for a library. The library is on three-and-a-half acres of rolling oak-studded hills. The building, designed by architect Woody Stockwell, is constructed of warm woods, lots of glass to allow an open outdoor feeling, and a wide deck with a rustic view. In the meeting room is a beautiful mural painted by Glen Dines, who was a local author and artist. A plaque on the fireplace notes that it and other library materials were donated by the Peter Arrigoni family in memory of Peter's mother and father, Rose Divita and Peter S. Arrigoni.

    Many people come to Fairfax for the excellent riding stables in the area (see chapter 12), and to play tennis and swim at the Cañon Swim and Tennis Club located at 135 Mitchell Blvd. The

FAIRFAX LIBRARY
Hours: 453-8092
Reference:
453-8151

club was purchased by the Fairfax Chapter of the Native Sons of the Golden West in 1998 and carefully restored. It contains a near-Olympic-size pool, eight tennis courts and a club house.

Another popular sports facility in Fairfax is the famous Meadow Club, at 1001 Bolinas Road, a private golf course with a beautiful old clubhouse used by local residents for wedding receptions and parties. The club members celebrated their 80th anniversary in the year 2000.

Other visitors come to picnic in the almost five acre Fairfax Town Park on Bolinas Road and Park Road adjacent to the Town Hall. The park has a creek and majestic old redwood trees, picnic tables, a children's playground and tennis courts. Besides the Town Hall, the building houses the fire department and police station. It was originally built in 1926, but was remodeled after a $300,000 bond issue was passed in 1973. In 1999 a large stone fountain was placed in front of the Fairfax Town Hall with money bequeathed by resident Isabella Abelleira. Local trades-

The Olympic-size pool at the Cañon Swim and Tennis Club in Fairfax.

The Meadow Club in Fairfx.

men and businesses donated resources for the project which was built by Buchholz Construction.

The fifty-four-acre Deer Park is reached by driving four-tenths of a mile south on Porteous Avenue off Bolinas Road. This is also the location of the Deer Park Elementary School now used by the Fairfax-San Anselmo Children's Center. Picnic tables are scattered under tall redwoods beside a creek. Facilities include barbecues and privies. There are several scenic hiking trails, but beware of poison oak.

Above Fairfax is Camp Tamarancho, owned by the Marin Council of Boy Scouts of America. Besides the usual camping and hiking, the property is the site of an annual Marin Knobular bicycle race, the third of five events sponsored by the Off Road Bicycling Association tour. The Marin Knobular draws around 900 to 1,000 riders in a race that stretches nearly six miles around Camp Tamarancho.

To learn more about the history of Fairfax, look up this website: http://www.marindirect.com/fxhistory. For more current information: http://www.mo.com/fairfax/

TO LEARN MORE ABOUT THE HISTORY OF FAIRFAX, WEBSITE: http://www.marindirect.com/fxhistory.

FOR MORE CURRENT INFORMATION: http://www.mo.com/fairfax/

Downstream face of Alpine Dam looking south—July 7, 1918. (From the collection of Nancy M. Skinner)

THE WATER DISTRICT LAKES

Five pristine alpine lakes are maintained by the Marin Municipal Water District on watershed land. Two additional lakes, Nicasio and Soulajule, are located on private water-shed lands devoted primarily to agriculture. The lakes are reservoirs for the county's drinking water, so neither boating nor swimming is allowed. Fishing is permitted with a valid California Fishing License and avid fishermen can always be found along the banks.

The most popular fishing lakes—Bon Tempe, Lagunitas, and Alpine—are also the easiest to reach. Drive south on Bolinas Road from Fairfax for one and a half miles. Turn left at a sign that says "Lake Lagunitas." You will pass through a gate which is open from 7:00 a.m. to sunset and continue straight to reach the lakes. Half a mile later you will arrive at The Sky Oaks Ranger Station (945-1181), where you will be charged an entrance fee. A sign will direct you to the parking area and to Lake Lagunitas, just a short hike.

THE SKY OAKS
RANGER STATION
945-1181

You can reach all the lakes (except Nicasio and Soulajule) from this trailhead on connecting trails. Phoenix Lake is also accessible through the town of Ross. Kent Lake may be reached by hiking east from Sir Francis Drake Boulevard near the town of Lagunitas. The lakes are regularly stocked with trout and special fishing regulations apply to Lake Lagunitas. At Lake Lagunitas you will find several picnic areas with tables scattered among redwood trees. A picturesque covered spillway leads up to the lake. You may walk up the trail next to the spillway or use the road which leads up the left side of the dam from the parking lot, marked "Protection Road." Horse trails encircle both Lake Lagunitas and Bon Tempe.

Alpine Dam, built in 1917 primarily by Italian-American labor and raised twice to its present level, may be reached by driving south on Bolinas Road from Fairfax for a distance of six miles. This road continues to Route 1 on the Pacific coast near Bolinas. It is a beautiful ride, but the road is narrow and exposed to strong winds. It may be closed for several days at a time in summer and fall because of fire hazard. The dam itself is an interesting structure, with a cubist honeycomb design on the south side. It has been compared to an ancient amphitheater.

San Rafael   8

From Mission Town to County Seat

S an Rafael, seventeen miles north of San Francisco, is the oldest and largest of Marin's cities, and also serves as its county
seat. The downtown area, built up around the old mission, is
nestled below San Rafael Hill. In the last four decades the city
has spread beyond the downtown to adjacent areas: to the
southeast on either side of the San Rafael Canal; to the east along
Point San Pedro Road; north to Santa Venetia and the Frank
Lloyd Wright-designed Civic Center; and beyond to the large
residential areas in Terra Linda, Marinwood, and Lucas Valley.

The city of San Rafael had its beginnings in 1817 with the
founding of a Spanish mission (the twentieth in the chain of
twenty-one in California), built as a northern outpost against
the threat of a Russian invasion into Spanish territory. At this
time the Russian American Company had established a fort in
Sonoma County, and Russians were occupying Bodega Bay on
the north. They were occupied with the slaughter of sea otters.
Initially, the Mission San Rafael Archangel, named for Saint
Raphael, the angel of bodily healing, was an *asistencia* or
"helper" mission used as a sanitarium for Indians from the Mission San Francisco de Asis (Dolores). When the Spanish
founded the San Francisco mission in 1776, they used Indian
labor to do the actual construction. Many were Coast Miwok

◀ *St. Raphael's Church in downtown San Rafael. The replica of the Mission
San Rafael Archangel is on the right.*

West End, San Rafael looking down 5th Street. (4th Street on the right)
Mansion Row is upper left, known then as 6th Street. Across the street in
front is H Street (1880s). (Courtesy Marin Historical Society)

Indians who were taken from their homeland in Marin (see
Miwok Indian Village, Kule Loklo, Chapter 11).

By the time the mission was complete, the Spanish had converted many of the Indians to Catholicism. Despite their supposed spiritual health, the Indians were often sick and many
died from their forced dislocation. Changes of food, clothing,
housing and an unfamiliar damp climate proved deadly to
them. In addition, thousands died of tuberculosis, measles and
chicken pox. In 1812, at Mission Dolores, every child under the
age of twelve died, and Presidio soldiers were sent out to dig
mass graves. Final records show that out of 6,536 Indians bap-
tized at the San Francisco mission, 5,037 died.

Father Gil y Toboada, a padre with some medical knowledge, took over the *asistencia* in San Rafael from 1817 to 1819. A
hospital, chapel, priests' quarters, and storeroom were built of
adobe. Reportedly, the mission building consisted of a chapel
and a long single-story structure forming an L shape. It had a
red tile roof with rafters held together by strips of rawhide.

Father Gil began planting an orchard of pear trees. The surrounding hills were stocked with cattle and sheep, horses and hogs. Indians were taught to care for the animals and to farm, cook, clean, spin wool, and make clothes. In 1822, the little *asistencia* became a full-fledged mission. That was also the year that Spain's rule of California was assumed by Mexico. As the Spanish missions grew in power, their rivalry with the new Mexican authorities became intense.

By 1828 the Mission San Rafael Archangel could boast of 1,140 Indian converts living there. The mission lands thrived. Two years later there were eight buildings, 2,000 horses and cattle, fields of wheat, barley, and corn, plus ten acres of orchards and vineyards.

Not all the Native Americans gave in without a struggle to serving the Spanish padres. One, named Pomponio, a San Rafael area native, defied the Spaniards and even cut off his own heel to escape a leg iron. In 1823, Pomponio was captured for the second time and executed in Monterey. Around the same time, a band of a thousand Native Americans, enraged over the killing of an Native boy by a riotous Mexican soldier, attacked the Mission San Rafael and burned several buildings.

Chief Marin, for whom the county is reportedly named, (the county also may have gotten its title from the Latin word 'Marinera' which was part of a name on a 1775 map), and his war chief, Quintin, attacked the mission in San Rafael. Marin's successful raids resulted in an expedition being sent to subdue him. He was captured in Bodega and taken to the San Francisco Presidio to be converted, but escaped and continued raiding until he was recaptured nine years later. In the end, according to legend, Chief Marin and Quintin were eventually subdued and worked as skilled mariners for the padres. Marin died at Mission San Rafael Archangel in 1834.

The year 1834 also saw the mission taken over by the Mexican civil government. Rivalry between the Spanish missionaries and the Mexicans had reached a crisis, and the Mexican government passed a decree of secularization which transferred all mission lands to the state. The Spanish Franciscan friars were exiled and replaced with Mexican Franciscans. General Mariano Vallejo was appointed administrator of the San Rafael mission. He used his position to confiscate much of the mission's equipment and land.

A group of the remaining Coast Miwok Indians was taken to a parcel in Nicasio called 'Tinicasia' (now Halleck's Valley) given to them by General Vallejo who "forgot" to file the Indian claim at Monterey. Genial Don Timoteo Murphy, a kind Irishman who spoke the Coast Miwok language with an Irish brogue, was made overseer of the Indians. Murphy, a muscular man who stood at least six feet, two-and-a-half inches (one report says six feet, seven inches) did his best to help the Miwok, but few made the adjustment to "civilized" life.

Murphy was rewarded for his work with the Indians with a land grant of three leagues (nearly 22,000 acres) from the Mexican governor, Micheltorena. The grant was called *San Pedro, Santa Margarita, y Las Gallinas* (Saint Peter, Saint Margaret, and the Hens). This area included what is now known as northeast and east San Rafael to San Pedro Point, and north to the subdivisions of Terra Linda, Marinwood, and Lucas Valley.

In the late 1830s and 40s, despite Murphy's kind efforts, the Indians were taken advantage of in every way possible. Some Indian children were forcefully taken from their parents and sold as servants to California ranchos farther south.

The end of the Coast Miwok Indians came during the Gold Rush, 1849-1855, with three laws passed by the new California state legislature. The first law stated that an Indian could not testify in court. The second declared that any white man could bring an Indian to court and have the Indian declared a vagrant, thus subjecting him to sale by auction to the highest bidder. The third law stated that any native child or adult could be bound over to a white citizen. This made it possible for the Indians to be used as slave labor. The Indians, already decimated by illness, now had no rights in this new society, no way to defend themselves against the white man and keep their way of life intact. A civilization that had evolved over thousands of years was thus destroyed in half a century, though some descendants remain.

By 1840, the Mission San Rafael Archangel was all but abandoned. The only life came from the orchard trees that continued to bear fruit. In 1846, the California Bear Flag replaced the Mexican flag and was in turn replaced by the Stars and Stripes.

Prosperity came to San Rafael with the Gold Rush. Saloons, hotels, and boardinghouses were built almost overnight. Streets, identified by numbers and letters, were laid out and lots divided up. In 1850, Marin became one of the twenty-seven original counties in California, and San Rafael was awarded the county seat. One of the old mission buildings was converted into a town meeting hall, court, and jail. In 1853, when Don Timoteo Murphy passed away, the new county government was moved into his two-story adobe house on the corner of Fourth and C streets.

The last old mission building was razed around 1860 for salvageable timbers. The remaining orchard became a campground for passing gypsies and a park for picnicking and for political rallies.

In the 1860s, the town continued to grow. The first public school opened in San Rafael in 1861, and a newspaper began publication. The Civil War broke out, creating conflicts between Marin citizens, some sympathizing with the North, others loyal to the South.

By the end of that decade, the San Rafael and San Quentin Railroad was completed, making fast access to San Francisco a reality. Suddenly, San Rafael became the retreat of wealthy residents of San Francisco. Elegant new mansions were built, many near the center of town. Fashionable resort hotels were constructed, including the luxurious 200-room Hotel Rafael built on a twenty-one-acre site by James M. Donahue and William Tell Coleman in what is now the Dominican area. Patrons of Hotel Rafael enjoyed leisurely meals, attended dances, and played tennis. They could also go to see productions staged in Gordon's Opera House at Fourth and D streets. (This later became a movie house, the Star Theater.)

In keeping with the town's prosperous look, a new Marin County courthouse was dedicated August 3, 1872, and construction began on a new county courthouse. Completed in March 1873 at a cost of $51,000, it was designed in a Greek Revival style with tall columns and an imposing set of steps. The building lasted nearly one hundred years, finally being destroyed by fire in 1971.

In 1874, San Rafael incorporated. For the next several decades, it experienced the same spurts of growth as did other areas of the county. A tent city was erected in San Rafael for survivors of the 1906 earthquake and fire in San Francisco. Many refugees stayed permanently, increasing the population of San Rafael by 60%. Other boosts in population came with the building of Hamilton Field between 1933 and 1935, the opening of the Golden Gate Bridge in 1937, and World War II. New housing developments were welcomed with enthusiasm.

Throughout all these years, the trees in the old "Priest's Orchard" on the former mission grounds continued to bear fruit. In 1929, Richard Lohrmann, a San Rafael nurseryman, took a graft from one of the last pear trees just before an apartment house was built on the orchard site at Fifth and Lootens streets. By 1934, there was only one pear tree left. In 1946, The Marin Historical Society began to campaign to resurrect the mission, and three years later a replica of the Mission San Rafael Archangel was built with money from the Hearst Foundation. The last mission pear tree was knocked down by a bulldozer in 1963 in the interests of progress and a new parking lot. The graft the nurseryman had taken grew into a tree which can now be seen adjacent to the Jose Moya del Pinto Library at the Marin Art and Garden Center in Ross.

CENTRAL SAN RAFAEL

The downtown area of San Rafael is crisscrossed by a grid of one-way streets. At the center of town, on the spot where the old courthouse once stood, is a high-rise bank building with a grassy plaza in front. The mission is a block away, and behind it is "Mansion Row." Many of the old elegant estates remain as private homes, clubs, schools and community centers. In town there are also parks, children's playgrounds, and a wildlife center.

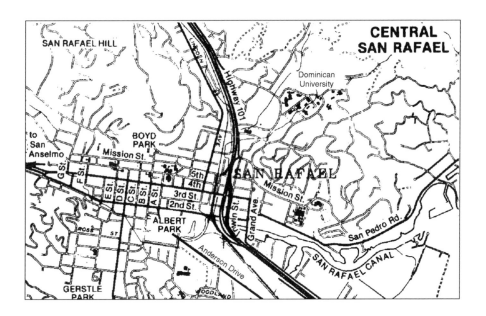

The main shopping area in central San Rafael is along Fourth Street. For many years, if you happened to be on Fourth Street on a Friday or Saturday evening, you might be surprised to see teenagers in cars cruising along the thoroughfare and up side streets. This 1950s custom was revived after movie producer George Lucas, now a resident of Marin, used Fourth Street (as well as Petaluma) to film *American Graffiti*. In May the custom is revived for one night when visitors can see the cars again on the streets of San Rafael.

Fourth Street is experiencing a Renaissance as part of a downtown development project adopted in 1993 called "Our Vision of Downtown San Rafael." Thirty-three organizations and 600 residents contributed their ideas to the plan. As part of it, The Macy's Store on Fourth Street, just past the old court-house site which was vacated in 1996, was torn down in 1999 to make way for the construction of a twenty-seven million dollar project. A five- and six-story complex in the shape of a U is being built in the year 2000. It consists of 113 studio and residential apartments, 30,000 square feet of retail and office space and 247 on-site parking spots. Farther down, at 1337 Fourth

Street, the Gordon's Opera House was purchased for $2.8 million in 1999 by Art Works Downtown, Inc., a nonprofit group whose members promote art. The 30,000 square-foot building provides a permanent gallery and space for classes, workshops and long-term affordable housing for thirty artists-in-residence.

At 118 Fourth Street, the old Rafael Theater reopened in 1999, having been transformed into a $7.5 million dollar three-screen movie palace. This showplace theater is now the home of the Film Institute of Northern California which runs the Mill Valley Film Festival. The four year project was the brainchild of Ann Brebner, who formerly had a talent agency in San Francisco, San Rafael Mayor Al Boro, and Mark Fishkin, the founder and director of the Northern California Film Institute. The architect was Mark Cavagnero of San Francisco who also did the renovation for San Francisco's Palace of the Legion of Honor. Today the popular Rafael Theater shows independent, foreign-language, and classic films as well as documentaries. In their first eight months of opertion, the remodeled movie theater welcomed over 100,000 moviegoers, not counting the 25,000 who attended various festivals, proving the project a hugh success.

The Mission San Rafael Archangel

The white adobe building with its red tile roof on Fifth Avenue and A Streets is the replica of the Mission San Rafael Archangel. Signs will lead you there from the Central San Rafael exit off Highway 101. The mission is a good place to begin a walking tour of downtown San Rafael.

Mansion Row

"Mansion Row" in San Rafael was the street behind the mission where many elegant homes were built. Several of these are now open to the public. From the mission, walk west on Fifth Avenue to B Street and turn right one block to Mission Avenue. Begin at the Gate House, which houses the Marin Historical Society Museum, then continue walking west past Maple Lawn, now privately owned by the Elks Club, and go on to Falkirk, the San Rafael Community Center. Just beyond is Foster Hall, part of the coeducational high school, Marin Academy. Along the way you may also want to visit the San Rafael Library, a block south on Fifth Avenue, and the San Rafael City Hall, just to the east of the library.

At 1125 B Street (where B Streets ends at Mission), is the former gate house or guest lodge to Maple Lawn, an estate built by Mrs. Theodocia Cook Arner, sister to Seth and Dan Cook. These two brothers came out from New York in 1850 and made a fortune in silver in the Comstock Lode in Nevada. Maple Lawn, named for the Japanese maples planted on the estate grounds, was built in 1875. Three years later, Seth Cook purchased six more acres from Joseph Angelotti. The Gate House, built on this site, is a High Victorian Gothic-style structure, constructed in 1879 by Ira Cook, the two brothers' father, who moved out to join them. Eventually this lodge, then called "Park Lodge," was given to Ira Cook's granddaughter, Louise Arner Cook, and her husband, John Franklin Boyd.

Park Lodge was described by the *Marin County Journal* at that time as being the "most perfect and costly of its size in the town . . .

Gate House to Maple Lawn, the old Louise Boyd Estate in San Rafael. Now the Headquarters of the Marin Historical Society.

rich in finish and ornamentation . . . Enclosed with an iron fence, having granite piers, and the large gate, forming the main entrance to the grounds, [the house] will be very imposing."

Today, the Gate House is the home of the Marin County Historical Society Museum, which contains a fascinating collection of artifacts, photographs, and drawings of Marin's early pioneers. Several displays are devoted to Louise Boyd, whose family once owned all this property. Miss Boyd became an internationally renowned explorer, and her strategic maps of the Arctic regions were used by the United States government during World War II.

Behind the Gate House is Boyd Park, presented to the city of San Rafael in 1905 by Louise Arner Boyd and her husband John in memory of their sons, Seth Cook Boyd and John Franklin Boyd, who both died at an early age. Robert Dollar later donated two parcels of land on the east slope of San Rafael Hill, adding 10 acres to the park for a total of 23 acres. Today, Boyd Park is a marvelous green oasis in the midst of busy downtown San Rafael. It includes a newly remodeled children's playground structure, tennis court, picnic area, barbecues and restrooms.

The Marin Historical Society is planning to build a 7500 square-foot museum in this area as an element in the revitalization plan for San Rafael. Plans also include new picnic areas and playground equipment, landscape improvements and added parking near the hilltop reservoir and below the museum building. A storytelling area for children is also envisioned around a historic fir tree. Displays in the new museum will include photographs and a large archive of books and local newspapers. The hours of the Gate House are Thursday through Saturday, 1:00 p.m. to 4:00 p.m. 454-8538; website: www. marinweb.com/marinhistory.

GATE HOUSE
454-8538
www. marinweb.com/
marinhistory.

Continue west on Mission Avenue past Maple Lawn—The Boyd estate now owned by the Elks Club—to Falkirk Cultural Center of San Rafael, at 1408 Mission Avenue. There was once a house here owned by railroad magnate James B. Walker. It was purchased by Ella F. Nichols (Mrs. Trenor) Park who auctioned off Walker's furniture and had the house removed. In 1888 she built a mansion typical of the Queen Anne style with porches, gables, dormers, and rounded and slated bays, at a cost of $30,000. The architect was Clinton Day, who also designed the famous City of Paris department store in San Francisco and the Stanford University Chapel in Palo Alto.

The mansion was purchased in 1906 by Captain Robert Dollar, who owned a worldwide steamship line. He lived in the house until his death in 1932. The estate remained within the family until it was purchased and given its name "Falkirk" after Captain Dollar's birthplace in Scotland, by the city of San Rafael in 1974.

Falkirk has seventeen rooms and is surrounded by eleven acres of gardens and hillside. The interior of the mansion has fine wood paneling of Sierra pine, burled ash, and redwood. There are lovely stained glass windows, damask-patterned brocade stretched over the walls in the parlor, an ornate Persian rug, and white lace curtains.

The mansion is used today by a variety of Marin County groups for meetings, musical concerts, and lectures. On the second floor are galleries with changing contemporary art exhibits.

Mary Case Dekker and her husband, Fred, of San Rafael were directly responsible for saving Falkirk. Upon hearing that the old mansion might be torn down, Mrs. Dekker organized the San Rafael Preservation Committee in May 1972. This group later was absorbed in Marin Heritage, which worked with the city of San Rafael in preserving the mansion.

You may visit Falkirk from Monday through Friday, 10:00 a.m. to 5:00 p.m.; Thursday until 9:00 p.m. and Saturday, 10:00 a.m. to 1:00 p.m. The facilities may be rented for meetings, retreats, weddings or community functions. Call 485-3328; website: www. falkirkculturalcenter.org/info.html.

FALKIRK
485-3328
website:
www.falkirkcultur-
alcenter.org/
info.html

In December 1999 the San Rafael City Council voted to sell the Menzies parking lot next door to Falkirk at Mission Avenue and E Streets, to the Marin Community Foundation for $1.1 million to build a 22,800 square-foot building for the Foundation offices. Part of the deal will include the Foundation helping with a remodel of Falkirk through the Marin Arts Council who will lease the mansion's third floor. The roof needs to be replaced, and the drainage, electrical and plumbing systems need work. In addition, the mansion needs a complete seismic

PROFILE: Ann Brebner

Ann Brebner of San Rafael is credited with the miraculous four-year effort in the successful refurbishing of the Rafael Theater. This seven- and-a-half million dollar three-screen movie palace at 1118 Fourth Street in San Rafael opened on April 16, 1999, and was an instant smash success. Many people, neighboring merchants in particular, felt the project would never succeed, especially after seismic problems were discovered and asbestos had to be removed, adding to the initial cost estimates. Internal murals were also found which needed restoration, further escalating the final costs.

But Ann Brebner, who was chairman of the entire construction project, was able to secure a last minute loan from Bank of Marin which enabled construction to go forward. Her patience through the long years of haggling over designs and desperately seeking funds was finally rewarded with the completion of this showplace home to the Film Institute of Northern California.

Large donations which helped finance the project included $850,000 from the San Rafael Redevelopment Agency, $600,000 from film editor Marcia Lucas, $750,000 from the Marin Community Foundation, $500,000 from LucasFilm and $500,000 from Tiburon philanthropist Chris Smith.

Ann Brebner was born in rural New Zealand and raised by her father and a great aunt. At the University of New

Zealand she earned degrees in abnormal psychology and music. Following graduation, she moved to London where she studied the art of directing at the Old Vic Theater for two years. She met her husband, John Brebner, in England and they immigrated to the United States, where she worked as a director and an actress. The couple had two sons; they were later divorced and she raised the children alone.

Ann founded the Brebner Agency, Inc., in San Francisco which represented actors and writers for the motion picture industry. She worked there full time and was enormously successful until she decided to sell the agency in 1981.

She has written a book, *Setting Free the Actor,* which she is now revising as well as writing another book. She is still involved in the Film Institute of Northern California and serves as a member of the Board of Directors. Her other activities include being a member of the Advisory Boards of Bread and Roses and The Marin Arts Council. In recognition of her many achievements, she was also inducted into the Marin Women's Hall of Fame.

Falkirk Cultural Center of San Rafael

retrofit. The design for the new Marin Community Foundation building was drawn by Hanuum and Associates of San Francisco and will include 6,000 square feet of space for public use.

At the west end of Mansion Row is Marin Academy, the third school to be located on this historic spot at Mission and Cottage avenues. The Mount Tamalpais Military Academy opened in 1890 in the Gilbert House. In 1892, Trustee A.W. Foster donated to the school the adjoining three-story mansion built by Thomas O' Conner in 1870. It was known thereafter as Foster Hall. This school was taken over by new owners in 1925 and renamed the San Rafael Military Academy. Four surplus World War I army barracks located in Vallejo were floated up the San Rafael Canal and brought onto the Academy grounds to be used as dormitories. They are gone today.

When the San Rafael Military Academy closed in 1971, the property was purchased by a group of parents who wanted to form a coeducational private high school. Thus Marin Academy began classes in the fall of 1972. It is a college preparatory school, grades nine thorough twelve, and is committed to a

strong academic program as well as outdoor sports and activities. At the heart of the nine and one-half acre campus is Foster
Hall, a fine old building with white columns and a broad front
porch. The driveway encircles a lawn shaded by mature sequoia
trees. Foster Hall itself is said to be haunted, and faculty members living in the second-floor apartments have become well-
acquainted with the "spirits" of the house—including a woman
in a long dress and a child.

For tours of the school or other information, call 435-4550.   MARIN ACADEMY
435-4550

San Rafael Improvement Club

At Fifth and H streets, just west of Mansion Row, is a building
that was originally the "Victrola Pavilion," representing the Victor Talking Machine Company in the Panama-Pacific International Exposition of 1915 held in San Francisco. The building
was described by one architect as "an irregular-shaped Neo-
Classical-Revival style structure with fluted Doric columns, a
Doric frieze, and simple pediment."

When the exposition was over, Leon Douglass, a resident of
San Rafael and chairman of the board of directors of the Victor
Talking Machine Company, had the building dismantled, placed
on rafts, and floated to San Rafael. A few weeks later, in January

Marin Academy on "MansionRow" in San Rafael.

1916, the San Rafael Improvement Club (which had been organized in 1902 for the purpose of planting trees and annihilating
mosquitoes) arranged to buy the building for a clubhouse. A large
fund-raising drive was launched to bring the building to the
property leased from A.W. Foster. The pavilion was completely
reconstructed, and a roof, back wall and extra pillars were added
for support. A circular front and large plate glass windows completed the conversion to a clubhouse. This was all done within six
months for only $3000. The formal opening was June 3, 1916. In
1922, A.W. Foster deeded the property to the club for $10.

In 1998 the San Rafael Improvement Club members, who
had reached an average age of 70, dismantled their association
after 96 years of outstanding community activities. The property has been taken over by the San Rafael Rotary Club, whose
members are renovating the building back to its original condition and adding a catering kitchen, covered pavilion, courtyard,
restrooms, lobby and outside chapel.

A new copper cover has been installed on the domed roof
and a portable stage made available for special events. The
Rotary Manor Corporation uses the property to serve one daily
meal to residents at the neighboring Rotary Manor senior housing complex. The Rotary Club has also promised to continue a
club scholarship to a graduate of San Rafael High School. San
Rafael Improvement Club archives were given to the Marin
County Historical Society along with a $10,000 gift. Seven hun-
dred dollars were also given to the nearby Sun Valley School to
pay for student music lessons.

Dominican University of California

Dominican University of California is an independent, four-
year, coeducational college which the Dominican Sisters began
as a school for girls in Monterey around 1850. The school moved
to Benicia, then to San Rafael in 1889. A convent was built at
1520 Grand Avenue on ten acres purchased from William T.
Coleman. The convent was a white, four-story Victorian building constructed of redwood. It remained in use until July 12,
1990, when the upper stories were set on fire by a crew using a
blow torch to remove old paint. The five-alarm fire caused an

estimated one million dollars in damage. After much agonizing, the Sisters decided to raze the old convent, or "Motherhouse," and build a much smaller redwood-shingled convent which opened in 1995. The 17,000 square-foot building is only one-third the size of the original convent but provides the Dominican Sisters with separate living quarters, a fireside lounge, modern kitchen, dining room, elevators, a courtyard and a chapel.

Other buildings were gradually added to the original school. The brown-shingled Meadowlands, located on Palm Avenue and Olive Street, was purchased by the Sisters in 1918. Meadowlands was a summer home for Michael de Young, cofounder of the *San Francisco Chronicle*. For a time the Meadowlands library was turned into a chapel by the Sisters; the main rooms were used for classrooms, and the upper floor was a residence. In 1924, a wing of twenty-seven bedrooms with adjoining baths was added, and eventually Meadowlands developed into the students' favorite residence hall. In 1998 groundbreaking ceremonies were held for a new Recreation Center named for for-

The former convent house (or "Motherhouse") of the Dominican order in San Rafael, which was located on the Domincan University campus, was built in 1889 and burned down on July 12, 1990.

Meadowlands at Dominican University, San Rafael.

mer College President Sister Samuel Conlan. This building, now completed, includes a gymnasium, swimming pool, weight room, department offices and classrooms. About the time this building was completed, the school officials changed the school's name from "Dominican College" to "Dominican University of California. The change, announced April 29, 2000, became official for the fall 2000 semester.

Across Grand Avenue from the original convent is an area called Forest Meadows. Tucked in among the trees is a small amphitheater where Dominican University holds commencement exercises every spring. There are also several tennis courts and a soccer field. Forest Meadows has been used by many groups over the years for outdoor drama productions, summer camp, and group picnics.

Dominican University covers nearly eighty acres of campus and woods in an exclusive part of San Rafael. A wide variety of students come to Dominican from all over the world for bachelor's and master's degree programs. In keeping with a recent trend, nearly one-third of those enrolled are women returning to school to seek careers after raising a family, or to pursue a change of careers. New courses have been added in nursing, occupational therapy, E-studies, communications, environmental science, and pre-med. Many evening and weekend classes are proving popular. The school would now like to build a chapel and a science and technology building.

Dominican University invites the public to its many and varied programs and events. The outstanding music department presents a large number of productions and concerts yearly. There are also continually changing art exhibits, drama productions, and guest lecturers, many free of charge. From the Central San Rafael exit off Highway 101, signs will direct you to the campus at Grand and Acacia Avenues, San Rafael. Call 457-4440 for further information.

DOMINICAN
UNIVERSITY
457-4440
www.dominican.edu

Marin WildCare Center

To reach the Marin WildCare Center, drive south on B Street, then east (or left) on Albert Park Lane (a one-way-street) to number 76. Walk across a small bridge that spans a freshwater creek

The Marin WildCare Terwilliger Nature Education and Wildlife Rehabilitation across from Albert Park, San Rafael.

to reach the museum grounds. The facilities here have had a variety of names and purposes. They began in July 1953 as a junior museum with the idea of creating exhibits and putting a small collection of animals on display for children. An old parish hall from St. Paul's Episcopal Church, owned by the Optimists Club, was leased for one dollar per year. Two new homes, condemned because they were sliding down hillsides, were purchased for a dollar each. Weekend work parties and donations by local contractors, labor unions, and tradesmen put the whole thing together for less than $5000. The doors opened May 22, 1955. Through the years financing has been a continuing problem for the museum. It is supported by the efforts of members and volunteers, and by fund-raising activities.

In 1961, the name of the museum was changed to the Louise A. Boyd Natural Science Museum in honor of the famous Arctic explorer. Until her death in 1972, Miss Boyd came often to visit the museum and donated several of her awards and mementos.

In 1978, the name of the museum was changed again, this time to the Marin Wildlife Center. Later it became the California Center for Wildlife. It is now WildCare Terwilliger Nature Education and Wildlife Rehabilitation which combined the organization created honoring Marin naturalist and educator Elizabeth Terwilliger with the California Center for Wildlife. The Center sponsors hikes and wildlife classes; in fact, education programs reach 6000 school children annually through in-class visits and other programs. Staff members answer hundreds of telephone calls weekly, giving information on ecology and on the handling of injured wildlife. The clinic cares for thousands of wild animals every year and claims a release rate of rehabilitated animals of 70% after 72 hours.

A walk through the grounds will acquaint you with the animals the Center has taken in but for various reasons has been unable to release. There are pelicans, eagles, gulls, hawks, ravens and many other birds. The Marin WildCare Center is open from 9:00 a.m. to 5:00 p.m. daily. WildCare Hotline: 456-7283 or call 453-1000.

Jousting at Albert Park.

Albert Park

The 11.5-acre Albert Park is adjacent to the Marin WildCare Center. Facilities here include baseball and softball diamonds with viewing stands, four tennis courts, four picnic areas, a basketball court, children's playground, bocce ball courts, and the San Rafael Community Center. The land was given to the city of San Rafael in 1937 by Jacob Albert, a Marin businessman. Albert owned the large Albert's department store, eventually bought out by Macy's, and he built the first "skyscraper" in Marin, the present Albert Building on Fourth and B streets. A supreme community effort to refurbish Albert Park was led by Dolly Nave in the early 1980s. Dolly and her husband Richard raised five boys and spent 28 years involved with Little League Baseball. Since much of the Nave's time was spent at Albert Park, Dolly found herself running the snack bars and hiring young people to staff them as part of an out-of-school work opportunity.

In 1977, a master plan was drawn up to refurbish the playing fields in the park which would have included proper drainage and irrigation. The estimated cost was $400,000.

PROFILE: **Gloria Duncan**

Gloria Duncan has been serving the public of Marin for the past twenty-five years as an elected Councilwoman in Fairfax, and as a member of numerous city and county boards and commissions. Her expertise runs the gamut from Bobby Sox girl's softball, which she coached for nine years, winning the Northern California Championships, to conservation issues and solid waste disposal.

She became involved with land use and solid waste through a League of Women Voters' educational program and went on to advocate curbside recycling. She worked with Joe Garbarino, owner of Marin Sanitary Service, in setting up Marin's excellent recycling program and has served on the Marin County Waste Management Advisory Committee since 1985. Because she developed expertise in this field, she was called on to serve on the Hazardous Materials Committee for the Marin Conservation League and the Solid Waste Management Committee for the League of Women Voters, State of California.

Another project involving the League of Women Voters was the Advisory Committee to Study the Feasibility of a Refuse Derived Fuel Project. This was an appointment made by the Marin County Board of Supervisors, as was Gloria's appointment to the Litter Control, Recycling and Resource Recovery Committee, set up to implement California Senate Bill 650—the County's Solid Waste Management element. She served as Chairman from 1978 - 85. The League also sent her to work as a member of ABAG (Association of Bay Area Governments) on their Environmental Management Plan dealing with air, water, and solid waste problems of the Bay Area.

Gloria Duncan was born in Oakland, as was her husband, Bruce Duncan. They were were married in 1959 and moved to Fairfax that same year. The Duncans reared two daughters, Lisa and Amy. Lisa, a chemical engineer, lives in Sausalito, while Amy, who was a star pitcher in the girl's softball league, is now married, works as a CPA and lives in Santa Clara.

In addition to her political activities, Gloria Duncan enjoys snorkeling off the coast of Honduras at Roatan and fly fishing on the Umpqua River in Oregon. She likes traveling, but gardening is her true passion. She also worked for twelve years as store manager at Heath Ceramics in Sausalito.

Duncan's political career began with an appointed term on the Fairfax Planning Commission, 1971-73, followed by an appointment to the Marin County Planning Commission, 1973-80, of which she served as Chairman in 1979. She then won an election to the Fairfax Town Council and served from 1984-88, with a term as Mayor in 1987-88.

In 1991 she was inducted into the Marin Women's Hall of Fame, and from 1992 to the present has served on the Steering Committee for the organization that handles the appointments and arranges the annual dinner.

Other organizations in which she has been involved include the Marin County Economic Commission; The Board of the San Francisco Bay Model Association; The Board of the Marin Conservation Corps; President of the Environmental Forum; Marin Citizens for Energy Planning; Bureau of Land Management District Advisory Council; Executive Committee of the City County Planning Council and Member and Chairman of the Marin Countywide Plan Committee, which in 1978-88 revised the original Countywide Plan. She also served on the Community Partnership 1990 Committee for the Marin Community Foundation. Between 1990-1994 this committee worked to strengthen a sense of community through awards given for neighborhood accomplishments. They also gave personal recognition to individuals who contributed to a better quality of life in Marin. In addition, they helped fund the restoration of the Fairfax bridges and the Landsdale Playground in San Anselmo.

Gloria Duncan was selected as the Grand Marshall for the Twentieth Annual Fairfax Festival Parade for her outstanding service to and participation in the community of Fairfax. Her active service in both town and county government, boards and commissions earns a highly deserved "Thank you, well done!" from all Marin residents.

Some years later, $100,000 was set up by the city of San Rafael as part of the city's interest in refurbishing the fields. When Dolly got involved as coordinator and manager of the project, she enlisted the aid of a group of 88 people and managed to obtain $525,000 in donated labor, material and equipment from the business community. The results were impressive. The playing fields were done over using a sand turf. All new irrigation equipment and drainage lines were installed, and the area was subjected to hydroseeding. A batting cage was added.

In the softball area, the grandstand was repaired and repainted and a press box added. The baseball stadium was given a new roof, and a PA system and score board were installed. New dressing rooms and restrooms were built. The old bathrooms were also painted along with the light standards, and security lighting was installed in the park. A paved area was put in around the baseball and softball grandstands and walkways. Finally, a cage-type sand box for small children was built and park benches added. The tennis courts were also resurfaced and landscaped. All this work was completed by 1985.

Major contributors to the Albert Park project included T&B Sports; Ghilotti Brothers, who provided the grading; Maggiora-Ghilotti, who supplied the drainage lines; Ray Forester, drainage; James McDonald, architect for the press box; Brian Whittenkeller, landscape architect; McPhails-Shamrock, drainage material and sand; Joe Pedrolli and Son, masonry for the tennis area; Dean Rhodes, engineer for the field; Jack Estes and Gene Carter, surveyors; Thomas Swan, signs; DeMello Roofing, the roofs on the press box, stadium, two snackbars, and the new bathrooms; Zappetini and Son, the park benches; Cagwin and Dorward, irrigation and hydroseeding; Muzinich Plumbing, bathrooms; Marvin Larsen, basalt; San Marin Lumber, wood; and Denny Coleman, painting.

In 1993 Dolly Nave was back at Albert Park supervising the construction of eight bocce ball courts. Six were opened in 1994 and another two in 1999. Currently there are 16 teams playing on several nights and around 1200 people who use the courts each week, nine months of the year. The complex received the

"Most Beautiful Public Bocce Facility in America" award and also the "Presidential Renew America Award of Environmental Achievement" in 1999.

Gerstle Park

Gerstle Park is a lovely, quiet area for resting or for playing. There are four picnic areas, one holding 200 and another accommodating 80 people. There is also a tennis court hidden in a redwood grove, a basketball court, and a children's playground. To get there, drive south on D Street to San Rafael Avenue. Turn right and go two blocks to Clark Street. The park was once the grounds of a summer home called "Violet Terrace," where four generations of the Gerstle family lived, beginning in' 1881. Lewis Gerstle emigrated from Bavaria, lived for a while in San Francisco, and then moved to Sacramento, where he met Louis Sloss. The two men became fast friends and established a partnership which continued throughout their lives. They even married sisters—Lewis Gerstle wed Hannah Greenbaum, and Sloss married her older sister, Sarah.

In 1897, when the Alaskan Gold Rush was on, Gerstle and Sloss formed the Alaskan Commercial Company. They secured a lease from the government to conduct sealing operations off the Pribilof Islands and made a fortune. The Sloss family bought property in San Rafael adjoining Violet Terrace so the two families could spend summer vacations together. The children would race from one house to another, through orchards and under arbors. Lewis Gerstle died in 1902, but his widow Hannah continued to enjoy the house for summer vacations until her death in 1930. At that time, the Gerstle heirs gave the property to the city for a park. Caesar Bettini, a gardener, was kept on to tend the estate. (His son, Paul, eventually became the mayor of San Rafael.) The house was used as a retirement center, then as lodging for the Army Air Corps from Hamilton Field during World War II. In 1955, it was destroyed by arson.

On the park's six acres are nearly fifty different species of trees, including a variety of acacia, laurel, myrtle, oak, redwood, basswood, buckeye, madrone, magnolia, maple, redbud,

For a permit to rent a picnic area in Gerstle Park or any San Rafael park, phone 485-3333

silk tree, smoke tree, toyon, walnut, and an assortment of fruit trees. The Sloss house served as a lodge for the park until it too burned in 1955.

For a permit to rent a picnic area in Gerstle Park or any San Rafael park, phone 485-3333.

EAST SAN RAFAEL

On the east side of town a canal comes in from the bay. The San Rafael Canal parallels Point San Pedro Road and is lined with homes, condominiums, yacht clubs, boat yards, and restaurants. The canal ends near the freeway behind the Montecito Shopping Center, built in the late 1950s and completely remodeled in the 1980s. This was once a municipal yacht harbor but was filled in, all in the name of progress.

Beyond the canal, Point San Pedro Road heads east, following the shoreline of San Rafael Bay; it passes the Peacock Golf and Country Club and arrives at McNear's Beach County Park. The road then becomes North San Pedro Road as it curves northwest to China Camp State Park, now following the shore of San Pablo Bay. Eventually the road turns inland and runs through Santa Venetia, ending at the spectacular Marin County Civic Center. The entire loop, beginning and ending at the freeway, is about ten miles and takes just over a half-hour by car. This scenic ride is especially popular with bicyclists.

San Rafael Canal Area

South of the San Rafael Canal is a residential section known as "The Canal." It is an area where many Hispanic immigrants have settled in Marin. Tucked in among the commercial establishments on East Francisco Boulevard is tiny Beach Park. The park recently underwent upgrading with two sand volleyballs courts added, a bocce ball court and a renovated dock for small boats and canoes.

Two more small neighborhood parks are located in "The Canal." Pickleweed Park, at the junction of Kerner Boulevard and Canal Street, consists of 6.2 acres running between Canal Street and the San Rafael Canal. Park facilities include benches, a sport field, play equipment, rest rooms and the Pickleweed

Park Community Center where there is now a teen center, and a child care and learning center with a library for children. Call 485-3077.

Tiny Schoen Park, about one-tenth of an acre, overlooks San Pablo Bay on East Canal Street. It has a picnic area, some play equipment, and benches.

Peacock Gap Golf and Country Club

On the north side of the canal, Point San Pedro Road heads to the east, past yacht harbors, the Marin Beach and Tennis Club, and the Loch Lomond marina and shopping center. The Peacock Gap area is 3.4 miles from the Montecito Shopping Center. Turn left on Biscayne Drive to get to the Peacock Gap Golf and Country Club, a semi-private golfing facility. Here is an eighteen-hole golf course covering 128 acres of rolling hills, with lakes and creeks. For golf information, call 453-4940. The clubhouse at 333 Biscayne Drive has a restaurant, bar, and banquet facilities, and is open to the public, 453-4122.

Peacock Gap Park

Peacock Gap Park is located at the end of Peacock Drive off San Pedro Road and sits adjacent to the golf course. It contains a grassy multi-use field, jogging trail, picnic area and a children's playground with play structures, two tennis courts and restrooms.

Victor Jones Park

This small neighborhood park located at Robinhood and Maplewood Drives contains a ball field, basketball court, and arbor overlooking a picnic area with a large barbecue, playground, shuffleboard courts and restrooms. For more information, call 485-3333.

McNear's Brickyard

On Point San Pedro Road, a block or so past Peacock Drive, you will see the entrance to McNear's Brickyard. The pioneers in Marin soon discovered that the clay soil was ideal for producing bricks. In 1868, John A. McNear and his brother George

Patent Brickyard, McInnis Park, 1880s. (California Room, Marin County Library, Marin County Civic Center)

bought 700 acres in this area for $35,000. When their partnership dissolved, John kept the property in Marin and increased his holdings to 2,500 acres; his land ran from McNear's Point to Santa Venetia near the Civic Center. Later he acquired the Fortin Brick Company brickyard which was being worked by Chinese labor. This impressive private company continues today but according to Scott McNear, a fifth generation member of the family, the ore has run out. In November 1988, the family purchased 327 acres off the Petaluma-Point Reyes Road just outside of Hick's Valley which was to be used for supplying clay, but according to Dan McNear, the family found they did not need this clay and are grazing cattle on the property. Clay for bricks is still available in Marin from contractors who need to get rid of the clay soil they dig out. This arrangement works out well for both the contractors and the brickyard.

McNear's Beach

McNear's Beach, a popular picnic and swimming area for the past century, lies in a sheltered cove on San Pablo Bay. In 1970 the County of Marin purchased the old resort and, after some remodeling, the beach was opened to the public. The park is kept in pristine shape. McNear's Beach covers approximately 70 acres and includes large areas of green lawns, picnic sites, a 500-foot concrete pier with wood railings, 3,000-square-foot swimming pool, two tennis courts, a swimming beach, restrooms, changing rooms, and a snack bar. McNear's Beach is about a

mile beyond the brickyard. Turn right on Cantera Way and follow the long drive lined with eucalyptus trees into the park.
There is a fee for entry.

China Camp State Park

Half-a-mile beyond McNear's Beach is China Camp State Park.
This location began as a Chinese settlement in the 1860s after
the American Civil War. It was a debarkation and relay point
for Asian laborers being smuggled in at night to work on construction of the Central Pacific Railroad. After the completion of
the railroad in 1869, the Chinese returned to China Camp and
began shrimp fishing. The *1880 History of Marin County* describes China Camp at the time:

> . . . *you hitch your team to a fence, and a walk of two or three
> hundred yards brings you upon the scene of the fishing grounds of
> Point San Pedro. This industry is entirely in the hands of China-
> men, who conduct a very extensive business, employing upwards
> of two hundred and twenty-five men. The land occupied by the
> fishermen is owned by McNear and Bro., and leased to Mr.
> Richard Bullis for one thousand dollars a year, and by him leased
> to the Chinamen for nearly three thousand dollars.*
>
> *From ten to fifteen acres are occupied, the shore line serving for
> houses, boat building, shipping, etc., and the side hill for drying
> the fish, and preparing them for market. Shrimps constitute the
> principal catch, and of these from twenty to thirty tons per week
> are taken. The shrimps are dried on the hillsides, threshed, "a la
> Chinois," to get off the hull, winnowed through a hand mill, and
> sent to market.*
>
> *The fish sell for eight to fourteen cents per pound in the San
> Francisco market, at wholesale, and the hulls are shipped to
> China, and sold for manure where they bring twenty dollars per
> ton, affording a profit over all expenses of five dollars. It is said to
> be an excellent fertilizer. Other kinds of fish are taken in great
> quantities, as flounders, perch, etc, and some of which are used
> only for dressing soil. The stakes to which the fishers attach their
> nets extend out into the bay a mile or more. There are thirty-two
> houses on the beach, and more all the time building. Two boats are*

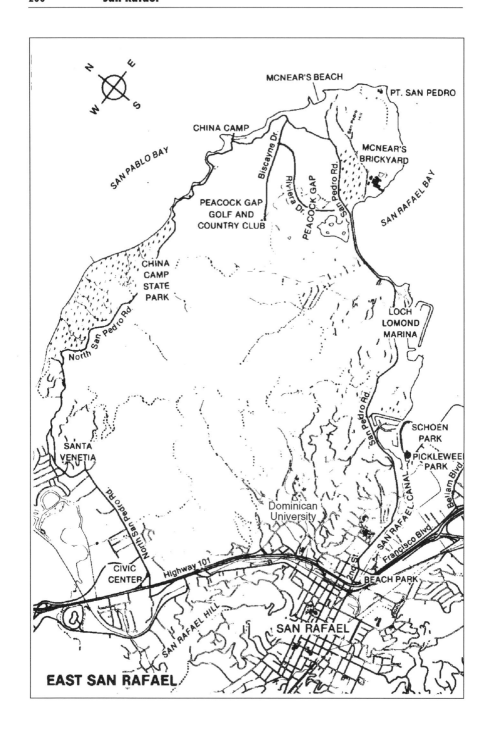

The old pier at China Camp State Park.

now on the ways, one forty feet long, and the other thirty. Nine hundred cords of wood have been used this season, which they buy in Redwood City and ship themselves to their fishing grounds. Captain Bullis makes a weekly trip to the city with a cargo, the law requiring a white captain on a forty-foot craft.

In the 1906 San Francisco earthquake and fire, Chinatown burned to the ground and thousands of Chinese refugees fled to China Camp. Shanties built on stilts filled the shoreline and extended out into the water. The beach and hillsides were covered with makeshift camps. Many of the refugees stayed at China Camp, while others eventually returned to San Francisco to help with the rebuilding of the city. In 1910, the state of California planted bass in the shrimping area and put restrictions on the nets, thereby wiping out the industry practically overnight. A disastrous fire in 1913 burned most of the shanties, and the Chinese began to leave.

Then in the 1920s, Frank Spenger invented a special cone-shaped net that allowed large fish to escape but retained the shrimp. Quan Hock Quock, using a fleet of thirty-six motor-boats equipped with this new net, reportedly hauled in a thousand pounds of shrimp per boat. He also operated a small store built out over the water adjacent to the pier.

Henry Quan and his wife Grace took over the shrimping business and store after the death of Quan Hock Quock. Although mud began to cover the shrimp grounds, the Quan heirs remained for many years and Frank Quan is still there today. He is the last resident in China Camp. His father was a shrimp fisherman and his grandfather the store owner. While the rest of his family has left, he plans to spend the rest of his life here. In 1954, a movie was filmed at China Camp, *Blood Alley,* starring John Wayne and Lauren Bacall. For years after, hundreds of people came out to see the site of what was to become a film classic.

China Camp is now part of a 1512-acre park. The land was purchased by the state of California between the years 1976-78 from Hawaii developer Chinn Ho, who donated the thirty-six acres that contain the shrimp village. The Marin Chinese Cultural Group believes this site to be the only remaining authentic Chinese fishing village left in California. The village is located about a half-mile beyond the park boundary sign. There is a fee for parking, which is in a lot overlooking the bay. From there a walk leads down a dirt road to the village itself. The hours are 8:00 a.m. to sunset.

The village is a photographer's delight. A long, rickety wooden pier stretches out into the bay. On shore are shacks and dilapidated old buildings, dinghies and fishing boats. A museum and visitors' center are open daily from 10:00 a.m. to 5:00 p.m. Nearby is a small beach with a few picnic tables.

Water activities include fishing, swimming, windsurfing and boating. Tours can be arranged for school groups and twelve miles of trails are available for hiking. Thirty walk-in campsites in the Backranch Meadows area north of the village contain picnic tables, food lockers, fire bells, running water and toilets. More picnic sites are located along the bay front. At Miwok Meadows there is a picnic area for up to 200 people with 25 picnic tables, chemical toilets, barbecue pits, horseshoe pits and poles to string up volleyball nets. (See Campgrounds, Chapter 16.) For information or to reserve the group facility, Miwok

MIWOK MEADOWS
456-0766
or for reservations:
800-444-7275
www.reserveamerica.com

Meadows, call the Park Office at 456-0766. To make a camping reservation call ReserveAmerica at 800-444-7275, or go on-line at www.reserveamerica.com. The California State Park Website is: www.cal-parks.ca.gov.

As you leave the village site, the park continues along San Pablo Bay to Rat Rock Cove, where wooden shanties were once built out over the water. These houses burned around 1904. North San Pedro Road continues to follow the shoreline, past the Backranch Meadows and through a broad pickleweed marsh, still part of the park.

NORTH SAN RAFAEL

After leaving China Camp State Park, North San Pedro Road goes on to Santa Venetia, a residential area named after Venice, Italy. In 1914, a real estate developer had planned to use Las Gallinas Creek to create a canal lined by elegant homes. There would also be a palatial clubhouse, miles of bridle paths, and authentic gondolas as a final perfect touch. World War I and the Depression killed this romantic plan. Houses were eventually built here on a more modest scale, and in the past few years very large homes have also been constructed.

As you drive through Santa Venetia, look off to the right for a golden spire to appear over the treetops. Then, the blue dome and roof of the Marin County Civic Center comes into view.

Just beyond the Civic Center is Highway 101, which at this point climbs Puerto Suello Hill, the geographic division between Central and North San Rafael. From the crest of the hill there is a sweeping view of the Las Gallinas Valley, originally a land grant of 22,000 acres of old mission land, and known today as the residential areas of Terra Linda, Marinwood, and Lucas Valley.

Marin County Civic Center

The famous architect Frank Lloyd Wright designed the unusual and beautiful Marin County Civic Center as his last commission. The 160-acre site was purchased by the county of Marin in

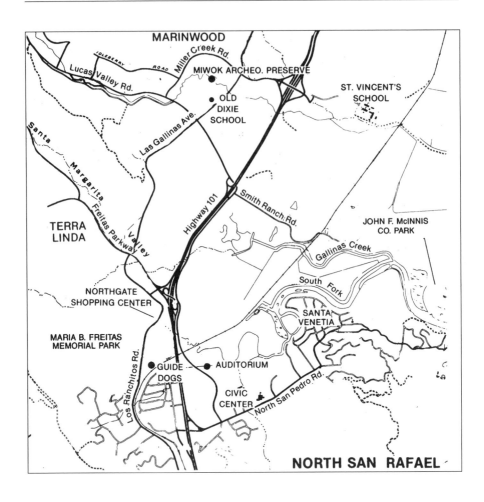

April 1956. Another 80 acres were later added. Presentation plans were submitted to the county by Wright the following March, and were followed a year later with additional plans for a fairgrounds with an amphitheater, pavilion, playground, lagoon, and general civic area.

Wright's plan was to unite three isolated hillcrests by way of one horizontal building line. The two buildings (Administration Building and Hall of Justice) would span the valleys in between and blend into each hill by means of a series of gracefully-moving arches. They would have the effect of floating from hill to hill.

The Marin County Civic Center designed by Frank Lloyd Wright.

Not everyone liked the new plans, or the cost, and a bitter fight ensued. Soon the lines were drawn. Against the Wright plan were members of the American Legion, an irate taxpayers' group, County Supervisor William Fusselman, and George Jones, the powerful county clerk. Supporting the plans were Supervisors Vera Schultz, Walter Castro, William Gnoss, and James Marshall, plus Planning Director Mary Summers and conservationist leader Caroline Livermore.

Proponents of the plan gave slide shows around the country in an effort to consolidate public support. As people took sides, animosity grew; intrigues, plots, and counterplots developed.

Then, Frank Lloyd Wright died suddenly on April 9, 1959. If the Civic Center were built, the people of Marin would have his last masterpiece. Six days later, the Board of Supervisors voted to continue working on the project with the Wright Foundation, and plans proceeded to submit the blueprints out to bid. Architect Aaron Green, representing the Wright Foundation, estimated the administration building would cost $3,379,000, and the bids received were right in line. Groundbreaking ceremonies were held in February 1960.

Marin County Civic Center.

Disaster struck when in the June elections two of the supervisors supporting the plan—Vera Schultz and Jim Marshall—were defeated in their reelection campaigns by anti-tax candidates J. Walter Blair and George Ludy. Suddenly, Fusselman had a 3-2 majority on the Board of Supervisors opposing the new Civic Center. Mary Summers, planning director for the county for twenty years, resigned in protest, as did County Counsel Leland Jordan and County Administrator Donald A. Jensen.

The bulldozers were working and the steel girders were up in January 1961 when the new Board of Supervisors was sworn in. Fusselman, a candy-maker from San Anselmo, was elected chairman. On January 10, a stop-work order on the Marin County Civic Center was voted through the Board. The Civic Center Committee was dismissed, and discussion began on the possibility of converting the administration building into a county hospital.

Marin citizens erupted with rage at this high-handed action. People who had paid little attention to local politics suddenly found their county the laughingstock of the whole Bay Area and demanded that something be done about it. A grand jury investigation was called for. Meetings turned into shouting matches.

An *Independent Journal* ballot showed disapproval of the stop-work order to be running 8-to-1. Picket lines were set up.

Finally, upon receiving an independent committee's report that converting the administration building into a hospital would cost more than finishing the original building, Supervisor George Ludy changed his vote, and construction was allowed to continue.

But the political controversy had not ended. In another attempt to foil the plans, the board voted, on a motion from J. Walter Blair, to abolish the office of county administrator. Again, the citizens of Marin took up arms. Blair was recalled by his Mill Valley district—the first successful recall election against a supervisor in California history—and Peter Behr, a lawyer and recent Mill Valley councilman, was elected. The result of the election was the completion of the entire Civic Center complex. (Peter Behr's popularity in the county continued. He went on to the state senate, where he served eight years until his voluntary retirement.)

Inside the Marin County Civic Center looking down from the fourth floor of the Adminsitration Building.

Marin County was rocked to its foundations by the Civic Center controversy, and afterwards much was changed. The result was the demise of one kind of leadership in the county and the rise of another force, that of citizen involvement and participation.

As you begin your tour of the Civic Center, stop for a look at the original Frank Lloyd Wright model on display on the ground floor of the administration building, which is the closest to San Pedro Road. Then, as you explore the grounds, you can see which parts of the original dream came true. Tours are also conducted through the Civic Center Volunteer Office which is run by Grace Holley. Visitors can drop in on Wednesday mornings at 10:30 a.m., or groups can be shown around by appointment. A small donation is requested for the tour. Call 499-6646.

CIVIC CENTER
TOURS
499-6646

The volunteer group operates a gift shop on the second floor of the Hall of Justice next to the cafeteria. The shop carries Frank Lloyd Wright inspired books and items specific to Marin County. In addition, there are some museum reproduction items. The gift shop is open from 9:00 a.m. to 4:00 p.m. Monday through Friday.

This complex was the culmination of the majority of Wright's ideas and shows his fascination with the use of circles, long horizontal lines, contrasting textures, and crescent shapes. These motifs are built into the outside of the buildings: wide crescents look like half-moons stretched over driveways that pass right through the buildings. On each consecutive floor going up, the crescent shapes used in balconies become smaller. On the top floor, they turn into round circles, a motif continued in the blue round and horizontal roof.

The exterior color, a buff pink, is continued inside and contrasts with a highly polished brick-red floor, gold/brass-colored fixtures, and ornamental grillwork. The gold/brass color is also used in the futuristic-looking spire built in the shape of a four-sided needle-like pyramid that towers majestically above the complex.

Wright liked the use of balconies, fountains, and patios, and incorporated these features into his design. As you enter the

The County Civic Center Auditorium.

administration building, you are struck by its vast openness—
three floors of balconies illuminated by a crescent-shaped sky-
light. Exotic tropical and subtropical plants grow in profusion
down the middle of the ground floor and continue into the Hall
of Justice building. There are massive schefflera (the Australian

Marin County Civic Center

umbrella tree), dieffenbachia, bird of paradise, Wandering Jew, and maranta (prayer plants that fold up at night).

There are two exhibition galleries—one in the connecting hall from the administration building to the hall of justice, and another on the third floor of the administration building outside the board of supervisors' chambers. Supervisors' offices look down on a landscaped patio with a circular fountain next to the cafeteria. This cafeteria is open to the public and has excellent, inexpensive food. You can eat lunch outside, around the fountain.

The main branch of the county library is on the fourth floor of the administration building. It features an extensive collection of books and the unique Anne Kent California History Room, which contains a variety of books on history, old photographs, and Marin County historical documents. In 1999 the Anne Kent California History Room was awarded a $10,000 California Library Service Act grant to help fund the cataloging of Marin's historical documents. It is estimated the collection contains 2400 items and oral histories.

On the south end of this building, the fourth floor opens up to the hillside where there is an attractive, carefully labeled "drought garden" containing plants that require little water. A short path leads to the top of the hill—an excellent spot to take photographs. There is a beautiful view all the way to the bay, and a unique perspective on the roof lines of the buildings.

Connecting with the Administration Building is the Hall of Justice, with its long halls and round courtrooms. It is now open to the public, but for years it was closed off and resembled an armed camp. During a trial in 1970 involving San Quentin inmates, this visionary building was the scene of a shootout. Guns were smuggled into the courtroom by Jonathan Jackson, 17-year-old brother of the convict author, George Jackson. Hostages were taken, and Marin County Superior Court Judge Harold Haley was killed in the melee that followed. Assistant District Attorney Gary Thomas was shot and paralyzed from the waist down, while San Quentin convicts James McClain, William Christmas and Jonathan Jackson

(continued on page 216)

The Marin County Civic Center Lagoon.

PROFILE: **Robert Roumiguere**

R obert Roumiguiere, a Marin County Supervisor from 1972 to 1994, was a mover and shaker in Marin's political scene for over twenty-five years. He was appointed to the Marin County Board of Supervisors to represent the First Supervisorial District by California Governor Ronald Reagan to fill the vacancy left when Supervisor John McInnis unexpectedly passed away while still in office.

Roumiguiere reflects back now that during those years he most enjoyed working on projects that improved the quality of life in Marin. What he achieved in securing large parcels of open space will remain a lasting monument to his leadership and powers of persuasion. In addition, he is credited with leading the battle to obtain the railroad right-of-way between Paradise Drive in Corte Madera which runs all the way north to Willits and over to Napa. He also chaired the 101 Corridor Action Plan developed and approved by the Marin and Sonoma County Board of Supervisors and their nineteen cities. It was a five year effort that Roumiguiere believes someday will be implemented.

He worked with homeowners groups in Terra Linda, Santa Venetia, Marinwood, Upper Lucas Valley, Sun Valley and San Marin residential areas whose members wanted to save the surrounding hills from being overrun with housing developments. He put together packages of bonds and open space funds to finance the purchase of the land. The homeowners raised their own property taxes and paid half the cost of the land. The bonds ran for twenty years and are now retired, while the hills are secured in open space forever. This formula was used six to eight times in Roumiguiere's district, saving an incredible amount of land.

To preserve the open space around Peacock Gap, Bayside Acres, Loch Lochmond, Villa Real and Santa Venetia, Roumiguiere led the successful effort to create China Camp State Park. After completing the negotiations for the major acreage, including a mile of bay front for the park, he worked with land owner Chinn Ho to donate the famous fishing village as a key part of the park.

Roumiguiere's goal was to preserve forever the quality of life in the residential communities of his district, and this was his way to provide growth management. He was dubbed the " Father of the Terra Linda Open Space Preserve." He also fought hard for transportation improvements and led the battle to build the HOV lanes on Highway 1. He was then responsible for Cal Trans reducing the carpool lanes from three to two people.

Roumiguiere was successful in raising nearly ninety-million dollars in Washington, D.C., for transportation, flood control, park acquisition, and other worthy projects such as removing the old wooden dry docks from Richardson Bay.

He was also a force in working to obtain McNear's Beach for a county park even before his appointment to the Board of Supervisors. In addition, the county had been working to secure the land for McInnis Park in San Rafael, a project which Roumiguiere helped spearhead and saw through to completion with the golf course and clubhouse.

Bob Roumiguiere was born in San Francisco in 1925 and moved to Laurel Avenue in San Anselmo with his family at age five. He remembers the joy of flying kites in the Hawthorne Hills and believes that is one of the reasons he worked so diligently to save the hills as open space for the enjoyment of all Marin residents.

He rode the train to Tamalpais High School in Mill Valley and after graduation joined the World War II effort by working at Marinship in Sausalito. This was followed by two-and-a-half years in the United States Navy Seabees in the South Pacific.

After the war ended, he returned home and enrolled at College of Marin and later at California State Polytechnic University in San

PROFILE:　**Robert Roumiguere** (continued)

Louis Obispo. His major was Dairy Husbandry and Business Administration. Upon graduation, he and a partner went into the dairy business in Templeton, south of Paso Robles. After three years of working sixteen hours, seven days a week with no time out for dating, he sold out to his partner.

He returned to Marin to help his father, Alphonse Roumiguiere, who owned a mortgage banking business, A.R. Roumiguiere, Inc. This company financed residential and commercial properties. (The elder Roumiguiere and two partners had started Ross Valley Savings and Loan Association which later became Santa Barbara Savings.) The business included real estate sales. What started out as a temporary job for Bob, lasted for thirty years.

In 1952 he married Barbara Norvell, a student he had met at College of Marin who, by then, had become a successful airline stewardess. They raised a wonderful family of three boys and two girls: Rob, John, Mark, Audrey and Lynn, and they now have six grandchildren.

In 1980 Roumiguiere purchased a vineyard in Lake County and he was suddenly back in the farming business. He now owns four ranches producing over five-hundred acres of wine grapes which are operated by his two oldest sons, Rob and John. The former supervisor jokes that he only has charge of firewood and cash flow.

Vacations in Puerto Vallarta led to some real estate investments in Mexico. ("I got bored after sitting on the beach for three days and went out looking at real estate.") He now owns a small company there with a Mexican partner, so divides his time between Mexico, Marin and Lake County.

Looking back at his active years in Marin, Roumiguiere is proud of the time he spent as a member and president of the Marin Council of Boy Scouts of America when they had 4500 to 5000 boys in the program; the undergrounding of utilities along East Francisco Boulevard. in San Rafael; his work with the California Association of Realtors in keeping county property taxes from being raised more than 5% annually in the pre-Prop 13 days; and his involvement with the North Coastal County Supervisors Association (representing eight counties reaching to the Oregon border), which fought successfully, during his presidency, for the HOV freeway lane in Marin and to build the Cloverdale Bypass. He also enjoyed the work on behalf of youth organizations, and the baseball field in Terra Linda is named "Bob Roumiguiere Field" in his honor.

Roumiguiere still serves as a trustee, and is current Chairman of the Marin County Employees Retirement Association whose assets now exceed nine-hundred millions dollars. The association also administers the assets for the employees of the city of San Rafael and the Novato Fire District employees.

In a recent interview, Roumiguiere was asked what he enjoyed most about his years of service. Without a moment's hesitation, he replied, "The people, they were wonderful. It was always a tremendous pleasure to begin one of my 'shirt sleeve roundtables' and find that the people attending represented six or eight different philosophies on how to solve the problem at hand. And by the time we would end what was usually a series of meetings, we would develop a solution almost all, if not all, could live with. Because, given the opportunity, most citizens will try hard to understand each other's views and there was a tremendous amount of give and take. We solved tons of problems with that spirit and a lot of hard work. I never allowed a meeting to last over two hours. We didn't waste a lot of time crying about the problem. We just got right down to crafting a solution."

Nearly one-thousand people showed up at Bob Roumiguiere's retirement party from the Board of Supervisors held at the Marin County Civic Center in San Rafael. His leadership was honored, his accomplishments listed and promises given that his achievements in Marin would always be remembered. A bronze bust of Roumiguiere, contributed by the citizens of Santa Venetia, was installed by the Board of Supervisors on a knoll off the fourth floor of the Administration Building at the Civic Center in recognition of his service.

were all shot to death. Gary Thomas went on to serve as a Marin County judge presiding from a wheelchair.

For years after what was called the "Marin County Shootout," the doors to the court floors were kept locked, the halls patrolled by armed deputies, and metal detectors used to screen everyone entering.

In addition to the two main buildings, the Civic Center complex contains a post office (the only one ever designed by Wright), an 11-acre landscaped lagoon (a favorite spot for feeding ducks), exhibit building, two theaters (including the 2,003-seat Veterans Auditorium and Showcase Theater next to the Exhibition Hall), and fairgrounds. A 20-acre informal Civic Center Lagoon Park contains picnic areas and children's play structures and allows fishing. Non-motorized boating is permitted.

A $20 million fund raising drive is currently going on to build a Museum of Art and the Environment on two acres of the Civic Center grounds north of the lagoon. The 40,000 square foot building would be the same as an earlier design by Wright for a museum at Arizona State University in Tempe, Arizona, that was never built.

When addressing the citizens of Marin with his preliminary plans, Frank Lloyd Wright had this to say about his design for the Civic Center:

> *Beauty is the moving cause of nearly every issue worth the civilization we have, and civilization without a culture is like a man without a soul. Culture consists of the expression by the human spirit of the love of beauty.*
>
> *We will never have a culture of our own until we have an architecture of our own. An architecture of our own does not mean something that is ours by the way of our own tastes. It is something that we have knowledge concerning. We will have it only when we know what constitutes a good building and when we know that the good building is not one that hurts the landscape, but is one that makes the landscape more beautiful than it was before that building was built. In Marin County you have one of the most beautiful landscapes I have seen, and I am proud to make the buildings of this County characteristic of the beauty of the County.*

Here is a crucial opportunity to open the eyes not of Marin County alone, but of the entire country, to what officials gathering together might themselves do to broaden and beautify human lives.

Guide Dogs for the Blind

North of the Civic Center and to the west of Highway 101, at 350 Los Ranchitos Road, is Guide Dogs for the Blind, an institution that trains dogs to aid people who have lost their sight and prepares people to use these highly trained dogs.

The eleven-acre campus contains kennels, an office building, and student dormitories. The dogs—Labradors, German shepherds, or golden retrievers—are often seen in downtown San Rafael as they are being trained to lead people across streets in heavy traffic conditions.

The public is invited to the graduations which take place every five weeks. Visitors may tour the kennels and see a demonstration of working guide dogs. Call 499-4000 for pre-arranged tours.

GUIDE DOGS FOR
THE BLIND
499-4000

Northgate Mall Shopping Center

The popular Northgate Mall Shopping Center is farther north on Los Ranchitos Road and is also accessible from the Freitas Parkway exit off Highway 101. Opened in 1965, it is an area of forty-five acres with over 100 stores, shops, and restaurants. Anything you want to buy—clothing, furniture, books, or gifts— can be found at Northgate.

The shopping center was completely remodeled in the 1980s with a grand opening in 1987.

Maria B. Freitas Park

Beyond the shopping center is the Maria B. Freitas Park. Stay on Freitas Parkway, then turn right on Montecillo Road toward Kaiser Hospital. The park is located near the hospital's Parking Lot 2.

Once known as the "Water Park," the city of San Rafael closed the tiered fountains because of new health and safety codes. The park reopened September 10, 2000, after a $520,000 facelift designed by Gerald Mitchell that includes terraces and four red metal rings that spray water.

Terra Linda Community Center

The Terra Linda Community Center is located at Del Ganado and Freitas Roads. These public facilities contain a swimming pool, tiny tot pool, basketball court, playground, and a picnic area with barbecues and restrooms. Call 485-3344 for information.

Jerry Russom Open Space Area

The 184 acre Jerry Russom Open Space Area is located off Lucas Valley Road. The land was saved from development in the early 1970s when the Mont Marin Homeowners formed an Open Space Assessment District through the city of San Rafael to purchase two parcels to keep in open space. It was dedicated as a park to Jerry Russom, President of the Mont Marin Homeowners and the driving force to save the land, after he died. In 1994-95 the City of San Rafael combined the land with open space in Terra Linda and Sleepy Hollow.

Visitors can walk along a road which follows a creek past a lower playing field. This field is still owned by the City of San Rafael and is used for passive recreation only. You can also climb up to a water tower and hike along a fire road that divides Terra Linda and Sleepy Hollow.

To get there drive north on Highway 101 and take the Las Gallinas exit. The first left will be Canyon Oak Drive. Drive along the creek until you get to the sign that says, "Jerry Russom Park."

Miwok Archeological Preserve of Marin

Located along Miller Creek near Las Gallinas Avenue is a site where the Coast Miwok resided for more than two thousand years. This village, called Cotomkotca, was a political and ceremonial center as well as a burial site. More than 500 old Coast Miwok village sites have been identified in Marin and southern Sonoma counties, mostly near San Francisco, Drake's and Tomales Bays. Nearly 90% of these have been destroyed by road and structure building.

To get to the preserve, take the Marinwood exit off Highway 101 to Miller Creek Road, then turn left at Las Gallinas. The site is behind the Miller Creek Middle School at 2255 Las Gallinas, beyond the basketball courts. You will see a round mound surrounded by a wire fence with a double gate. It is identified as "MRN 138" which means "Marin" plus the number of the archeological site.

These mounds are the remains of a Coast Miwok dialectic troupe or tribelet. At this place, archeologists have found human remains as well as animal, bird and fish bones, bone tools and ornaments, stone arrow and spear points, acorn grinding mortars, and shell tools and ornaments. All are clues to the way of life of these early Marin citizens.

Primitive beads were made from olivella shells, those of a small snail. After about 1200 A.D., the Coast Miwok used clam shells to make small round beads called clam disc beads, or money beads. Strung with abalone ornaments, these became ceremonial jewelry. They were also used as a medium of exchange and traded as far as western Nevada. Wide belts made of thousands of clam beads were used as dance regalia. Bird feathers were used in dance skirts and headdresses, ear ornaments and belts, as well as basket ornaments.

The Miwok did not make pottery but were expert basket makers. Their waterproof baskets were used for cooking, and a wide variety of carrying baskets served every purpose pottery served in other cultures. Cordage and net making were also highly developed arts.

After archeological studies were completed, all the remains were reinterred. The sign at the site says: "This is their resting place—here they will remain." Also found at Miller Creek were six ceremonial structures and a floor covered with a thousand pounds of a fallen clay roof. This village was a ceremonial center for all the tribes in the Gallinas Valley.

Old Dixie School

In front of the Miller Creek Middle School is the historic Old Dixie School, built by pioneer James Miller in 1864. The school originally stood north of Miller Creek Road on Highway 101, but was moved to Las Gallinas Avenue in 1972.

The little white schoolhouse with its high, black-trimmed windows makes a picturesque sight surrounded by green lawn and a picket fence. It is furnished as an old-fashioned school complete with textbooks (including replicas of the McGuffey Readers), slates, slate pens, desks, a blackboard, antique clock, pictures of Presidents Washington and Lincoln, a thirty-seven star flag, and a school bell.

The building is used as a community meeting house for several groups. It is open to the public the first Sunday of every month between 2:00 p.m. and 4:00 p.m. and can be rented for parties. For information or a docent tour, call 472-3010.

OLD DIXIE
SCHOOL
472-3010

John F. McInnis Park

At the end of Smith Ranch Road, eight-tenths of a mile from Highway 101, is the John F. McInnis Park, named in memory of a former San Rafael City Councilman and Marin County Supervisor who died in office in 1972. The park covers an area of 441 acres beyond the Marin County Civic Center. It contains two softball fields (one lighted), two soccer fields, canoe launch, four tennis courts, a group picnic area and nature trails. Dogs are allowed under immediate verbal control.

Located here also is the McInnis Park Golf Center which has a nine-hole, 1900-yard, par 31 golf course. In addition, there is a tiered driving range, practice putting green, short game practice area, 20-hole miniature golf, batting cages, clubhouse, pro shop and a restaurant called The Club. The address is 350 Smith Ranch Road, 492-1800. To arrange a party call 491-5961.

PRO SHOP
492-1800
To arrange a party

St. Vincent's School

On the east side of Highway 101 at the Marinwood exit is St. Vincent's School, a California Historical Landmark.

St. Vincent School, San Rafael.

When pioneer Timoteo Murphy died in 1853, he left 317 acres of land to the Roman Catholic archbishop of California, Joseph Alemany, to establish a "seminary of learning." On January 1, 1855, the Daughters of Charity of St. Vincent de Paul came to Marin from San Francisco to establish a school for six orphaned girls. This did not work out, and the children returned to San Francisco that same year, but the name "St. Vincent" remained.

The girls were replaced by 14 orphaned boys at the new "St. Vincent's Orphan Asylum of San Francisco," a name used until 1975. The orphan asylum grew rapidly, and by 1890 there were 600 boys living at St. Vincent's. Buildings were added and a large farming operation developed.

From 1868 to 1890, the Dominican Sisters taught at St. Vincent's before moving into their new convent facilities on Grand Avenue in San Rafael. The strict Christian Brothers were brought in and stayed from 1894 to 1922. At that time Dominican Sisters from the Mission San Jose took over and are still teaching at St. Vincent's.

Today, the number of children living at St. Vincent's School is up to sixty-six. They are neither orphans nor delinquents, but boys ages seven to fourteen who have severe emotional and social adjustment problems.

The boys now live in cottages which provide a more home-like atmosphere than the old dormitories. On weekends they may participate in a "Visiting Family Program" in which they are invited into homes of people interested in the school. It helps prepare the boys for the adjustment they will make when they are placed with a foster family or return to their own homes after leaving St. Vincent's.

The school also sponsors a "Foster Family Agency Program" which serves 20,000 children, while their Catholic Youth Organization includes an athletic program for another 5,000 children. In addition, there is an outdoor environmental education program.

The entrance to St. Vincent's is a lovely, eucalyptus-lined drive. It is like taking a journey into the past, into a quiet world of Spanish missions, formal gardens, palm trees, and fountains.

A sign in the front parking lot, half-a-mile from the freeway, advises you to check in at the main office. To reach it, walk straight back under a long, cool portico, then turn left. In this

St. Vincent's School, San Rafael.

area there are extensive gardens, benches, iron gates, graceful archways, colorful bougainvillea, statues of lions, and a round fountain with water lilies. Old buildings of yellow stucco with green tile roofs surround a central court, reminiscent of a California mission. As you stand in this quiet spot, remember that over 50,000 boys have lived here in the last hundred years.

At the main office you can arrange for a tour of the Chapel of the Most Holy Rosary, or call 507-2000 for a docent tour for not less than ten people, or more than forty. A small donation is requested.

CHAPEL OF THE
MOST HOLY
ROSARY
507-2000

The chapel is the familiar landmark, the richly-carved spires and ornate church facade, seen fleetingly through tall eucalyptus trees from the freeway. It was completed in 1930, part of a large building program initiated by Father Francis P. McElroy.

In front of the chapel, up under the eaves, are dozens of swallow nests. Hundreds of the industrious birds swoop around with great speed. Unlike the swallows at the famous Mission San Juan Capistrano in Southern California, the birds at St. Vincent's never leave. When the church was cleaned and painted in 1979, they hovered around nervously and watched the progress. The minute the paint was dry, the swallows began rebuilding their mud nests exactly as they were before.

Inside the chapel, one is immediately impressed with fifteen beautiful stained glass windows depicting the life of Jesus. Paintings marking the Stations of the Cross line the wall, and the ceiling is ornately carved and painted. The center aisle is inlaid with tile, and there is generous use of intricately-carved white marble and stone along the walls and in the high columns. The altar is also of white marble, carved in a simpler design.

As you leave the quiet beauty of the chapel and look again at the graceful old buildings, cool porticos, fountains, and flowers, it seems a long way to the hurtling tempo of the twenty-first century.

North Marin   9

The Old West

N ovato, Marin's northernmost city, lies in a sheltered inland
valley surrounded by hills. Away from the coastal fog, it is
warmer here than in the rest of the county.

This is a sprawling western town with wide streets and
boulevards. The actual city limits encompass twenty-three
square miles, taking in what was once Hamilton Air Force Base,
portions of Ignacio, and Black Point, while the Greater Novato
Area is a tremendous seventy square miles encompassing several large residential areas, parks, and the county airport.

The ranch land in the northern part of the county was the last
area open to development. While many homes and industrial
parks have been built here, Novato still retains its friendly,
small-town atmosphere, and there is a strong sense of community. New development includes the building of homes at
Hamilton, sixty units behind San Marin High School, and fifty-
plus units and a golf course at the 18-hole StoneTree Golf Club
at Black Point.

HAMILTON FIELD

I n 1929, the federal government decided a major military
installation was needed in Marin, and a site known as Marin
Meadows in North Marin was picked to build an air base.

◀ *Tall palm trees mark the site of Olompali State Historic Park north of
Novato.*

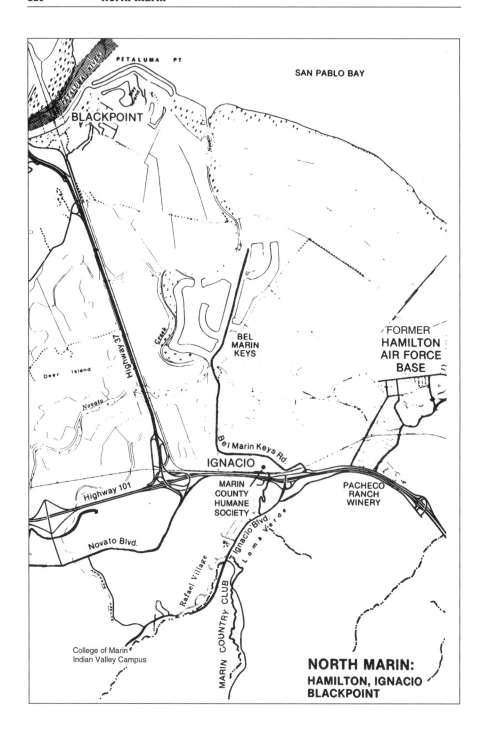

PETALUMA PT

SAN PABLO BAY

BLACKPOINT

FORMER
HAMILTON
AIR FORCE
BASE

BEL
MARIN
KEYS

Highway 37

Creek

Deer   Island

Novato

Novato

Bel Marin Keys Rd.

IGNACIO

MARIN
COUNTY
HUMANE
SOCIETY

PACHECO
RANCH
WINERY

Highway 101

Ignacio Blvd.

Loma Verde

Novato Blvd.

Rafael Village

MARIN COUNTRY CLUB

College of Marin
Indian Valley Campus

NORTH MARIN:
HAMILTON, IGNACIO
BLACKPOINT

President Hoover signed the bill and work began in December 1933. Coming in the heart of the Depression, these new jobs were a great boon to residents of the county.

From 1935 to 1940, Hamilton Field was used as a bomber base. Then it became a fighter base and was particularly important to the country throughout World War II as a jumping-off point to the Pacific. In 1947 it was renamed Hamilton Air Force Base. Hamilton eventually occupied 2,010 acres and became the home of the 78th Fighter Wing (Air Defense), including the 83rd and 84th Fighter Interceptor Squadron, part of the U.S. Air Force Aerospace Defense Command.

In 1974 the Air Force declared 1600 acres of the military base to be surplus, and the housing and ancillary facilities were taken over by the Navy, in addition to a large hanger and runway operated by the Army. These portions of the base became surplus again in 1996. The operations portion of the base, the hangers and other historic buildings , are being preserved and reused for other purposes by the New Hamilton Partnership. The overall plan for the reuse of the whole base includes 2122 residential units to be built, 100 acres to be used for park land, 50 acres for community facilities, and a transitional facility to aid the homeless. The old runway is to be converted to wetlands.

In 2000 the City of Novato purchased a 550-acre parcel from the United States Navy for 8.13 million dollars to be developed by the Novato Community Partners. Shea and Centex Homes are building approximately 1287 homes and 2.2 acres of commercial space. The houses will be a mix of townhouses, duplexes, market rates houses and affordable senior units.

Meanwhile, the New Hamilton Partnership is developing 935 new homes and 500,000 square feet of commercial development on their 408 acre parcel. This alliance is made up of The Martin Group and the Whitehall Fund #1 (Goldman Sacs Pension Fund). The four principal men involved include Peter Palmisano (marketing and sales); Todd Wright (project manager); Thomas Gram (legal matters); and Michael Covarrubias (financing). The 1930s Spanish style buildings at the old base have influenced the design of the new housing and town center.

Seven original Air Force hangers and two adjacent acres are being remodeled by the Barker Pacific Group, Inc., into retail businesses which will be called "Hamilton Landing." This property was purchased from the New Hamilton Partnership. The project has attracted other businesses, including a Marriott Hotel, new facilities for the Marin Airporter, a fast food outlet and a large supermarket complex.

The airplane runways, which are part of 700 acres of bay front land adjacent to the old base, will be flooded to create wetlands, a project estimated to cost 55 million dollars. This can only be done when a massive clean up, started in 1995 by the military, has been completed.

Residents in Hamilton's new subdivisions are able to use abandoned recreational facilities once used by the military. These include a swimming pool, community center, sports court, Little League field, gymnasium and racquetball courts. The Hamilton Community Center at 203 El Bonito Drive was once the Officer's Club. It is now run through the Novato Parks and Recreation Department and used for wedding receptions, parties, senior activities and children's recreation, such as lessons in music, dance, and yoga. Call 884-4900 for more information.

HAMILTON COM-
MUNITY CENTER
884-4900

The homeless were housed in a warehouse at Hamilton Field since 1998, which led to the construction of an 80 bed permanent facility called The New Beginnings Center. In 1999 the U.S. Department of Veteran's Affairs granted $620,000 to the shelter to help with construction and provide programs for veterans. The shelter opened April 8, 2000, and is run by Homeward Bound of Marin, which has been helping the homeless since 1987.

The year-round facility, consisting of five buildings located on over five acres, provides lodging and job training. One project called "Homeplate" consists of growing organic fruits and vegetables that are sold to restaurants and grocery stores in Marin. There is also job training dealing with food preparation. For information call New Beginnings Center at 382-3532.

NEW BEGINNINGS
CENTER AT
382-3532.

A museum is also being planned that will be located in the 1933 Spanish style military firehouse. The new 9,000 square-foot Hamilton Field History Museum will tell the story of people who were stationed and worked at the old base. Displays will include a working World War II Link Trainer used to train fighter pilots, a large collection of photographs, uniforms, documents, medals and even the original bell from the entrance gate. The period covered in the displays will run from 1935 to 1974, during the time that Hamilton Field was an Army Airfield and then an Air Force Base.

IGNACIO

Adjacent to Hamilton Field, at the Highway 101 exit just past Hamilton Field, is Ignacio. This area was named for Ignacio Pacheco, who received the Mexican land grant *Rancho de San Jose* in 1834. The grant, consisting of 6,659.25 acres, may have been named for Pacheco's birthplace, the village of San Jose in Santa Clara County.

Pacheco's parents had come to California from Mexico with the de Anza expedition in 1776. Ignacio grew up to become a Mexican army sergeant and later a justice of the peace in San Rafael.

Today, the Ignacio area contains apartments, industrial parks, and some interesting restaurants. In 1970 a new enterprise began in Ignacio which was wine making. This was actually a return to an old Marin tradition started by the Spanish padres. Herbert Rowland, a direct descendant of Ignacio Pacheco, and his family have created the Pacheco Ranch Winery on 75 acres across from the old Hamilton Air Force Base. Rowland planted seven acres of Cabernet Sauvignon grapes which now produce 1,000 cases a year. Local connoisseurs applaud the production and look forward to many fine Marin wines.

Drivers on Highway 101 can still glimpse the white Victorian house which was built on the property in 1878. The public is welcome to stop by the ranch by appointment. Call 883-5583. The address is 235 Alameda Del Prado, Novato.

PACHECO RANCH WINERY 883-5583

Ignacio was also the location of a large bowling complex called Nave Lanes, built by "Papa" Bill Nave and his sons Bill, Bob and Rich in 1958. The Nave family has been in Marin since "Grampa" Pete Nave arrived in 1880 from a little town outside

PROFILE: **Dolly Nave**

I n 1988, Dolly Nave was named "Citizen of the Year" by the SanRafael Chamber of Commerce for her tremendous contributions as coordinator and manager in refurbishing Albert Park. This project, completed in 1985, included drainage, irrigation and sand turf for the playing fields.

There was also a new softball press box built, a new roof for the baseball stadium, the installation of a public address system and scoreboards, construction of modern dressing rooms and rest rooms, the emplacement of security lighting, and the building of an enclosed children's sandbox. The tennis courts were then resurfaced and beautifully landscaped. (The tennis courts at Boyd Park, Gerstle Park and Freitas Park were also resurfaced at this time.) After that project was completed , Dolly has never stopped and her efforts have continued to benefit Marin parks and schools.

Dolly did not originate from Marin. She was born Dolores Wright in San Antonio, Texas, and came to Marin at age 11 when her father, who was in the Air Force, was sent to Hamilton Field. The family lived in Fairfax, where she organized a teenage canteen. Her first two high school years were spent at Tamalpais High School in Mill Valley. When her father was transferred again and her parents were ready to move, she elected to stay in Marin to finish at San Rafael High School.

She was working at Hamilton Air Force Base when the Korean War broke out. In 1955 she married Rich Nave, a member of a pioneer Marin family. Dolly and Richard raised five boys and three girls.

The building of the Marin Community Fields in Larkspur next to Redwood High School was Dolly's next project after Albert Field. Opened in September 1987, the facilities included 17 acres of public playing fields providing for softball, baseball, rugby, soccer, a beep ball (softball) field for the blind, and a 1,000-seat amphitheater.

In 1989 Dolly became the San Rafael High School Alumni Association Project Coordinator. Projects included refurbishing the swimming pool, working on the football field to allow for night games, and a long-term project to paint the entire high school which took several years to complete. In later years she added an "all weather"regulation track to San Rafael High School.

In 1994 she dreamed of bringing "World Class" bocce ball to Albert Park in San Rafael. She succeeded beyond everyone's expectations. By 1999 there were eight courts and a Marin Bocce Federation providing recreation for over 1200 players each week for nine months of the year. The project was named the "Most Beautiful Public Bocce Facility in America" and received the "Presidential Renew America Award for Environmental Achievement."

Dolly Nave was chosen Woman of the Year for the third Senate District for the State of California in 1991. She was inducted into the Marin County High School Hall of Fame in 1993.

Nave Patrola in the 1983 Elk's Parade, 4th and A Streets, San Rafael.

Genoa, Italy. In 1890, he purchased land from Ramon Pacheco which was part of the Pacheco land grant. It was fondly known as the "cabbage patch" for all the vegetables he raised and delivered to local stores by cart. Today, it is the site of the Nave Shopping Center in Novato.

The architect for Nave Lanes was Gordon Phillips, a former pupil of Frank Lloyd Wright, and he used many of the same features incorporated in the Marin Civic Center. It was easy to recognize similar curves, round holes, round pillars, and even a stucco atrium. In 1999 the Naves sold this property to American Stores, who are planning a new shopping area with a grocery store, drug store and other businesses.

Rich Nave, a San Rafael City Councilman between 1983-1987, his brothers Bob and Bill, other members of the family and their friends organized the "Nave Patrola." This "Italian" military marching unit has delighted residents of Marin for the past thirty years in parades from Point Reyes to San Rafael and all over the state of California.

Indian Valley Campus of the College of Marin

The Indian Valley Campus of the College of Marin opened in 1975 (interim classes began in 1971) under the Marin Community College District. It is located at the west end of Ignacio Boulevard, to the northwest of the private Marin Golf and Country Club.

The campus covers 333 acres of rolling, oak-studded hills and contains clusters of two-story wooden buildings nestled beneath the trees. Architects Nepture and Thomas of Pasadena, California, won an Award of Merit in 1977 for their design of the college buildings.

The campus has an enrollment of 2,000 to 2,500 credit students and also schedules community education and services on campus. The three centers of the campus are named Miwok, Ohlone and Pomo.

Indian Valley Campus has the only Olympic-size swimming pool in the county which is open to the public. There are also six tennis courts, hiking and bicycle trails.

The Marin Humane Society

The Marin Humane Society, organized over ninety years ago, is located at 717 Bel Marin Keys Road, to the east of Highway 101 (take the Ignacio/Bel Marin Keys Boulevard exit, bear right at the fork, then make an immediate left on Bel Marin Keys Road). Under a contract with the County of Marin, the Humane Society has responsibility of the Animal Control Services; if your dog or cat has roamed, this may be where you can locate your pet.

The Marin Humane Society is a progressive animal shelter offering refuge and rehabilitation to nearly six thousand animals each year through a myriad of community services including: adoptions, foster care, education, hotlines for lost and found pets, and low-cost medical care. The shelter hosts a monthly low- cost vaccination and microchip clinic, as well as a spay-neuter clinic. The Society finds homes for nearly 2000 animals yearly.

The Humane Society is open Tuesday through Sunday, 10:00 a.m. to 5:30 p.m., Wednesdays until 7:00 p.m. For information and to hear the lost-animal recording, call 883-4621.

HUMANE SOCIETY
883-4621

BLACK POINT

This hilly, wooded point of land fronts on the Petaluma River near where it flows into San Pablo Bay. Black Point was settled in 1853, and most of the pioneers were engaged in wood cutting and dairying. A few schooners were built here, and in the 1960s, fine oak was sent to Mare Island for the construction of naval ships. The thick oak forests were soon gone, but the area remained an important shipping point on the Petaluma River. A branch railroad connected it with Ignacio.

Black Point today is residential with many homes scattered through the hills. For many years the widely known Renaissance Pleasure Faire was held here annually in late summer and early fall, but the Faire moved to Vacaville in 1999.

In 1998 voters overwhelmingly approved the Black Point proposal for a golf course on the Renaissance Faire parking lot, and 53 homes on the site's middle ridge. Plans also call for planting 13,077 trees for the 4,282 cut, and three acres of wetlands created for every acre lost to development. Out of a total of 238 acres, 64.5 acres will be left in open space.

To get to Black Point, drive north on Highway 101 and then east on route 37 (just north of Ignacio). Turn off on the Black Point-Atherton Avenue exit.

COUNTY OF MARIN PARKS DEPT. FOR BLACK POINT PUBLIC FISHING ACCESS 507-4045.

The Black Point Public Fishing Access is a mile farther on the Petaluma River. Operated by the county of Marin, this one-acre site under the Petaluma River bridge contains one large ramp, two docks, picnic tables, barbecues, portable toilets, a hose to wash boats, and a parking lot. This public fishing access was developed by the Wildlife Conservation Board. The other side of the river is Sonoma County and the Port Sonoma Marina. For information call the County of Marin at 507-4045.

NOVATO

The Novato area was originally part of five Mexican land grants. The first came three years after the secularization of the Spanish missions, when the Mexican government was strengthening its hold on California by awarding land to citizens who had proven their loyalty and dedication to Mexico.

According to the *1880 History of Marin*, the first grant here was *Rancho de Novato*, awarded in 1839 to Fernando Feliz, whose family had come to California from Mexico with the de Anza expedition of 1776. Feliz was born in Los Angeles Pueblo in 1795. He served in the army and was awarded this land grant of 8,876.02 acres.

The other land grants were: *Rancho San Jose*, 1840, awarded to Ignacio Pacheco in exchange for a Sonoma grant he had obtained; *Corte Madera de Novato*, 1840, 8.878.02 acres awarded to John Martin, a Scotsman who married Tomasa Cantura; *Rancho Olompali*, 1843, 8,877.43 acres awarded to Camilo Ynitia, a native American and son of the Miwok chief, Olompali; and *Rancho Nicasio*, 1844, 56,621.04 acres awarded to Don Pablo de la Guerra and John Cooper.

The early land grantees set about their peaceful business of building homes, raising families, planting crops, and tending their animals. They raised cattle and hunted the plentiful local game, such as elk, bear, deer, and game birds. Generally, the land barons lived a very good life, entertaining often at gay fiestas in their adobe haciendas. The men have been described as tall and vigorous. Their typical Spanish costume was a wide-brimmed hat, short, decorated jacket, and deerskin leggings. The black-haired Spanish women wore loose, short-sleeved gowns of silk, crepe, or calico, complemented by colorful belts and jewelry. Since they had Indian maids to cook and clean their houses, the ladies spent their time knitting and doing needlework.

The only flaw in the serenity of rancho life was the continuing migration into California of American citizens. Tension and jealousy grew into hatred; the Mexicans feared an American takeover of California, and the new settlers feared they would be expelled by the Mexican California officials.

Violence broke out in 1845 when Captain Elliott Libbey, of the American ship *Tasso*, was stabbed and beaten in Yerba Buena. Groups of Americans began forming makeshift armies whose members patrolled the northern countryside.

In June 1846, Mexican General Vallejo and others were captured in Sonoma by these American vigilantes in what came to be called the Bear Flag Revolt. By July, a state of war existed between the United States and Mexico. The American troops were led by Captain J.C. Fremont. The Mexican leader was Jose Castro, lieutenant colonel of cavalry in the Mexican army and acting commandant of the Department of California.

The United States finally acquired California in a settlement with the Mexican government at Guadeloupe Hidalgo on February 2, 1848.

Novato was soon transformed from a sleepy Mexican community to an American frontier town. As the town is farther inland than other portions of Marin and free from strong sea breezes, the early pioneers found its milder climate perfect for

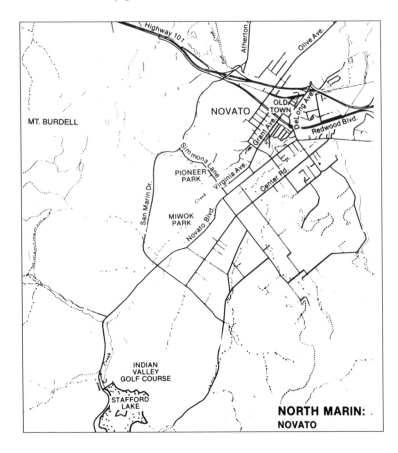

NORTH MARIN: .
NOVATO

growing fruit. Joseph B. Sweetser and Francis De Long bought 15,000 acres in the mid-1850s. De Long eventually bought out his partner and by 1880 had 20,000 apple trees, 3,500 pear trees, 3,000 apricot trees, 200 cherry trees, 600 peach trees, 500 almond trees, and a vineyard with 8,000 vines. Dr. Galen Burdell's wife planted an orchard of tropical fruit with orange trees from Los Angeles, Japan, Florida, and Tahiti.

The center of town was originally around Novato Creek on the old country road now called South Novato Boulevard. Local products were shipped out by barge and scow to San Francisco and to points east and west. The same water transports brought supplies to Novato and the North Marin area.

Trains came to Novato in 1879, connecting Sonoma County to Novato, Ignacio, and San Rafael. The railroad enabled school children to attend high school in San Rafael, and workers could commute to San Francisco by a variety of connections.

Produce could now be shipped quickly, and it found a ready market. Frank Gnoss, a Swiss immigrant to Novato, raised hens and planted fruit trees such as peaches and apricots. (Two of his sons have served as county officials: William A. Gnoss was a county supervisor from 1952 to 1971, and George Gnoss was county clerk from 1962 to 1974.)

Trains arrived in Novato in 1879. (Arrigoni Family Collection)

The area around the railroad station—where there were hotels, a blacksmith, a grocery, livery stables, and a cheese factory—was then referred to as "New Town," and the area around Novato Creek became "Old Town." The first Novato school was built in 1859, and the picturesque Presbyterian church was erected in 1896. The school was located at the corner of Grant Avenue and US 101 at what is now called Redwood Boulevard.

In 1918, an area of lots named the Sweetser Subdivision Number One, in the district of First through Seventh streets, was offered for sale. The population of Novato continued to increase, especially in the 1930s, with the construction of Hamilton Field, though the Depression nearly wiped out Novato's big orchards and poultry farmers. Prices for products dropped so low that orchards were left to die, and many small farmers lost their land.

After World War II, tract homes began to be built for the big population boom. The freeway was constructed and ran right through the heart of town (the bypass was not built until the 1970s). In 1948, the North Marin Water District was formed, making Novato independent of the Marin Municipal Water District. A drive to incorporate the city began in the 1950s and finally succeeded in 1960. The city now could exercise control over the housing development. Novato continues to grow but does so in an orderly, planned fashion.

Old Town Novato

Old Town Novato is the part of town that grew up around the old train depot at the east end of Grant Avenue at Railroad Avenue (it was known then as "New Town"). The picturesque depot, painted in mustard and brown colors, was built in 1917 to replace an earlier station. It closed in 1959 as there were no more passenger trains running through Novato, although occasionally a freight train still passes through.

Near the train station, at 701 Scott Court, is the historic Flatiron Building. This elongated, triangular-shaped structure has had a checkered career as a Wells Fargo office, drugstore, news-

Gina Burrafato at the old Novato train station.

paper office, antique shop, real estate office, bookstore operated by the John Birch Society, and sandwich shop.

The remodeled stores of Old Town Novato are along three blocks of Grant Avenue east of Redwood Boulevard. There is a western theme, even an antique metal hitching post. On this tree-lined street are antique shops, a saddle shop, restaurants, and many specialty stores.

Novato's Municipal Buildings

Two blocks north of Old Town are several historic buildings now being used by the community. When in 1960 Novato voted to incorporate, the old Presbyterian church, located at the southwest corner of Sherman and De Long, became its city hall. The interior was remodeled for offices and the outside painted red with white trim. The entrance foyer is now decorated in a turn-of-the-century decor with old photos of the Novato area and two heavy wooden church pews for seating.

North of the city hall are two houses also taken over by the city for offices. One was the church parsonage, used for many

The Novato City Hall.

years by the police department, which is now occupied by the finance department.

The Novato Community House, built in 1923, is west of the city hall on Machin and now houses the city council chambers. Painted a deep red to match the city hall, the Community House still has iron horse-head hitching posts in front. This building has always been the nucleus of Novato's cultural and social life. Senior citizen groups meet here for bingo, cards, and pool, and the Novato Community Players present their productions here. Preschool children also use the facilities for a variety of programs.

Across De Long Avenue from the city hall is the Novato History Museum and Archives at 815 De Long Avenue, founded and directed for many years by Novato volunteer city historian, Peg Coady. The Novato Historical Guild, which she organized, runs the museum. Peg now lives in Auburn, California. The Novato History Museum was then directed by Jacqueline Moore for the next fourteen years, but she has also retired.

This pioneer house, built around 1850, was once the home of Henry Jones, the local postmaster. Its style of architecture is called "eclectic pioneer," which incorporates various European architectural styles remembered by the pioneers and used when they built their homes.

The house was originally located in Old Town. On June 11,1972, it was donated to the city by Fabian Bobo and moved to

The Novato History Museum.

its present location where restoration began. The museum opened on June 6, 1976. The archives and collection of artifacts cover the period from post-Indian to the present and include a section upstairs designated the "Hamilton Field Room." It contains a collection of photos and artifacts about the former active air base. The museum also has many oral history tapes made by members of Novato pioneer families.

You may visit the Novato History Museum on Wednesdays, Thursdays and Saturdays from 12 noon to 4:00 p.m., except holidays. For an appointment for group tours on other days, call 897-4320.

NOVATO HISTORY
MUSEUM
897-4320

Next door to the museum, at 807 De Long Avenue, is the Novato Chamber of Commerce, located in what was a Queen Anne-style cottage purchased in 1902 (or 1904) by Charles Edgar Carlile. Close to the house is a three-story wooden water tower.

Restoration began in 1973 by Landmark Associates. The water tank was moved slightly and connected to the house, and unique offices were built in both. The "tank house" now features a circular staircase, exposed beams, redwood walls, and three offices on three separate levels; the house has five offices. Call 897-1164 for more information.

NOVATO CHAMBER
OF COMMERCE
897-1164

NOVATO CITY HALL
897-4311
website:
www.ci.novato.ca.us

The phone number of the Novato City Hall is 897-4311 and their website is: www.ci.novato.ca.us.

Pioneer Park

About a ten-minute drive from Old Town is Pioneer Park and the old Pioneer Cemetery. Go west on Grant Avenue, which runs into Virginia Avenue at a slight right angle. Virginia Avenue ends at the park, whose entrance is on Simmons Lane.

The nine-acre Pioneer Park was constructed by volunteers in 1971-72. The city has made regular upgrades to the facility and it has become the community's premier park, hosting the summer music series, the city's annual tennis tournament and a series of special events.

The restoration of the old cemetery which had been heavily-damaged by vandals was led by a citizens' group formed by Peg Coady. The original plan was to level off the knoll and remove all the old headstones, but the citizens' group saved the historical cemetery and restored it with a budget of $2,600 plus thousands of hours of volunteer time. (In 1974, Peg Coady and Will Lieb won an award from Novato for the "best citizen project of the year" for their work.)

Today, the park can be enjoyed by all with its well-groomed, sloping lawns, picnic tables under tall shade trees, a children's playground, a gazebo, and four tennis courts. The park is open between 6:00 a.m. and 10:00 p.m. Note that dogs must be on a leash, and fires may be built only in barbecue pits.

The old cemetery is at the top of a knoll and you can reach it by climbing stairs made of railroad ties. Towering above the marble gravestones are two obelisks marking the burial sites of the cemetery's earliest occupants, Mrs. Charlotte C. Haven (1861) and Maria Ingalls Sweetser (1876). Other members of the Sweetser family, who originally owned the land, as well as many prominent Novato pioneers, are buried here.

Walking among the gravestones and reading the names and epitaphs of these early settlers, you can begin to imagine what it was like one hundred years ago in the frontier town of Novato.

Miwok Park

Miwok Park, which includes a Coast Miwok village archeological site, is just west of Pioneer Park at 2200 Novato Boulevard. Here, on thirty-four acres, are lawns and shaded picnic areas, a creek, a banquet-sized barbecue with sink facilities, a preschool children's playground, and two bocce ball courts.

A garden identifies "California Native Plants used for tools, food, shelter, clothing and basketry by Coast Indians." Remains of the archeological dig have been moved inside, but occasionally arrowheads and other artifacts are found under the trees along the creek.

The Marin Museum of the American Indian (formerly the Miwok Museum) was opened in 1973 as the Novato Prehistory Museum in a small two-story house donated by Crocker Bank. The museum contains artifacts found in the archeological site, plus collections of Indian art of the Americas from Alaska to

South America. There are tools and baskets, mortars and pestles, collections of obsidian arrowheads and clam shell beads, a quiver with bow and arrows, and fishing equipment. A display shows the uses the Indians made of tule, a low, bulrush marsh plant. Tule was woven into receptacles for serving food, deermask hunting disguises, and leggings and moccasins. It was also used for constructing houses and building canoes.

In addition to the permanent exhibit showing the life of the Coast Miwok, there are changing exhibits on other North American Indians. Programs include demonstrations in basket weaving, puppet shows of Indian tales, Indian games, a Miwok discovery hunt and hands-on activities such as grinding acorns in authentic stone mortars.

MARIN MUSEUM
OF THE AMERICAN
INDIAN
897-4064

Admission to the museum, located at 2200 Novato Boulevard is free, although a small donation is requested. Hours are 10:00 a.m. to 4:00 p.m. Tuesday through Saturday, and noon to 4:00 p.m. on Sunday; closed Monday and most holidays. Special tours and field trips may be arranged. Call 897-4064.

Indian Valley Golf Course

Opened in 1958, this 212-acre public golf course is most famous for its elevator (which looks like a tram) running between the thirteenth green and the fourteenth tee. The clubhouse, with a fully-stocked pro shop plus the "19th Hole" Bar and Grill, has a lovely view of Stafford Lake. The turnoff to the Indian Valley Golf Course is 1.8 miles west of Miwok Park on Novato Boulevard (which becomes Hicks Valley Road). If you are driving north on Highway 101, take the last exit, the San Marin/Atherton Avenue off-ramp. Turn left over the freeway and drive for three miles The last stop sign will be Novato Boulevard. Turn right on Novato

INDIAN VALLEY
GOLF COURSE
897-1118

Boulevard and drive for 1 1/2 miles. The entrance will be on the left. Call 897-1118.

Stafford Lake County Park

The entrance to Stafford Lake County Park is on Hicks Valley Road, approximately half a mile beyond the entrance road to the Indian Valley Golf Course.

Indian Valley Golf Course.

The park covers 139 acres, and many picnic areas lie scattered about on the manicured lawns sloping down to the lake. Several of the picnic tables are protected from wind by semicircular wooden structures. In the winter, visitors will find a flock of Canada geese.

Other facilities here include barbecues, a children's play structure, softball field, volleyball court, and horseshoes. Two large picnic areas are each capable of accommodating up to five-hundred people, but a permit must be obtained.

A new game called disk golf consists of throwing a frisbee into baskets. Players must go around trees and rocks to reach the baskets on a course spread out like a golf course. The baskets are about 100 yards from the starting point, and par is 2, 3 or 4. There is also a 2 1/2 mile Terwilliger Nature Hike. Annual fireworks are displayed on the Sunday before Labor Day.

The park is open from 7:00 a.m. to 8:00 p.m. in summer and 9:00 a.m. to 5:00 p.m. in winter, and there is a parking fee. Rules prohibit boats, pets, open fires, swimming and wading. For more information call the Marin County Parks Department at 499-6387.

MARIN COUNTY PARKS DEPARTMENT 499-6387.

The children's playground at Stafford Lake County Park.

GNOSS FIELD—MARIN COUNTY AIRPORT

The Marin County Airport, originally called the Novato Airport, was started by Paul W. "Woody" Binford, a flight instructor in World War II. In 1946, Woody leased farmland two miles north of Novato, built a dirt runway and a T-hanger, and with one airplane—an Aeronca Champion—began teaching students to fly.

In 1947, Binford took in a partner, Jack Lewis, who added his own plane, and the two men built a second hanger. Binford had found that the angle of the runway was not quite right for the heavy winds whipping around Mt. Burdell, so they carved out another one 3,000 feet long in a east-west direction.

Now the airfield met the requirements of the Civil Aviation Administration (now the FAA), and they could teach flying to ex-GIs, who could use service benefits to pay for lessons. Eventually, the flying school grew to six planes and fifty students.

In 1949, the government changed the rules; GIs enrolled in flight training had to prove they were specifically going to use the skill in their vocation. This killed the program, and by Octo-

Marin Builders Exchange Picnic at Stafford Park in Novato.

ber 1949, Binford and Lewis had given up their lease on the land. Harry Tollefson, another flight instructor from World War II, took over and ran the airport facilities until the county of Marin bought him out in 1968.

The new Marin County Airport was named "Gnoss Field" for North Marin's popular supervisor, William Gnoss, who had worked hard for many years to expand aviation in Marin. At the dedication ceremonies, Woody Binford flew the first plane into the airport—a large, single-engine Navion that seated four people. Bill Gnoss was his special passenger.

The current major runway was paved in 1968 with asphalt six inches thick, and upgraded in 1995 with new runway reconstruction and better lighting. The runway lies north to south, is 3,300 feet long, 75 feet wide, and stands two feet above sea level.

A helipad was constructed and lighted in 1996 and the taxiway reconstructed and lighting upgraded in 1998. AWOS III P, which is a weather system, was installed in February 1999. It can be reached at 897-2236 or 120.675 on VHF radio.

AWOS III P 897-2236 or 120.675 on VHF radio.

The biggest problem pilots face here are seasonal strong rolling gusts of winds from the western hills, especially in the spring and fall. The master plan at Gnoss Field calls for a runway extension to a possible 4400 feet, a possible parking ramp expansion, and construction of a cross-wind runway. All prospects are pending environmental studies and FAA funding. A control tower may someday be constructed at the direction of the FAA, pending adequate traffic to meet the criteria for the need of one.

A rotating beacon of light showing the location of the airport shines from sunset to sunrise. The runway and taxi ways are lit at night, and there are VASI (Visual Approach Slope Indicators) red and white vertical approach beams.

Gnoss field has around thirteen aviation-related companies: North Bay Aviation and Airward, flight schools; Sunset Aviation, an aircraft management and charter company; the T.J. Aircraft Sales and Wingover Enterprises, aircraft sales; Northern Lights Aviation and Flight Wash, aircraft maintenance; Sky Ranch Upholstering; Pilot Testing, pilot flight exams; EDMC Petroleum, aircraft fuel service; Direct Avionics, aircraft radio and avionic sale and service; Prichard Corporate Air Services Inc., helicopter flight instruction; and Briles Wing and Helicopter, helicopter charter.

An estimated 50,000 annual takeoffs and landings occur at the county airport, and all of the 235 privately and county owned hangers were occupied at the end of the Twentieth Century.

The address is 451A Airport Road, Novato. For information call 897-1754. Weather reports for landing may be obtained by calling 897-2236.

GNOSS FIELD
897-1754

Weather reports
for landing
897-2236

THE BUCK INSTITUTE FOR AGE RESEARCH

The Buck Institute for Age Research celebrated its grand opening September 30 to October 1, 1999, in its I.M. Pei designed facilities at 8001 Redwood Boulevard, Novato. Two buildings, encompassing Phase One, were dedicated for scientists to conduct their research on the problems of aging.

The complex is being built on 488 acres on the eastern slope of Mt. Burdell. Phase One includes the Research, Support and Education building which houses the 238-seat Drexler Auditorium, the epidemiology study, administrative offices, the library, and the future site of the bioinformatics group. The second building contains a laboratory consisting of 104 lab benches, three reading rooms and offices for twelve faculty. Three more laboratory buildings and one-hundred and thirty affordable housing units for Buck Institute staff will be built in Phase Two.

The Buck Institute for Age Research was founded in 1987, the result of a court case in which the County of Marin sued the San Francisco Foundation which was handling a twelve million dollar bequest left by Beryl Buck to benefit Marin. When the San Francisco Foundation tried to break the will so they could spend the money elsewhere, the County of Marin sued. Using their own County Counsel, Douglas Maloney, Marin battled for two years before the San Francisco Foundation withdrew from the fight.

The court settlement established the Marin Community Foundation plus three major projects, including the Buck Institute for Age Research, Beryl Buck Institute for Education, and the Marin Institute for the Prevention of Alcohol and Other Drug Problems.

The Buck Institute for Age Research is the only project to have its own facilities built so far, though the Marin Community Foundation will soon build on a site in San Rafael next to the Falkirk Community Center on Mission Avenue. According to Tom Peters, The CEO of the Marin Community Foundation, the building will be started in the spring of 2000, and the Foundation will move in during the summer of 2001. The Foundation headquarters will be built of recycled materials such as wood from an East Bay army base. Peters calls it a "green building" and there will be no air conditioning except for two meeting rooms. People will be expected to open their windows for fresh air. Owning their own building will save the Foundation money instead of leasing space for offices, approximately four million dollars over twenty years.

Beryl (Hamilton) Buck was a nurse who married one of her patients, Leonard Buck. She was from Marin and grew up in Sausalito with her mother, May, and brother, Ray Hamilton. Her father, Charles Frank Hamilton, was an engineer on the North Shore Railroad until a fatal accident in July 1903. According to a July 3 local newspaper account, his train hit a cow on the tracks between Ocean Roar and Tomales.

Hamilton was struck by a shower of wood from the tank and was hurled out of the cab. His head was crushed and five ribs were broken, his death occurring instantly...

When Hamilton died he left his wife, May, and two children: Beryl, age eight, and Ray, age 2.

After Beryl's father died, the family moved to Oakland where her mother worked as a milliner. Beryl trained as a nurse in Berkeley at what is now Herrick Hospital. There she meet Leonard Buck, a University of California student recovering from a back injury. They were married in 1914. Leonard was the son of oil industrialist Frank Buck.

Beryl and Leonard had no children, but raised their two nephews, Lee and Leonard, through their school age years.

Beryl held onto some holdings in an obscure oil property in Kern County, Belridge Oil, which had originally been developed by her father-in-law. In her will she gave some of this stock to be used for the benefit of Marin County. Her estate grew over 70 times after her death to the unexpected and lasting benefit of Marin.

The probate of Beryl Buck's will was complete in 1979, the same year Shell Oil bought out Belridge Oil. In 1984 the San Francisco Foundation sued to break the will, a trial ensued and after a two-year battle in which lawyers billed their clients for over 10 million dollars, the San Francisco Foundation eventually withdrew.

The Marin Community Foundation took over the distribution of the trust in 1987 and the site on Mt. Burdell was purchased to build the Institute for Age Research. It consisted of 488 acres and cost 5.8 million dollars. In 1989 I.M. Pei was selected as the architect to design the institute.

Lawsuits in 1991 and 1992 by the Bay Area Legal Foundation and some animal rights groups, including the Humane Society, challenged the legality of the project. The lawsuits lost, but an environmental report suggested there might be earthquake problems with the site and a new one was selected.

In 1995 a countywide referendum on the Institute lost, but a similar one voted on by the residents of Novato won and the site was annexed to the city. Another lawsuit challenged that action and was tossed out of court. Construction began in 1996 and a dirt berm was built to block a view of the Institute by residents of a subdivision, Partridge Knolls. In the following year landslides damaged houses in the subdivision and the berm was removed. More suits were filed and are pending.

By June 1999 the trust had grown considerably to 1.136 billion dollars and the Marin Community Foundation has become the third-largest community foundation in the nation. The Buck Institute for Age Research currently receives five-and-one-half-million dollars annually from the Buck Trust and also seeks funding from other corporate, government and foundation sources.

The Buck Institute for Age Research hopes to extend the healthy, productive years of human life through basic research and education. Specifically, they are working . . ."to delay the onset of diseases like Alzheimer's and Parkinson's by developing early, predictive tests coupled with therapeutics to treat these diseases."

BUCK INSTITUTE FOR AGE RESEARCH 209-2000; Website: www.buckcenter.org.

For information on the Buck Institute for Age Research, call 209-2000; website: www.buckcenter.org.

The Buck Institute for Age Research north of Novato.

PROFILE: **Douglas J. Maloney**

Doug Maloney's contributions to Marin are legendary. He was appointed County Counsel of Marin at the young age of 29 after two years as the Assistant County Counsel and went on to serve for another thirty years. His victory over hordes of corporate lawyers in the Buck Trust Litigation, dubbed "The Super Bowl of Probate," would have been enough to distinguish any career. He retained the one-half billion dollar bequest in Marin (which has now grown to over a billion) for the benefit of its citizens and formed the Marin Community Foundation, after six months of trial on live television. During the trial Maloney told the judge, "If Lorenzo de Medici had adopted the same policies as the San Francisco Foundation, there would have never been a Renaissance."

His victory was hardly a surprise. Shortly after Maloney became County Counsel, he argued the question of reapportioning Marin's supervisorial districts in the California Supreme Court. Fresh from that challenge, he led the team of government lawyers who attacked and obliterated San Francisco's attempt to impose a commuter tax on Marin citizens. With typical audacity, he told the court that the brown lunch bags the commuters threatened to carry to the city symbolized the bags of tea that colonists threw into Boston Harbor, and that Mayor Joe Alioto was King George III in disguise.

When the Golden Gate Bridge District ignored the pleas of commuters and hiked tolls, Maloney was back in court, calling the late October increase a "treat" for the bridge directors and a "trick" on the commuters. The rate hike was invalidated, and the Bridge District was forced to allow free passage on the bridge for a month to reimburse the riders.

Any County Counsel of Marin is immersed in land use, and Maloney led the way, helping to devise the A-60 zoning which has kept West Marin rural, and then going to Court and defending it in Barancik v. The County of Marin, a major national legal precedent upholding agricultural zoning. At the same time, he helped acquire thousands of acres of open space by purchase and condemnation, and raised money to create the Marin Open Space District. He also negotiated the purchase of land for the Indian Valley Campus site, Mc Innis Park, and the Buck Institute for Age Research.

Few lawyers could hope to equal Doug's legendary win in the Buck Trust lawsuit, but on May 15, 2000, he went on to achieve one of the highest jury verdicts in Marin History. The Las Gallinas Valley Sanitary District tried to grab 82 acres of the historic Silverira Ranch for a pittance. They offered the land owners a scant 650,000 dollars. Doug took them to court and conviced a blue-ribbon jury to award the Silveira family 15,663,000 dollars.

Outside of Maloney's duties as County Counsel, he found plenty of time to contribute to the community. He has written fourteen plays and musicals which have raised tens of thousands of dollars for groups such as the Women's Political Caucus and the Marin Conservation League, as well as for several political campaigns. He was a member of the Board of Directors and legal counsel for the Marin Symphony for twenty-five years, and most recently President of the Marin Shakespeare Company. As President of the Buck Institute for Age Research, he convinced the fabled architect I.M. Pei to come to Marin and design its magnificent buildings.

Marin is magical. Doug's wonderful Irish sorcery is one of the reasons why.

OLOMPALI STATE HISTORIC PARK

M arin County residents who have been involved with archeological studies of the Miwok Indians claim that the Indian
mounds at Rancho Olompali, north of Novato, are even older
than Site #38 at Miller Creek, which goes back 2,600 years. Archeologists have spent several years at Olompali, but much more
research needs to be completed. Some people claim the Indians
occupied the site between approximately 6000 BC and 1852 AD.

An interesting theory of the history of Olompali was put
forth in 1979 by Dr. Robert C. Thomas, an East Bay physician. In
his book *Drake at Olomp-ali,* he claims that Sir Francis Drake, on
his circumnavigation of the world in 1579, anchored his ship,
the *Golden Hinde,* in the Chol-Olom harbor on the Petaluma
River, then sojourned for a month on the Rancho Olompali site.

Thomas traces his ancestry back to Camilo Ynitia, the last
Indian chief at Olompali, who received the rancho as a Mexican
land grant in 1843. Thomas's great-grandmother was Maria
Antonia Ynitia, daughter of Camilo Ynitia. Thomas suggests
the name Novato originated with Drake, who called the area
"Nova-Albion" and added the Indian word "ko" to identify the
native people. "Nova-Albion-Ko" became shortened over the
years to "Nova-Ko" which eventually became "Novato,"
(Another theory is that Novato was named by a priest in honor
of Saint Novatus.) One piece of evidence supports Thomas's
claim: in 1974 an Elizabeth I coin, a silver sixpence showing the
image of Queen Elizabeth I and dated 1567, was unearthed at
Olompali by anthropologist Charles Slaymaker, a San Francisco
State graduate student.

Slaymaker, who obtained a doctorate at San Francisco State,
went on to become an independent archeologist and also worked
at the Miller Creek site. The artifacts he collected at Olompali
between 1972 and 1977 amounted to between 50,000 to 100,000
beads, bones, bottles, obsidian flakes and other specimens which
are now in storage at the University of California, Davis.

Ruins of adobe buildings used by the Indians still stand at
Olompali. When they were built is in question, but it was most

likely in the 1830s. An account in the *1880 History of Marin* states that members of a Spanish expedition taught the Indians to make adobe during a stop there in 1776. Subsequent historians claim it would have been impossible for the adobe bricks to have been mixed, formed, sun-dried, and placed in construction in the short time the Spanish were there.

Probably these Indians learned the construction of adobe when they helped build a new church for the San Rafael mission. After its completion in 1824, some of the Indians were allowed freedom. They returned to Olompali and constructed the first adobe there sometime before 1828.

The application for the Olompali land grant was actually made by Mariano Vallejo, commandant at Sonoma, in the name of Camilo Ynitia. It was awarded on October 22, 1843. James Black, originally from Scotland, who at this time was assessor as well as coroner, set the grant at 8,456 acres. Camilo Ynitia sold James Black the property in 1852 for $5,000 in gold coin.

Recreation of a native American village at Olompali State Historic Park.

Black gave the land to his daughter Mary when she married Dr. Galen Burdell, a dentist, in 1863. The couple moved onto the property three years later. In 1874, Mary visited Japan and came back with plants and Japanese gardeners who laid out the first formal garden in Marin.

In 1913 their son James and his wife Josephine remodeled the old timber house into a stucco mansion, incorporating the old adobe within its walls. This house remained in the Burdell family until 1942. After changing hands several times, the house burned in 1969. Some of the original adobe walls survived.

For about a year previous to the fire and for a short time thereafter, the mansion and surrounding acreage were occupied by a hippie commune called the "Chosen Family." The commune was financed by its founder, houseboat-builder and real estate speculator Donald C. McCoy, Jr. Among the inhabitants were show people including the Grateful Dead, and school teachers—even a former nun. McCoy's relatives fought in the courts to prevent him from spending his entire fortune on the venture, and the police made raids on the dwellings in search of drugs. Because the members of the commune frequently wore no clothing, especially around the pool, the Chosen Family became a curiosity, but the members were rarely seen in town except for occasional visits to the local ice cream parlors.

Tragedy and near tragedy always hovered close to the Chosen Family. In a short time two children drowned in the pool. Commune members escaped injury when the house burned on February 2, 1969, but Novato Fire Chief George Cavallero died when his car plunged off Highway 101 as he sped to the fire following a fire truck. With hopes for an idyllic life dashed by internal problems and tragic events, the Chosen Family left Olompali not long after the fire.

In 1972, Rancho Olompali was designated a Historic Place on the National Register and became a State Historical Landmark.

Charmaine Burdell, the granddaughter of James Burdell Sr., lived at Olompali as a child. She is very interested in history and has studied the life of Olompali's original owner, Camilo Ynitia. The Burdells enjoyed lovely formal gardens, several magnificent old magnolia trees, agaves, pomegranate trees, date palms, and other majestic palms. There was also a handsome circular rock grotto with a fountain and a miniature volcanic rock mountain in the middle, once topped by a stork. As a child, Charmaine Burdell swam in this grotto; when it was emptied, she used it for roller skating.

The old adobe walls built by the Indians are fenced-in and protected under a makeshift wooden roof. This is all that remains of the Miwok who lived quietly on this land until the Spanish padres came and changed their lives. The marsh where the Indians once canoed was filled years ago to make way for Highway 101.

In October 1990, the 700 acre site opened to the public as the Olompali State Historic Park. Some restoration of the formal gardens was accomplished by Marin County youths working for the Youth Conservation Corps.

A group called the "Olompali People," led by June Gardner, raised some money to commission a general plan for the park which called for a visitor's center, a restored blacksmith shop, and the building of a model Miwok village. A glass conservatory would also be built and the formal gardens completely restored. This plan was approved by the state in 1988.

The park is the site of some interesting history. Besides the possible Drake visit, Olompali is remembered as the site of the only skirmish of the Bear Flag Revolt. William Todd, believed to have been the nephew of Mary Todd Lincoln, was taken prisoner along with other Americans and held by the Mexicans at Rancho Olompali. (Todd had designed the flag for the revolt, which is now the California state flag.)

Today visitors can still see the adobe ruins and the remains of the gardens. The park is being restored, including the Burdell buildings and the barn, and a Miwok village is being built. The park is west of Highway 101 about 2.3 miles south of San Antonio Road, north of Novato. From the south, drive to San Antonio Road and make a U-turn back to the entrance. For information call 892-3383.

OLOMPALI STATE
HISTORIC PARK
892-3383

Old St. Marys
OF NICASIO VALLEY
ESTABLISHED 1867

Mass 11:15

West Marin　　　　　　　　　　　　　　　10

The Pastoral Inland Valleys

The pastoral valleys of West Marin have changed very little in the past 140 years. Today, there are dairy ranches and a scattering of small towns. Visitors and residents delight at the open hills and fields dotted with grazing cattle, horses, and deer.

The valleys were part of two Mexican land grants awarded in 1844: *Rancho de Nicasio*, granted to Pablo de la Guerra and Juan Cooper, and *Rancho Canada de San Geronimo*, given to Rafael Cacho.

Early California pioneers ranched this country, hunted the plentiful game, and fished for steelhead trout and salmon in Lagunitas Creek. The trains reached the valley in 1875, and many travelers decided that this was the perfect vacation spot. Early settlements were tracts of summer homes; later these were converted to year-round residences.

The peaceful rural existence continued undisturbed until 1967 when suddenly there was talk of a major freeway going through the Ross Valley and continuing west. It threatened to open up West Marin to big real estate development.

For the next six years, preservation of this land became a dominant issue in Marin politics. The freeway was stopped with the election of Peter Arrigoni and Michael Wornum to the Marin County Board of Supervisors in 1968. Their leadership resulted in the Board of Supervisors acting on a request to the State of California in 1971 that this stretch of road be eliminated

◄ *Old St. Mary's Church, Nicasio.*

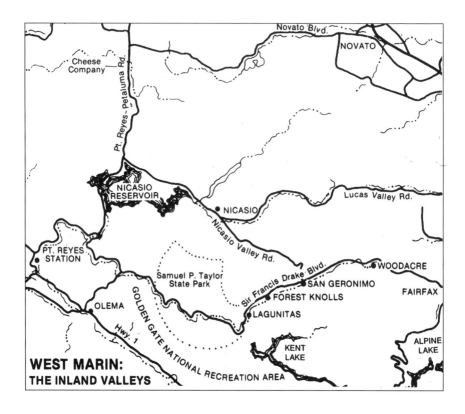

from the state freeway system. In 1973, in a series of controversial votes, the Board created a new agricultural zoning which provided that only one residence could be built for every sixty acres. The votes were three to two with Arrigoni, Wornum and Arnold Baptiste voting for the A-60 zoning and a new County-wide Plan. This overturned the West Marin General Plan of 1967 which had included proposals to build freeway routes from Highway 101 to West Marin. The new zoning applied to a large portion of West Marin's 350,000 acres, and resulted in assuring that the rural flavor of this area would be preserved.

The next critical election came when Gary Giacomini was elected to the Board of Supervisors, taking office January 1, 1973. He defeated pro-development candidate Michael Peevey to represent West Marin. Giacomini served as the watchdog of the agricultural interests and coastal preservation for the next twenty-four years and proved to be one of the most effective supervisors ever elected in Marin.

The West Marin valleys are just over the hill from Fairfax. After passing through the town of Fairfax, Sir Francis Drake Boulevard begins the climb up and over White's Hill. This mile-and-a-half of curvy two-lane road is a continuing problem for the highway department, as it cracks and slides regularly. The hill was an even larger problem in the early 1870s when the railroad was being built. Rather than going over the top, railroad officials used Chinese labor to build a 1,200-foot-long tunnel through the hill near the summit. In 1904 they opened a second tunnel, 3,190 feet long, and eliminated a 4.7-mile climb. Both tunnels are closed today.

As you cross White's Hill, you leave the suburbs behind. The open hills are before you, gold in summer and fall, green in winter and spring. Though only seven miles from the freeway, the valleys are a peaceful change from busy, suburban Marin.

As the road levels out at the bottom of White's Hill, a sign points to the left. This is San Geronimo Drive, leading to the tiny hamlet of Woodacre.

WOODACRE

The land around Woodacre was once owned by Adolph Mailliard, grandson of Joseph Bonaparte, Napoleon's brother. Mailliard maintained three dairy ranches as well as a mansion here. (The Mailliard home later became the Woodacre Lodge and the Woodacre Improvement Club until it burned in 1958. The family remained prominent in Marin affairs for many years. Adolph's great-grandson, William Somers Mailliard, represented Marin in Washington, D.C., as a congressman from 1955 to 1974.)

When the North Pacific Coast Railroad arrived in 1875, the valley was suddenly opened up to San Francisco commuters. Two stations were eventually built in Woodacre: the Woodacre Lodge Station (near the old grocery store on what is now Railroad Avenue, south of Carson Road) and the Woodacre Station

The train station in Woodacre. (Old postcard, courtesy of Bill Allen)

(to the northwest, just south of Park Street). The tracks came straight from the tunnel through White's Hill and into the heart of town. Carson Road crossed under the tracks and was called the "subway." You can still see evidence of the abutments.

In 1907, the railroad changed to a broad gauge and became the Northwestern Pacific. Two commute trains ran morning and evening with a midday freight; train time to San Francisco was one-and-one-half hours.

In 1913 the Lagunitas Development Company built a summer-home tract here, and Woodacre could then be called a "town." The Improvement Club was organized in 1924, and a post office was opened a year later.

Train service was discontinued in 1933 and since then, although the population has increased, little else has changed. Woodacre is still a small country town, and it is not at all unusual to see kids riding horses down the middle of the main streets.

The Woodacre Improvement Club (also known as the San Geronimo Valley Swim and Tennis Club) offers sports facilities which include two tennis courts, a basketball court, an adult swimming pool heated all year, a children's pool heated from April to October, ball fields, and a clubhouse. Classes for children include trapeze, master swim classes and a swim team; there is a children's playground which the community built on land donated by the club. This is open to the public, as is the ballfield. The pool is open to the public for a fee on Tuesdays between 1:00 p.m. and 5:00 p.m.

The Woodacre Improvement Club is located at One Garden Way. To get there take the Woodacre exit off Sir Francisco Drake Boulevard and go to the stop sign on Railroad. Turn right toward Carson and immediately take a left turn onto Castle Rock. The club is located on the right at Garden Way and Castle Rock.

WOODACRE
IMPROVEMENT
CLUB
488-0708

The Spirit Rock Meditation Center at 5000 Sir Francis Drake Boulevard in Woodacre was built on 412 acres of land purchased from the Nature Conservancy in 1988. Today there are four residence halls, a dining room, council house and meditation hall, but the structures cannot be seen from Sir Francis Drake Boulevard. Spirit Rock offers meditation classes and retreats. Call 488-0164 for information, or see their website at: www.spiritrock.org.

SPIRIT ROCK
488-0164
website:
www.spiritrock.org

Above Woodacre and running clear to Lagunitas is the 1549 acre Gary Giacomini Open Space Preserve, formerly known as the Skye Ranch. This preserve borders Marin Municipal Water District property, as well as the Marin County Open Space District's White's Hill preserve.

While 88 acres were acquired in 1991 in Forest Knolls, the bulk of the preserve was purchased from developers in December 1995 for 2.1 million dollars. The purchase was made with 1.05 million dollars from the Marin Open Space District and 1.05 million dollars from the Marin Community Foundation.

The Gary Giacomini Open Space Preserve is open to the public for hiking, but access and parking are problems. Visitors can park in downtown Woodacre and hike a mile from Railroad Avenue up to Carson Road, Conifer Way or Buckeye Circle to enter. Access is also possible by hiking up from the Shafter Bridge near Samuel P. Taylor Park.

PROFILE: **Gary Giacomini**

Gary Giacomini served on the Marin County Board of Supervisors for twenty-four years, longer than any Supervisor in Marin or even in the State of California. He took the oath of office at the age of 33 on January 1, 1973, then won five more elections, serving until January 1997. His District Four represented three-fourths of Marin, including twenty communities in West Marin, Muir Beach, Muir Woods Park, Homestead Valley, Larkspur, Corte Madera, East San Rafael and West Novato.

Giacomini voted as a conservationist while serving on the Marin Board in addition to twenty-five other boards and commissions. He worked diligently to see that the A-60 zoning was upheld and agriculture protected. He was also a driving force to enlarge the Point Reyes National Seashore and the Golden Gate National Recreation Area. One of his proudest accomplishments was being among the founders of the Marin Agricultural Land Trust (MALT), an organization created to buy up development rights to property, mostly in West Marin, to save land in perpetuity.

Giacomini was a hero, along with County Counsel Douglas Maloney, in saving the Buck Trust for Marin County when the San Francisco Foundation tried to break Beryl Buck's will. She designated a certain amount of money be spent for charitable and religious causes in Marin only. The court battles lasted between 1984-1986 when the San Francisco Foundation withdrew, and the Trust has now grown to over a billion dollars.

The outcome of this expensive court victory was that three special projects were established under the auspices of the Marin Community Foundation established in 1986. Giacomini is credited with shepherding through the building of the new I.M. Pei designed research facilities in Novato for one of them, the Beryl Buck Institute for Age Research, which opened in 1999.

Giacomini also spent twenty years as a Director on the Golden Gate Bridge, Highway and Transportation District and was serving as president at the time of the bridge's 50th Anniversary, May 24, 1987. An estimated 500,000 to 800,000 people showed up to walk the bridge and celebrate. The day ended with Tony Bennett crooning "I Left My Heart In San Francisco," and 20,000 fireworks shells being launched from six barges anchored in the bay. Giacomini was instrumental in installing the lovely soft lights that were put in place at that time and now illuminate the bridge at night, a reminder of this special celebration.

Gary Giacomini grew up in Belvedere and San Rafael, attended Marin Catholic High School and St. Mary's College in Moraga. He went on to law school at Hastings College of the Law, graduating in 1965. He then took a job with the Freitas Law Firm, but after being elected to the Board of Supervisors dropped his practice to become a full-time supervisor.

One of the government bodies on which he has had a lasting impact is the California Coastal Commission. During the ten years he spent serving on this organization, he attended meetings up and down the State of California, helping to protect the coast from big development such as designs on Pebble Beach, a proposed West Marin golf course and off-shore oil drilling.

After his retirement from the Board of Supervisors, Giacomini took a position with the Golden Gate Bridge's law firm, Hanson-Bridgett, and opened a Marin County office for them on Wood Island in Larkspur. His practice concentrates mainly on agriculture, land-use and coastal issues.

Gary Giacomini lives with his wife, Linda, in San Geronimo in a house once owned by Van Morrison. For the past twenty years he has devoted most of the time not already committed to public service to his love of gardening and the endless outdoor projects on his twelve-acre property. He tackles his begonias and other favorite flowers with the same enthusiasm and passion as he did his many West Marin projects and problems.

Giacomini has two sons, Andrew and Antony, and three grandchildren. In 1997 he was named the Marin Citizen of the Year by the Citizen's Foundation of Marin and the Marin Council of Agencies. In the same year he received an honorary degree from Dominican University.

COUNTY OF MARIN
PARKS
DEPARTMENT
499-6387
For more information, call the County of Marin Parks Department at 499-6387, and ask for an Open Space Ranger. A book titled *Open Spaces, Lands of the Marin County Open Space District*, by Barry Spitz, copyright 2000, is helpful in finding your way around all thirty-two preserves in the county.

SAN GERONIMO

SAN GERONIMO
WATER TREATMENT
PLANT
945-1505
From Woodacre, Sir Francis Drake Boulevard continues on through the rolling hills of this lovely valley. Just past Woodacre, on the parallel San Geronimo Valley Drive, is the San Geronimo Water Treatment Plant. It was built in 1962 by the Marin Municipal Water District and serves the residents of the San Geronimo Valley and all areas north of Corte Madera to what was Hamilton Air Force Base. It is open to the public by appointment from 9:00 a.m. to 3:00 p.m., and an interesting tour acquaints visitors with the procedures for purifying and filtering water. Call 945-1505 for an appointment.

Farther on is the tiny town of San Geronimo, on the south side of Sir Francis Drake Boulevard. Adjacent to the Valley Community Church is the old railroad station. The building was moved west from its original site for the safety of the children who attend the church nursery school.

Half a mile west of the San Geronimo train station was a gold mine begun in 1878 by Adolph Mailliard. By 1880, the mine was being operated by fourteen men who worked in three shifts of eight hours each, plus two engineers who worked twelve-hour shifts. The *1880 History of Marin County* reported that the value of the ore averaged from $30 to $40 per ton, although it had yielded up to $90. The ore contained gold, silver, iron, manganese, antimony, and tracings of nickel.

On the north side of Sir Francis Drake Boulevard is the clubhouse of the San Geronimo Golf Course. This attractive public course, covering 150 acres of the old Roy ranch, began operation in 1965. A subdivision was created at that time, allowing a few homes to be built around the golf course on lots of one to ten acres. The golf course was closed for several years, then

The San Geronimo Golf Course.

reopened in 1986. For information on the golf fees call the pro shop at 488-4030; for restaurant, cocktails, and clubhouse rentals, 488-8180. All facilities are open to the public.

SAN GERONIMO GOLF COURSE 488-4030; for restaurant, cocktails, and clubhouse rentals, 488-8180

Here at the golf course, Nicasio Valley Road intersects Sir Francis Drake and leads north toward the town of Nicasio, at the geographic center of Marin County.

To visit the Roy's Dam fish ladder, turn south off Sir Francis Drake (or left as you are driving toward West Marin) onto Nicasio Valley Road, then left again on San Geronimo Valley Drive. Just a short way down is the fish ladder reconstructed in 1999 to benefit the coho salmon and steelhead. You can drive into the San Geronimo Golf Course and park, then walk over to a viewing area on a bridge. The project was spearheaded by the Marin Chapter of Trout Unlimited with the help of businesses and other volunteers who gave their money energy, supplies and labor.

As you look down from the bridge, you will see four large pools running down plus an old narrow fish ladder on the side. A large stone with a plaque identifies the project as "Roy's Dam to Roy's Pools Restoration Project, November 20, 1999." It also lists and thanks the major contributors.

FOREST KNOLLS

Continuing west on Sir Francis Drake, Forest Knolls is approximately one mile away. This is another area where one-time summer homes are now year-round residences. There are also a few shops.

LAGUNITAS

Lagunitas is just a short distance past Forest Knolls and marks a change in terrain—from open hills to redwood forest. Again, as a result of the railroad, people began buying cottages in this area around 1905.

Just past Lagunitas, the public may view salmon spawning in an area set up for that purpose by the Marin Municipal Water District and named in honor of a former director. It is called the "Leo T. Cronin Fish Viewing Area." Cronin is remembered as "the fish's best friend" for a life dedicated to improving its habitat. The area also has an informational display on coho salmon (silver) and rainbow (steelhead) trout.

The salmon begin coming up streams in Marin to spawn when the first rains start, usually in October and running through February. The viewing area is open from dawn to dusk from December 1 to February 28 with sixty minutes of parking allowed.

The Leo T. Cronin Fish Viewing Area is below Kent Dam right off Sir Francisco Drake. Cross the long green bridge before Samuel P. Taylor State Park, and you will see a parking lot on the left. Usually there is a locked gate barring the road, but the Water District leaves it open for the public during the time the fish are spawning.

SAMUEL P. TAYLOR STATE PARK

The road is now shaded by thick stands of redwood trees, with lush ferns growing beneath. Seven-tenths of a mile past Lagunitas, a sign welcomes you to Samuel P. Taylor State Park. The Irving Picnic Area, the park office at the main entrance to the camping area, and the Madrone Picnic Area are all just off Sir Francis Drake Boulevard.

Picnicking, hiking, swimming in Papermill Creek, and camping under the redwoods are just as popular here today as they were over a hundred years ago when the North Pacific Coast Railroad deposited vacationers at the two-story hotel and into the Camp Taylor grounds.

At that time there was a paper mill here, built along the creek by Samuel Penfield Taylor, a transplanted Easterner. It supplied newsprint, bags, manila wrapping, election ballots, and other paper products for San Francisco.

Taylor's first mill opened in 1856 using a waterwheel. A larger mill was built in 1884 using steam power. Chinese supplied rags from San Francisco for the paper, and some of them worked at the site.

A small town emerged known as "Taylorville," which consisted of about a hundred families, a boardinghouse, store, hotel, post office, blacksmith, and a carpenter.

The old paper mill at Samuel P. Taylor State Park. (Courtesy of Bill Silverthorne Photo Collection)

State Park Ranger Jim VanCott welcomes visitors to the Samuel P. Taylor State Park.

Taylor died in 1886, leaving his widow, sons, and brothers to run the business. Using the land as collateral, Mrs. Taylor borrowed money from Alexander Montgomery; when the country suffered a depression in 1893, she was unable to repay the loan. After Montgomery died, his widow Elizabeth married Arthur Rodgers, who eventually gained control of the property by foreclosure.

The land became a park in a very roundabout way. Boyd Steward, a West Marin rancher from a pioneer family, remembers the story well. In 1924, a year after his family bought their ranch, Boyd, then a student at Stanford, was sent by his father to visit Elizabeth Rodgers in her suite at the Fairmont Hotel in San Francisco.

Boyd was understandably nervous. He was to discuss a mutual boundary between their lands which had not been clearly established. At that time, Mrs. Rodgers owned about 25,000 acres in the Camp Taylor-Devil's Gulch area. When Steward told her what he wanted, the widow consulted a set of books and thumbed through several before finding the papers that identified this property. Then she asked him to do something for her. She had decided she would give the land encompassing Camp Taylor to the county for a park. Boyd was to present the offer to the Marin County Board of Supervisors.

Stewart carried out her request, but the Board of Supervisors refused the offer, preferring instead to collect the taxes. Rebuffed, Mrs. Rodgers countered by refusing to pay taxes on the parcel. This eventually resulted in default on the land to the county.

The Marin County Conservation League then became interested and urged the county to forego the taxes and let the state take over the land. The League put up money for legal fees, waged a large campaign, and emerged victorious; the area became a state park in 1946.

Today there are 3000 acres, many picnic sites, sixty campsites, two group camp areas located in the Madrone Group area which have a combined capacity of 75 people, a picnic area for groups of up to eighty people, and a special area set aside for backpackers and bicyclists. Facilities in the park include rest rooms, potable water, hot showers, picnic tables, and barbecue pits. Horsemen use the Devil's Gulch Camp, which has a hitching rack, eight pitted corrals, three wire and post corrals, watering troughs, pits toilets, and camping facilities for up to 24 people and twelve horses. Reservations are necessary. (See chapter 16 on camping and chapter 12 on horses.)

The old mill burned in 1915, and all that is left are rock walls covered with moss and fallen leaves. The mill site is a short distance north of the main picnic area adjacent to the creek; a sign marks the trail down to the ruins. At the site there is a historical plaque and an exhibit of old photographs of Taylorville in its heyday. Iron straps buried in the ground between the mill and the creek once held a redwood flume that brought water to the waterwheel.

Other trails follow Paper Mill Creek and the old narrow-gauge railroad bed. One takes you up to Barnabe Peak, which is 1,498 feet high and has a wonderful view.

The Paper Mill Dam and Fish Ladder are marked by a plaque stating that this was the first fish ladder of its kind on the Pacific Coast. It was designed and built by Stephen Schuyler Stedman in 1887. Duplicates were later constructed elsewhere in California, Oregon, and Washington.

CAMP TAYLOR
488-9897

For more information on Camp Taylor, call 488-9897.

From Samuel P. Taylor Park, Sir Francis Drake Boulevard leaves the thick forest and winds through open hills, meeting Highway 1 at the town of Olema (see Chapter 11).

NICASIO

To reach the town of Nicasio, return to Nicasio Valley Road at the San Geronimo Golf Club. This road goes north through ranchland and redwood trees to Nicasio, approximately 4.2 miles from Sir Francis Drake Boulevard. Lucas Valley Road intersects Nicasio Valley Road about half a mile before the town; this connects with Highway 101.

Nicasio was once a populous village inhabited by the Nicasio Indians, a powerful tribe numbering many thousands. Then the Spanish and the Americans came, and by 1880, only eight wickiups (tule huts) remained.

By the late 1800s, ranching, dairying, and logging the redwood forests were important enterprises in this area. The village of Nicasio was thriving. There was a three-story hotel with twenty-two rooms, a bar, dining room, kitchen and parlor.

Other buildings sprang up—a Catholic church, blacksmith shop, general store, meat market, livery stable, and boarding-house. The post office was established in 1870, followed later by a racetrack and a creamery. A stagecoach from San Geronimo connected Nicasio to the rest of Marin. Nicasio's great ambition was to be the county seat, but this did not happen. It lost that bid to San Rafael in 1863.

Then the railroad came to Marin and roads began to be built, but not to Nicasio, isolated in the center of the county, away from the harbors and centers of commerce. The town was locked in time, and today Nicasio appears more rural than it did in 1880. The center of town is a large open square donated by William J. Miller for the courthouse that was never built. Today it is used for baseball games and town barbecues. St. Mary's Catholic Church stands facing the square. This small white church was built in 1867 of locally-milled redwood. In 1967, St. Mary's parishioners celebrated their hundredth anniversary and were presented by the Native Sons and Daughters of the Golden West with a plaque declaring the structure a historical monument.

The pioneer Nicasio School.

Dairy cattle can be seen throughout West Marin.

Across the square is Druid's Hall, built in 1933. It is used for private meetings of the Nicasio Grove of the Druid's Lodge. The building next door was a pioneer butcher shop that opened for business one hundred years ago.

The only commerce left in Nicasio is the Nicasio Land Company, founded by the late Peter Edwards and now owned and operated by his son, Marc Edwards. A bar and restaurant, Rancho Nicasio, on the site of the old Nicasio Hotel, offers good meals and live entertainment on weekends. The post office, a deli and a public telephone are located in this building.

The old Nicasio School, just north of town on Nicasio Valley Road, was built in 1871 to replace an earlier version erected in 1866. It was declared a historical site in 1959. The building was remodeled and painted red by its owner, the late local judge and avid horseman, Ray Shone. The old school is still a private residence of the Shone family.

Nicasio is the home of artist George Sumner, who came to national prominence in 1985 with his painting titled *Sweet Liberty*. This picture was reproduced as the official poster commemorating the centennial for the Statue of Liberty, July 4, 1986. Sumner is also famous for his "environmental-impressionist" paintings of whales, dolphins and seascapes. He and his wife, Donnalei, a voice artist, work together and have studios in Nicasio and Sausalito. You may tour their studios by appointment, 332-0353.

Tiny Nicasio is also the headquarters of the ever expanding LucasFilm, Ltd., at Skywalker Ranch on Lucas Valley Road. George Lucas is most famous for his *Star Wars* films, but has founded other companies located in Marin and the Bay Area.

In October 1996, the Marin County Board of Supervisors approved a plan for Lucas to build an eighty-seven million dollar office complex to accommodate the growth of LucasFilm in Nicasio. An 184,694 square-foot office building complex is to be constructed on the Big Rock Ranch adjacent to Lucas' Skywalker Ranch. Envisioned are several wings two and three stories high surrounding a courtyard and adjacent to a lake and lagoon. It is designed in the prairie style developed by architect Frank Lloyd Wright with long low roofs with deep overhangs.

In exchange for being allowed to build business facilities in an area essentially zoned for agriculture, Lucas agreed to donate 2,300 acres of land to the Marin Agricultural Land Trust for open space. When construction starts on the adjoining Grady Ranch, another 800 acres will also be donated. This facility will be in addition to the new training institute, visual effects archive and several additional company office headquarters planned by LucasFilm for the Presidio in San Francisco. The facilities in Nicasio are not open to the public.

Nicasio Reservoir

Just past the old Nicasio School, the Nicasio Reservoir begins. Built in 1960 by the Marin Municipal Water District, the reservoir at maximum covers 869 acres of the Nicasio Valley.

The Water District maintains a 100-foot-wide strip around the reservoir and allows fishing and hiking from sunrise to sunset. Fish are no longer stocked by the California Department of Fish and Game, but fishermen can still find crappe, bluegill, and catfish, the latter seeming to thrive in warm, slightly muddy water. Also found are large carp introduced from

PROFILE: **George Lucas**

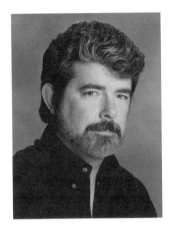

The arrival of George Lucas in Mill Valley in 1969 marked the beginning of what has become a major motion picture empire in Marin. Only two years out of the University of Southern California film school, Lucas had already worked on one film, *The Rain People*, with Francis Ford Coppola, when he and his then-wife, film-editor Marcia Griffin Lucas, rented a house on Varnal Avenue. It was here he edited his first made-in-Marin film, *THX 1138*, a dark and moody look into an oppressive future.

In 1971 the young filmmaker incorporated LucasFilm Ltd. and then began work on the nostalgic *American Graffiti*, filmed in downtown San Rafael and Petaluma. In 1974 he bought a small home in San Anselmo, followed by the purchase of a larger Victorian house in the same town where he established his film headquarters. This Victorian is still his home today.

In 1975-76 Lucas filmed the classic science-fantasy movie, *Star Wars*, which won seven Oscars. It opened in 1977, making movie history and three-million dollars in profit which Lucas used to purchase land for a new headquarters on Lucas Valley Road in Nicasio. He also expanded into four buildings in the Canal area of San Rafael.

In 1985 LucasFilm Ltd. moved into a 50,000 square foot white Victorian mansion built on his 6,000 acre Skywalker Ranch. The house overlooks Lake Ewok and is surrounded by lawns, gardens, vineyards and gardens of organic vegetables plus an olive tree grove. The mansion itself is famous for its glass work, including beveled glass doors and a stained-glass dome in the library. Other buildings were added, including the technical building. At Lucas's request, this massive 120,000 square foot building was designed to look like a winery by the architectural firm of BAR (Backen, Arrigoni and Ross) of San Francisco. Other buildings include stables, a fire department, day-care center, a fitness center, guest facilities and three restaurants.

Meanwhile, Lucas made more films and created several technical companies, including Industrial Light & Magic which has won 14 Academy Awards for Best Visual Effects. Some of his films have included *The Empire Strikes Back, More American Graffiti, Raiders of the Lost Ark, Return of the Jedi, Indiana Jones and The Temple of Doom, Tucker: The Man and His Dream, Indiana Jones and the Last Crusade,* and *Star Wars: Episode I. The Phantom Menace.*

Other companies were formed which assured the continuing prosperity of the company, including LucasArts Entertainment Company, a leading developer of interactive entertainment software; Lucas Digital Ltd., which consists of Industrial Light & Magic; Skywalker Sound, which has been honored with 15 Academy Awards for Best Sound and Best Sound Effects Editing; *THX* (home and theater sound systems); Lucas Licensing; Lucas Learning; and Lucas Online.

A television series, the *Young Indiana Jones Chronicles,* won critical success and many awards, including 26 Emmy nominations and 12 Emmy Awards. Lucas has also created the George Lucas Educational Foundation to explore how technology can facilitate learning. He wants to try to develop more interesting teaching methods for students than those he experienced growing up and attending the public schools in Modesto, California.

George Lucas, born May 14, 1944, in Modesto, California, has been married and divorced and is raising three adopted children as a single parent. His films and merchandise marketing have grown enormously over the years, making him one of the great success stories in the movie business. In 1992 he was honored by the film industry with the presentation of the Irving Thalberg Life Achievement Award.

Lucas purchased more land on Lucas Valley Road, including the Grady Ranch and Big Rock Ranch where he is now building an eighty-seven million dollar office complex to accommodate the growth of LucasFilm.

In June 1999 Lucas was selected as the developer for former military land in the Presidio in San Francisco, some twenty-three acres called the Letterman Complex. He plans to build a large training

PROFILE: **George Lucas,** continued

institute, visual effects archive and a five acre "Great Lawn" open to the public. He will move several of his Marin companies to the new facilities, including Industrial Light & Magic, LucasArts Entertainment Company, Lucas Learning Ltd., the THX Group, Lucas Online and The George Lucas Educational Foundation. His buildings will total 900,000 square feet and include offices, a dining room, child-care facility, employee fitness center and general store in addition to underground parking for 1500 vehicles.

George Lucas has made many contributions to the Marin Community. His companies have participated in the Marin County Fair for many years and have provided computer services to several public schools. In October 1999, he surprised patrons of the Mill Valley Film Festival with a very generous gift of $500,000 to help pay off the two-million dollar debt run up by the refurbishing of the Rafael Theater. In 2000, Lucas donated 800 acres on the southern sloped of his Big Rock Ranch in Nicasio to facilitate an 11-mile trail, part of the Bay Area Ridge Trail. He is considered a good neighbor in Nicasio, and has definitely added a touch of glamour to the county.

Skywalker Ranch.

Europe centuries ago. They are especially popular in the Asian community, and were probably introduced here when fishermen brought them as minnows for bait.

The Nicasio Point Nature Preserve, northeast of the dam site and just off the Point Reyes-Petaluma Road, consists of twenty-two acres of open space. It was donated to the county of Marin in 1968 by William Field. The County Parks Department once envisioned a regional park in this area, but tight budgets precluded its development. There are no public facilities here, but hikers are welcome.

Marin French Cheese Company

The Marin French Cheese Company, founded in 1865, produces the world famous "Rouge et Noir" brand of Camembert cheese based on the famous "Camembert veritable" of Normandie, France. A brochure from the company states that this variety of cheese was named by Napoleon after the tiny hamlet of Camembert in Orne, France, where it originated.

To get to the cheese company, continue on the Nicasio Valley Road 2.7 miles past the reservoir to the intersection of the Point Reyes-Petaluma Road. Turn right and drive 3.2 miles. The curvy road follows a picturesque creek called Arroyo Sausal which flows through hilly ranch country.

Visitors are invited to sample cheese and tour the factory from 10:00 a.m. to 4:00 p.m. daily (except for some holidays.). There are large picnic areas next to a duck pond where picnickers can enjoy their cheese along with wine, beer, sodas, bread and other deli snacks sold inside.

In 1977, a plaque was placed here, dedicated to the California Pioneer Cheese Makers by the Petaluma Parlor of the Native Daughters of the Golden West. The Marin French Cheese Company is open daily from 8:30 a.m. to 5:00 p.m.; it is closed on selected holidays. For information, call (800) 292-6001; website: www.sfnet.net/cheesefactory/

MARIN FRENCH CHEESE COMPANY (800) 292-6001 website: www.sfnet.net/ cheesefactory/

West Marin   11
The Rugged Pacific Coast

The coast of Marin is separated from the rest of the county by high mountains, hills, and the San Andreas Fault. It is an area of inspiring beauty, a world apart. This is a wild and rugged place, with towering cliffs, white beaches, pristine lakes, and thick forests.

Most of the acreage lies within the boundaries of the Golden Gate National Recreation Area and the Point Reyes National Seashore. Except for enclaves of state land and private land at Muir Beach, Stinson Beach, and Bolinas, the Marin coast line is preserved for public use.

A drive from Muir Beach to Tomales, with time out to explore the Point Reyes Peninsula, is an unforgettable experience. Highway 1, the Shoreline Highway, goes up the coast from Muir Beach to Stinson Beach. This narrow road winds along the ridges high above the ocean, and the scenery is breathtaking, the equal of that of Big Sur.

North of Stinson Beach and the Bolinas Lagoon, the road takes an inland route through the rolling hills of the Olema Valley, following the San Andreas faultline. From the little town of Point Reyes Station, Highway 1 continues north along the eastern shore of Tomales Bay. Sir Francis Drake Boulevard, which joins Highway 1 at the town of Olema, goes up the opposite shore of Tomales Bay, then turns west toward the ocean, ending at the remote tip of the Point Reyes promontory.

◄ *The Point Reyes Lighthouse.*

MUIR BEACH

egin your drive up the coast at Muir Beach, which is quite close to Mill Valley in Southern Marin. This semicircular cove on the Pacific Ocean has a lovely sandy beach, creek, lawn, and picnic area with barbecue grills and privies. It is a popular place to fish for surfperch and various species of rockfish. Swimming is discouraged as there are no lifeguards on duty. Dogs are allowed but must be kept under control. Camping is prohibited.

Muir Beach Overlook

One and a half miles north on Shoreline Highway is Muir Beach Overlook. Turn left at a sign that reads "Vista Point" and go through a residential area to the parking lot. The street is also called Muir Beach Overlook. From this small park there are spectacular unobstructed views of the ocean with San Francisco to the south and Duxbury Reef to the north. Whale watching is good from this overlook in December and January when the gray whales are migrating south to their spawning lagoon in Mexico. You can see them spouting far out to sea as they swim by (bring your binoculars).

Military buffs will want to explore the World War II gun emplacements in what were called "Base End Stations." Built in 1940, the stations were used as range finders for coastal defense artillery batteries. They became obsolete after the war.

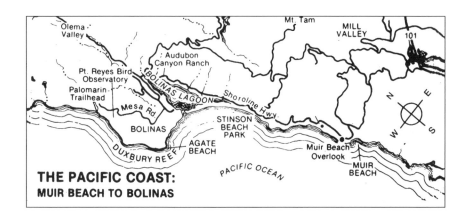

THE PACIFIC COAST:
MUIR BEACH TO BOLINAS

Picnic tables and privies are available here for public use. Several steep paths lead down to rocks below, but watch out— it is a dangerous climb.

Slide Ranch

Two miles past Muir Beach on the winding Shoreline Highway is Slide Ranch, a center for environmental education, nestled above the Pacific Ocean on 134 acres of land slanting down toward the ocean and covered with coyote bush, mustard plant and cypress trees. The property began as a dairy ranch operated by Portuguese immigrants in the early 1900s. It was owned by private families until 1969, when the ranch was purchased by the Nature Conservancy to keep the land from being developed into a housing subdivision.

In 1970, Slide Ranch was launched as a non-profit organization and a few years later became part of the Golden Gate National Recreation Area. Today the Ranch provides farm-based hands-on environmental education through a variety of programs to more than 10,000 Bay Area residents annually.

Visitors to Slide Ranch can participate in school field trips, weekend family programs, and group overnight camps. Facilities include a large remote group campsite at The Dome (located near the farmstead) which can be used for cooking, eating and food storage. Sleeping in this geodesic dome is not allowed. Another structure is The Yurt, which is a circular canvas space for up to 40 people. The Yurt has electricity and drinking water. The public can also rent the sweat lodge and fire circle. The site is a wonderful setting for parties, workshops, wedding and meetings.

Visitors to Slide Ranch learn about where their food comes from, and about caring for ranch animals such as sheep, goats and chickens. Some visitors, especially children, may participate in chores such as milking a goat, baking bread, planting or harvesting vegetables, collecting eggs, making cheese, spinning wool into yarn, or even turning a compost pile. For today's urban and inner city youngsters, these experience can be exciting new adventures.

Visitors are also taken on hikes down to the Pacific Ocean to explore the tidepools. On the way they may see varieties of wildlife such as deer, skunks, and bobcats, plus hawks, gulls and other birds flying overhead.

SLIDE RANCH
381-6155

In late 1999, the Marin Community Foundation awarded $100,000 to reconstruct the old buildings on Slide Ranch, some of which are around one-hundred years old. Plans for the future include building a new farmhouse, staff cabins and a new visitor center.

The address of Slide Ranch is 2025 Shoreline Highway, Muir Beach, Ca. 94965. Call 381-6155 between the hours of 10:00 a.m. and 5:00 p.m. for information and to register for programs.

Steep Ravine

STEEP RAVINE
RESERVATIONS
1-800-444-PARK

Website :
www.reserveamerica.
com
or
www.cal-parks.ca.gov.

For local information,
call Mt. Tamalpais
State Park
388-2070.

Steep Ravine is a state park site on Highway 1 just south of Stinson Beach which contains ten cabins built on cliffs overlooking the ocean. While the cabins are primitive, they are also very popular to rent because of their spectacular views and proximity to great hiking trails. Each cabin can sleep five people and contains a wood-burning stove, table, benches and sleeping platforms. A toilet and water source are located outside, and there are no showers. There are also six small campsites.

The road to get to Steep Ravine is kept locked except for those with reservations. Only one vehicle may be brought in per site. To make reservations, call Destinet at 1-800-444-PARK which is the California Campground Reservation System. Their Website is: www.reserveamerica.com or www.cal-parks.ca.gov. For local information, call Mt. Tamalpais State Park at 388-2070.

STINSON BEACH

Continue on Highway 1 to Stinson Beach. The road from Muir Beach to Stinson Beach is narrow and curvy and needs full attention, so stop at one of the turnouts to enjoy the view of this rugged coastline. As you continue down the road, suddenly you see Stinson Beach below you—a three-mile crescent of white sand, one of the finest beaches in Northern California.

Route 1 becomes the main street of the charming shoreline village of Stinson Beach. You will be delighted with the antique stores and art galleries, many featuring works of local artists. The heart of town is the general store, Beckers-By-The-Beach, which

*Eight-foot dolphin by sculptor Peter Allen in front of the Claudia Chapline
Gallery and Sculpture Garden in Stinson Beach.*

carries groceries, some deli sandwiches, kitchen supplies and just
about anything you might need. Stinson Beach Books is also well
worth a stop; in addition to books and cards, it carries a good
selection of local field guides, nature books, children's books and
toys. You can even find art supplies, housewares and gifts. The
book store stays cozy in winter with a wood burning stove which
is appreciated not only by customers, but by Max, the friendly
resident black lab dog.

PROFILE: **Peter Bishop Allen**

Peter Bishop Allen, born in 1943, lives and works as a sculptor in Stinson Beach. As a member of an old Marin family (his grandfather was founder of Frank Howard Allen Real Estate), Allen grew up around the beaches of the county where he has enjoyed fishing, boating and surfing. His love of the ocean has carried over to his art; he specializes in carving marine mammals such as harbor seals, dolphins, whales, sharks, otters, and sea lions out of recycled old growth redwood. He also has had some sculptures cast in bronze. A sample of his work, a harbor seal sculpture fountain, may be seen in front of the Frank Howard Real Estate office at 505 Sir Francis Drake Boulevard, in Greenbrae (just past the service station west of the Bon Air Shopping Center), while another over-sized harbor seal greets visitors ouside the Seadrift Realty Office in Stinson Beach.

Peter learned to carve from his father, Charles Howard Allen, a sculptor and painter, as did his brother, Wheatly Allen, who sculpts birds. The family boasts of five generations of talented artists.

Peter Allen has had many group and one-man shows in places such as the Bohemian Club, the Hall of Flowers in San Francisco's Golden Gate Park, the California Academy of Sciences, where he was named an honorary field associate, and First World Wilderness Congress in Johannesburg, South Africa. In addition, he has exhibited at several private galleries in New York, Texas, California and Johannesburg. His works may be found all around the world in such diverse places as the private collections of pianist George Shearing, former Philippines President Corozon Aquino, the mayor of Cork, Ireland, and California State Senator Dianne Feinstein.

Peter Allen's sculptures may currently be seen at the Claudia Chapline Gallery and Sculpture Garden in Stinson Beach. The beauty and creative genius of his art brings pleasure and appreciation to all who view his magnificent work.

Marine mammal sculptures by Peter Allen.

A new community library opened in December 1999 in a closed-down convenience store located at 3521 Highway One. Around nine-thousand books, videos, music compact discs and audio tapes can be found in the library's 2400 square feet, which is six times larger than the old facility. The Stinson Beach Library also contains six public Internet stations and two Web-based catalog terminals. Community volunteers raised over $390,000 to get the library up and running. Some 600 donors' names are etched on a glass wall which is on permanent display.

Stinson Beach Park

Beyond the town is the Stinson Beach Park, once known as Easkoot's Beach. Captain Alfred Easkoot, the county's first surveyor, ran an overnight "tent camp" here in the 1870s and 1880s. He supplied dressing rooms and organized parties and fishing trips.

Around 1880, Nathan Stinson and his wife Rose opened a resort that became known as Willow Camp. A dance floor was the main attraction, and guests flocked to the area by wagon and stageline.

Stinson Beach Park.

This was followed by another tent city erected in the early 1900s by Archie Upton, Nathan Stinson's stepson. Upton gave beach property to the county in 1932; seven years later, Marin County bought Willow Camp from Eve Stinson Fitzhenry. The area was maintained as a county park until the state of California took it over in 1950. The beach is now part of the Golden Gate National Recreation Area.

Stinson Beach Park is a popular area for swimming, picnicking, surf fishing and sunbathing. The beach can become crowded on a hot day (a rare occurrence), but you can always find a spot for a solitary walk.

Bird watchers are delighted by the many species here—gulls, sooty shearwaters, pelicans, western grebes, swallows, killdeer, willets, and sandpipers. In winter, thousands of fluttering monarch butterflies cluster in the trees near the beach, displaying their brilliant orange-and-black wings.

Lifeguards are on duty during the summer and on holidays. They sometimes have to close the beach when there are shark alerts which seem to happen every year or so. Facilities include tables, charcoal-grill stoves, and rest rooms. Hours are 9:00 a.m. to 6:00 p.m. in winter, 9:00 p.m. in spring, and 10:00 p.m. after Memorial Day. There is no entrance fee. Call 868-1922 for weather reports, tides, and surf conditions. No camping or pets are allowed.

STINSON BEACH
PARK
868-1922

BOLINAS LAGOON

J ust past Stinson Beach, Highway 1 curves around the 1,034-acre Bolinas Lagoon. This quiet body of water, a Marin County Nature Preserve, is one of the most important of the state's surviving lagoons. It is one of the least disturbed tidelands of California, a rich feeding ground for migrating great blue herons, great egrets, snowy egrets, ducks and other waterfowl.

In the early 1800s, the Bolinas end of the lagoon was a harbor for small ocean-going vessels. "Lighters," or very shallow-draft scows, were used for carrying wood down and across the lagoon to be loaded onto larger vessels at Bolinas.

Later, the lagoon began to be filled up by sedimentation from erosion caused by heavy logging and excessive grazing and planting. The Bolinas mesa was an area of intensive potato growing from around 1860 to the 1920s. Farmers planted their potatoes in straight rows instead of following the curvature of the hills, and soil washed down the furrows into the lagoon during winter rains. Tidal mud flats now comprise around 70 percent of the lagoon's acreage.

Located within the lagoon are Kent and Pickleweed islands, both wildlife sanctuaries. The islands have a permanent colony of harbor seals which increases after pupping season in June, July, and August. More fish are also found in the lagoon during the summer months. The seasonal migration is thought to originate from San Francisco Bay, but may also include seals from other coastal hauling-out grounds such as Drake's Estero.

Pickleweed Island, only one hundred meters from Highway 1, has been used both as a whelping site by the females and a retreat by mothers and pups who prefer to haul out away from the main herd on Kent Island.

To view Pickleweed Island from the edge of Bolinas Lagoon, follow the Shoreline Highway 1.7 miles from the entrance of Stinson Beach Park. There is a small parking area on the right, adjacent to the point where a creek flows under the highway and into the lagoon. Walk across the road past two large posts for the best view of the island. Caution: signs there warn against disturbing the marine mammals, and a fine of up to $10,000 will be levied for each violation.

In the late afternoon the seals often swim out through the entrance of the lagoon into the ocean to feed. People strolling along Stinson Beach at this time can see seal heads bobbing up and down as the marine mammals swim and fish along the shoreline.

A study by the United States Corps of Engineers to be released in 2001 will identify what is causing the sedimentation which continues to fill the Bolinas Lagoon, and suggest possible solutions. The study is being funded by federal, state and local agencies supported by Marin citizens concerned with the lagoon's fragile ecology.

Audubon Canyon Ranch

The world-famous Audubon Canyon Ranch is located along Highway 1 on the Bolinas Lagoon 3.3 miles from the Stinson Beach Park entrance.

Assisted by the Marin, Golden Gate, Sequoia, and Madrone Audubon Societies, the 1,000-acre ranch was purchased in segments over an eighteen-year period in order to preserve the famous heron and egret rookery. The driving force behind the purchases was Dr. L. Martin Griffin who recently wrote a fascinating book about the circumstances of obtaining this priceless site. (The book is titled *Saving The Marin-Sonoma Coast, The Battles for Audubon Canyon Ranch, Point Reyes, and California's Russian River,* copyright 1998, by L. Martin Griffin, M.D., Sweetwater Springs Press, P.O. Box 66, Healdsburg, Ca. 95448, (707) 431-1910.)

Visitors to Audubon Canyon Ranch may hike the half-mile Rawlings or Alice Kent Trails, a steep 250 foot rise, and look down on the nesting birds from a special observation point called Henderson Overlook. Mounted telescopes and binoculars are available for closer viewing.

The four canyons in the ranch are rich in wildlife. As you hike, watch for such species as band-tailed pigeons, hawks, great horned owls, vultures, squirrels, gray foxes, raccoons, badgers, bobcats, and deer.

Several trails lead hikers through forests of Douglas fir, redwood, and other native California trees. Wildflowers present an array of mixed colors in the spring—purple and white iris, blue hound's-tongue, blue lupine, and orange poppies.

Headquarters for the ranch is a two-story 1875 white frame house. Historical and environmental exhibits and a nature bookshop are housed in an old milking barn.

Volunteer Canyon borders on Highway 1 and is open to the public by special arrangement. This is the location of another pioneer house, built around 1852. The canyon was named in honor of the volunteers who fought to save the Bolinas Lagoon from a disastrous oil spill in 1971.

Audubon Canyon Ranch is open 10:00 a.m. to 4:00 p.m. weekends and holidays from the middle of March to the middle of July. This is the time of year when the white great and snowy egrets and great blue herons are nesting in the tall redwood trees. Facilities here include picnic tables and restrooms which are wheelchair accessible, as are the displays. For more information call Audubon Canyon Ranch at 868-9244. There is no charge, but contributions are welcome.

AUDUBON
CANYON RANCH
868-9244.

BOLINAS

The beach town of Bolinas was the busiest spot in Marin in the 1850s. Now it lies hidden down an unmarked road on the west side of the lagoon adjacent to the ocean. Road signs mysteriously disappear in the vicinity of Bolinas as soon as they are put up. The little town is surrounded by parkland and, while not unfriendly, the residents value their privacy.

To visit Bolinas, follow Highway 1 to the north end of the lagoon, just over a mile past the Audubon Canyon Ranch. Turn south, or left, on the Olema-Bolinas Road which is opposite the sign marking the "Rancho Baulines." Historians disagree on the origin of the name "Baulinas" or "Baulenes." In her book, *Bolinas, a Narrative of the Days of the Dons,* Marin W. Pepper states that the name meant "whales playground" in the Indian language. The Spanish word for "whale" is "ballena." Others say that the work simply refers to the Indians who lived in that area. Some sources trace the name to a pilot on the Vizcaino expedition.

The original settlers were a Mexican family. In 1836 Rafael Garcia was awarded a Mexican land grant of nearly 9,000 acres, which he called the *Rancho Tomales Y Baulenes*. A few years later, Garcia turned the area over to his brother-in-law Gregorio Briones and moved north into the Olema Valley. The earliest days were bucolic, with the main occupations being dairy ranching and cattle raising.

When the gold rush boom hit California in 1849, Bolinas was affected immediately. There was a virgin forest here, and lumber was urgently required in the exploding city of San Francisco. Thirteen million board feet of lumber were cut during the next thirty years. Sawmills, wharves, lumber schooners, and steamers became part of Bolinas.

The rugged coastline of the Pacific Ocean. ▶

Along with lumber, other exports—firewood, dairy products, potatoes, chickens, and eggs—brought in big profits. Hundreds of thousands of murre eggs from the Farallon Islands were collected by Bolinas residents and sold, nearly wiping out that unique bird colony.

At this time Bolinas was connected to the rest of the county by boat, wagon road, and horse trails. A road, part of the Shoreline Highway, was opened in 1870. The railroad never made it this far.

Today the way to Bolinas is the same—by water or by the single road. When driving into town, watch on your right for the old Bolinas School built in 1907. At first glance, Bolinas will remind you of a small New England village.

On Wharf Road, which is at the end of the Bolinas-Olema Road, are a variety of shops. Some of these buildings date back to the 1880s. Beyond them is Bolinas Beach, a rocky area which runs between the Bolinas Lagoon and Duxbury Reef.

The Bolinas Museum at 48 Wharf Road is worth a visit to see historic items of the area including documents from the Gregorio Briones family, and memorabilia of Bolinas and West Marin's history. A special exhibit titled "The Living Artists Project Resource Center Gallery" showcases local artists. The Bolinas Museum is open on Friday from 1:00 p.m. to 5:00 p.m., and on Saturday and Sunday from 12 noon to 5 p.m. For information call 868-0330.

BOLINAS MUSEUM
48 WHARF ROAD
868-0330

On your left you will see a row of summer homes built on pilings which jut out over the water. In the 1906 earthquake, buildings in this area were dumped right into the Bolinas Lagoon. Also on Wharf Road is the College of Marin Marine Biology Laboratory, located in an old Coast Guard station that began operation in 1917.

On Brighton Avenue (turn right at the intersection of the Olema-Bolinas Road and Wharf Road) is the two-acre Bolinas Park which has a tennis court, picnic tables, restrooms, and a drinking fountain.

Point Reyes Bird Observatory

On the way out of Bolinas, a side trip to the Point Reyes Bird Observatory will be of interest to all bird lovers. Founded in 1965, this private, nonprofit organization of ornithologists, both professional and volunteer, operate a bird observatory which is open year-round. Point Reyes Bird Observatory (PRBO) works to conserve birds and the environment, using science to find solutions to problems threatening wildlife populations and ecosystems. It also provides conservation and environmental education and participates in the study of marine mammals.

To reach the Point Reyes Bird Observatory Palomarin Field Station, turn southwest on Mesa Road from the Olema-Bolinas Road. In the winter, watch for monarch butterflies in the eucalyptus trees along here. Proceed for about four miles to the site, which is the old Palomarin Ranch and a former religious settlement. (The last half-mile of the road is gravel.)

The Station opens its mists nets and band lab every day except Mondays from May to November. They band three times a week (Wednesday, Saturday and Sunday) from December to April. The nets, which are located along a short loop trail adjoining the field station, are opened fifteen minutes after sunrise and closed between noon and 1:00 p.m. daily. Approximately every thirty minutes the nets are checked and any captured birds are gently extracted and brought to the band lab where they are banded, measured and released unharmed. For weather conditions, call 868-0655.

WEATHER
CONDITIONS
868-0655.

Inside the visitors' room are some interesting displays and information on the Point Reyes Bird Observatory's projects of studying birds and their habitats in the western United States. Included are displays on PRBO's ongoing research on the Farallon Islands. Personnel from the Point Reyes Bird Observatory also reside at a field station on the Farallon Islands, twenty-five miles off the Golden Gate, studying seabirds and marine mammals. Their staff are the sole guardians of this natural resource for the United States Fish and Wildlife Service.

Plans announced in 1999 for remodeling the Palomarin Field Station are now underway. The remodeled facilities will feature an interactive computer learning center, updated displays focused on the observatory's work with ecosystem themes, a membership and merchandise display, improvements to the banding lab, and a small deck with interpretive panels. The Nature Trails will also be improved and a viewing platform built looking at the Farallon Islands with panels describing the research going on there.

Visitors may pick up brochures and pamphlets with valuable information about wildlife in the immediate area and about the activities of the organization. A phone is available at the site, as well as a privy.

POINT REYES BIRD OBSERVATORY
868-1221

E-mail:
PRBO@aol.com

website:
www.prbo.org

The Point Reyes Bird Observatory also has offices located at 4990 Shoreline Highway, Stinson Beach, but they are not open to the public. Call 868-1221 for information; E-mail: PRBO@aol.com, or look at their website:www.prbo.org.

Palomarin Trailhead

Past the Point Reyes Bird Observatory is the trailhead at Palomarin. From here you have access to miles of trails in the southern end of the Point Reyes National Seashore, trails that lead inland and along the coast and to Palomarin Beach.

It is just 2.5 miles on the Coast Trail to Bass Lake, passing Abalone Point. Coast Trail then passes two lakes: Pelican and Crystal. Wildcat Camp, near the beach, is 5.4 miles from the trailhead; Glen Camp, in a protected spot between two ridges, is 7.4 miles. The trail continues along the ridges above the ocean to Coast Camp, 12.5 miles away.

Duxbury Reef and Agate Beach

Named for a steamer that grounded on it in August 1849, Duxbury Reef is often called a "living marine laboratory." Accessible only during a minus tide, the reef reveals a myriad of sea treasures. Tidepool collecting is illegal, as this area is now a marine preserve, called the Duxbury Reef National Marine Sanctuary.

Adjacent to the reef is Agate Beach, a 6.6 acre park providing access to almost two miles of shoreline at low tide. Collecting in not permitted here either as the beach is located within the sanctuary.

To get there from the Bird Observatory, take a right turn on Overlook Drive from Mesa Road (left if you are going directly to the reef from Mesa Road off the Olema-Bolinas Road). Then turn right on Elm and go to the end, where there is a parking lot. Again, do not depend on road signs, as the ones installed—like those leading to Bolinas—are often torn down.

Duxbury Reef is the largest shale intertidal reef in North America, running a mile long and 2,000 yards south into the sea. Its rocks are 28 million years old, though it has been only a million years since the reef was lifted up by an upheaval along the San Andreas Fault. The soft shale is especially fine for boring clams such as the rock piddock.

Be sure to check a tide table, for the reef can be explored only at low tide. You will see countless numbers of marine creatures: barnacles, periwinkles, rock snails, and black turban snails. Carpets of sea anemones look like squishy beds of sandy gravel and bits of shell because the tiny animals attach these materials to their outer surfaces to reflect heat and retain moisture.

Starfish are plentiful on the reef, as are purple urchins which look like lovely violet-colored flowers. Small limpets are found in many varieties, including the slipper, button, plate, dunce cap, and the owl limpet (though the latter is not common on this reef). Also visible are massive beds of California sea mussels and a few red and black abalone.

The priceless Duxbury Reef was endangered in January 1971 when a big oil spill occurred in San Francisco Bay. The reef took the brunt of the first heavy waves of oil that swept the Bolinas-Stinson area.

The great mussel beds were saturated with oil, and patches of tar were flung over the millions of barnacles, limpets, and urchins. Iridescent oily film spread colorfully across the surface of the tidepools. Surf grass and kelp lay in black streaks in the reef's crevices; mats of straw, brought in to absorb the oil, clogged the homes of rock crabs and starfish.

Volunteers began working around the clock to save the reef. They dug the oil out with pitchforks, shovels, and their fingernails. With the volunteers was the late Gordon L. Chan, a biology and zoology teacher at the College of Marin, who had been studying the reef since 1959. He looked for his huge pet sea anemone, Big Tony; he had been hand feeding this sea creature for thirteen years, and found him still miraculously alive after the spill.

To access the damage caused by the oil, Chan conducted a study of the reef, sponsored in part by Standard Oil, whose tankers had caused the spill. He found, in the years following, that life on the reef was gradually returning to normal. Today it has fully recovered and is again rife with sea life.

THE OLEMA VALLEY

From the Bolinas Lagoon, the San Andreas Fault runs north-west through the Olema Valley. Highway 1 follows the fault zone, winding through stands of eucalyptus and over the rolling hills. During the 1906 earthquake, buildings, fences, trees, and the road in the valley were heavily damaged and visibly dislocated. At one time, this slender tranquil valley abounded with wild game. Now, cows and horses graze on the hills though deer are plentiful and sometimes a bobcat can be

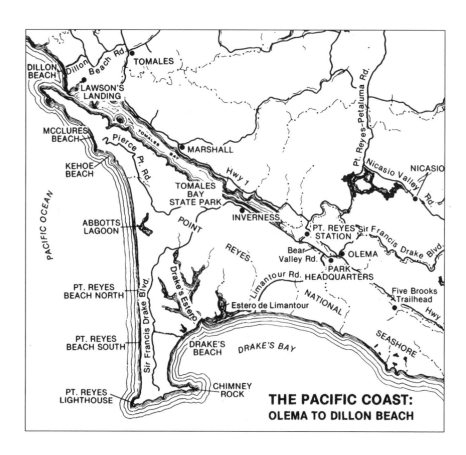

THE PACIFIC COAST:
OLEMA TO DILLON BEACH

seen. Although this is parkland, ranching continues here on a lease-back basis.

West of the faultline is the Point Reyes peninsula, heavily forested and foggy, a contrast to the sunny, open hills to the east. The ocean is cut off from view by the Inverness Ridge, but there are trails—mostly long and steep—that ascend to the ridgetops and lead to fishing lakes and to the coast.

Dogtown

Woodville, originally named by lumbermen, was nicknamed Dogtown for the dogs that hunters used to track bear and deer. The village is located on a curvy half-mile through fragrant eucalyptus trees past the intersection of the Bolinas Road and Highway 1.

In the 1880s, there was a lumber mill here. Reportedly over six million feet of virgin redwood was cut, sawed, and shipped by schooners to San Francisco. With all this activity, a saloon, blacksmith shop, grocery, and department store flourished.

In 1863, two copper mine companies were organized to bring out low-grade copper ore from the William W. Wilkins property at Dogtown. The mine did not produce much ore, though the Union Company dug down to 700 feet.

Wilkins lost a few head of cattle down the mine shaft and went to court in 1904 to clear his land of what was clearly a losing operation. He succeeded in getting a judgment, and peace returned.

The mine was reopened during the First World War when copper was so scarce that even this low-grade ore was mined. A reported 22,500 pounds were taken out by the Chetco Company during those years and ferried aboard the schooner *Owl* to the town of Pittsburg.

Today the old Wilkins Ranch is part of the Point Reyes National Seashore. You may hike into the area marked by a gate north of the Connolly property (a dangerous spot to park, so leave your car farther up the road).

The mine is about a mile northeast of Dogtown in an area old maps called "Copper Mine Gulch." Follow the small stream to the mine. Remnants of the old road are visible, though covered with fallen trees. Pieces of an old boiler and bits of other machinery may still be found on the site. The actual mine shafts have been sealed to comply with a federal law. These shafts are extremely hazardous and, during winter, full of water.

The name of the town was changed back to Woodville well over one hundred years ago to provide "a better image." It was renamed Dogtown by a resolution of the Marin County Board of Supervisors a few years ago.

Twin Lakes

As you continue along Highway 1, 2.8 miles past Dogtown, you may notice cars parked and people carrying picnic hampers headed up the hill to the east. They are going up to the ponds of the old Borello Ranch, called Twin Lakes but often referred to as the Hagmaier or Sieroty ponds.

A large wooden gate cuts off access by vehicle to an old ranch road, so visitors must hike in; it is about a five-minute walk. To reach the lake on the north, head up the old road, then turn left and walk down the hill. To arrive at the south lake, keep hiking uphill, then turn right and go down. This lake may also be reached by walking through a flat pasture to the right of the road. A fast-flowing creek runs adjacent to the pasture.

When you arrive at the lakes, do not be surprised if you encounter someone sunbathing "au natural." GGNRA rangers warn that there are no lifeguards on duty here, and the water can become stagnant in the summer. Except for garbage cans adjacent to the gate, there are no facilities here.

Five Brooks Trailhead

The Five Brooks Trailhead is located at the site of the old Five Brooks Stables. Facilities include a parking area and privies. Hikers may pick up a number of trails here to Bear Valley, Glen Camp, Wildcat Beach and Palomarin.

Stewart Ranch

The Stewart Horse Ranch is the private operation of a second- and third-generation Marin County family who raises Angus

Cattle and Morgan horses and operates under the name "Wood-side." The ranch begins two and one-half miles past Twin Lakes, and the main ranch house is eight-tenths of a mile beyond.

The National Park Service rents the Stewarts' approximately 1,000 acres in this location. Like other private ranchers within the Golden Gate National Recreation Area, the Stewarts retain grazing rights through a lease with the government on they land they once owned.

The family also retains a lifetime residency in the redwood ranch house, built in 1863 and 1864 by Horatio Nelson Olds, who had large land holdings in this area. The Stewart family bought the ranch in 1923, rebuilt the ranch house fireplace, and added barns.

Boyd Stewart, born early in the twentieth century, has lived all his life in West Marin and was a leader in the movement to create the park. He claims that talk about the park began as long ago as 1932. Stewart also notes that the ranches in the area are over 130 years old. The land was bought (not homesteaded) in the period when the great land grants were broken up.

OLEMA

The town of Olema was named after the Coast Miwok Indian village of Olemaloke, which meant "Coyote Village." This tiny hamlet, at the intersection of Highway 1 and Sir Francis Drake Boulevard, 2.5 miles past the Stewart ranch, gives little hint of the bustling activity that went on here 130 years ago.

Historical accounts of pioneer days in Olema mention two churches, seven bars, and a race track. Other services included a post office, grocery store, butcher shop, two hotels, stables, an express office, and a dry goods store. Druids Hall was built in 1881. The old Olema butcher shop, "Gamboni's," shall forever remain a historical relic. In 1967 the front of it was carted off to Washington, D.C., to be used in a display in the California section at the "Hall of Everyday Life in the American Past" in the Smithsonian's Museum of History and Technology.

Today in the town of Olema there are two restaurants, a grocery store, and a campground. The Olema Inn, the old Nelson's

Hotel, built in 1876, which once served as a local bank and stage stop, was remodeled and now contains six rooms, all with private baths. It features a restaurant with an outdoor deck and garden.

A second hotel, the Point Reyes Seashore Lodge (10021 Coastal Highway), opened in June 1988. It contains 21 rooms plus a sitting room downstairs with a stone fireplace and a lovely view of the valley. The Olema Store sells beer and wine, picnic supplies, "healthy munchies," and also has a boutique. The Olema Ranch Campgrounds are open to the public and provide gas, a post office and laundromat.

POINT REYES NATIONAL SEASHORE

Just past Olema is the headquarters of the Point Reyes National Seashore. Some thirty-five miles north of San Francisco, this wild sweep of land has been described as an "island in time."

The triangular-shaped Point Reyes peninsula, separated from the rest of the county by that fissure in the earth known as the San Andreas Fault, is indeed different from the "mainland." Not only the soil and plants but the granite and shale rocks here differ completely from the mixture of sandstone, chert, and serpentine found in the rest of Marin.

Geologists explain that the "island" is moving northwest an average of two inches per year and may have moved 300 miles in the past 80 to 100 million years, lurching ahead whenever there is an earthquake. Rocks matching those on Point Reyes are found an incredible distance south in the Tehachapi Mountains.

Point Reyes was named by Sebastian Vizcaino, who sailed along the California coast in early 1603. On January 6, the twelfth day of Christmas, he passed the peninsula and called it *Punta de los Reyes* for the Feast of the Three Kings.

At that time, there were reportedly over one hundred Coast Miwok Indian villages here. When the Spanish came, the Indians were sent to the missions and few ever returned.

In the days of the early settlers, Point Reyes contained rich cattle and dairy ranches which supplied products for San Fran-

The Bear Valley Visitor Center at the Point Reyes National Seashore.

cisco. Like the Bolinas area, it was also logged. A few attempts were made at developing the land, but these failed, perhaps because the peninsula is isolated and the weather is often cold, windy, and foggy. In any case, Point Reyes made it to the second half of the twentieth century as undeveloped as it was one hundred years before.

In 1935, the federal government began taking a look at this land for a park. In September 1962, a bill was finally signed authorizing the creation of the Point Reyes National Seashore, to include nearly 54,000 acres of the peninsula. The area is now 75,000 acres, and has about 2.5 million visitors annually. The plan for the park is to keep it wild, and with few roads, some leased ranchland, and much of the area formally designated as Wilderness.

Before setting out to explore Point Reyes, visit the park headquarters at the old Bear Valley Ranch. Here you can pick up general directions and maps for the hundred miles of trails and obtain information about fishing, clamming, and horse rentals.

BEAR VALLEY
RANCH
Reservations
663-8054
Headquarters
663-1092
Administration
663-8522

You may also make reservations for the four hike-in campgrounds Monday-Friday, 9:00 a.m. to 2:00 p.m. only at 663-8054. The headquarters is open from 9:00 a.m. to 5:00 p.m. On weekends and holidays it opens at 8:00 a.m., 663-1092. The administration office is 663-8522.

To get there, drive northwest from Olema and turn left on Bear Valley Road. The distance from the intersection to the parking lot is seven-tenths of a mile.

The Bear Valley Visitor Center was completed in 1983 at a cost of 1.4 million dollars raised entirely thorough donations. The center contains a seismograph used for monitoring earthquakes. You can select books, pamphlets, and postcards on the area and study exhibits on geology, natural science, Coast Miwok Indians, early explorers, ranching, shipwrecks, and the park itself. Public telephones, first aid, picnic tables, and restrooms are also available. There are food concessions in the park only during the summer months, so you may want to

The country club built by the Pacific Union Club, 1895. It was located in Bear Valley in the Divide Meadow. (Courtesy of Nancy Skinner)

bring your own picnic supplies. The nearest stores are in Olema, Inverness, or Point Reyes Station.

An educational facility called the Clem Miller Education Center was built in 1987 and accommodates up to 80 people. Located in the heart of Point Reyes National Seashore, this facility includes a commercial kitchen, dining hall, large meeting room, and covered deck. There is also a central bathroom building with heated showers and five recently built cabins, unfurnished except for wooden beds with mattresses. The cabins, with dormitory style accommodations, are without heat, electricity or running water, but can be used as an overnight place to sleep for people attending seminars at the environmental education center.

The trails that begin at the headquarters lead throughout the park, connecting with the Five Brooks and Palomarin trailheads. You can hike or ride horseback through dark forests and open meadows, up the ridges, and down to the beach. There is an easy, level walk along the Bear Valley Trail to the ocean, 4.5 miles away. For the more ambitious, Mount Wittenberg Trail leads up to Mt. Wittenberg for an exhilarating view of the Pacific Ocean, Tomales Bay, and the entire peninsula; farther on, this trail connects with the Coast Trail, following the cliffs along the shore.

For a short walk near the headquarters, try the Earthquake Trail, the self-guided Woodpecker Nature Trail, or the trail to Kule Loklo, a replica of a Coast Miwok Indian village. The Morgan Horse Farm is also open to the public.

A non-profit group called the Point Reyes National Seashore Association was established in 1964 to help support the park and has raised $3,000,000 for projects and programs. The Association is credited with construction of the Clem Miller Environmental Education Center; the interpretive displays at the Lighthouse, Bear Valley and Kenneth C. Patrick Visitors' Centers; wayside exhibits throughout the park; education programs, field seminars, Elderhostel, science and adventure camps for children as well as books and the publication of other materials. For information, write to the Point Reyes National Seashore Association, Point Reyes Station, CA 94956. The website for the Point Reyes National Seashore is: www.nps.gov/pore.

POINT REYES
NATIONAL
SEASHORE
663-1092
Website:
www.nps.gov/pore

Earthquake Trail

If you have ever wanted to know more about earthquakes and what causes them, walk the Earthquake Trail, which begins near the picnic area at park headquarters. This self-guided walk takes you right along the edge of the notorious San Andreas Fault.

Along the 0.6-mile trail, which is paved and wheelchair accessible, you will see the scars of the disastrous 1906 quake; this area, known as the old Skinner Ranch, was near the epicenter. In front of the main ranch house, the ground reportedly moved fifteen feet, nine inches. The garden path that led to the front steps of the farmhouse moved over to face a wall. A cow barn was torn in two when the east side was dragged sixteen feet.

As you walk along, interpretive signs explain the geology of this area and give interesting facts about earthquakes. You will see more evidence of 1906: a fence that was offset fifteen feet, a creek bed that shifted, and an exhibit about the internationally famous cow that was "swallowed up" at the Shafter Ranch, south of the Skinner place.

The cow story is questionable, but the official commission investigating the incident at the time wrote, "A fault crevice was momentarily so wide as to admit a cow which fell in head first and was thus entombed. The closure which immediately followed left only the tail visible." The trail is open daily from sunrise to sunset.

Coast Miwok Indian Kule Loklo Village

Indians have lived in Marin County for at least 5,000 years and in California for at least 10,000. The earliest dated site in Marin is on de Silva Island at the north end of Richardson Bay Bridge.

The Coast Miwok derived their name from a Sierra Miwok word meaning people, although the Coast Miwok used other terms for themselves. Linguists used the term for several groups with similar languages.

They were hunters and gatherers using spears and bows and arrows to kill deer and elk. Arrows were tipped with obsidian, a volcanic glass for which the Coast Miwok traded seashore products to inland tribes. Their diet also included fish and shell-fish, wildfowl, root vegetables, greens, berries and nuts. Food was abundant and varied. A mainstay of their diet was acorns which were ground, leached and cooked in baskets to make the starchy bland food which is represented in our diets by pota-toes, rice, bread and pasta.

The Coast Miwok constructed canoes by tying together bun-dles of tule rushes. These light craft were used for fishing and transportation on bays, but not on the open ocean. Dome-shaped houses constructed of tules and more permanent houses of redwood bark slabs were used for shelter. A men's sweathouse also served as a dormitory where men stayed when they were restricted from contact with women before important activities such as hunting and dancing. Smaller women's sweat houses also existed.

The principal structure in the village was the dance house or roundhouse, a round semi-subterranean structure with a long low entryway. A central hearth was used for fires on ceremonial occasions and dances, most of which were religious. Some dances took place outdoors on the round dance ground.

At Point Reyes, a replica of a Coast Miwok village has been constructed by the joint efforts of the Point Reyes National Seashore and the Miwok Archaeological Preserve of Marin; it is called Kule Loklo, which means "Bear Valley" in the Bodega Miwok language. The village was constructed with traditional materials and methods. Basket making and other traditional methods are often demonstrated on Saturdays. There is also a regular program of interpretive walks to the village.

The dance house is open to the public when the village is staffed. Visitors can enter the shelter through a low tunnel, and upon reaching the main room it is possible to stand upright. A small stone fire ring is in the center beneath an opening in the roof for the smoke to escape. Logs for sitting encircle the fire. Park rangers at Kule Loklo demonstrate Coast Miwok crafts and explain the way of life here centuries ago. Call the Park at 663-1092 for information. School groups may visit with prior reservations.

In 1776, there were 3,000 Coast Miwok living in this area. Then the Spanish missionaries arrived and recruited the Indians for slave labor and forced religious conversion on them. In less than sixty years, only 300 were still alive. Today there are no full-blooded Coast Miwok left, but hundreds of their descendants live in the Bay Area, particularly in Sonoma County, very much aware of their ancestry. Many Coast Miwok people married Pomo people in the 19th century.

In mid-July a traditional "Big Time" takes place at Kule Loklo with craft demonstrations, traditional dancing, food and cultural exhibits. Some of the crafts include basketry, clam disc beading, flintknapping and tule crafts. Indian goods are also for sale. A spring Strawberry Festival, a blessing for the first fruit, is also open to the public.

It is estimated that there are over eighty archeological sites related to Native American history in the Point Reyes National Seashore. The Miwok Archeological Preserve of Marin sponsors adult classes in traditional central California Indian skills at Kule Loklo in the spring and fall. Contact them at 2255 Las Gallinas Road, San Rafael, 94903.

Morgan Horse Farm

The Morgan Horse Farm in Point Reyes began with donations of Morgan colts from local ranchers with the intention that the grown horses would be used by park rangers.

The Morgan breed began in the state of Vermont in the early 1800s with a prodigious horse known as "Justin Morgan." He was only fourteen hands high and was thought to be a blend of thoroughbred and Arabian with some other elements. Today's Morgan horses are known for intelligence, good disposition, endurance, and extraordinary longevity.

Use of the Morgans has vastly improved the quality of contact with visitors to the parks, the rangers declare. People seem more comfortable talking to a ranger on horseback than they would be if the ranger were in a vehicle.

The Morgan Horse Farm has several interesting displays, including an old hay rake, grain driller, mower, and blacksmith shop with an anvil and forge. During summer weekends, visitors may be treated to a horse training and riding demonstration.

Limantour

On Bear Valley Road, about a mile northwest of the park headquarters, you will find the Limantour Road which winds its way over Inverness Ridge and down to the beach at Limantour Spit. It is a lovely, scenic drive to the beach about eight miles away. Going up the summit you pass through forests of Douglas fir and bishop pine.

Along the way, you may be surprised to see what appear to be white deer. These are fallow deer, seen in white and other colors. Imported to Marin in the 1940s, they are originally from the Mediterranean area of Europe. They have large palmate antlers, which are flat, like those of a moose, with up to fifteen points per side. The deer weigh from 130 to 170 pounds. They are usually seen in small herds or family groups of ten to fifteen. They breed in December, and the fawns are born in April or May.

The axis deer, another exotic species of deer that inhabit Point Reyes, were imported from India. These deer are reddish-brown with lines of conspicuous white spots, looking much like a giant fawn. The average adult weight is from 200 to 240 pounds, and they have long slender antlers, most with three points per side.

The axis deer are a herd animal and appear in groups of 5 to 150. This is a tropical species, and the deer breed at any time of the year. They have a strange but distinguishing bark when alarmed or when calling to other herd members.

Also seen with the fallow and axis species are the common California black-tailed deer, a subspecies of the mule deer. Their coat is a tawny yellowish-brown color in summer, with the winter coat being longer and grayer. They breed in the fall—October and November—and fawns are born in the spring. They do not form herds, although a buck may have a small harem during rutting season.

Other animals you might spot here and throughout the park are skunks, rabbits, bobcats, foxes, and raccoons. There are even mountain lions in Point Reyes.

Limantour Spit is a narrow strip of land with a gorgeous white beach. On one side is Drakes Bay and the Pacific Ocean; on the other side is the Estero de Limantour, which is part of the larger Drake's Estero (Spanish for "estuary"). Limantour is named for a French trader whose ship was wrecked here in 1841. The beach is a good one for fishing, swimming, and wading. The estero is spectacular for birdwatching, as it provides food and refuge for the estimated 450 bird species found on the peninsula. Visitors may recognize great blue herons, great egrets, several variety of ducks, sandpipers, cormorants, gulls, godwits, western grebes, and willits.

Now under federal protection—which means no clamming or collecting—the mudflats of the Limantour Estero contain string worms, clams, blue ghost shrimp, giant moon snails, sea slugs, and beds of eel grass.

In the Drake's Estero mudflats, clamming is legal with a California fishing license, and you can dig for horseneck

The schooner Point Reyes, which was owned by ranchers from Pt. Reyes. Approximately 1910-1932. (Courtesy of Nancy Skinner)

and geoduck clams. Hike along the rocky intertidal area and look for sea anemones, limpets, crabs, starfish, and a large kelp bed.

Drake's Estero is known for sharks, rays, and cod, and also for a colony of harbor seals that hauls out on the sandbars within the estero. During the pupping season (March through June), many pups have been sighted. The seals will tolerate humans at relatively close range—200 meters—without stampeding into the water. This provides a unique opportunity to watch mother-pup interactions. It is important to note that mothers often leave their pups alone on the beach, especially when the pups are quite young. Therefore, if you should find a lone pup, please leave it undisturbed.

With its beach, sand spit, and estero, Limantour is one of the nicest picnic areas in the park. Facilities are limited to primitive privies and a gravel parking lot located about a quarter of a mile from the beach.

Point Reyes Hostel

The Point Reyes Hostel is located south of Limantour Road in the former Laguna Ranch main house, about five miles from the headquarters. The hostel welcomes individuals, families, and groups. Please see chapter 16 for details.

INVERNESS

Return on Limantour Road to Bear Valley Road. Turn left and the road becomes Sir Francis Drake Boulevard. Continue 3.3 miles north past Inverness Park to the town of Inverness situated on Tomales Bay.

The San Andreas Fault runs north under Tomales Bay in a straight line all the way to Bodega Bay. In fact, Tomales Bay was formed when the rift opened up and water flowed in. During the 1906 earthquake, huge mud flows toppled piers, stores collapsed, and houses fell off foundations.

Originally a Mexican land grant to James Barry in 1836, *Rancho Punta de Los Reyes* consisted of eight square leagues adjacent to Tomales Bay and surrounded the area where the town of Inverness would be developed. The land grant went through complicated legal entanglements for over twenty years before being acquired in 1857 by two brothers, Oscar and James Shafter, and their law partners.

Thirty-two years later, James Shafter—by then a judge—established the town of Inverness, which he named for the home of his ancestors in Scotland. Judge Shafter died before substantial development was completed, but houses began to be built within the next five years.

Inverness attracted the wealthy from San Francisco, who came to build summer homes, especially after the disastrous 1906 earthquake. The city refugees must not have realized that the same fault that wrecked San Francisco ran right under the peaceful bay they viewed from their windows.

A huge calamity happened in 1995 when a fire, started by four teenage boys who were camping, erupted in Inverness on October 3 and burned for four days. Over 12,000 acres were swept by fire and 44 homes destroyed with losses estimated at over forty million dollars. Fire fighters from all over California were called in to help put out the holocaust which became known as the Vision Fire (after Mt. Vision), but miraculously no lives were lost.

Many of the well-built summer homes in Inverness are now lived in all year. This lovely little town, about three miles north of Point Reyes Station, is surrounded by parkland (Point Reyes National Seashore and Tomales Bay State Park).

The town offers visitors several motels. The Inverness Store supplies groceries, a full deli with hot and cold food to go, liquor, and such services as making duplicate keys and photocopies.

The Bellweather is one of the most photogenic buildings in the county. Built first as a general store in the 1890s, it was toppled by the 1906 earthquake and was rebuilt. The Bellwether has baskets, pottery, handmade items, books, maps, and postcards relating to the area.

Shaker Shops West, at 5 Inverness Way, is a unique furniture and kitchenware store selling furniture which replicates the famous 19th century Shaker crafts. This furniture was based on

Train crossing north of Tomales. (Photo by Roy Graves, 1929. Bancroft Library)

early American designs and was known for the simplicity of the work. The furniture is hand-finished, solid wood and includes chairs, tables, chests and benches. You will find the shop in a white frame house with a picket fence.

Marin historian Jack Mason and his wife Jean lived in Inverness in the first substantial house built here in 1894, which they named "The Gables." Mr. Mason had his own press, North Shore Books, which published his seven books on Marin County history. His home is now a museum located at 15 Park Avenue. Call for hours at 669-1099.

JACK MASON
MUSEUM
669-1099

Inverness has been famous for its two Czech restaurants: Manka's at the Inverness Inn and Vladimir's. Milan Prokupek and his wife Manka originated Manka's Restaurant over forty years ago, while Vladimir's is owned by the Prokupeks' daughter Alena and her Czech husband, Vladimir Nevi. In April 1989, Manka's and the inn were sold.

POINT REYES PROMONTORY

From Inverness, Sir Francis Drake Boulevard continues up the shore of Tomales Bay, then turns southwest and heads toward the ocean. Watch for Mt. Vision Overlook Road on your left. This is a narrow, winding, blacktop road pocked with pits and potholes, but the view of Drake's Estero and Limantour is worth the drive up the mountain.

Another mile and a half down the road is Johnson's Oyster Farm. It is on your left half a mile south on Schooner Bay, part of the Drake's Estero. The oyster farm, in business for over forty years, cultivates oysters by suspending them from wooden frames under water. These horizontal trays are more expensive than the sticks people originally used when they started cultivating oysters, but are safer from predators and easier to harvest. The oysters breed in the summer and take three to five years to grow to eating size.

Point Reyes Beach, North and South

When the road finally reaches the ocean, ten miles of windswept sands face the Pacific. There are north and south entrances 2.5 miles apart, and you will see the signs on Sir Francis Drake Boulevard. Both beaches provide parking lots and restrooms. Point Reyes Beach North is 2.8 miles beyond Johnson's Oyster Farm and about eight miles from Inverness.

Signs warn against wading or swimming since the surf is considered extremely dangerous, with riptides and undertows. In any case, the weather here is really not conducive to swimming. This is a rugged beach, usually cold and foggy, and the coastline is among the most dangerous, having claimed many ships through the years. But this is a fine place to beachcomb, fish and watch for birds and whales (in December and January).

Point Reyes Lighthouse and Sea Lion Overlook

Sir Francis Drake Boulevard ends at the very tip of the promontory at Point Reyes Lighthouse. Just before you reach the lighthouse, seven-tenths of a mile past Chimney Rock intersection, there is a wide space in the road with enough room for about five vehicles to park. This is Sea Lion Overlook.

Take the thirty-two steps down to the viewing area, a sandy spot surrounded by railing. You will hear barking coming from Sea Lion Cove below. Steller's sea lions, California sea lions, and elephant seals are found here. The elephant seal population has grown dramatically in the past ten years with hundreds of pups being born in nearby beaches in mid-January and February. These seals haul out on Limantour and Point Reyes beaches and the north end of Drake's Beach. Their breeding season lasts from December to March. Elephant seals also visit during their molting season from March to July, and the juveniles' haul out period, September to November.

To get a good view of these marine mammals it is best to bring binoculars. Their colors—a dark chocolate when wet and a sandy shade when dry—camouflage them as they swim in the surf or sleep on the rocks.

Beyond the Sea Lion Overlook is the Point Reyes Lighthouse, a very dramatic and exciting place to visit if the weather is clear. The lighthouse sits on the western tip of the promontory, high

Point Reyes Beach.

above the surf. This is one of the windiest, foggiest spots in the entire country, and a lonely and treacherous place for ships. Photographs on exhibit inside the Visitor's Center show ships crashed on the rocks or run aground and the rescues being made. Ten major ships are recorded as being wrecked in the Point Reyes area, and another dozen here at the lighthouse.

The first ship lost was the *San Agustin* at Drake's Bay in 1595. Eleven more ships went down during the 1800s. In 1903, the *S.S. Lurline* was wrecked at Point Reyes Beach, followed in 1910 by the *Annie Smale*. The last was the *Munleon*, which smashed up here in 1931.

The lighthouse was built in 1870 and a revolving three-ton Fresnel lens was installed. Consisting of more than 1,031 pieces of hand-cut crystal, the lens was made in Paris, brought around the Horn in a sailing ship, and hauled from Drake's Bay to the site by heavy oxcarts. The light beamed a one-second flash every five seconds and was visible for twenty-four nautical miles. The source of light was an oil-burning four-wick lamp.

An automated light station was opened in 1975, and it operates a rotating beacon twenty-four hours daily. Also installed here is an electronic diaphone foghorn and a radio beacon.

The old lighthouse, which has undergone extensive repairs, is open to the public from 10:00 a.m. to 5:00 p.m. (steps close at 4:30 p.m.) every day but Tuesday, Wednesday, and Christmas Day. It is closed when the wind exceeds forty miles per hour, so it is wise to phone ahead for weather information to the Lighthouse Visitors' Center, 669-1534.

To get to the lighthouse from the parking lot, walk down the old road, a 0.4 mile hike. Then climb down the long stairway—equal to that of a thirty-story building, says a sign. I counted 311 steps from the overlook picnic deck and Visitors' Center down to the lighthouse. The steps originally numbered over 400, but the climb is broken up by three cement ramps and rest areas with benches.

At the lighthouse you can walk around, looking out at the sea. On the rocks below are thousands of common murres, black and white seabirds about sixteen inches high which stand upright, penguin-fashion. In flight, the murre looks like a small

Hiking down to the Point Reyes Lighthouse.

loon with a slender head and pointed bill. Gulls and cormorants swoop down on currents of wind out over the glistening water.

From this most western spot in the continental United States you can view the spectacular sweep of the Point Reyes Beach, the long, curving line of cliffs toward the north, and the surf crashing upon the rocks. The sea is a graveyard of ships.

POINT REYES
LIGHTHOUSE
VISITORS' CENTER,
669-1534

J.P. Monroe-Fraser wrote in 1880 about a lighthouse:

> *When the winds of ocean sweep with fiercest fury across the trackless main, lashing with water into seething billows almost mountain high, when the black pall of night has been cast over the face of the deep, and ships are scudding along under close reef and storm sails, not knowing were they are or how soon they may be cast upon the rocks or stranded upon the beach, when the storm king seems to hold full sway over all the world, suddenly a flash of light is seen piercing the darkness, like a ray of hope from the bosom of God.*

From the lighthouse you can see whales going south the first two weeks of January and north again during the two middle weeks of March. On a clear day vehicle traffic can get heavy and a shuttle has been set up from the Drake's Beach Parking lot of the

Point Reyes National Seashore for a shuttle ride the last five miles to the lighthouse. This was mandated by Congress as a demonstration program and is still in operation. The service is only on weekends and holidays from January to mid-April when the weather is so good it brings out many people to see the whales. Call the park headquarters, 868-1092, to find out the current fee.

Chimney Rock

On the east end of the Point Reyes promontory is Chimney Rock, a huge sea stack that marks the entrance to Drake's Bay. Go to the Chimney Rock Road intersection, and continue 3.6 miles on this narrow, single-lane blacktop road to the parking lot (no facilities here, just a privy). From this spot it is a thirty-minute hike to the overlook.

In the last few years a new Elephant Seal Overlook has been set up near the parking lot of Chimney Rock. From the lot you walk down a paved trail one-fourth of a mile, pass through a cattle gate and continue on a gravel path to the Overlook. Free docent tours are given weekends and holidays from mid-December to March, which is the time the elephant seals are here to breed. Hour-long ranger led programs on whales or elephant seals are set up on weekends only.

When you walk to the Chimney Rock Overlook, you will pass an old life-saving station built after World War I which then included a five-bedroom house, boathouse, and lookout tower. The Coast Guard took over the station in 1939 and ran it until 1968. In October 1990, it was opened to the public as a National Historic Landmark.

On a metal plaque in the wall adjacent to the steps of the house is an illustration of Sir Francis Drake and a native American. The inscription reads: "On June 17, 1579, Sir Francis Drake landed on these shores and took possession of the country, calling it Nova Albion."

Past the house, the hike is mostly uphill. On the left are old ramps leading down to the water from the boathouse. These were part of the original life-saving station. Thirty-six foot motor lifeboats were carried down to the water on small railroad cars using these tracks.

About twenty minutes into your hike, you will see a sign directing you to an ocean overlook to the right and Chimney Rock to the left. At the end of the hike, your reward is a fabulous view of Drake's Bay with its magnificent white cliffs. The huge sea stack at the entrance to the bay is Chimney Rock.

A granite-boulder reef runs from the steep cliffs in this area out to Chimney Rock. The subtidal area supports a nursery of red abalone, chitons, sunstars, surfgrass, batstar, sea urchins, sea cucumbers, and a variety of crabs and snails. This is a natural preserve area that extends all the way to the lighthouse, and the sealife may not be disturbed.

A special warning: do not try to climb down the cliffs to the beach. They are crumbly and quite dangerous.

Drake's Beach

On the side of the promontory opposite windy Point Reyes Beach is Drake's Beach, facing on Drake's Bay. Swimming is possible here, as this beach is protected from heavy winds by the sheltering sea cliffs. Many small boats seek the quieter water here.

The Kenneth C. Patrick Information Center is open from 10:00 a.m. to 5:00 p.m. (Closed for lunch from 12:00 to 12:30 p.m.) Exhibits include a minke whale skeleton suspended from the ceiling and a 250-gallon saltwater aquarium with species of life from Drake's Bay, including tidepool creatures and mounted local birds. In 1990, the center was expanded to 1,200 feet and now houses fossils discovered in the Drake's Estero and the Drake's Beach areas. These fossil beds were formed from seven million to nine million years ago and are considered the richest whale fossil deposits in the world. Fossils of dolphins, porpoises and sharks are also found.

In addition, there are exhibits about the coast and the relationships between the ocean and the land such as currents, their effect on weather patterns and wildlife, and the geology of the area. The impact of the European explorers who visited here is also examined, such as the shards of Chinese porcelain found on beaches and sites of former Native American villages.

Rangers provide interpretive programs at the Kenneth C. Patrick Information Center, and there are displays on intertidal creatures and shells to touch. The facilities include a book shop, dressing rooms, rest rooms, and a telephone. The Drake's Beach Cafe, the only food concession in the park, is located here, 669-1297.

Look for a granite cross erected in 1946, "In commemoration of the landing of Sir Francis Drake... on these shores." Many historians and history buffs believe that this is indeed the spot where Drake came ashore in 1579.

Another plaque near the information center was dedicated in June 1979 in honor of the 400th anniversary of Drake's landing in Marin. A mile east along the beach at Drake's Cove, an anchor and still another plaque have been erected by the Drake Navigator's Guild, whose members believe he landed in that very spot.

In June 1994, the Marin County Board of Supervisors, without any additional proof, designated that it was official that Sir Francis Drake did land at Drake's Bay. The subject of Drake's landing is still highly controversial, however. Briefly, the story is as follows:

Sir Francis Drake, admiral of Her Majesty's Navy, knighted gentleman, sea pirate, and adventurer, provided the first known

Drake's Beach.

Barbecuing fresh oysters at Drake's Beach Cafe.

record of Marin on his famous circumnavigation of the world, 1577-80. Acting on private orders from Queen Elizabeth to find a suitable site for an English colony in the New World, he enlarged his mission by plundering Spanish ships, cities, and towns along the coast of South America. Although England and Spain were experiencing an uneasy peace, Elizabeth secretly welcomed the Spanish gold.

Drake survived an attempted mutiny, the treacherous water of the Magellan Straits and the loss of four of his five ships and finally arrived in the foggy waters off the Northern California coast in June 1579. He hunted desperately for a safe haven in which to repair his leaky ship.

On June 17, the *Golden Hinde* entered a protected harbor, and Drake's party was able to unload their treasures, overhaul the ship, and repair the leaks. While there, they explored the interior and met with friendly Indians who, according to Drake's reports, offered him their kingdom. He accepted in the name of Queen Elizabeth and left fastened to a large post a plate of brass that claimed the land for his queen. After thirty-seven days of resting and making repairs, they sailed out on July 23, 1579.

Exactly where Sir Francis Drake landed in Marin is a question that has been studied and argued for years. Some historians believe it was here at Drake's Bay, while others think it could have been in the Bolinas Lagoon, Tomales, Bodega, or Half Moon Bay. Others are adamant that Drake discovered San Francisco Bay and landed near San Quentin Point.

Whether or not you believe that Drake landed here, the beach named for him is a gorgeous spot for a picnic or barbecue, beachcombing, fishing, or just walking.

Gulf of the Farallones National Marine Sanctuary

Located off the beaches in this area is the Gulf of the Farallones National Marine Sanctuary, 948 square nautical miles established in 1981. This marine region includes the nearshore waters of Bodega Bay, Tomales Bay, Drake's Bay, Bolinas Lagoon, Duxbury Reef, Estero de San Antonio located north of Dillon Beach, and the Estero Americano which marks the boundary between Marin and Sonoma Counties.

In the middle of the Sanctuary are the Farallon Islands, a National Wildlife Refuge containing thousands of seals, sea

The accident-prone "Ida A" out of Point Reyes which sailed around the turn of the century, aground on the sand at Ten Mile Beach. (Jack Mason Library)

lions and breeding seabirds. The islands, which are adminis-tered by the National Oceanic and Atmospheric Administra-tion, are closed to the public. For information call 561-6622. Website: http://www.farallones.org.

GULF OF THE FARALLONES NATIONAL MARINE SANCTUARY 561-6622.

Website: http://www.faral-lones.org.

TOMALES BAY STATE PARK

After one visits the remote and rugged Pacific beaches, the warm, sandy coves of Tomales Bay seem especially inviting. Sheltered from the wind and fog by the Inverness Ridge, the beaches of Tomales Bay State Park are superb for picnicking, swimming, and boating. There are no boat launching facilities here but kayaks, canoes, and small sailboats can be carried in.

To get to Tomales Bay State Park, take Sir Francis Drake Boule-vard to the intersection of Pierce Point Road. Drive north for a mile to the park entrance. The park is open from 8:00 a.m. to sunset and there is an entrance charge per car. No dogs are allowed. This 2,000-acre park is not part of the Point Reyes National Seashore but is under the jurisdiction of the state parks department.

Upon entering the park, pick up a brochure, then drive a mile to the popular Heart's Desire Beach. Half-mile trails lead north-west to Indian Beach where Coast Miwok Indians used to camp, and southeast to Pebble Beach. You can also take the Johnstone Trail from Heart's Desire Beach to Shell Beach, a hike of four-and-one-half-miles, or hike to Shell Beach from Pebble Beach.

Away from the beaches there are trails through the woods. The Jepson Memorial Grove, a virgin stand of bishop pine, can be viewed from a mile-long trail that runs between the picnic area and Pierce Point Road. These craggy, grotesquely-shaped trees, close relatives of the Monterey pine, have survived here from pre-historic times. The grove is named for the botanist who founded the Division of Forestry at the University of California at Berkeley.

Nature lovers will identify many other native California trees in the park, a variety of berry bushes, manzanita, honey-suckle, and ferns, and over 300 varieties of wildflowers, includ-ing lilies, poppies, wild strawberries, lupine, and iris. Wildlife is plentiful, and bird lovers should look for the rare spotted owl, pelicans, woodpeckers, nuthatches, and many other species.

PROFILE: **Dr. L. Martin Griffin**

Residents of Marin who remember the proud opening of the Ross Valley Clinic in 1951, and the friendly, well-run Ross Hospital, will probably remember Dr. Martin Griffin, who practiced medicine in Marin for twenty years.

Dr. L. Martin Griffin, known to his friends as Marty, was one of the original founders of the Ross Valley Clinic, one of the owners of Ross Hospital and a founder of the Kentfield Psychiatric Hospital. He and his family lived in Kent Woodlands.

Marty was also active in early conservation efforts in the county and was a founder of the Richardson Bay Audubon Sanctuary. He was the driving force in the founding of Audubon Canyon Ranch, and the purchase and preservation of both Kent Island in the Bolinas Lagoon and the Cypress Grove Preserve on Tomales Bay. His award-winning book, *Saving the Marin Sonoma Coast* (1998, Sweetwater Springs Press, P.O. Box 66, Healdsburg, CA. 95448), describes these battles in detail.

In addition to his conservation efforts in Marin, Marty spent time in Nepal leading trips and working to establish a wildlife preserve on the Tibetan border.

On the island of Maui in Hawaii, he was the physician who accompanied the Nature Conservancy expedition that explored the uncut Kipahula Rain Forest. He then worked to establish the Kipahula Wildlife Preserve, which now runs from the Seven Sacred Pools on the Pacific Ocean to the top of Mt. Haleakala.

Marty moved up to Sonoma to become a gentleman farmer on a 240 acre ranch in Healdsburg he purchased in 1961, while still keeping a house in Belvedere. In 1975 he prepared to grow his own grapes at his Hop Kiln Winery (where hops were once grown for beer), and manufacture wine.

What he quickly found out was that starting a new winery can be a very expensive venture, so he went back to work, taking a job at Sonoma State Hospital. After his years in Nepal, he had become interested in public health and had received his Master in Public Health Degree from the University of California, Berkeley, in 1972. This was in addition to his Doctorate of Medicine earned in 1946 from the Stanford Medical School, and his Diplomate from the American Board of Internal Medicine which he received in 1953.

Marty's new job in public medicine was set to last six months. Instead, he stayed for fifteen years. Eventually Dr. Martin Griffin became the Chair of Hepatitis B and AIDS Task Force for all eleven state hospitals in California.

Marty is married to Joyce Griffin, a retired English professor and former head of the English Department at Santa Rosa Junior College. He especially likes to be involved with young people, specifically his four daughters and six grandchildren.

TOMALES BAY
STATE PARK
669-1140

Facilities in the park include picnic areas, restrooms, barbecue pits, and water. Rangers are on duty daily. A small campground is available for hikers and bikers and has a fee. Spaces are given out on a first-come, first-served basis. There are no reservations. Vehicles must be out of the park by sunset.

POINT REYES — THE NORTHERN TIP

N orth of Tomales Bay State Park, you are back in the boundaries of the Point Reyes National Seashore. Pierce Point Road continues north past Abbotts Lagoon and ends at McClures Beach.

There is a scattering of dairy ranches here, and you will see herds of cattle grazing on the gently sloping hills. Farther north you will see some other large creatures grazing: tule elk, once native to this area, were reintroduced here years ago.

Abbotts Lagoon

This quiet body of water is separated from the ocean by a sandbar, although occasionally there is a break and the saltwater comes flooding in. Fishing is good here—the catch includes surf perch, sculpins, starry flounders, and large sticklebacks. There are even rumors of some landlocked striped bass.

The still waters of the lagoon are perfect for canoeing, and the upper lagoon has long been a favorite swimming spot.

Kehoe Beach

The trailhead to Kehoe Beach is two miles past Abbotts Lagoon, and the hike to the beach is around half a mile. It is isolated and wildly beautiful.

Tule Elk Range

In the northernmost part of the Point Reyes National Seashore is a herd of tule elk brought here from the San Luis Refuge near Los Banos, California, to replace herds that roamed freely here

140 years ago. Legend has it that the last Marin County band of elk swam across Tomales Bay and headed north in a mass migration around 1860.

The mature bull tule elk weighs up to 425 pounds and has majestic antlers spanning three to four feet. His triumphant trumpeting call can be heard for long distances during rutting season in the fall. The color of these large but docile animals runs from sandy to darker brown with a buff-colored rump.

You enter the Tule Elk Range when you cross the wide cattle guard that runs across the road. High fences mark the boundary of the range which runs between the Pacific Ocean and Tomales Bay. The animals are free to roam in the Point, but not within the entire Point Reyes Peninsula. They can be seen from the road or trail all year long.

The elk have bred so successfully here that the herd has reached over 500; an experimental contraception program of shots began in 1997 to try to limit the herd to around 470. The program has been about 80% effective.

McClures Beach

As Pierce Point Road meanders north, there are lovely views of Tomales Bay, the Pacific Ocean, and to the far north, Bodega Bay. The road ends at McClures Beach. There is a parking lot here, as well as privies and a telephone.

Visitors are greeted by signs that warn of hazardous cliffs, dangerous surf, and sharks. But don't be frightened: the half-mile hike to the beach is worthwhile in spite of these warnings. Many people feel this is the most dramatic and beautiful of all the beaches in Marin. The cliffs are majestic, with towering granite rocks rising straight up and surf crashing against them. Walk through the tidepools at low tide and look for goose barnacles, sea anemones, sponges, snails, mussels, crabs, and worms. No collecting is permitted.

Birdwatching is excellent, and driftwood may be found after a storm. Surf fishing is permitted, but keep an eye out for incoming tides and watch for "rogue waves"—gigantic waves that sometimes sweep in without warning. And heed the signs—wading and swimming are not a good idea.

The "Samoa," a two-masted steam schooner bringing lumber from Eureka to San Francisco, went aground near Point Reyes on January 28, 1913. The people aboard were saved with a "breeches buoy." (Photo courtesy of Nancy Skinner)

POINT REYES STATION

P oint Reyes Station, originally called Olema Station and even Burdell's Station, was just a stop on the railroad when the trains began running in 1875. Within a year, Dr. Galen Burdell, a dentist and well-known Marin pioneer, had built a hotel and bar to accommodate the new trade. Then called "Burdell's," the building later became known as the Point Reyes Hotel.

The town grew quickly on Burdell's land. Within a short time there were a blacksmith, general store, livery stable, grain warehouse, and bank. Life revolved around the train, part of the North Pacific Coast narrow-gauge railroad, which brought passengers and supplies into town while exporting dairy products and livestock.

The railroad stopped running in 1933, and since then, Point Reyes Station has changed very little except for the growing number of tourists brought in by the Point Reyes National

Seashore. Agriculture is still the main industry, and the town has the appearance of a movie set—"the genuine western town."

To reach Point Reyes Station, follow Sir Francis Drake Boulevard north from Olema (at this point the road is also Highway 1). Just south of town the road crosses a green bridge and then turns left.

As it goes through the center of town, Highway 1 becomes A Street, also known as Main Street. For three blocks it follows the old railroad right-of-way, ending up at the railroad engine house. As you proceed through town, look for the old train station on your right; still painted yellow, it is now the post office. The old hotel, now closed, stands at A and Second streets.

Take some time to explore Point Reyes Station. Toby's Feed Store sells hay and grain to the local ranchers, but it also has some gift items—flowers, plants, sweatshirts and mugs. You can even purchase an original painting here.

Station House Gifts on Main Street sells books, stationery, cards, art and office supplies, and toys. Stop at the Station House Cafe for fried oysters, fresh from Tomales, or pick up picnic supplies at the Palace Market, which offers fresh seafood, natural foods and a deli. For a casual drink, there is the old Western Saloon.

Several shops carry original art created by local residents, including Flower Power, a nursery with local arts and crafts; Viewpoints, which sells local art and imported clothing and rugs; and Black Mountain Weavers, which carries knitted sweaters, quilts, handwoven clothing, and jewelry. The Tomales Bay Foods has delicious cheeses supplied by local farmers. They also sell ice cream and have a deli.

An outstanding photographer, Art Rogers, lives in Point Reyes Station. His work can be seen regularly in the *Point Reyes Light*, a weekly newspaper owned by David Mitchell and Don Schinske. Mitchell won the Pulitzer Prize in 1979, an honor seldom awarded a weekly paper. It was given for meritorious service for his investigative reporting on Synanon, a drug rehabilitation organization turned religious.

In 1989, a new Dance Palace designed to serve as a community center was built by volunteers. The contractor for the project

Train Depot in Point Reyes. (Postcard from Jack Mason Museum)

DANCE PALACE
663-1075
E-mail:
dance@svn.net
website:
www.svn.net/dance

was Jeff Long who, along with a two-person crew, directed the $650,000 project. The complex includes a 250-seat community theater, smaller meeting rooms, an art room and a kitchen. Today the Dance Palace Community Center provides recreation such as basketball, classes, meetings, senior activities and children's classes. For information, call 663-1075; E-mail: dance@svn.net; website: www. svn.net/dance.

Point Reyes Station is the location of Marin Agricultural Land Trust (MALT), a private non-profit organization created in 1980 by a coalition of ranchers and environmentalists to permanently preserve farmland in Marin. MALT purchases conservation easements in voluntary transactions with landowners. By January 2000, they owned forty conservation easements on 26,604 acres in Marin. MALT has produced a ninety-minute audio cassette tape titled, *An Abundant Land: The History of Ranching in West Marin,"* which is a driving tour of West Marin ranchland, from the Point Reyes National Seashore to Tomales. It is narrated by actor Peter Coyote and may be purchased at local book stores or directly from MALT. For information on MALT, call 663-1158; E-mail: farmland@malt.org; website: www.malt.org.

MALT
663-1158

E-mail:
farmland@malt.org

website:
www.malt.org.

Agriculture has always been important in this region, with dairy ranching being the prime occupation of West Marin ranchers. Today agriculture is becoming more diversified as new vineyards are being planted, as well as organic fruit orchards and vegetable farms. Some of the vegetables include organic lettuce, tomatoes and pumpkins.

Other major organic operations in West Marin are the Straus Dairy and the Straus Family Creamery in Marshall. They produce dairy products without the use of commercial fertilizers, pesticides, antibiotics or hormones. Their products include milk, cheese, butter, cream and ice cream.

In the very north of Marin near the Sonoma County border, thousands of olive trees imported from Italy have been planted at Nan Mc Evoy's Ranch and are producing fine oil for sale in restaurants and gourmet grocery stores. Another organic operation is the production of fleece, marketed as pure grown wool, now being grown on the Pozzi Ranch in Dillon Beach.

Still, the dairy industry is the anchor of Marin agriculture, supplying approximately twenty-percent of the milk consumed

Point Reyes Station.

in the Bay Area. Besides dairy cattle, Marin supports a healthy business in cattle and sheep ranching, chickens, eggs, turkeys and turkey eggs. Shellfish, including mussels, clams and oysters, are important seafood products coming out of the Tomales Bay area.

A new concept called subscription farming —selling directly to the consumer or restaurants—is being done by at least one farmer in West Marin. This helps with initial costs and shares the risks. Customers pay in advance in what is known as "community-supported agriculture."

Agritourism—combining agriculture with tourism—is also taking hold in West Marin as more bed and breakfast inns are open on ranches, thus supplementing the ranchers' income.

Giacomini Ranch

In February 2000 the National Park Service purchased the 550-acre Giacomini dairy ranch to become part of the Golden Gate National Recreation Area. It will be administered by Point Reyes National Seashore, as is any parkland north of the Bolinas-Fairfax

Train turned over in the 1906 earthquake at Point Reyes. (Bill King Photo, Jack Mason Museum)

road. The 4.65 million dollar purchase will improve estuary health and shorebird habitat once the wetlands adjacent to Tomales Bay are restored, a job that will begin in about 2002. The task is expected to take until about 2012. The restoration will also improve the flow of Papermill Creek (also called Lagunitas Creek) where coho salmon swim to go up to their spawning grounds.

White House Pool

One mile west of Point Reyes Station is the White House Pool consisting of twenty-four acres with a scenic trail for hiking along Papermill Creek. No fishing is allowed because the coho salmon, which are endangered, also swim through here on their way to spawning grounds. Benches and privies are available. This is also a great spot for bird-watching. For information, call the County of Marin, 499-6387.

COUNTY OF MARIN FOR WHITE HOUSE POOL 499-6387

THE EASTERN SHORE OF TOMALES BAY

On the other side of Tomales Bay, Highway 1 heads north along the curving eastern shoreline. About five miles from Point Reyes Station is the Tomales Bay Oyster Company, which specializes in homegrown Pacific and French oysters plus live clams, mussels, and fresh scallops. It is open daily from 9:00 a.m. to 5:00 p.m. (663-1242.)

TOMALES BAY OYSTER COMPANY 663-1242

Oysters have been cultivated in Tomales Bay since 1875, the year the trains reached here. Two stops on the line were Millerton and Bivalve, towns no longer in existence. At Millerton the oysters were protected from predators by picket fences built out in the water around the beds. Bivalve was established at the turn of the century by the Pacific Oyster Company and was serviced by the railroad, which made daily shipments of oysters to San Francisco.

Two miles past the Tomales Bay Oyster Company is the location of the old Marconi Wireless Company which built a trans-Pacific receiving station here after 1913. The buildings erected were in the Mediterranean style and included a two-story hotel, a warehouse and administrative residences. These buildings were once occupied by Synanon, a drug treatment community. In 1979, they were purchased by the San Francisco Foundation with money from the Buck Trust and are now part of the California Department of Parks and Recreation.

The Marconi Conference Center officially opened January 1, 1990. Located on 62 acres of grass and forests and overlooking Tomales Bay, this California State Historic Park can house up to 96 overnight guests in 40 rooms. All the guest rooms are remodeled and have private baths, telephones, modem ports, coffee makers and study desks. Most have bay, garden or courtyard views. Dining room patrons enjoy a view of Tomales Bay.

A mile past Marconi is the Marshall Boat Works and an impressive array of fishing boats are anchored near shore. A half-mile beyond is the hamlet of Marshall.

MARSHALL

The beginnings of a town—a wharf, hotel, and warehouse— were already in the area of Marshall when the railroad arrived in 1875. The place was named after five Irish brothers, one with a young wife, who had crossed the western plains and arrived in Tomales in the mid-1800s.

Today the town stretches along Shoreline Highway. Businesses include the Hog Island Oyster Company and the ever-popular Tony's Seafood Restaurant, owned by Anton Konatich, which was established in 1948. The Marshall Store, with two decks on the water, serves barbecued oysters, mussels, sandwiches, beer, and wine. Fishermen can also purchase bait here.

In July 1999 the historic 1873 Marshall Tavern was purchased by a real estate marketing consultant from San Francisco, Stephanie McNair. She has plans to restore the structure and open an inn and restaurant which could also be used as a community center.

Audubon Cypress Grove Preserve

North of Marshall (eight-tenths of a mile) is the Audubon Canyon Ranch Cypress Grove Preserve which began with ten acres called the Cypress Grove Promontory, donated by Clifford Conly, Jr., to the Ranch in 1971. The Grove's restored Victorian hunting lodge now houses Audubon's Tomales Bay headquarters as well as their educational and research facilities for salt and freshwater marsh and chaparral habitats. The preserve contains a rich marsh, tidelands, and bird-nesting areas. Subsequent land purchases and donations to Audubon Canyon Ranch enlarged Cypress Grove to 182 acres of tidelands, coastal chaparral and marshland habitat.

A portion of Cypress Grove has been named the Caroline Livermore Marshland Sanctuary; twenty-six acres were dedicated to her as one of the founders of the Marin Conservation League. Audubon Canyon Ranch also purchased Hog and Duck islands in Tomales Bay in 1972. Hog Island reportedly received its name when a barge broke up and its cargo of pigs landed on the island's deserted shores. These islands, along with other strategic pieces of tideland along Tomales Bay, were purchased to protect the shoreline from development. The islands were donated to the National Park Service in 1996.

Between 1968-1985, Audubon Canyon Ranch purchased 432 acres on Tomales Bay and more land was donated, though Audubon has not kept it all. Five acres were given to the California Department of Fish and Game for fishing access to the tidal estuary of Tomales Bay, and twenty-six acres were donated to the California State Parks Department bordering the bay north of Cypress Grove.

For details on how Audubon Canyon Ranch miraculously saved Tomales Bay from commercial subdivision even after a group called Land Investors Research had purchased 7,805 acres for major land development, read *Saving the Marin-Sonoma Coast* by L. Martin Griffin, M.D., Sweetwater Springs Press, P.O. Box 66, Healdsburg, Ca. 95448; (707) 431-1910.

As you continue north along the eastern shore of Tomales Bay where the old trains used to run, you will pass a boat works and marine laboratory. Three miles further is the six-acre Miller Park, developed by the Department of Fish and Game and operated by the County of Marin. Facilities include a long fishing pier, concrete boat launch ramp, parking lot, picnic tables, and privies. There is also a lovely view of Hog and Duck islands.

Marshall Boat Works.

Seven-tenths of a mile north of Miller Park is a place once known as Ocean Roar. No camping is allowed in this county park, but you can park overnight for a fee. If you plan on camping on a beach in the Point Reyes National Seashore and arriving there by boat from Miller Park, it is also necessary to pay a fee for a permit first at the headquarters. Rangers warn of heavy currents at the entrance to Tomales Bay from the ocean. There have been several drownings here because of the currents and a dangerous sand bar which sometimes causes people to lose their boats. The Rangers recommend that boaters go out to the ocean through Bodega Bay.

From the Ocean Roar stop on the railroad, the train turned inland through an area of marsh and tidelands to follow the old estero and creeks up to the town of Tomales. Highway 1 follows the same route, turning inland and heading east toward Tomales. Audubon Canyon Ranch purchased 97 acres in this area now called Keys Creek/Walker Creek Delta Saltwater Wildlife Sanctuary.

An ongoing problem with water quality in Tomales Bay which is being resolved concerns high mercury level and periodic fecal coliforms from livestock which have washed into the bay. The mercury has been running down Walker Creek into Tomales Bay from the old sixteen-acre Gambonini Mercury Mine run by the Buttes Gas and Oil Company between 1964-1970. The mine is located thirteen miles to the east. In January 2000, it was announced that environmental officials had plugged the leak of the toxic mercury in a three-million dollar cleanup. The Environmental Protection Agency filled in a two-acre pit, terraced slopes and added concrete drainage ditches. The Department of Conservation will revegitate the area with trees and grasses. Future tests will be taken on the toxic level of the fish, shellfish and other marine life in the bay.

TOMALES

Before reaching the town of Tomales, Highway 1 is intersected by the road to Petaluma. The original settlement, called Lower Town, was at this location. A hotel, warehouses, and a store were built here by an Irish immigrant, John Keys.

Keys' house still stands and will be to your left on a knoll opposite the Petaluma Road. The house is described in the 1976 Tomales Historic Resource Survey as a "Greek revival farmhouse with shiplap siding," circa 1850. (The house has now been rebuilt and plastered over.)

A post office using the name "Tomalles" (the second "l" was soon dropped) was opened in Lower Town in 1854. Present-day Tomales was once called Upper Town and began when Warren Dutton, Keys' partner, founded his own store here in 1858.

Tomales was a productive agricultural community, second in importance only to San Rafael. Large quantities of potatoes, grain, dairy products, hogs, and beef were shipped by schooner from Keys Embarcadero, down Keys and Walker creeks to Keys Estero, a finger of water reaching northeast from Tomales Bay.

Like Bolinas Lagoon, Tomales Bay was soon silted-up because of erosion, and navigation of the creeks and estuary became impossible. When the train service began in 1875, shipping switched from schooner to rail, and products were sent to the ports of San Quentin and Sausalito.

Upper Town prospered and grew, surviving the 1906 earthquake and a devastating fire in 1920. Sixteen buildings were totally burned in that fire, nearly destroying the town. Ten years later the railroad pulled out, leaving the town's future linked to the destiny of the automobile. Few buildings have been added to Tomales since then, and the town still serves the agricultural countryside as it did over one hundred years ago.

On your left as you enter the town of Tomales is the Catholic Church of the Assumption, built in 1860. Behind it, just barely visible, is the 1868 Tomales Presbyterian Church located on Church Street. One of the original trustees of this church was George W. Burbank, Luther Burbank's brother. Luther spent time in Tomales with his brother, and while here he developed a potato that he named "Bodega Red."

The downtown area of Tomales, which now has a population of around three hundred, contains Diekmann's General Store, now owned by Bill Diekmann and his sister, Kristin Lawson. The present store has been here since 1948 when it was opened by their father, and still has deer heads and rifles hanging on the walls. The original store was built in 1875 by Newburg and Kahn.

Another landmark is the U.S. Hotel, built in 1883, destroyed in the 1920 fire, and rebuilt in 1989. The hotel was purchased in December 1999 by Kate Foist, a software engineer from San Francisco who now rents out its eight, antique-filled rooms.

In 1978 a group of residents organized the Tomales Regional History Center which is located in the old refurbished Tomales High School at 26701 Shoreline Highway. Visitors are welcome to see the exhibits between 1:00 p.m. and 4:00 p.m. on Fridays, Saturdays or Sundays. Phone 707-878-9443.

TOMALES REGIONAL HISTORY CENTER 707-878-9443

Town meetings are held in the 1874 town hall erected by the Tomales Temperance Social Club. The building is also used for meetings, dance lessons, community affairs and weddings.

Church of the Assumption, Tomales.

DILLON BEACH

D illon Beach Road heads west from Tomales, ending about four miles away at Marin's northernmost beach. On the way, you will pass a picturesque Catholic cemetery a half-mile out of town on the right, and then some impressive rock formations known as Elephant Rocks (two miles farther). The road curves around them to the left and goes on to Dillon Beach on Bodega Bay.

The bay was named by the Spanish explorer, Bodega, who landed here in 1775. Dillon Beach was founded by an Irish pioneer, George Dillon, who built a hotel here in the late 1800s. The beach prospered as a resort area for many years under Dillon and other owners.

Sylvester Lawson arrived around 1923 and his family now controls local businesses, including the Lawsons' General Store which carries groceries, apparel, fishing gear, and other supplies.

To reach the bay, follow Beach Avenue. Dillon Beach is a beautiful wide, sandy strip with tall rocks rising dramatically out of the ocean to the north; to the south are the sand dunes covered with sea grass. Rows of old cottages and some modern homes are located to the north on a treeless hill overlooking the area. There is a beach admission fee and a lot for parking your vehicle. Public facilities include rest rooms (locked in winter) and picnic tables. The beach is open for day use only and closed entirely in January.

Dillon Beach.

Just beyond is Lawson's Landing. A toll road leads to a camping area. At the end of the road is a huge trailer park, pier, and boat launch. Overnight camping is available with a charge per night or by the week. Call (707) 878-2443 for information.

LAWSON'S
LANDING
(707) 878-2443

Lawson's Landing is at the mouth of Tomales Bay where it flows into the Pacific Ocean. The town of Bodega Bay is to the north in Sonoma County. You may reach Sonoma by continuing north on Highway 1. Here you will find the Russian River resort area, Jack London country (near Glen Ellen) and the beginning of the California wine-growing region.

Horses   12

Trails
Rental Stables
Riding Academies and Boarding Facilities
Staging Areas
Bay Area Ridge Trail
Horse Clubs

TRAILS

Marin County offers hundreds of miles of spectacular trails, making it one of the finest horseback riding areas in the United States. Equestrians can ride their horses from the shores of the Pacific Ocean to the Golden Gate Bridge, crossing mountains and ridge tops with breathtaking views.

In the last few years, new Marin portions of the 400-mile Bay Area Ridge Trail which will connect parks and open space in nine counties have been dedicated in the area of Loma Alta west of Fairfax and the Gary Giacomini Open Space Preserve.

Most trails in Marin are in the public domain: federal, state, county or a utility such as the Marin Municipal Water District or the Marin County Open Space District, which has 80 miles of fire protection roads. These are designated multi-use, meaning that they are available for horses, hikers and bicycles.

RENTAL STABLES

Three popular stables located in Northern, Southern and West Marin provide rental horses and guides for the public. All three facilities are connected to the hundreds of miles of trails.

Other stables, open to the public, have facilities for boarding horses and provide well-trained personnel who specialize in riding and jumping lessons. Many stables also sponsor trail rides and summer horsemanship camps.

Northern Marin

Sunset Corral   897-8212
2901 Vineyard Road, Novato

This complete horse facility in sunny Novato is owned and operated by Pat and Gail Martin. They offer around 20 horses for rent (more in the summer), in addition to guides to lead you along the 32 miles of trails through the North Marin Water District, Marin County Open Space

◄ *Alicia Arrigoni of Nicasio on her jumper, Clementine, at a local horse show on her way to being named Children's Jumper Reserve Champion of Northern California. (Photo © Jump Shot, 1996.)*

343

Kendra Hartnell of San Francisco and Deni Wetsel of the Wetsel Ranch hold Little Frosty and Big Frosty. The ranch is located on Lucas Valley Road in San Rafael.

and the 125 miles of fire roads adjoining the stables. There are hourly rides, day rides, and evening rides.

The Sunset Corral has about 150 horses (100 boarders), and offers Western and English lessons in both indoor and outdoor arenas. Summer horse camps run from the end of June through August.

The Martins, who have been in the horse business for 43 years, provide other care for their horses such as shoeing, shots, worming, leg wraps, dentistry and regular vet visits. They live on the premises (along with two families and two hired men), so they can keep an eye on things as well as be available in all emergencies.

The Sunset Corral is open seven days a week from 9:00 a.m. to 5:00 p.m. To get there drive north on Highway 101 and

take the Atherton Avenue/San Marin exit; drive west on San Marin Drive, which will become Sutro; Sutro dead ends at Vineyard Drive. Turn right on Vineyard Drive, go to the end of the paved road, continue a short distance down the dirt road and you will see Sunset Corral.

Southern Marin

Miwok Livery Riding Stables   383-8048
701 Tennessee Valley Road, Mill Valley

Linda Rubio owns the Miwok Livery, which is leased from the Miwok Valley Association, a cooperative of horse boarders. Since 1983 the riding school here has given lessons and sponsored summer camps (ages six and older) and outreach programs. There are two outdoor riding rings. Beginners and "rusty riders" are welcome, as are more skilled equestrians. Adult classes range from beginners to advanced. After-school programs are popular (no beginners), and certified instructors teach a variety of disciplines, including English riding, centered riding techniques and dressage.

Although primarily a riding school, Miwok Livery can arrange guided trail rides through the Marin Headlands and above the Golden Gate Bridge Monday through Friday, reservations required. These are for one to four riders, ages 12 and older with a 190 pound weight limit.

Miwok Livery is open from 9:00 a.m. to 5:00 p.m. Their website, www.miwok-stables.com, has much useful information about their programs. To get to the sta-

bles, take Highway 101 to the Stinson Beach exit, go west one quarter mile from the exit and turn left on Tennessee Valley Road (at the fruit stand); go two miles to the end of the road and the GGNRA parking lot; turn left into the stables.

West Marin

Five Brooks Ranch   **663-1570**
8001 State Route #1, Olema
P.O. Box 99, Olema 94950

Open daily from 9:00 a.m. to 5:00 p.m. and located in the Point Reyes National Seashore, the Five Brooks Stables offers English riding lessons for all abilities and ages, guided trail rides for groups and individuals, as well as hay rides for children, adults, and the disabled. The rides include one- and two-hour, half-day and all-day excursions. Horses may be

Outdoor arena at Miwok Stables in Tennesse Valley.

Andrew Loose, manager of Five Brooks Stables, rides Geronimo, a thoroughbred owned by Avelina Flanders of Tomales. (Photo by Avelina Flanders)

boarded overnight or by the month. Boarding includes feed, water and "mucking out" the stall or paddock once daily. A tackroom and arena are also available. About 26 horses are available for rent to the public, and you can join their sponsorship program, where, for a fee, you may sponsor one or more of their horses for unlimited riding during weekdays. Trails cover 350 miles and run all the way to the Golden Gate Bridge. Reservations are recommended, and hay rides should be reserved at least a week in advance. To get to Five Brook Stables, take Highway 101 to the San Anselmo exit; head west on Sir Francis Drake Boulevard for several miles to the town of Olema; turn left onto Highway 1 and drive approximately six miles. Visit their website at **www.fivebrooks.com**.

RIDING ACADEMIES AND BOARDING FACILITIES

Baywood Canyon Equestrian Center
460-1480
59 Baywood Canyon Road, Fairfax

This state-of-the-art boarding/training facility was purchased in November 1999 by three Marin women: Patti Covell, Elza Porter Lawrence, and Beth Graham. Features include a newly constructed large, lighted indoor arena and Grand Prix outdoor arena. There are facilities to board 69 horses, and trail access to hundreds of miles of open space.

Jumping is taught by hunter/jumper trainer Laura O'Connor, a top international Grand Prix rider and past junior AHSA final winner. Dressage trainer

Elza Porter offers equal emphasis on the concepts of the riding and the training of your horse. Classes for both include beginners to more advanced riders.

Bonty Ranch at Meadowbrook Inc.   662-2288
2800 Nicasio Valley Road, Nicasio

The seventy-five acre Bonty Ranch, with its redwood, bay, and oak forests, large lake, creek, and ponds has been the setting for several films and commercials. You will find buffalo and South African Longhorn cattle on the hillsides, and riders can see Point Reyes from the ridge trails.

This boarding and training facility has fifty horses and five trainers. Equestrians focus on competition, and trainers often schedule shows. Facilities include a hunter/jumper arena, an indoor and outdoor dressage arena, and an event arena.

Chevalle Ranch   898-2068
404 Gage Lane, Novato

Owned by Jim Naugle who specializes in training horses for their riders to participate in horse shows. Naugle breeds Tennessee walking horses, spotted saddle horses, Arabians and others. Indoor arena.

Creekside Equestrian Center   488-4006
5001 Sir Francis Drake Boulevard, Woodacre

The 46 horses in these new stables are fed three times daily, and someone is there day and night to care for them. Creekside gives lessons in dressage, hunter/jumper, Western and English for all ages. (The public is welcome for lessons.) There are indoor and outdoor arenas, and extensive trails nearby.

Dickson Ranch   488-0454
182 San Geronimo Valley Drive, Woodacre

The historic 50-acre Dickson Ranch, founded in 1855, is still owned and operated by fourth generation family members Grace Dickson Tolson and her husband Chuck. They offer boarding, lessons and about ten shows a year. Facilities include four arenas, including one indoors and a cross country course for beginning jumpers. In 1870, Grace's great-grandmother built a Vermont-style house on the property; it is still occupied today.

Dougherty Arabians   662-2031
700 Nicasio Valley Road, Nicasio

Bob and Diana Dougherty raise Arabians and board over 50 horses at their very fine ranch in Nicasio. Facilities include a lighted indoor arena, a large outdoor arena, pipe paddocks as well as runs located adjacent to the stables, a four-horse "hot walker," turn-out paddocks and a separate hay barn. Horses are turned out daily to pasture for exercise. Three trainers provide lessons in jumping, dressage, and Western and English riding. There is good access to open space trails. Dougherty Arabians can also furnish two stallions for breeding and will foal out mares.

Golden Gate Dairy Stables   381-6263
1760 Shoreline Hwy., Muir Beach

(These stables are sometimes called "Muir Beach Stables" and also the "Dairy.")

These stables provide overnight facilities for 10 horses with another 6 horses on pasture land at Green Gulch Farms. They also provide the opportunity for B & B riders from the Pelican Inn in Muir

Beach to stable their horses here during the dry season.

The facilities and land are now owned by the National Park Service which has given a one year interim lease to the Ocean Riders at the stables. The lease is based on water quality testing.

Nearby is a horse camp located in Franks Valley which is part of the state lands and is operated through Mt. Tamalpais State Park. Organizations may contact the state to rent the camp. In the immediate area also is an arena which may only be used by members of the Ocean Riders who pay the insurance.

In the summer of 1999 a pilot Wilderness Program was set up between the Ocean Riders, National Park Service and the San Francisco Police Department to bring inner-city children out to the park for hikes, environmental training and to ride on horses which were being led by hand. The program was considered successful and it is hoped that this outreach program for inner-city children will be continued.

The Ocean Riders are continuing to work diligently with the National Park Service to improve environmental concerns with their horses which are on park land.

Kilham Farm   662-9678
3431 Nicasio Valley Road (at Windfield Station) Nicasio

Trainer Lumpy Kilham specializes in horse sales, training, and lessons in hunting and jumping. See Winfield Station for facilities.

Mar-Ghi Arabians   662-2135
2501 Nicasio Valley Road, Nicasio

Owned by Mario and Eva Ghilotti who sell feed and tack such as saddles, bridles, blankets and other horse care products.

Marin Stables   459-9455
139 Wood Lane, Fairfax

Jim McDermott leases land from the Marin Municipal Water District, which has excellent riding trails. Facilities include boarding stalls – he presently boards 35 horses – paddocks, a small covered arena and a new round pen. Boarding, lessons and training are the specialties of Marin Stables.

Morning Star Farm   897-1633
885 Sutro Avenue, Novato

Vicky and Kevin Byars provide quality boarding, English riding instruction, jumping, dressage, and cross country. They also sponsor shows and clinics in their four arenas.

Morning Star specializes in children's riding and training lessons. They have summer horsemanship camps, birthday riding parties, and pony parties for children under seven.

Adult lessons are also available, and extensive trails are easily accessed from this central location.

Pencil Belly Ranch   898-0802
1671 Indian Valley Road, Novato

Frank and Elaine Sanders board 20 horses in their private boarding stable, but do not offer lessons or shows. Facilities include covered stalls with paddocks, double-sized pipe corrals and a large open arena. The four-acre ranch borders the Pacheco Open Space District and is near the private Indian Valley Riding Club. Families can join the club, which offers over 2,300 acres for riding, special rides and barbecues. Frank stresses that there are no streets to cross to get into the open space district from the Pencil Belly Ranch and you do not have to trailer your horse.

Presidio Stables 332-9712
Bunker Road, Fort Cronkhite, Sausalito

These stables were established in 1966 for horses being ridden at the Presidio in San Francisco. All horses stabled here must be used by persons affiliated with the military or their families or guests as dictated by the National Park Service, under which the stables have operated for the past five years. The stables are actually run and expenses paid by the

non-profit Presidio Riding Club, a group which would like to see the stables opened up to the public. The club takes care of maintenance and repairs.

While there are 45 stalls, the National Park Service restricts the club to using only 19, so the empty facilities are sometimes used for "overnighters."

A special feature is the indoor riding ring built in 1921 which is on the National Register of Historic Buildings. It was built by the military as a hanger for an observation balloon. The balloons were not successful because of the high winds in the area and the program was ended by 1940. The hanger was then used for the motor pool of Fort Cronkhite, as were two other buildings constructed in 1940 and now used for horse stalls. There is also an outdoor horse riding ring.

Show exhibitor gracefully clears the jump at a San Domenico School Show.
(Photo courtesy of San Domenico Riding School)

Members of the Presidio Riding Club are proud to say they have the cleanest stables in California, and the public is invited to stop by any time to tour the facilities.

San Domenico Riding School   459-9126
1500 Butterfield Road, San Anselmo

San Domenico School, tucked away in a secluded valley at the end of Butterfield Road in Sleepy Hollow, is surrounded by 550 acres of rolling hills and dedicated open space. The riding school provides boarding stables for students and members of the public; it has a lighted indoor arena and two outdoor arenas. Students are encouraged to compete in local horse shows.

San Domenico teaches its students hunt seat equitation and the fundamentals of horsemanship. Group lessons are given every afternoon, Monday through Saturday, at 3:30 and 4:30. Individual lessons may be arranged for the morning and early afternoon hours. The 10-week summer camp, consisting of one-week sessions, attracts both beginners and advanced riders. Year-long clinics with trainers stress riding, horsemanship, and stable management. Each spring and fall a horse show is held on the grounds of San Domenico.

Sky Ranch,   459-9925
106 Crest Road, Fairfax

Nancy Sandy provides boarding facilities including pasture, paddock and stalls. Boarders enjoy pleasure trail riding all the way to the Pacific Ocean through MMWD lands, Mt. Tamalpais, Pine Mountain, and the Point Reyes National Seashore. Sky Ranch has a common fence with the Marin Municipal Water District. No lessons are available.

Stewart Ranch   663-1362
8497 State Route No. 1, Olema

The Stewart Ranch, operated by Boyd and his daughter Joanne Stewart, provides a horse camp and boarding adjacent to the beautiful trails in the Point Reyes National Seashore.

The Stewart Horse Camp operates between April first and late October. Bring your recreational vehicle, or choose from their tent sites. The camp holds 125 people and has barbecue pits, picnic tables, and a bathhouse with hot showers. They provide water and a high-line post for your horse; box stalls are available, also. Bring rope and feed. Reservations required.

Vanishing Point Ranch
581 Evergreen Rd., Bolinas
Barn, 868-9019, 868-1693
Fax: 868-9472
P.O. Box 781, Bolinas, CA 94924

The Vanishing Point Ranch is owned by Sally Stearns Peacock, who offers boarding stables and English riding training to students of all ages. There is room for 20 horses with eight 12X14' sheltered box stalls and a variety of paddocks, some sheltered. A 100'X200 outdoor arena offers all-weather footing and a spectacular view of the Farrallon Islands. In the vicinity are many local riding trails, and it is only one mile to the Point Reyes National Seashore.

The Marin County Pony Club meets here.

Wetsel Ranch   472-4938
2200 Lucas Valley Road, San Rafael,

This ranch is owned by Deni Wetsel and run by King Dexter. It includes a horse

Ashley Mangus rides Dolly, a gentle mare with a soft gait at San Domenico Riding School. (Photo courtesy of San Domenico Riding School)

training center specializing in natural horsemanship, instead of the usual offerings at a boarding facility. King Dexter says, "We look at things from the horses' viewpoint." A one-of-a-kind arrangement has been set up whereby boarders pitch in to help with feeding their animals and cleaning stalls. Facilities include an outdoor arena and round pen, five stalls with paddocks and 19 more paddocks. The stalls and paddocks are all sheltered. There is a huge pasture turn-out area for the horses and trail access.

Willow Creek Stables   **892-6226**
545 McClay Road, Novato

Owned by Dorothy Scott. Lessons are given on quarter horses.

Windfield Station   **662-2232**
3431 Nicasio Valley Road, Nicasio

Winfield Station boards up to 60 horses in fine facilities on sixty acres in Nicasio. Facilities include stables, a lighted and covered arena, a large outdoor arena, turn-out paddocks, two extra-large foaling stalls, a new 20-stall barn, and a storage barn for hay and tack. They are building a new grand prix arena which will be the largest in Northern California, with permanent water jumps and bank jumps.

See Kilham Farm for training and lesson information.

STAGING AREAS
(HITCHING POSTS AND WATER TROUGHS)

Staging areas are places where groups of riders meet to leave for a ride. Facilities usually include an ample area to park vehicles and horse trailers, hitching posts, water troughs and rest rooms.

Golden Gate National Recreation Area

Next to Miwok Livery Riding Stables, 701 Tennessee Valley Road, Mill Valley. Parking and privies. The water trough is up the driveway and next to the small arena.

Marin Municipal Water District

(It is forbidden to ride or water horses in the lakes.)

Only Lake Lagunitas and Sky Oaks Staging Area have all of the amenities listed above; the following listings include water troughs and hitching rails that are on fire roads.

Victoria Arrigoni of Nicasio on her junior jumper, Pensacola. Victoria was Children's Jumper Champion of Northern California. (Photo by John C. Totton © Stock Photography Services, 1995.)

Bear Wallow (alongside a fire road on Eldridge Grade)—water trough.

Lake Lagunitas—Parking, water, hitching rails adjacent to picnic area, rest rooms. Laurel Dell Fire Road—Hitching rails (north of Rock Springs), water trough, rest room.

Portrero Picnic Area—Hitching rails by rest rooms.

Rifle Camp Picnic Area—Water trough (access via Lagunitas/Rock Springs Road east of Portrero Meadows).

Rock Spring—Hitching rails and rest rooms (north of the Mountain Theater area).

Sky Oaks Staging Area—Entrance of the Water District (Lake Lagunitas and Bon Tempe) above Fairfax. Parking is about 100 yards west of the Sky Oaks Ranger Station. Rest rooms and water troughs. Fee for horse trailers is $7.00.

West Point Inn—Hitching rails and water troughs. (Access via the Old Railroad Grade or Eldridge Grade.)

MT. TAMALPAIS STATE PARK

Franks Valley Road (also called Muir Woods Road) —Horseman's Arena at Santos Meadow.

This special arena was built by Ocean Riders of Muir Beach on state park land. In addition to being a staging area, it is also a horse camp for two to twelve horses and riders. It has 12 pipe corrals, water faucets, water troughs, picnic tables, a fire ring and pit toilets. For reservations and trail information, call 388-3215 or 388-3653.

Old Stage Road—A watering trough is located on the Old Stage Road below Bootjack Trail.

POINT REYES NATIONAL SEASHORE

Five Brooks Trailhead is immediately adjacent to Five Brooks Ranch, 8001 State Route 1, Olema.

Water troughs, hitching rails, rest rooms and good access from State Highway 1.

Bear Valley Visitors Center, off Highway 1 near Olema, has a parking lot reserved for horse trailers. Horses are allowed on the 150 miles of trails daily, except for three shorter trails (Bear Valley, Meadow, and Old Pine) which are closed to riding on weekends and holidays. The Visitors Center has trail maps, suggestions for rides in the park, and information about camping with horses. They can also tell you about horse rentals in the area.

Sky Camp and Wildcat Campgrounds, a water trough in each.

BAY AREA RIDGE TRAIL
(ABOUT HALF COMPLETED)

A 400-mile trail link through nine counties will connect parks and open space following the ridges and mountains that circle the Bay Area. Besides horses, the trail corridor will be used by hikers and bicyclists. Alternate parallel routes will be assigned where necessary. This region-wide project was started in 1988, and the first sections were dedicated in 1989. In Marin, the recreational corridor runs

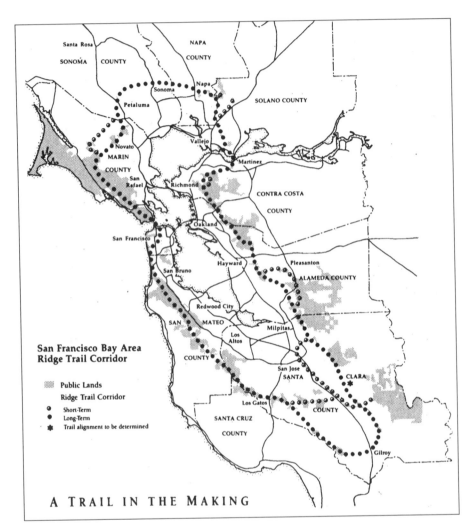

Santa Rosa

SONOMA   COUNTY

NAPA

COUNTY

Sonoma

Napa

Petaluma

SOLANO COUNTY

Novato

MARIN

COUNTY

San
Rafael

Vallejo

Richmond

Martinez

CONTRA COSTA

COUNTY

San Francisco

Oakland

San Bruno

Hayward

Pleasanton

ALAMEDA COUNTY

Redwood City

SAN   MATEO

Los
Altos

Milpitas

**San Francisco Bay Area
Ridge Trail Corridor**

COUNTY

San Jose
SANTA   CLARA

Public Lands
Ridge Trail Corridor
○ Short-Term
● Long-Term
✱ Trail alignment to be determined

Los Gatos   COUNTY

SANTA CRUZ

COUNTY

Gilroy

A TRAIL IN THE MAKING

through several parks and water district land and most of the trail in public domain has now been dedicated. It will take years, however, for the trail running through private property to be added. For more information contact: Bay Area Ridge Trail Council, 26 O'Farrell Street, Suite 400, San Francisco, CA. 94108. Phone; 415-391-9300; Fax: 391-2649; website: **www.ridgetrail.org.**

A SPECIAL MARIN RIDE
THE POINT REYES BRIDGE RIDE

Since 1976, riding enthusiasts in Marin have sponsored a popular three-day ride beginning at Pierce Point Ranch, Tomales Point, and ending at the Golden Gate Bridge overlooking the Golden Gate National Recreation Area Headlands. Riders cover approximately twenty miles per day along the following route: Tomales Bay, Point Reyes, Bear Valley, Bolinas Ridge, Mt. Tamalpais, Muir Beach and the Golden Gate National Recreation Area.

Much of the trail runs on top of ridges providing stunning views of San Francisco Bay and the Pacific Ocean. Other parts traverse beaches, forests of Douglas fir, redwood trees and fern groves.

The nights are spent at Toby's Pasture in Point Reyes and Rancho Baulinas in Bolinas. Each rider brings camping gear for personal use. Food and liquid refreshments for horse and rider are provided, and trailer transportation is available. The ride is limited to 50, and it is important that all riders and horses be well conditioned, as the trails are mostly up and down hill. For more information on future rides, write Sandra Sullivan, P.O. Box 1536, San Anselmo, Ca. 94979.

HORSE CLUBS

Halleck Creek 4-H Riding Club for the Handicapped, Halleck Creek Ranch, Nicasio. P.O. Box 189, Inverness, CA 94937. Program Coordinator: Julie Cassel, 662-2488.

In 1977, Duane Irving and Joyce Goldfield started a horseback riding club for the disabled at Irving's Nicasio Ranch; the two taught "hippotherapy" (therapeutic horseback riding) to children riding ponies. Today the club has several hundred members, some 100 volunteers and its own land in Nicasio. An average of 25 handicapped riders of all ages participate in the free one-and-a-half-hour

Saturday sessions, which include lessons and trail rides. The club is a Marin 4-H Club, and several fund raisers are given during the year to support not only equestrian offerings, but rafting expeditions, camping, Easter egg hunts, and attending horse shows.

Joyce Goldfield says, "We welcome adults and kids, anybody with any and all disabilities." She also stresses that volunteers at any level are needed and welcome. Both she and Irving have been widely recognized for their outstanding innovations and contributions.

Horseman's Association of Sleepy Hollow, 1317 Butterfield Road, San Anselmo, 94960

This group organizes rides throughout the year in addition to two clinics dealing with worming and dentistry. The members maintain a public ring on the grounds of Brookside School, Upper Campus, in Sleepy Hollow.

Marin County Pony Club Terry Fairman, 668-9786

This pony club currently meets every other week at the Vanishing Point Ranch in Bolinas. Though members live all over the county, most are from Bolinas, Point Reyes, and Nicasio. The members, ages 6-21, are eligible for membership as soon as they can walk and trot their pony. They are taught stable management, how to care for their ponies or horses, and are given riding lessons, including dressage, cross country, and show jumping. Many members go on to compete on regional and national levels. Discipline, working as a team and taking responsibility are all part of the Marin Pony Club's program.

Marin Horse Council
171 Bel Marin Keys, Novato, CA 94947. Call 883-4621 ext. 361 during business hours

The 200-member Marin Horse Council, formed in 1981, is a non-profit group which promotes the interests of horse enthusiasts and horse-related activities in Marin County. Its members publish a newsletter and appear before government bodies such as city councils, county and state agencies, federal agencies such as the GGNRA and utilities. Their all-day January Horse Seminar, now in its 18th year, features experts in areas such as stable management and safe trailering; demonstrations, booths, and lunch are also offered. The 12-member Board of Directors meet at the Humane Society Library at the above address on the third Tuesday of each month at 7:30 p.m. Those interested are welcome to attend.

Marin Sheriff's Posse, Larry Weiland (Past Captain and current SAR Operations Manager), 457-1622. P.O. Box 1234, Novato, CA 94948

The Marin Sheriff's Posse, founded in 1942, has about 35 members, both men and women. The main focus of the organization is search and rescue for the Marin County Sheriff's Department. The rigorous training is ongoing, and it typically takes a year to 18 months before riders are qualified. Members are volunteers of the Sheriff's Department.

In addition to being on call for an emergency, activities include assisting in certifying riders for such organizations as the Marin Municipal Water District and the Marin County Open Space District in a trail test, and holding an annual mock search each summer. This all-day event is coordinated with the Marin County Sheriff's air patrol, the Marin Search and Rescue ground team, and other groups.

In addition to equestrian skills, members need to be proficient in such areas as radio communications and other techniques necessary for successful search and rescue operations.

Middle Marin Hunt Pony Club
Margot Szabo, 457-7821

This pony club meets every other Sunday at Creekside Equestrian Center in Woodacre. Members receive riding lessons, instruction in veterinary care, and stable and horse management. The children, ages 8-18, also participate in one or two fox hunts every year out of Windfield Station in Nicasio. The riders chase a scent which has been dragged instead of a live fox. It is not mandatory for members to own their own horses or ponies, but they should have access to one when they want to ride. The club is non-profit and considered quite inexpensive for all the benefits it provides.

Ocean Riders
Mareen Pinto, President, 388-7670

This group rides out of the Golden Gate Dairy Stables in Muir Beach and uses the arena in Franks Valley. Along with the National Park Service and the San Francisco Police Department, they conduct an outreach program for inner-city children to hike, learn about the environment and ride on a horse which is being hand led.

Tamalpais Trail Riders,
P.O. Box 63, San Anselmo, 94960.

Founded in 1939 to protect equestrian usage of trails on the Mt. Tamalpais watershed, this club built many of the fine trails enjoyed by equestrians and hikers today on the mountain. They hold day rides in addition to a trail test every year.

Volunteer Mounted Patrol of the Open Space Lands in Marin County
Ranger Leonard Page, Volunteer Coordinator, 499-3778.
Open Space VIEW
3501 Civic Center Drive #417, San Rafael, 94903-4155
Attn: Lucas Valley Field Office

The "County Mounties," as they call themselves, were formed in 1984 under the direction of the 12 rangers of the Marin County Open Space District. Working with rangers, these 30 equestrians perform a variety of services on district lands extending from Richardson Bay in Mill Valley to the San Geronimo Ridge. They answer visitors' questions, direct those who are lost, provide first aid, promote law awareness and proper use of the preserves, deal with erosion and maintenance problems on trails, work on special projects such as replanting and repair, and even herd cattle. These volunteers are trained both in classrooms and in the field. They have no set hours, but you can usually find someone on patrol in Marin's open spaces. For more information, contact Ranger Page (see above).

Dog Parks   13

Parks, Trails, and Open Space Where You Can Exercise Your Dog

Marin County is definitely a pet-friendly place. A spokesman at the Marin Humane Society says that half of all Marin households have cats, dogs or both. While there are only 20,000 licensed dogs in Marin, the Humane Society estimates that in reality 70,000 dogs and 50,000 to 60,000 cats live in the county.

Dogs need exercise, and in the past few years, seven dog parks have been developed where these animals can socialize and run off-leash in a safe, secure environment.

Dave Wilkinson, Recreation Director in Larkspur, is proud of the fact that his department was the first to develop a dog park in 1990. It is called Canine Commons and is located in Piper Park, and you don't have to be a resident to use it. The dogs are divided into areas for large or small animals, and there are designated areas for waste and pooper scoopers. Canine Commons is open from dawn to dusk and is free.

Nearby Corte Madera refers to Piper Park as the closest place for dogs to exercise since the town has a leash law for the entire city and no facilities for dogs.

In Novato the dog park is in O'Hair Park, located off Sutro Avenue across from San Marin High School. All dogs must be on a leash in Novato public parks.

Mill Valley offers a four-acre dog park in Bay Front Park, located at the end of Sycamore Avenue past the Middle School. The dogs must be kept on a leash until they reach the dog run area and this is strictly enforced. Once in the run area, animals also have access to swimming in the bay. Dogs walked in other parks in Mill Valley must be on leashes.

A group of dog owners have been trying to develop a dog park in San Anselmo but cannot find a suitable property. Meanwhile, the San Anselmo School District has allowed them to temporarily use the three-acre Red Hill School site behind the Red Hill Shopping Center. The organization of dog owners has put up a bulletin board with rules, while the town has helped out by bringing in two picnic tables and water barrels.

Two other open space parks in San Anselmo, Sorich Ranch Park and Faude

---

◀ *Marin is a dog-friendly county with thousands of these pets bringing joy to their owners. In this photo Sophie chases a ball at a beach in West Marin.*

Ruphert is walked by his master at O'Hair Dog Park in Novato.

Park, allow dogs to run without a leash under voice control. All other parks have rules posted at their entrances and require dogs to be on a leash.

Dog etiquette for visiting the dog parks, according to the Humane Society, requires dogs to be licensed, vaccinated and have a handler present. Spay/neutered animals are recommended, and puppies under four months are prohibited (due to immature immune systems.) No aggressive dogs are allowed and owners must clean up after their pets.

The Marin County Dog Park Groups are as Follows: Canine Commons, Piper Park, Larkspur; D.O.G. (Dog Owners' Group), Remington Park, Sausalito (3 dogs per person maximum); D.O.G. B.O.N.E. (Dog Owners' Group Bettering Our Novato Environment), O'Hair Park, Novato; Field of Dogs, Civic Center Drive, San Rafael (located behind the Civic Center Post Office); McDOG, McInnis Park, San Rafael; Park, People & Dogs, Bayfront Park, Mill Valley; San Anselmo Dog Park, Red Hill School site behind the Red Hill Shopping Center.

California State Parks—These parks do not allow dogs on trails. These include: Angel Island, China Camp, Mt. Tamalpais, Olompali, Samuel P. Taylor, and Tomales Bay State Parks.

Marin County Open Space—Steve Petterle, Open Space and Park Planner for the County of Marin, warns that a leash is necessary on all trails as dogs have been known to injure or even kill deer when only under voice control. He also mentions a preserve behind Indian Valley College in Novato where dogs can be exercised. Maps of Marin's Open Space Preserves including North, Southern, Central and Western, are available at the Marin County Civic Center in San Rafael, Room 415, for $2.00.

Dogs can be under voice control on fire roads and controlled by a leash on trails or in sensitive areas (though there are areas that do not allow dogs).

Golden Gate National Recreation Area— Dogs are allowed on selected trails and beaches, but you need to get a map at the Marin Headlands Visitor Center. Rodeo Beach at Fort Cronkhite is a popular exercise area.

Marin Municipal Water District—Dogs on a leash are allowed on trails and roads.

Muir Woods National Monument—No dogs allowed.

Point Reyes National Seashore—Some beaches allow dogs on a leash 6' or shorter including Kehoe, North, South and Limantour. No dogs are allowed on the trails except the Bolinas Ridge Trail.

Bailey (front), Rosie (back), and Sophie rest after their morning walk.

Sports: Golf, Tennis, Swimming, Fishing 14

GOLF

The five public golf courses in Marin have one thing in common—their settings all reflect the beauty, tranquillity and diversity of Marin's landscape. Call for tee time reservations, green fees, and cart rental prices. A former Marin County Women's Champion, who prefers anonymity, offers a golfer's view (see italics) of each course.

PUBLIC GOLF COURSES

Indian Valley Golf Club   897-1118
3035 Novato Boulevard, Novato

Yardage: Men, 6,100, Par 72, Course Rating 67.4. Women: 5,900, Par 72, Course Rating 70.9.

The scenic course at Indian Valley is located in the rolling hills near Stafford Lake. The elevator which takes players from the 13th green to the 14th tee allows the player a few moments of relaxation while enjoying the spectacular views of the course. The three-tiered 16th green is the largest in Marin. The topography of the golf course creates different lies and is a challenge for golfers. Though hilly in spots, the course is walkable, and golfers have no trouble carrying their clubs or pulling a golf cart.

There is a fully stocked pro shop, putting green and driving range, and lessons are available for all ages and abilities. Fundraising tournaments are held throughout the year. The clubhouse's **19th Hole Bar and Grill (892-5885)**, has great views, features affordable sandwiches and salads and is open for breakfast and lunch. For sketches of the course and each hole, or to preview the menus, go to the website at **www.ivgc.com.**

Interesting golf course. The player will use all his/her golf expertise to score well. Good course for the higher handicap player.

◀ *Erik Johannson, the Tennis Pro at the Cañon Swim and Tennis Club in Fairfax, watches play in the Marin Grand Prix Tennis Circuit from the club's deck. Johannson and George Zahorsky also run "Tennis in Marin", which offers tennis clinics, junior camps, lessons, and tournaments throughout Marin.*

McInnis Park Golf Center   492-1800
350 Smith Ranch Road, San Rafael

Yardage: 1,700, par 31. Course Rating 60.

One mile east of Highway 101 past San Rafael, the McInnis Park Golf Center has a wide variety of offerings. The 9-hole executive course itself has expansive rolling greens with water hazards on three holes and panoramic views of San Francisco Bay and Mt. Tamalpais.

The year-round Golf Academy has a comprehensive program of individual and group instruction for all ages and abilities with a small student to teacher ratio. The two-tiered driving range of 52 stations has weather screens on the lower deck for protection in rainy weather.

Additionally, there is a practice area for pitching and chipping, and a pro shop stocked with clubs, bags and shoes. Adjacent to the club house is a 9-station baseball batting cage and a 20-hole miniature golf course. Nearby is a snack bar for the entire family to enjoy. **The Club Restaurant (491-5959) has** an outdoor heated terrace in addition to a large indoor dining area and offers lunch, full course dinners, weekend brunches, and a well-stocked bar. This facility can handle up to 300 people for special events. You will find their tempting menus on the club's website, **www.mcinnisparkgolf.com**.

The perfect course for the beginning golfer and also the player who wishes to practice his or her short game. Interesting and challenging holes. Level, and players can easily walk and carry their bags.

Mill Valley Golf Course   388-9982
280 Buena Vista Avenue, Mill Valley

Yardage: Men, 4,185, Par 65, Course Rating 63.1. Women: 4,123, Par 69, Course Rating 62.8.

In the heavily-populated area of Southern Marin you'll find this tranquil course just minutes from downtown Mill Valley. You will play among redwoods and rolling hills and the gully-like arroyo that runs through the course. Mt. Tamalpais is just above you on this nine-hole, executive length challenging course.

There is a putting green and a pro shop, but no lessons are given and driving carts are not available in winter. Junior clinics are offered every summer.

Open all year, seven days a week during daylight hours. Either metal or soft spike golf shoes are required from October through April.

This course is fun to play, with short iron accuracy required.

Peacock Gap Golf   453-4940
and Country Club
333 Biscayne Drive, San Rafael

Yardage: Men, 6001, Par 71, Course Rating 68.3. Women: 5629, Par 73, Course Rating 71.9.

Just across from San Pablo Bay in San Rafael, this picturesque 18-hole course is in a valley ringed by mature pine, oak and eucalyptus trees. You'll play around a natural lagoon and a creek, and water is involved on 12 holes. Plan to use all the clubs in your bag for the variety of approach shots.

Amenities in this semi-private club include a pro shop, a 25-stall driving

The club house at the San Geronimo Golf Course

range and putting green. Lessons are available for members and the public, as well as summer golf camps. Open all year during daylight hours. Yearly memberships are available.

The clubhouse's **Bar and Grill Room** serves lunches daily except Monday from 10:00 a.m. to 3:00 p.m., and breakfast is served Saturday and Sunday beginning at 7:00 a.m. The clubhouse is also available for banquets, weddings and parties, and can accommodate up to 500 people. For further catering information call **453-4122.**

An easy course to walk. Though this course is primarily level, it has many challenges for the player. There are water canals on 15 of the 18 holes and a lake to be carried on one hole. No two holes are alike and the player will make full use of all of his or her clubs.

San Geronimo Golf Course   **488-4030**
5800 Sir Francis Drake Boulevard
San Geronimo

Yardage: Men, 6,003, Par 72, Course Rating 69.8. Women: 5,140, Par 72, Course Rating 74.6.

This 18-hole championship course is "built on the site of a ranch where Alexander Graham Bell hooked up the first telephone in California." It has been called the most challenging course in Marin. You'll play near redwood and oak forests and next to streams that in winter hold steelhead and coho salmon. Golfers find a marked difference between the deceptively easy front-nine and the more challenging back-nine, where there are more elevation changes and some really difficult holes.

Amenities include a putting green, a chipping area, a pro shop, both private and group lessons, summer junior clinics and a snack bar. The clubhouse restaurant, **The Eagle's Nest at San Geronimo (488-8189),** serves breakfast and lunch seven days a week and has a full bar. It is available for banquets and holds up to 200 people.

Tournaments are welcome seven days a week, and the club sponsors The Marin County Amateur Tournament each summer. The tournament is open to both men and women amateurs. The club's website, **www.bayinsider.com,** has informative photographs and descriptions of each hole.

A great course. If you score well here you know you have played well. Water trouble on many holes. Good course for long irons and woods.

PRIVATE GOLF COURSES

Meadow Club   **456-9393**
1001 Bolinas Road, Fairfax

Yardage: Men, 6,324, Par 71, Course Rating 71.4. Women: 5, 923, Par 73, Course Rating 75.2.

In 1927 this was the first course in the United States designed by Alister MacKenzie, who also designed Scotland's St. Andrew's Golf Course and Cypress Point on the Monterey Peninsula. The landscaping was designed by Frederick Law Olmstead, creator of New York's Central Park.

The road to the Meadow Club winds up the mountain from Fairfax and it will take you about 15 minutes to get to the course. Once there, the golfer will see no houses, no roads—only rolling hills, red-

woods and a serene setting which includes deer wandering the fairways. There is a full pro shop, driving range, putting green and a clubhouse for members only.

Non-members are welcome for lessons, and outside tournaments may be booked on Mondays. A junior clinic is held in the summer; participants must be accompanied by a member. Reciprocal privileges are available on Tuesday and Thursdays. The waiting list for membership extends for several years.

A beautiful golf course with interesting and challenging holes. Greens are moderately contoured and on the fast side in summer. Well-bunkered greens and fairways make for a true test of golf.

Marin Country Club   **382-6700**
500 Country Club Drive, Novato
(Pro shop: 382-6707)

Yardage: Men, 6,205, Par 72, Course Rating 71.7. Women: 5,807, Par 72, Course Rating 74.8.

A lovely course surrounded by homes and hills provides many vistas for the golfer. Undulating fairways and greens with tree-lined fairways make this a very challenging course. Water comes into play on 8 holes providing a true golfer's test.

Amenities include full pro shop with driving range and practice putting green. Non-members are welcome for lessons. Large swimming pool with children's smaller wading pool plus tennis courts. Clubhouse includes full banquet facilities. Several different types of memberships are offered, and reciprocal play is available for members of other private clubs.

A great course to play. Tough but fair. Excellent condition with greens having many breaks. Some tight fairways, putting a premium on the straight drive.

PUBLIC TENNIS COURTS

Tennis is a popular sport for all age levels in Marin County. Courts are available at various schools, private clubs, and neighborhood parks. The following listing includes the telephone number of each town's recreation department, where you may receive information about tennis lessons, reserved times for local groups, and the policies regarding keys. (In some communities, you must obtain a key at the local recreation office in order to play on locked courts.)

Several local communities work with the teachers and programs of **Tennis in Marin** (457-9217). Their website, **www.tennisinmarin.com**, offers information about lessons on municipal courts, junior and adult programs and leagues, free tennis clinics, round robin tournaments, and much more.

NEIGHBORHOOD PARKS

Corte Madera Town Park   927-5072
Tamalpais & Pixley Avenue

2 lighted courts; **Granada Courts**, Prince Royal and Granada Streets, 2 unlighted courts.

FAIRFAX
Peri Park   453-1584
Park Road between Bolinas Road and School Street

2 unlighted courts.

LARKSPUR
Piper Park   927-5110
Doherty Drive near Magnolia Avenue

4 unlighted courts; **Magnolia Avenue Park,** Magnolia and Alexander Avenues, 2 unlighted courts.

MILL VALLEY
Boyle Park   383-1370
East Blithedale Avenue & East Drive

5 lighted courts.

Strawberry Recreation Center   383-6494
East Strawberry Drive & Tiburon Boulevard

4 lighted courts.

NOVATO
Pioneer Park   897-4323
Simmons Lane & Novato Boulevard

4 lighted courts.

ROSS
Town Courts   453-6020

2 unlighted courts. For use by Ross residents only. Key required.

SAN ANSELMO
Memorial Park   258-4645
1000 Sir Francis Drake Boulevard

4 courts: 2 lighted courts and two unlighted courts; **Red Hill Tennis Courts,** Red Hill School at Shaw Drive off Sir Francis Drake Boulevard, 2 unlighted courts. Key required.

SAN RAFAEL   485-3333
Albert Park, Albert Park Lane & B Street, 4 lighted courts.

Boyd Memorial Park, B Street & Mission Avenue, 1 lighted court.

Gerstle Memorial Park, San Rafael Avenue & Clark Street, 1 lighted court.

John F. McInnis County Park (446-4423), Smith Ranch Road, 4 unlighted courts.

Maria B.Freitas Memorial Park, Montecillo Road &Trellis Drive, 2 lighted courts.

McNear's Beach County Park (446-4424), Cantera Way & San Pedro Road, 2 unlighted courts.

Peacock Gap Park, end of Peacock Drive, 2 unlighted courts.

SAUSALITO   289-4100, ext.152
Martin Luther King Park
Columa Street off Bridgeway,

5 unlighted courts; Marinship Park, Harbor Drive and Marinship Way, 3 lighted courts; North Street Park, North Street at West Street, 1 unlighted court.

TIBURON
Del Mar Courts   435-4355
Tiburon Boulevard at Miraflores

2 unlighted courts; Lagoon Courts, Lagoon Road across from Lyford Drive, 2 unlighted courts; Point Tiburon Courts, Beach Road and Tiburon Boulevard, 2 unlighted courts. Key required for all courts.

PRIVATE TENNIS AND SWIMMING CLUBS

The tennis courts listed below for private clubs are outdoors, unless otherwise noted. Most of these clubs are accepting new members, while a few have a waiting list. Group and individual lessons given by tennis professionals are popular in many of these clubs. Several clubs have amenities such as swimming pools, fitness centers, locker rooms, clubhouses and food service. Junior programs and league participation are often given special attention. Call for specific information.

Belvedere Tennis Club   435-4792
700 Tiburon Boulevard, Tiburon

Seven tennis courts, two lighted. Outdoor swimming pool is open all year. The Junior Program runs throughout the year, including after-school clinics. The club has active men's and women's league matches. Summer snack bar, and active social events. The clubhouse is available for rental by members and non-members.

Cañon Swim and Tennis Club   457-7766
135 Mitchell Drive, Fairfax

Eight courts, three lighted, in a memorable setting: at the end of a cul-de-sac surrounded by several hundred acres of open space. Year-long junior and adult tennis programs and league play. (There is a large deck overlooking the three lower courts for viewing tournament play.) Backboard and ball machine. Lessons available for members and non-members. The outdoor Olympic-sized pool, solar and gas heated, is open all year, and the club has on-going swimming programs for both juniors and adults. There is also a two-story clubhouse with a kitchen and separate locker rooms for men and women, each with a sauna. The clubhouse can be rented for parties. Tennis hours 8:00 a.m. to 10:00 p.m. year-round.

Dave Kregel Tennis Center   389-8522
99 Lowell (off North San Pedro Road)
San Rafael

Four individually-fenced courts, three lighted. In a sunny, quiet location, this small club is devoted exclusively to tennis. Private and group lessons available. Free use of ball machine. Open all year, 8:00 a.m. to 10:00 p.m.

Harbor Point Racquet
& Beach Club   383-3448
475 East Strawberry Drive, Mill Valley

Seven courts, four lighted. Primarily an adult club, members are active in local leagues. Lessons available for members and non-members. There is an outdoor pool heated all year, an outdoor 12-person Jacuzzi, as well as a fitness center. The **Harbor Point Bar & Grill,** open to the public, serves lunch daily. The clubhouse overlooks nearby Richardson Bay and has a view of San Francisco. Tennis hours are 8:30 a.m. to 10:00 p.m.

Marin Beach and Tennis Club   457-2844
250 Point San Pedro Road, San Rafael

Three unlighted courts. Outdoor swimming pool with separate swim memberships available, hot tub, and clubhouse (available for outside rental). Junior program includes pee-wee tennis for four to six year olds and summer camp. No restaurant, but members have dining privileges at the nearby Marin Yacht Club on Friday and Sunday nights. There is a large family membership. The club operates during daylight hours.

Marin Tennis Club   457-5160
925 Belle Avenue, San Rafael

Twelve outdoor courts, three lighted. Sauna and Jacuzzi, outdoor swimming pool. A junior tennis program for both members and non-members operates year-round, including all-day summer camps and after- school clinics for juniors aged 4-17. (For rates call **457-8015.**) Weekend breakfasts and lunch daily, except Monday, are available in the restaurant. Hours are 7:00 a.m. to 10:00 p.m.

Mill Valley Tennis Club   388-2010
285 Manor Drive, Mill Valley

Five courts, none lighted. This long-established club, started in 1929, also has an outdoor swimming pool, children's pool, and clubhouse. Junior and league programs are popular. Open all year during daylight hours.

Mt. Tam Racquet Club   924-6226
Number 1 Larkspur Plaza, Larkspur

Eight outdoor courts, six are lighted, and five indoor courts. Indoor and outdoor swimming pools, basketball gym, sauna, nursery and day care, bar and restaurant, pro shop. Open from 6:00 a.m. to 11:00 p.m. weekdays, and 7:45 a.m. to 10:00 p.m. weekends. Family oriented.

Rafael Racquet & Swim Club   456-5522
95 Racquet Club Drive, San Rafael

Nine courts, none lighted. The club has an outdoor pool and sponsors a summer swim team. Tennis members are active in league play, and the club offers a junior summer tennis camp. Clubhouse and snack bar, which is open all year. Daylight hours.

Rolling Hills Club   897-218
351 San Andreas Drive, Novato

Twelve courts, six lighted. Junior programs and adult league. Pro shop, entertainment center, restaurant. A complete health and fitness center on seven acres, this club has a multitude of offerings, from swimming and racquetball to yoga and massage. Their outdoor recreation program includes hiking, skiing, and kayaking. Social programs for all ages, including a 50+ group. Tennis hours are

8:00 a.m. to 10:00 p.m.
website:www.rollinghillsclub.com

Ross Valley Swim   461-5431
and Tennis Club
235 Bon Air Road, Kentfield

Nine courts, none lighted. This club is very family-oriented, and special attention is given to children's swim and tennis lessons. There are on-going children's programs, with clinics and inter-league play, and an active adult league play program. Three pools include a diver pool, lap pool and toddler pool. Summer snack bar. Summer hours 8:00 a.m. to 7:00 p.m., winter hours 8:00 a.m. to 5:00 p.m.

Scott Valley Swimming
and Tennis Club   383-3483
50 Underhill Road, Mill Valley

Six courts, four lighted, and a ball machine court. The outdoor six-lane swimming pool uses a low chlorine mixture. (In winter, the pool is covered with a large bubble so that it can be used all-year long.) There is also a wading pool, and the club is adding a weight room and Jacuzzi. Popular junior swim program and teams, summer tennis camps, and year-long tennis clinics for juniors and adults. Salad and snack bar, clubhouse. Year-long hours: Pool, 7:00 a.m. to 8:00 p.m.; tennis, 7:00 a.m. to 10:00 p.m.

Tiburon Peninsula Club   435-0968
1600 Mar West   (tennis: 435-0106)
Tiburon

One of the oldest clubs in Marin County, often with a waiting list, this club has ten courts; six are lighted. It also has two

swimming pools, a fitness center, and a summer snack bar. Family memberships only. Summer tennis and swim camps along with other activities, such as arts and crafts. Several adult league teams. Non-members may take advantage of lessons and programs such as the swim team. Tennis court hours, 8:00 a.m. to 9:00 p.m.

FISHING

Whether you want to drop your line into the salty waters of the Pacific Ocean or toss your bait at a freshwater lake, Marin offers a variety of settings and experiences for the angler.

Caruso's Sportfishing Center   332-1015
Foot of Harbor Drive, Sausalito

Seven party boats during salmon season—March through October—are available at this Sausalito landmark, which is also a deli, fish market and tackle shop. The boats fish as far out as the Farallon Islands, 26 miles, and along the Pacific Coast, as well as in San Francisco and San Pablo Bays. Catches include salmon, halibut, striped bass, sturgeon, sea bass and albacore. During salmon season, the deli opens at 5:00 a.m., and the staff can make sandwiches for your trip. Boats leave daily at 6:00 a.m. Reservations are strongly suggested **(332-1015)**, especially on weekends. (Party boats are not regularly scheduled during the winter months.)

Caruso's sells licenses and day licenses, in addition to saltwater tackle and bait; rod and reel rentals are available on board. The fish market is known for the live crab and lobster cooked on the premises.

Loch Lomand Live Bait 456-0321
Loch Lomand Marina, San Rafael

Keith Fraser has several party boats and a launch area, and is an expert on bay fishing. The boats operate all-year long. Anglers on these boats, which go to San Pablo and San Francisco Bays, fish primarily for sturgeon, striped bass, halibut, and salmon. You may rent rods and reels; all kinds of salt-water tackle and bait are available, as well as fishing licenses and free tide books.

Don't miss the tame birds—egrets, herons and pelicans—which are here, especially in the early morning. The nearby **Fo'c's'Le Cafe** serves early breakfasts in addition to lunches. For party boat information and reservations, which must be made in advance, call **456-0321.**

Western Boat and Tackle 454-4177
101 3rd Street, San Rafael

Western Boat and Tackle, owned for 40 years by the same family, has a knowledgeable staff to help you with a complete line of saltwater fishing supplies, including those you might need in Hawaii or Baja California. Private boaters can find anything from fuel to boating and marine supplies to a new fishing boat. There is a full-service seafood market here with live and cooked crab and year-round local fish.

From November through the winter months a charter fishing boat, the *Bathtub,* skippered by second-generation captain **Erik Anfinson (456-9055)** is available for anglers. Sturgeon and striped bass are the most popular catches.

Western Boat and Tackle's hours are: Friday, Saturday, Sunday, and holidays, 6:00 a.m. to 5:00 p.m. Other days, 7:00 a.m. to 6:00 p.m. Their website is **www.westernboatshop.com** (with good links to fishing reports).

Western Sport Shop 456-5454
902 3rd Street, San Rafael

In business for over 50 years, the Western Sport Shop has a staff knowledgeable about fishing Marin's lakes. They are familiar with Kent, Alpine, Bon Tempe, Phoenix and Lagunitas lakes, and the tactics you will need for catching trout, bass or blue gills. (You can also get advice about fishing for steelhead, salmon and trout in the rivers of Northern California.) The shop stocks a full line of equipment, including flies, bait, and lures. You will also find outdoor sports clothes and hunting gear.

Many people sign up for the fly-fishing class, Fly-fishing 101, offered all-year long.

Marin Restaurants

15

There are many outstanding restaurants in Marin, but I will mention only a selection of special ones I have enjoyed over the years in addition to a few recent arrivals. Call to check on the days that they are open, since restaurant hours often change.

CORTE MADERA

Baby Sal's Seafood Grill   927-0149
60 Corte Madera Avenue

Established 1983, fresh seafood and diverse menu, well-prepared. Cozy surroundings. Good wine list.

Benissimo Ristorante Pizzeria   927-2316
18 Tamalpais Drive

Dinners in this classic Italian trattoria include choices of pasta, pizzas and other entrees. Moderately priced.

California Cafe Bar & Grill   924-2233
Village at Corte Madera

Diverse changing menu, along with traditionals.

Il Fornaio   927-4400
223 Corte Madera Town Center

Creative Italian cuisine with a Tuscan flair in an authentic atmosphere. Some dishes cooked in wood burning ovens. Breads from the Il Fornaio bakeries. Try the angel hair pasta.

Marin Joe's   924-2081 and 924-1500
1585 Casa Buena Drive

A traditional Joe's Restaurant opened in 1954 by the Della Santina family. Italian and continental cuisine, charcoal broiled steak and chops. Try the "Joe's Special." A lot of food for your money and excellent service. Full bar. Valet parking available.

Max's Restaurant   924-6297
60 Madera Boulevard
(Formerly the Peppermill)

Innovative breakfast, lunch and dinner. Super desserts. Full service bar.

Savannah Grill   924-6774
55 Tamal Vista

Mixed grill, pasta and seafood. Nice setting. Live jazz in the bar Wednesday-Saturday nights.

FAIRFAX

Cafe Amsterdam   256-8020
23 Broadway

Popular local dining spot with the younger crowd. Live jazz performed Sunday nights.

Deer Park Villa   456-8084
367 Bolinas Road

A lovely garden setting perfect for weddings and parties. Serves traditional prime rib, steak, seafood and Italian cuisine. Special nights: Wednesday,

◀ *Roy Murrin and Paul Fradelizio, owners of Fradelizio's Ristorante Italiano in Fairfax.*

Head Chef Phil Baldwin, Deer Park Villa in Fairfax. (Photo by Don Walker)

"Family Fare" and Thursdays, "Supper Club" with live music. Dinner dining open to everyone Wednesday through Sunday. Expanded catering service throughout the Bay Area. Open seven days a week for parties.

Fradelizio's Ristorante Italiano   459-1618
35 Broadway (Formerly Pucci's)

A cozy and somewhat funky family-style Italian restaurant with outstanding Northern Italian cuisine. Very reasonable prices. Try the chicken sauté, chicken forno, the seafood fettucine or calamari fritti. Excellent service and one of my favorites.

Ghiringhelli Pizzeria   453-7472
45 Broadway

Some of the best pizza in Marin.

Koffee Klatch   454-4784
57 Broadway

For the early riser, try the delicious full-breakfasts with wide selection of omelets. Hamburgers, sandwiches, chicken, fish or salads for lunch. (Closed for dinner.)

Pancho Villa's   459-0975
1625 Sir Francis Drake Boulevard

A popular Mexican restaurant. The food is always delicious with fresh ingredients, extra large servings and low prices. Full liquor bar also offers a wide choice of Mexican beers and grand-sized margaritas.

Ross Valley Brewing Company   485-1005
765 Center Boulevard

Innovative continental. Fresh produce, seafood and meats served with beer brewed on the premises. Friendly service. Highly recommended.

GREENBRAE

Chevy's Mexican Restaurant   461-3203
302 Bon Air Shopping Center
(Also in Novato: 128 Vintage Way, 898-7345)

Popular Mexican restaurant with delicious fresh chips and salsa. Mesquite-broiled fish. Outdoor patio dining.

Joe LoCoco's Ristorante   925-0808
300 Drake's Landing Road

Creative and delicious Italian cuisine. Excellent anti-pasto and special pasta dishes. Try the risotto with truffles.

IGNACIO

Maya Palenque   883-6292
349 Enfrente Road.

Great atmosphere and excellent Mexican food. Take the Ignacio Road exit.

Ristorante Orsi   883-0960
340 Ignacio Boulevard

Popular lunch spot for North Marin. Outdoor dining on terrace. Pastas, salads, fresh fish, steaks, veal, lamb and house-made desserts. Full service bar.

INVERNESS

Barnaby's By The Bay   669-1114
12938 Sir Francis Drake Boulevard

Seafood, barbecued ribs and oysters.

Manka's   669-1034
Callender Way and Argyle

For forty years this was a Czech restaurant. Now owned by Margaret Grade, who offers dinner with a fixed priced menu and a single entree on Fridays and Saturdays. Fresh local produce. Wild game a specialty.

Vladimir's Czechoslovakian   669-1021
Restaurant
12785 Sir Francis Drake Boulevard

A fine Czech restaurant owned by Alena and Vladimir Nevi; a real Inverness tradition.

KENTFIELD

Half Day Cafe   459-0291
848 College Avenue

Popular with the early morning crowd. Good breakfast choices. Now open for dinner and brunch on weekends. California cuisine, fresh fruits and vegetables in addition to organic beef.

Maya Palenque Restaurant in Ignacio

Pacific Cafe   456-3898
850 College Avenue.

One of the best seafood restaurants in Marin. Specialties are pan-fried oysters and seasonal fresh fish dishes. All well-prepared. Family oriented and reasonable prices.

LARKSPUR

El Quixote   925-9392
125 East Sir Francis Drake Boulevard
(Formerly Bolero.)

Traditional Spanish with good paella. Great atmosphere in old brick kiln. Live flamenco on weekends. Dinners only.

Fabrizio Ristorante   924-3332
455 Magnolia Avenue

One of the best Northern Italian restaurants in Marin. Superb daily specials and great pastas. Try the crab cioppino or lamb shank with polenta. Beautifully prepared desserts.

Lark Creek Inn   924-7766
234 Magnolia Avenue.

Chef Bradley Ogden's and partner Michael Dellar's famous restaurant is always outstanding. Try their signature dish, the house smoked fish. Menu changes daily. Specializes in seasonal farm-fresh American cooking. Oak burning oven, all American wines, full service bar.

Left Bank   927-3331
507 Magnolia Avenue

Country style French cooking, hearty and delicious in a light and airy atmosphere. Try the cheese plate, especially the Humboldt fog sheep cheese. Several "Heart Healthy" items. Sandwiches and delicious desserts. Outdoor dining. Moderate prices.

Marin Brewing Company   461-4677
1809 Larkspur Landing Circle

Good variety of sandwiches including burgers and a large selection of beers.

Marvin Gardens Cafe   461-2241
1000 Magnolia Avenue

Enjoy outdoor dining and an excellent meal.

Rulli's   924-7478
464 Magnolia Avenue

A great place to stop in downtown Larkspur for coffee, tea and a dessert or pastry. If you are hungrier, the soups are good.

Yet Wah Restaurant   461-3631
2019 Larkspur Landing

Owned by Chef Hoon Sing Chan and his family. Diners may select from 300 authentic Mandarin dishes— six dinners or a-la-carte soups, fish, beef, pork, lamb, chicken and duck selections. Nice decor and view from some tables. Cocktail lounge, banquet room, food to go and deliveries.

MARSHALL

Tony's Seafood   663-1107
18863 State Route 1 on Tomales Bay

Fresh seafood meals. A special treat is barbecued oysters every Saturday and Sunday. The restaurant and bar have a lovely marine view through blue-tinted glass.

MILL VALLEY

Buckeye Roadhouse   331-2600
15 Shoreline Highway

No longer German-American cooking, the Buckeye now offers trendy, up-market American cuisine. Great steaks and barbecued baby back ribs. Delicious salads. Try the appetizer "Oysters Bingo." Full bar.

The Cantina   381-1070
651 East Blithedale Avenue

Mexican food and delicious margaritas have been served in an authentic atmosphere for the past twenty years. Try the enchiladas, quesadillas or fajitas. Patio dining available. Friendly service.

Dipsea Cafe   381-0298
200 Shoreline Highway

The breakfast spot in Southern Marin. Good luncheon menu also.

El Paseo   388-0741
17 Throckmorton Avenue.

Located in the El Paseo shopping complex. Excellent French cuisine.

Frantoio Ristorante   289-5777
152 Shoreline Highway

Located in the Holiday Inn Express, this outstanding restaurant is famous for its White Truffle Dinner, which is only served once a year. Contemporary Italian meals. Olive oil pressed on the premises.

Gira Polli   383-6040
590 East Blithedale Avenue

Try the whole chicken roasted on the spit. Excellent takeout.

India Palace Restaurant   388-3350
707 Redwood Highway

Good friends rave about this restaurant, especially its specialties, shahi khorma (lamb curry), and tikka kabob, boneless chicken cubes marinated and roasted in a Tandoori clay pit oven.

Jennie Low's Chinese Cuisine   388-8868
38 Miller Avenue
(Also at 120 Vintage Way, Novato. 892-8838)

Tasty home-style Chinese cooking. Dim sum lunch specials. Very popular with locals.

La Ginestra   388-0224
127 Throckmorton Avenue

Owner Maria Aversa from Sorrento, Italy, serves a delicious variety of hearty Neapolitan food. Try the veal: veal piccata or veal parmigiana with eggplant. Pizza a specialty. Wide selections of wine and a full bar.

Mountain Home Inn   381-9000
810 Panoramic Highway

Enjoy lunch and dinner on top of Mt. Tamalpais with fabulous views from the terrace, or dine inside by a cozy fireplace. New American cuisine. Try a pasta dish or the salmon. Weekend breakfast or brunch.

Piatti Restaurant   380-2525
625 Redwood Highway

Good Italian food with an influence of California cuisine. Try the risotto or the spit-roasted chicken. Friendly service by a staff which seems to have little turnover.

Piazza D'Angelo   388-2000
22 Miller Avenue

One of the better Italian restaurants in Southern Marin. Good variety.

Strawberry Joe's   383-1400
320 Strawberry Town and Country Village

Italian-American cuisine. Full bar.

Szechuan Flowers of Marin   388-8886
505 Strawberry Village

Traditional Chinese with a flair. Lunch and dinner at reasonable prices.

Thep Lela Thai Restaurant   383-3444
411 Strawberry Village

Great Thai food. Intimate and attractive surroundings. Try the hot and sour seafood soup. Reasonable prices.

Vasco   381-3343
106 Throckmorton

Named for owner Paul Lazzareschi's father, Vasco offers choice Northern Italian cuisine favoring classic Tuscan dishes. Wood burning oven, full bar and counter. Pleasant decor. Very reasonable prices.

MUIR BEACH

The Pelican Inn   383-6000
10 Pacific Way

Opened in 1978, this replica of an authentic English inn and pub offers such traditional British dishes as shepherd's pie, ploughman's lunch and fish and chips. Cozy atmosphere with low ceilings and a fireplace which burns year-round. Specialty is wild boar sausage.

NICASIO

Rancho Nicasio   662-2219
1 Old Rancheria Road

Popular western-style bar and restaurant featuring wagon wheel chandeliers, an oak carved bar and mounted animal heads. Now open daily with live entertainment on weekends. Try the hearty beef or ribs.

NOVATO

Cacti Restaurant   898-2234
1200 Grant Avenue

American-southwest grill. Lunch on Monday—Friday; dinners nightly. Features prime rib on Friday and Saturday.

Roga Patoja, Veronica Cruz, and MaElena Patoja enjoy lunch at Las Guitarras, their Mexican and seafood restaurant in Novato.

Also specializes in "Grande Margaritas" and great tostados. Good atmosphere.

Hilltop Cafe — 892-2222
850 Lamont Avenue

Nice view of surrounding hills. Popular with North Marin business crowd. Good extensive menu.

Jennie Low's — 892-8838
120 Vintage Way

Offers a selection of traditional and upscale Chinese cuisine including new and "light" creations cooked with chicken or vegetable broth instead of oil.

Las Guitarras — 892-3171
1017 Reichert Avenue

Mexican and seafood restaurant. Delightful patio dining with attractive iron garden furniture and a bubbling fountain. Try the tasty tostada.

OLEMA

Olema Farm House — 663-1264
Highway 1 and Sir Francis Drake Boulevard
Open daily

Located in a former carriage house built in 1845. Barbecued oysters daily, hot lunch specials, plus salads and sandwiches. Dinner offers fifteen regular entrees in addition to specials. Patio, deck, and full bar.

Olema Inn and Restaurant — 663-9559
Highway 1 and Sir Francis Drake Boulevard

Lunch and dinner are now being served in this 1876 restored Victorian hotel. Chicken, pasta and fresh seafood dishes are featured. Sunday brunch. Picturesque outdoor deck.

POINT REYES STATION

Station House Cafe — 663-1515
11180 State Route 1

Favorite with locals. Light and airy atmosphere. Try the Hangtown Fry. Breakfast, lunch and dinner.

Taqueria La Quinta — 663-8868
11285 State Route 1

Diners will find the menu on the wall and have to order at the cash register, but the food is very tasty. Try the combination plate of a taco, enchilada or the vegetable nachos with beans and cheese, guacamole, sour cream and salsa.

SAN ANSELMO

Bubba's Diner — 459-6862
566 San Anselmo Avenue

Old time San Anselmo. Excellent large standard breakfast, lunch and dinners offering American cuisine such as pot roast and meat loaf. Small space and usually crowded with happy local diners.

Comforts Cafe — 454-9840
335 San Anselmo Avenue

Good take-out and several small tables for customers ordering from the deli. Superb Chinese chicken salad.

Insalata's Restaurant — 457-7700
120 Sir Francis Drake Boulevard

A popular gourmet restaurant offering one of the most creative menus in Marin. Always delicious. Try "Insalata's Cataplana," a Portuguese clam dish with chorizo and fresh tomatoes sauted.

"Making the Most of Marin" book designer, Janet Bollow, author, Patricia Arrigoni, and editor, Carroll Dana enjoy lunch in San Anselmo. (Photo by Rachel Epstein.)

Lococo's Pizzeria   453-1238
638 San Anselmo Avenue
(Also at 631 Del Ganado Road, Terra Linda. 472-3323.)

Tasty pizza which can be ordered by the slice. Generous toppings and crisp crusts. Friendly service.

Ming Garden   453-2468
340 Sir Francis Drake Blvd. at the Hub

Healthy Szechwan and Hunan cuisine. Salad and fresh fruit bar. Pleasant atmosphere with classical music. Try the lamb with basil and onion, the mango chicken or beef rib-eye steak. Will deliver take-out.

Orchid Thai Restaurant   457-9470
726 San Anselmo Avenue

One of the better Thai restaurants in Marin. Friendly service.

Riccardo's Ristorante   457-0616
and Pizzeria
411 San Anselmo Avenue

A fine Italian restaurant in the Courtyard. Antipastos, veal, chicken, seafood specialties, pasta dishes and a wide selection of pizza.

Rosetti Italian Restaurant   459-7937
510 San Anselmo Avenue

Simple, authentic Italian food. Wood burning oven, house-made ravioli, popular deli. Brunch on weekends.

Shiraz Persian Cuisine   460-0391
205 San Anselmo Avenue

Owner Farzad Aliabadi offers a wide selection of delicious Persian dishes including dinner kababs, basmati rice, seafood, stews, salads and appetizers. Try the delicious chelo-kabab soltani which combines ground lamb and beef with pure filet mignon. Affordable and popular buffet lunches served week-days. Outdoor dining and take out.

Taco Jane's   454-656
221 Tamalpais Avenue

A favorite for Mexican food. Fresh with ample servings and always delicious. Patio dining in good weather. .

SAN GERONIMO

Two Bird Cafe at the Valley Inn   488-0105
625 San Geronimo Valley Drive

Favorite valley restaurant with American, vegetarian and Italian food.

SAN RAFAEL

Anita's Kitchen   454-2626
534 Fourth Street

Good Thai food.

Art's Pier 15   459-3228
15 Harbor Street

Located on the water with a lovely view. Seafood, Italian cuisine, full bar. Orders to go.

Cafe Ristorante Italia   459-3977
1236 Fourth Street

Bright airy atmosphere in downtown San Rafael. Extensive selection of Italian dishes including good pastas and pizza. Delicious seafood. Full service bar. Reasonable prices.

Casa Manana   456-7345
711 D Street

A popular Mexican restaurant for many years. Wide selection and delicious entrees.

Celia's Mexican Restaurant   456-8190
1 Vivian Way

A favorite in the Canal area. Fresh Mexican food with plentiful portions and good service.

Centro Stelle   485-4422
901 Lincoln Ave.

A Tuscan trattoria with indoor and outdoor dining. Excellent choices. Open for dinner daily and lunch Monday through Friday.

The Club Restaurant   491-5959
350 Smith Ranch Road

Located at the McInnis Park Golf Course and popular for Marin groups and private parties. A big screen TV draws patrons to watch sporting events, especially the San Francisco 49ers. Pasta is featured with daily specials. Buffet brunch on Sundays. Open to the public seven days a week.

Flatiron Grill   453-4318
724 B Street

Crowded but fun. Sports bar with a good selection of beer and inexpensive burgers, fried calamari, chicken wings, sandwiches, salads and fruit pies. Breakfast served on weekends.

Giovanni's   454-8000
999 Anderson Drive

Serving good Italian food since 1975. Specials are veal, chicken, and "tutto mare" with rock shrimp, clams, mussels and calamari served over pasta with a red sauce. Other favorite dishes include seafood cannelloni with salmon, seabass piccata and sweetbreads sauté. Full bar. Friendly service.

Il Davide   **454-8080**
901 A Street

Consistent outstanding Italian cuisine. One of the best in Marin featuring wonderful pastas and good Tuscan fare. Owner David Haydon has added ten sidewalk tables which will seat 30 diners.

India Village   **456-2411**
555 East Francisco Boulevard.

Their low-priced luncheon buffet is terrific for lovers of Indian food. Extensive dinner menu.

Kamikaze Sushi Bar   **457-6776**
and Japanese Cuisine
223 Third Street
in the Montecito Shopping Center

Chinese owner Gene Su serves absolutely fabulous sushi and impeccably fresh fish. Great personalities behind the sushi bar. Fine quality.

Kasbah Moroccan Restaurant   **472-6666**
200 Merrydale Road

An exquisite selection of Moroccan dishes. Diners may elect to eat with their fingers or with knives and forks. Friends

Carlo Farina and his sister, Cynthia Richardson, and their cousin, Head Chef Chez-Bornia, who jointly own San Rafael Joe's along with their parents, Guido and Theresa Farina.

say their meal was wonderful, a totally different experience. Open for dinners except for Monday.

Las Camelias Cocina Tradicional   **453-5850**
912 Lincoln

Traditional Mexican food and a longtime favorite of San Rafael diners.

La Toscana   **492-9100**
3751 Redwood Highway

Popular Italian cuisine. Pastas, beef, seafood and other specials. Warm and welcoming staff. Always delicious and one of my favorites. Full service bar.

Mayflower Inn   **456-1011**
1533 Fourth Street

Authentic old English pub. Fish and chips and other British offerings plus hamburgers. Piano sing-alongs on weekends, dart games and trivia games played on Thursday evenings.

Panama Hotel   **457-3993**
4 Bayview Street

Older remodeled hotel with lots of atmosphere and delightful patio dining. Very interesting wine list. Fresh seafood of the day and a good selection of salads. Live jazz by "Swing Fever" on Tuesday nights.

Pasta Pomodoro   **256-2401**
421 3rd Street

Light and airy restaurant located in the Montecito Shopping Center. Tile counter and floors with posters on the walls. Customers can watch the cooks perform behind the counter. Cheerful fast service. Try the capellini pomodoro or the healthy seafood linguine with bay scallops, zucchini, peas, fresh tomatoes, garlic and basil. (Healthy pastas are low in oil and butter.) Wine list could be expanded. Very reasonable prices.

Peking Low   456-9416
411 3rd Street

Excellent Chinese cuisine for lunch and dinner daily. Extensive selections and reasonable prices with food to go.

Phyllis' Giant Burgers   456-0866
2202 4th Street

Friends think Phyllis' serves the best hamburgers on sourdough bread in Marin. Also great: veggie burgers, chicken burgers and onion rings cooked with lots of pepper in the batter.

Pier 6   457-1733
1559 Fourth Street

Great Chinese food. Specializes in Mandarin cooking. Try the princess squid or the princess prawns. Very reasonable.

Ping's Mandarin Restaurant   492-1638
817 Francisco Boulevard West

Delicious Mandarin cooking.

Rice Table (The)   456-1808
1617 Fourth Street

Sumptuous Indonesian feasts.

Royal Thai   485-1074
610 Third Street

Voted best Thai restaurant in the Bay Area by *San Francisco Focus* and Channel 5 TV.

Salute Ristorante   453-7596
706 Third Street

Simply one of the best Italian restaurants in Marin. Several specials on a daily basis. Gino La Motta is a gracious host.

San Rafael Joe's   456-2425
931 Fourth Street

All-around good restaurant and popular bar which has been serving Marinites for a long time. Italian food, steaks and seafood at reasonable prices. Makes a

M'hamed Ba'het, General Manager of The Seafood Peddler Restaurant and Oyster Bar in San Rafael.

great hamburger. Generous portions, well-prepared.

Scopazzi's Restaurant   453-7877
1613 Fourth Street

Traditional Italian. New owner has a flair for innovation.

Seafood Peddler   460-6669
507 East Francisco Boulevard
(Was Dominic's)

Specializes in fresh seafood, lobster. On the order of Eastern seafood houses. Full service bar and deck with view of the San Rafael Canal. Two stories and outdoor dining in good weather. Live music on weekends.

Sushi To Dai For 721-0392
869 Fourth Street.

Good variety of Japanese luncheons.
Super sushi.

Yu Shang Mandarin Restaurant 457-9199
and Sushi Bar
180 Bellam Boulevard

Very good selection of authentic
Chinese. Excellent sushi bar.

SAUSALITO

Alta Mira Hotel 332-1350
125 Bulkley Avenue

Classic Marin hotel with a stunning view
and terrace. American and Continental
cuisine. Famous for Sunday brunch.

Chart House 332-0804
201 Bridgeway

Standard fare, well prepared. Good service. Great view of San Francisco and the
bay. Dinners nightly and Sunday brunch.

Guernica Restaurant 332-1512
2009 Bridgeway

Basque cooking with some outstanding
dishes including paella, patés, game,
escargot and fresh seafood. Live classical guitar and wine bar.

Horizons 331-3232
558 Bridgeway

Located in old San Francisco Yacht Club.
Fantastic views of San Francisco and the
bay. Fresh seafood and daily brunch.
Indoor and outdoor dining. (Will be
remodeled and changed back to the
Trident Restaurant in 2001)

Houlihan's Old Place 332-8512
660 Bridgeway

Dining with a panoramic bay view. Specializes in fresh seafood while you enjoy
the view of the bay and San Francisco.
Rear patio for warm weather. A chain
restaurant popular with locals and
tourists alike. Reasonable prices. Try the
grilled pork ribs or the cioppino.

Scoma's, Horizons, and Ondine restaurants in Sausalito.

Margaritaville Restaurant 331-3226
1200 Bridgeway

Delicious Mexican cuisine. Full bar, cozy fireplace and gorgeous views of the Sausalito Yacht Harbor. Spacious deck with heaters. Reasonable prices and free parking.

Ondine 331-1133
558 Bridgeway

Upscale restaurant which has returned to the former San Francisco Yacht Club. Great views of San Francisco.

Mikayla 331-5888
at Casa Madrona Hotel
801 Bridgeway

Glass-enclosed dining room on the top floor of this hilltop hotel offers spectacular views of Sausalito and the bay. French influenced cuisine with a Mediterranean touch. Homemade breads and desserts. Selection of heart healthy and vegeterian entrees. Dinners and Sunday brunch.

North Sea Village 331-3300
300 Turney Street

Popular authentic Hong Kong seafood. Specializes in delicious dim sum. Gorgeous waterfront views of Richardson Bay.

Saylor's Landing 332-6161
305 Harbor Drive

Popular local hangout built of natural woods with lots of glass. Skylights, a stone fireplace, brick floors and plants everywhere. Good selection of soups, salads and sandwiches, seafood daily and tasty pasta dishes. Full bar and "Happy Hour."

Scoma's 332-9551
588 Bridgeway

Seafood specialties, salads, steaks and Italian dishes. Built out on a pier over-looking the bay with great views. A Sausalito tradition for over twenty years.

Seven Seas Restaurant 332-1304
682 Bridgeway

Complete fresh seafood selection served in a greenhouse dining area with a retractable roof. Also fresh homemade pizza.

Spinnaker 332-1500
100 Spinnaker Drive

Excellent seafood menu and good pasta dishes. Spectacular views right on the bay. Good service. On-site parking.

STINSON BEACH

Parkside Cafe and Snack Bar 868-1272
one block west of Highway 1

This local favorite was remodeled in January 2000 and has become more upscale. Try their delicious oyster chowder, mussels and crème bruelle.

Sand Dollar 868-0434
3458 Shoreline Highway.

Bob and Juiliann Temer own this popular eating house where locals and visitors have enjoyed dining for over 30 years. Full bar.

Stinson Beach Grill 868-2002
3465 State Route 1

Regular local hangout owned by Tom Horton and his son, Michael. Menu has a wide selection of delicious entrees, all reasonably priced. Recommendations: clam chowder, Chinese chicken salad or chicken burrito. Full bar.

The Parkside Cafe in Stinson Beach.

TIBURON

The Caprice   435-3400
2000 Paradise Drive

This recently remodeled restaurant sits overlooking San Francisco Bay and has spectacular views. Good selection of seafood.

Guaymas Restaurant   435-6300
5 Main Street

Unique regional Mexican dishes. Wide selections and all delicious. Gorgeous views of the bay. Popular with locals and tourists alike.

Milano Restaurant   388-8100
1 Blackfield Drive

Located in the Cove Shopping Center. Tasty traditional Italian/American cuisine. Generous portions, excellent service. Reasonable prices.

Rooney's Cafe and Grill   435-1911
38 Main Street

California cuisine and garden dining. Try the Rueben sandwich for lunch. Dinner specialities include seared, spice-rubbed pork chops with raspberry red-onion marmalade and sesame herb crusted salmon. Open daily for lunch and Wednesday through Sunday for dinner.

Sam's Anchor Cafe   435-4527
27 Main Street

Started in 1920 by Sam Vella, this popular Marin restaurant has grown to the point that they now can serve up to 2,000 customers on a sunny day when diners can enjoy the deck. Co-owned by Steve Sears and Brian Wilson, who offer fresh seafood and a selection of American classics. Hamburgers are popular as are some pasta dishes, such as linguine with smoked salmon and mussels. Gorgeous view of yacht harbors and bay. Full service bar.

Guaymas Restaurant in Tiburon overlooks Racoon Straits and San Francisco Bay.

Servino Ristorante   435-2676
9 Main Street
(Next to Guaymas)

Italian cooking with a southern flair. Brothers Angelo and Carlo Servino originate from Calabria where their family owned a restaurant. They opened a smaller restaurant in Tiburon in 1987, then moved to their larger, current location in 1999. Delicious entrees include pasta, pizza, stuffed and baked mushrooms, seafood, chicken and steaks. Friendly service. Reasonable prices.

TOMALES

William Tell House Restaurant
Highway 1   707-878-2403

The restaurant in this historic hotel opened in 1983, while the bar has been serving locals since 1877. Now under new management, Kirk Furlong offers prime ribs, steaks and seafood, including barbecued oysters. Moderate prices and good food.

Lodging, RV Parks, Camping, and Youth Hostels

RENTAL EXCHANGES

In the past few years, accommodations have sprung up in the form of bed and breakfast inns and cottages and homestays in Marin residences. Several exchanges have been organized to help people make reservations.

Bed and Breakfast Exchange   485-1971
of Marin
45 Entrada Avenue, San Anselmo, CA 94960

This exchange is owned by Suellen Lamorte, who personally inspects every property. She specializes in homestays and handles about 25 properties, including cottages and houseboats.

Coastal Lodging of West Marin   663-1351
P.O. Box 1162, Pt. Reyes Station, CA 94956
Website: www.coastallodging.com

Six cottages available in Bolinas, Point Reyes and Inverness.

Coastal Getaways   1-888-663-9445
P.O. Box 681, Pt. Reyes Station, CA 94956
Website: www.coastalgetaways.com

Handles five cottages near Point Reyes Station.

Inns of Marin   663-2000
Reservations: 1-800-887-2880
P.O. Box 547, Pt. Reyes Station, CA 94956
E-mail: innmarin@best.com
Website: www.innsofmarin.com

Free lodging referral and reservation service for over 30 inns, cottages and bed and breakfast accommodations in western Marin County.

Inns of Point Reyes   663-1420
P.O. Box 176, Pt. Reyes Station, CA 94956

Handles five of the original bed and breakfast inns and cottages of Point Reyes.

Point Reyes Lodging   663-1872
Reservations: 1-800-539-1872
P. O. Box 878, Pt. Reyes Station, CA 94956
Website: www.ptreyes.com

Doris Ferrando will help you with 14 properties – small hotels, country inns and cottages in addition to a lodge.

West Marin Network   663-9543
P.O. Box 834, Pt. Reyes Station, CA 94956
E-mail: westmnet@svn.net

With one call, you can get area and lodging information for 50 properties in West Marin

West Marin Vacation Rentals   663-1776
P.O. Box 160, Pt. Reyes Station, CA 94956
E-mail: vacation@west-marin.com
Website: www.west-marin.com/vacation

Specializes in one to three-bedroom Inverness vacation homes, all with well-equipped kitchens. Weekend, weekly and monthly rentals.

◀ *Casa Del Mar, Stinson Beach.*

HOTELS, MOTELS, INNS, BED AND BREAKFAST COTTAGES AND HOMESTAYS

BOLINAS (94924)

Blue Heron Inn, 11 Wharf Road (868-1102)

Bolinas Bed and Breakfast, 15 Brighton Avenue (868-1757)

One Fifty Five Pine, 155 Pine Street, P.O. Box 62 (868-2721)
website: www.angelfire.com/ ca4/bolinas/flames.html

Smiley's Schooner Saloon & Hotel, 41 Wharf Road (868-1311)

Thomas' White House Inn (868-0279)
website: www.coastallodging.com

CORTE MADERA (94925)

Corte Madera Inn—Best Western,
1815 Redwood Highway (924-1502) or reservations (800-777-9670)

Howard Johnson Express Inn, 1595 Casa Buena Drive (924-3570)

Marin Suites Hotel, 45 Tamal Vista Boulevard (924-3608),
website: www.marinsuites.com.

FAIRFAX (94930)

Fairfax Inn B & B, 15 Broadway (455-8702), website: **www.fairfax/inn.com.**

INVERNESS (94937)

Abalone Inn, 12355 Sir Francis Drake Boulevard, Inverness Park (663-9149), website: www.abaloneinn.com

The Ark, P.O. Box 273 (663-9338), reservations (800-808-9338), website: www.rosemarybb.com

Blackthorne Inn, 266 Vallejo Avenue, Inverness Park, P.O. Box 712 (663-8621), website: www.blackthorneinn.com

Dancing Coyote Beach, P.O. Box 98 (669-7200)

Fairwinds Farm, Box 581 (663-9454), e-mail: fairwind@svn.net

Golden Hinde Inn and Marina, 12938 Sir Francis Drake Boulevard (669-1389), reservations (800-339-9398)

Hotel Inverness, P.O. Box 780 (669-7393), website: www.hotelinverness.com

Inverness Valley Inn & Tennis Ranch, 13275 Sir Francis Drake Boulevard (669-7250), reservations (800-416-0405), e-mail: info@invernessvalleyinn.com, website: www.invernessvalleyinn.com

Manka's Inverness Lodge, Callendar Way and Argyle (669-1034), reservations (800-585-6343), website: www.mankas.com

Motel Inverness, 12718 Sir Francis Drake Boulevard (669-1081), e-mail: Inverness@ispchannel.com, website: www.coastaltraveler.com\motelinverness

Rosemary Cottage, P.O. Box 273 (663-9338), e-mail: rosemarybb@aol.com

Sandy Cove Inn, 12990 Sir Francis Drake Boulevard, P.O. Box 869 (669-2683), reservations (800-759-2683) e-mail: innkeeper@sandycove.com, website: www.sandycove.com

Ten Inverness Way, P.O. Box 63 (669-1648), e-mail: inn@teninvernessway.com, website: www.teninvernessway.com

The Tree House Bed and Breakfast, 73 Drake Summit Road, Inverness Park (663-8720), reservations (800-495-8720), website: www.treehousebnb.com

LARKSPUR (94904)

Courtyard by Marriott, 2500 Larkspur Landing Circle (925-1800), website: www.marriott.com

MILL VALLEY (94941)

Acqua Hotel, 555 Redwood Highway (380-0400), reservations (888-662-9555), e-mail: mgr@acquahotel.com, website: www.acquahotel.com

Fireside Motel, 115 Shoreline Highway (332-6906)

Fountain Motel, 155 Shoreline Highway (332-1732)

Holiday Inn Express, 160 Shoreline Highway (332-5700), reservations (800-258-3894), website: www.hiexmv.com

Mill Valley Inn, 165 Throckmorton Avenue (389-6608), reservations (800-595-2100), e-mail: mgr@millvalleyinn.com, website: www.millvalleyinn.com

Mountain Home Inn, 810 Panoramic Highway (381-9000), website: www.mtnhomeinn.com

Travelodge, 707 Redwood Highway (383-0340).

MUIR BEACH (94965)

Pelican Inn, Shoreline/Highway 1 (383-6000), website: www.pelicaninn.com.

NOVATO AREA (94947)

Best Western Novato Oaks Inn, 215 Alameda Del Prado (883-4400), reservations (800-625-7466), e-mail: novoaks@ reneson.com, website: www.renesonhotels.com

Courtyard by Marriott, 1400 North Hamilton Parkway (883-8950), reservations (800-321-2211) website: www.marriott.com

Days Inn, 8141 Redwood Boulevard (897-7111), reservations (800-DAYS-INN)

Inn Marin, 250 Entrada Drive (883-5952), reservations (800-652-6565), website: www.innmarin.com

Skylark Motel, 275 Alameda Del Prado (883-2406)

Travelodge, 7600 Redwood Boulevard (892-7500), reservations (800-255-3050).

OLEMA (94950)

Bear Valley Inn, 88 Bear Valley Road (663-1777)

Olema Inn, 10000 Sir Francis Drake Boulevard at junction of Highway 1 (663-9559), website: www.olemainn.com

Point Reyes Seashore Lodge, 10021 Highway 1 (663-9000), website: www.pointreyesseashore.com

Ridgetop Inn & Cottages, P.O. Box 40 (663-1500), website: www.ridgetopinn.com

Roundstone Farm Bed and Breakfast Inn, 9940 Sir Francis Drake (663-1020), website: www.roundstonefarm.com

POINT REYES STATION (94956)

Bay View Cottage, P.O. Box 638 (663-8800), e-mail: bayview@nbn.com, website: www.abayview.com

Berry Patch Cottage, P.O. Box 712 (663-1942), reservations: (888-663-1942), e-mail: berry@nbn.com, website: www.coastalgetaways.com

Carriage House, 325 Mesa Road (663-8627), reservations: (800-613-8351), e-mail: felicity@nbn.com, website: www.carriagehousebb.com

Cherry Tree Cottage, 50 Cherry Tree Lane, P.O. Box 1082 (663-1689), website: www.cherrytreecottage.com

Cricket Cottage, P.O. Box 627 (663-9139), e-mail: pinc@nbn.com, website: www.permacultureinstitute.com

The Country House, 65 Manana Way, P.O. Box 98 (663-1627), e-mail: innkeeper@ ptreyescountryhouse.com, website: www.ptreyescountryhouse.com

Ferrando's Hide-Away, 12010 Highway 1 (663-1966), reservations: (800-337-2636), website: www.ferrando.com

Holly Tree Inn, 3 Silverhills Road (663-1554), website: www.hollytreeinn.com

Horseshoe Farm Cottage, P.O. Box 332 (663-9401), website: www.horseshoefarm-cabin.com

Jasmine Cottage, P.O. Box 56 (663-1166)

Knob Hill, P.O. Box 1108 (663-1784), website: www.knobhill.com

Neon Rose, P.O. Box 632 (663-9143), reservations: (800-358-8346), e-mail: neonrose@nbn.com, website: www.neonrose.com

Point Reyes Station Inn, 11591 Highway 1 (663-9372), website: www.p-r-s-i.com

Point Reyes Vineyard Inn, 12700 Highway 1 (663-1011), website: www.ptreyesvine-yardinn.com

Pt. Reyes Country Inn & Stables, 12050 Highway 1 (663-9696), website: www.ptreyescountryinn.com

Seamist Cottage, P.O. Box 834 (663-9543) (Cottage located in nearby Marshall)

Thirty-Nine Cypress Bed and Breakfast Inn and **Redwing Cottage,** 39 Cypress Road, P.O. Box 176 (663-1709), e-mail: bartlett@svn.net, website: www.Great ViewInn.com

Terri's Homestay, P.O. Box 113 (663-1289), reservations (800-969-1289), website: www.terrishomestay.com

Windsong Cottage, P.O. Box 84 (663-9695), reservations (800-663-9695), website: www.windsongcottage.com.

SAN ANSELMO (94960)

San Anselmo Inn, 339 San Anselmo Avenue (455-5366), reservations (800-598-9771), e-mail: info@sainn.com, website: www.sananselmoinn.com.

SAN RAFAEL (94901)

Colonial Motel, 1735 Lincoln Avenue (453-9188), reservations (800-554-9118)

Embassy Suites, 101 McInnis Parkway (499-9222), website: www.embassy-marin.com

Gerstle Park Inn, 34 Grove Street (721-7611), reservations (800-726-7611), e-mail: innkeeperatgerstleparkinn.com, website: www.gerstleparkinn.com

Panama Hotel, 4 Bayview (457-3993), reservations (800-899-3993), website: www.panamahotel.com

Villa Inn, 1600 Lincoln Avenue (456-4975)

Four Points Barcelo Sheritan, 1010 North-gate Drive (479-8800; fax 415-479-2342) website: www.fourpoints.com.

SAUSALITO (94965)

Alta Mira Hotel, 125 Bulkley Avenue (332-1350)

Casa Madrona Hotel, 801 Bridgeway (332-0502),
website: www.casamadrona hotel.com

The Gables Inn, 62 Princess Street (289-1100), reservations (800-966-1554), website: www.gablesinnsausalito.com

Hotel Sausalito, 16 El Portal (332-0700), reservations (888-442-0700),
e-mail: hotelsaus@aol.com,
website: www.hotelsausalito.com

The Inn Above Tide, 30 El Portal (332-9535), reservations (800-893-8433), e-mail: inntide@ix.netcom.com, website: www.innabovetide.citysearch.com.

STINSON BEACH (94970)

Casa del Mar, 37 Belvedere Avenue, P.O. Box 238 (868-2124), reservations (800-552-2124),
e-mail: inn@stinsonbeach.com,
website: www.stinsonbeach.com

Ocean Court Motel, 18 Arenal Avenue (868-0212)

The Sandpiper, 1 Marine Way, P.O. Box 208 (868-1632),
e-mail: sandpiper@sfbay.net

House Rentals, Seadrift and Calle del Arroyo contain a colony of private beach homes, several of which are rented through Seadrift Realty (868-1791),
e-mail: cristina@seadrift realty.com, website: www.seadriftrealty.com. Seadrift rentals are also available through Stinson Beach Realty (868-9637), e-mail mareljanel@aol.com, website: www.stinsonbeach realty@aol.com.

TIBURON (94920)

Tiburon Lodge, 1651 Tiburon Boulevard (435-3133),
website: www.tiburon lodge.com.

Waters Edge Hotel, 25 Main Street (789-5999),
website: www.marinhotels.com

RECREATIONAL VEHICLE AND TRAILER PARKS

Golden Gate Trailer Park, 2000 Redwood Highway, Greenbrae 94904 (924-0683).

Sixty-five spaces with 38 spaces for overnight trailers. Complete facilities: hookups, showers, laundry rooms.

Lawson's Landing Campground, at Dillon Beach (94929) on Bodega Bay (707-878-2443), website: www.lawsonslanding.com.

Five hundred trailer or camper spaces. No hookups. Summer docking, rental boats, clam digging, rock and pier fishing, and a safe beach.

Marin Park, 2140 Redwood Highway, Greenbrae 94904 (461-5199), reservations: (888-461-5199), website: www.campgrounds.com.

Eighty-nine mobilehome and 89 RV sites in two separate parks. Complete facilities: hookups, showers, heated pool, laundromats.

Novato RV Park, 1530 Armstrong Avenue, Novato 94945 (897-1271), reservations: (800-733-6787), e-mail: novatorvpark@aol.com, website: www.campgrounds.com/novatorvpark.

Sixty-eight RV sites, full hookups and utilities. Big Rig and Pull-Through sites in this new park. Convenience store/deli, pool, laundry, showers, and office services, including computer, fax and telephone.

Olema Ranch Campground, State Route 1, Olema 94950 (663-8001), website: www.campgrounds.com/olemaranch.

One hundred fifty trailer, RV and tent sites. Barbecue pit and picnic table at each site, recreation hall, full hookups, showers, laundry rooms and RV supplies. Pads at all water/electric sites, firewood, ice, shuffleboard and horseshoes.

CAMPGROUNDS

(Detailed information on California state campgrounds can be found on the following websites: www.cal-parks.ca.gov, as well as the reservation site, www.reserveamerica.com.)

ANGEL ISLAND STATE PARK
in San Francisco Bay. General information: 435-1915 Park ranger: 435-5390

There are nine environmental sites; each one can hold up to eight people. The East Sites are partially wooded and away from the wind; the three Ridge Sites have a San Francisco vista; the Sunrise Sites have unobstructed East Bay views.

Campers must carry all of their equipment two miles, some parts uphill, to the sites. Facilities include picnic tables, food lockers, water, (no showers), pit toilets, and a barbecue at each site. No pets or wood fires are allowed.

Transportation to the island is by the Angel Island - Tiburon Ferry Service, **435-2131.** (There is no scheduled ferry service on weekdays in winter. Call the Tiburon Ferry to join a weekday charter run.)

For reservations, call **ReserveAmerica** at **1-800-444-7275.** If a campsite is not reserved, it is sold on a first-come, first-served basis in the park. You can also reserve on-line at: **www.reserve america.com.**

CHINA CAMP STATE PARK
four miles from downtown San Rafael on North San Pedro Road (456-0766)

Originally settled centuries ago by the Coast Miwok Tribe and in the 19th century by Chinese shrimp fishermen, China Camp, on the shore of San Pablo Bay, offers a variety of activities: camping, picnicking, hiking, bicycling, horseback riding, swimming, fishing, boating, windsurfing and bird-watching. The park has no rental facilities; you must supply your own equipment.

Within its 1,512 acres, more than 18 miles of trails, including fire roads, are available for bicyclists, equestrians and hikers. (Dogs are not allowed on trails; on leash, they are allowed in developed areas.)

Thirty developed campsites (some wheelchair accessible) in a peaceful laurel/oak forest have running water, pay showers, flush toilets, picnic tables, food lockers, and fire rings. Firewood may be purchased from the Camp Host or at the entrance station. No open fires are allowed anywhere in the park. Overnight stays (one night only) for self-contained recreational vehicles are permitted in the parking lot from 6:00 p.m. to 9:00 a.m.

Five day-use picnic areas and Miwok Meadows, a reserve day-use facility that can hold up to 200 people, are also popular destinations.

The site of the old shrimp-fishing village has a small museum with exhibits of China Camp's history; it is open daily from 10:00 a.m. to 5:00 p.m.

Reservations for camp sites may be made by calling ReserveAmerica at **800-444-7275,** or on-line at www.reserveamerica.com. Unreserved sites are available on a first-come, first-served basis. From

November through March reservations are not taken, and all camp sites are on a first-come, first-served basis. For seasonal campground hours and to reserve the group facility, Miwok Meadows, call the **Park Office at 456-0766.**

GOLDEN GATE NATIONAL RECREATION AREA

This park offers five walk-in or backpacking campgrounds located in the Marin Headlands, on the northern side of the Golden Gate Bridge. (No car-camping). Except for Kirby Cove, campgrounds are open all year **(331-1540)**.

All sites have picnic tables and chemical toilets, but none have drinking water or showers. Some have barbecue pits or fire rings. (The knowledgeable staff at the **Marin Headlands Visitor Center, 331-1540,** can answer specific questions, especially about group accommodations for autumn or winter camping at the first two campgrounds listed below.) The maximum stay in campgrounds in the GGNRA is three nights per campsite annually per permittee.

Haypress Camp , in Tennessee Valley, has five sites accommodating up to four people each. It is a relatively easy half-mile walk from the parking lot – good for beginning backpackers and families. No barbecue grills or water available. Fires are not allowed. No fee.

Hawk Camp has three sites for four people each. It is a steep 3.5 mile hike up the Bobcat Trail, but you will be rewarded with spectacular views of the Headlands and San Francisco Bay. It is the most remote of the campgrounds; bring your own water and camp stove. Fires not allowed. No fee.

Bicentennial Campground, near the Point Bonita Lighthouse, is automobile accessible with a short walk to the campground. This small campground has three sites, maximum two people per site. Water is located at the Visitor Center one mile away, and barbecue grills are close by. Fires not allowed. No fee.

Kirby Cove, just west of the Golden Gate Bridge, is in a grove of cypress and eucalyptus trees along a sandy cove. With an automobile permit, you may park and walk in 100 meters. Four sites hold a maximum of 10 people. Group sites are available, and campground hosts are at this site. No water is available, but there are fire rings and barbecue pits. (Bring your own firewood and kindling). No pets. Because of its popularity, advance reservations are recommended for this site. A fee is charged.

Battery Alexander Group Site is an indoor converted mortar battery close to Point Bonita. This site is especially popular with groups such as the Boy Scouts. Minimum of 15 people, maximum of 80. Bring your own bedding. Outside fire pits (bring your own firewood) and barbecues, drinking water and electricity available. No pets. Groups must have a responsible leader 21 years or older for every ten children under the age of 18. A fee is required.

Permits for the non-fee sites (Haypress, Hawk and Bicentennial) are available at the Marin Headlands Visitor Center between 9:30 a.m. and 4:30 p.m. The Center is located on Field Road at the Ft. Barry Chapel, Building 948, three miles from the Bunker Road Tunnel. Permits for Kirby Cove and Battery Alexander (fee sites) are available by mail and must be secured at least a week in advance.

Reservations may be made through the **Special Park Users Group, 561-4304.**

Reservations are suggested for all campgrounds, but for the non-fee sites they are also available on a first-come, first served basis at the Visitor's Center if there is availability. For camping reservations call **331-1540** between 9:30 AM and 4:30 p.m., or come to the Visitor's Center during the same hours. Reservations are accepted no more than 90 days in advance.

The National Park Service website for this area is: **www.nps.gov/goga/camping.htm.**

MOUNT TAMALPAIS STATE PARK
Adjacent to Mill Valley on Panoramic Highway (388-2070)

Pantoll Campground, at the Pantoll Ranger Station, has 16 sites available on a first-come, first-served basis. Open all year, the campsites are complete with tables, elevated fire pits, charcoal grills, piped water and restrooms, but no showers. Pets are allowed for an extra dollar. Self-contained RVs under 25 feet may stay one night in the nearby lower parking lot. (No hookups.)

Rocky Point—Steep Ravine Environmental Campground has six walk-in campsites and 10 rustic cabins on a bluff that over-looks the ocean. One car and five persons maximum are allowed at the cabins. The cabins have no running water; nearby are primitive toilets and piped drinking water.

Alice Eastwood Group Camp , in the redwoods near Muir Woods, can accommodate up to 75 people.

Except for Pantoll Campground sites, reservations must be made at least ten days in advance : **ReserveAmerica, 1-800-444-7275, or on-line at: www.reserve america.com.** You may also call the park directly **(388-2070)** for detailed camping availability and fee information.

POINT REYES NATIONAL SEASHORE
Entrance to the Bear Valley Camping Area is at the Point Reyes National Seashore Headquarters, a quarter mile west of the town of Olema on Bear Valley Road (663-1092)

Accessible only by hiking or biking, there are four back-country sites in the park: **Skycamp, Coast Camp, Glen Camp,** and **Wildcat Camp**. They vary in settings, elevation and in distance from park headquarters. Some are available as group sites (up to 25 people); most individual sites hold up to six people. The helpful staff at the Bear Valley Visitor Center is available for more detailed information **(663-8054).**

Each campsite has a picnic table, food storage locker, charcoal grills, pit toilets and a water faucet (water may have to be treated). No pets are allowed. Wood fires are permitted only on beaches, and with a free fire permit.

Camping permits, available at the Visitor Center, are required. Reservations may be made up to three months in advance of your stay by calling 663-8054 between the hours of 9:00 a.m. and 2:00 p.m., Monday through Friday. (VISA/Mastercard accepted.) You may also make reservations in person at the **Bear Valley Visitor Center** seven days a week during its hours of operation. Week-end reservations are strongly recommended; first-come, first-served permits are often available Sunday through Thursday nights. website: **www.nps.gov/ pore**

SAMUEL P. TAYLOR STATE PARK
in Lagunitas (488-9897)

There are 60 individual campsites within the redwood groves, and two group camps located in the Madrone Group Area which have a combined capacity of 75 people. The Redwood Grove Group Picnic Area may be reserved for day use only.

Facilities in the park include restrooms, hot showers, picnic tables and barbecue pits.

Devil's Gulch Camp is maintained for horseback riders using the state riding and hiking trails. The camp has a corral, hitching racks, watering troughs, and a cleared camping area for up to 25 people and their horses.

For reservations, call **ReserveAmerica at 1-800-444-7275.** Reservations may also be made on their website: **www.reserve america.com.**

TOMALES BAY STATE PARK
four miles north of Inverness off Sir Francis Drake Boulevard to Pierce Point Road (669-1140).

Open all year from 8:00 a.m. to sunset, this 2,000 acre park which is adjacent to the Point Reyes National Seashore has four surf-free beaches, picnicking, swimming, clamming and boating, as well as six miles of trails. (Dogs are not allowed on beaches or trails.) It offers a self-guided nature trail that will give you information about Native American use of indigenous plants.

Within the park, there are six hiker/biker campsites in an oak and bishop pine forest. No reservations are taken, so availability is on a first-come, first-served basis, and a fee is required. A mile-long hike brings you to the campsites, which have food lockers and a shared fire pit. (Bring your own wood.) Nearby are picnic tables,

running water, changing rooms, cold showers and flush toilets. Be sure to wear layered clothing, since the weather changes quickly. For more information, call the ranger station at **669-1140,** or visit the website at **www.cal-parks.ca.gov.**

YOUTH HOSTELS

The **Marin Headlands Hostel** (Hosteling International), part of the Golden Gate Council, is located within Fort Barry in the Marin Headlands. Open all year, its amenities include 103 beds, a common room, kitchen, family room, laundry and internet access.

Private rooms for families and couples are available, as well as men's, women's and coed dormitories. Reservations may be made by writing **The Marin Headlands Hostel, Building 941, Ft. Barry, Sausalito CA 94965. You may also telephone 331-2777 or 800-909-4776, #62.** Credit cards are accepted for reservations. website: **www.norcalhostels.org/**

Point Reyes Hostel is located two miles from Limantour Beach in the Point Reyes National Seashore, and may be reached by car, foot, or bicycle. It was once a working ranch house and is open all year. Accommodations include dormitory sleeping for 44 people, hot showers, a spacious, fully-equipped kitchen, dining room, common room, and an outdoor barbecue and patio.

Reservations may be made by writing **Point Reyes Hostel, P.O. Box 247, Point Reyes Station, CA 94956,** or by telephoning **663-8811. Reservations may also be made at 1-800-909-4776 (#61).** Master Card/ VISA accepted for reservations. website: **www.norcalhostels.org/**

Transportation, Tours, and Entertainment 17

TRANSPORTATION

Angel Island State Park Ferry provides transportation between Tiburon and Angel Island daily from April through October, a trip that takes only 10 to 15 minutes. During winter the service is available on weekends and by arrangement during the week. For information call **435-2131. Website: www.angelis-landferry.com**

Golden Gate Transit operates daily buses within Marin County to nearby San Francisco and Sonoma Counties, with modified services on weekends and holidays. Daily service also connects San Rafael with the El Cerrito Del Norte BART station in western Contra Costa County. The fares very according to the distance traveled, and various discounts are provided to regular commuters, students, senior citizens and persons with disabilities. All GGT bus service is operated with lift-equipped buses; however, not all GGT bus stops are wheelchair-accessible.

Golden Gate Ferries, which include a high-speed catamaran, operate from the Sausalito and Larkspur terminals to the San Francisco Ferry Building at the foot of Market Street. Ferries operate daily except Thanksgiving, Christmas, and New Year's Day. Family fares are available on weekends, and refreshments are for sale on board. Discounts are available to seniors, youth, and to persons with disabilities; the ferries are accessible to passengers using wheelchairs.

Golden Gate free shuttle buses operate weekdays, except holidays, during peak commute periods throughout the communities in Eastern Marin to the Sausalito and Larkspur ferry terminals.

For bus and ferry schedules and information, call **455-2000** in Marin, **923-2000** in San Francisco. **Website: www.golden-gate.org**

Marin Airporter has two terminals, and offers daily shuttle service between Marin County and the San Francisco International Airport. Parking is available at each terminal. Buses stop at Mill Valley and Sausalito.

The Larkspur Terminal is located at 300 Larkspur Landing Circle. Buses run every half hour between 4:30 a.m., (5:30

◄ *The Hubbard Street Dance Company is just one of the groups appearing at the Marin Center.*

a.m. from San Francisco) up to and including 11:00 p.m. from Larkspur with the last bus leaving San Francisco at 12 midnight. Information: **461-4222.**

The Ignacio Terminal, at 1455 North Hamilton Parkway, Ignacio, has hourly service beginning at 4:00 a.m., up to and including 10:00 p.m.. Information: **884-2878.**

Connecting shuttle service is available from Embassy Suites, Four Points Barcelo Sheritan, North San Rafael, and the transportation center (2nd & Tamalpais, San Rafael) to the Larkspur Terminal. **Website: www.marinairporter.com**

TOURS AND CHARTERS

SIGHTSEEING BY BOAT

One of the best ways to see Marin County is from a San Francisco Bay cruise.

In addition to their Tiburon-Angel Island ferry service, the *Angel Island-Tiburon Ferry* has two vessels for charter, the elegant *Tamalpais* , a luxury yacht accommodating 97 guests, and the larger *Angel Island* , for 200, with a fully-open upper deck. Weddings, corporate events and family celebrations are held on these boats. The one-and-a-half hour Sunset Cruise is a popular tour, and private groups may arrange for a 45 minute historic guided cruise to learn the history of Angel Island.

Information: 435-2131. Website: www.angelislandferry.com

The Blue and Gold Fleet's bay cruises leave Pier 39 in San Francisco beginning at 10:00 a.m. Tickets may be purchased at the dock or, for an extra fee, in advance. (In addition to the bay cruise, weekday

service between Tiburon and the San Francisco Ferry Building is offered.)

The ships ride smoothly and offer glass-enclosed lower decks, open-air top decks, and snack bars. The narrated cruise lasts about one hour. The ship passes many San Francisco landmarks, sails under the Golden Gate Bridge and past Alcatraz, Sausalito, Belvedere, Tiburon, and Angel Island.

Blue and Gold also offers charter trips to Muir Woods, Angel Island, Sausalito and Tiburon, among other destinations.

For advance tickets, call **705-5555.** The number for group rates, 15 or more, is **705-8214.** For a recorded schedule, call **773-1188.**

Website: www.blueandgold.com

The *Hawaiian Chieftain* is an impressive 103-foot square topsail ketch, built in the 1790s period style. Her home port is Marina Plaza in Sausalito. From April through October you can choose among the scheduled Wednesday, Thursday and Friday Sunset Sails, the Saturday Adventure Sail, where you are encouraged to help sail the ship under the crew's supervision, or the Sunday Brunch Cruise, complete with live music. Food and beverages are included in the price for all cruises. There are many special events throughout the year, and the ship is also available for private charter. For reservations and information, call **331-3214.**

Website: www.hawaiianchieftain.com

The *Ka'iulani* is docked in Sausalito and named for Princess Ka'iulane, the last heir apparent to the Hawaiian throne. It is a luxurious 86-foot classic wooden schooner and modern replica of an 1850s coastal trading ship. Scheduled cruises from April through October include a Friday Sunset Sail, 6:00 p.m. to 9:00 p.m., and a Sunday Adventure Sail, 10:00 a.m. to 1:00 p.m.. Reservations are required. The *Ka'iulani* may also be reserved for corporate events, weddings, and private celebrations.

For reservations and information, call 331-1333. Visit the website at **www.sfyacht.com**

For powerboat and sailboat charters, see "Boat Renting and Leasing" in the Yellow Pages.

SEAPLANE TOURS

San Francisco Seaplane Tours, now in its 50th year, offers two popular flights from its Sausalito seaplane base. The 30 minute Golden Gate Tour flies you out to the Pacific Coast and then over the Golden Gate Bridge and points of interest in San Francisco and Southern Marin. The Champagne Sunset Flight lasts about 40 minutes, bringing you back at dusk as you pass between Sausalito and the Tiburon Peninsula. Reservations are necessary for the Sunset flight.

The seaplane base is at 242 Redwood Highway, Mill Valley, adjacent to Highway 101. For reservations, call **332-4843.** Website: **www.seaplane.com**

MOTOR COACH TOURS

Marin Charter and Tours , a division of the Marin Airporter, offers scheduled and chartered bus service. Scheduled minitours have included destinations such as Hearst Castle, Lake Tahoe, Yosemite, and Las Vegas. Muir Woods and wine country tours are scheduled daily in conjunction with the Blue and Gold Fleet. In addition to large coaches, 21 passenger

buses are available for individually arranged charters.

For information, call **256-8830.** Website: **www.marinairporter.com**

ENTERTAINMENT

The Belrose Theater   454-6422
1415 Fifth Avenue, San Rafael

Since 1954, Margie Belrose has been producing comedies, classical drama, and original shows which run throughout the year at her San Rafael theater and school. The productions draw from professional and community actors, as well as an established company of performers. (A recent addition is the 7:30 p.m. Thursday "Open Mike" show for singers, comics, and poets.) The Belrose Theatrical School offers a variety of dance and acting classes, and the costume shop has a wide array of costumes. Call for information about current productions and for tickets.

College of Marin   485-9385
835 College Avenue, Kentfield

On its Kentfield campus, College of Marin sponsors two professional-quality stage productions each fall and spring. These range from *Peter Pan* to classical Greek drama, and the actors are chosen from the community as well as from the college. Actors Robin Williams, David Dukes and Kathleen Quinlan are College of Marin theater alumni.

A new series of productions, "Fresh On Fridays," produced and performed by students, plays in the Studio Theater most Fridays during the school year at 8:00 p.m. Hotline for information: **485-9556.**

The award-winning College of Marin Dance Department offers a major dance performance each fall and spring.

The College of Marin Music Department performs a variety of musical offerings each semester: choral and piano concerts, orchestra and band concerts, including jazz productions, chamber ensembles, and a Handel's *Messiah* sing-along each December.

Art and photography exhibits as well as film festivals are also sponsored by the college.

The website, which lists performances, exhibits and other events, is **www.marin.cc.ca.us**

Dominican University of California   485-3215
50 Acacia Avenue at Grand Avenue, San Rafael

Dominican University offers a variety of events in its 859-seat Angelico Hall. These include lectures, dramatic productions, concerts and other musical offerings, and travel film series. The acclaimed Winifred Baker Chorale is based at the school, which also sponsors art exhibits and dance performances. Shakespearean productions are held at the Forest Meadows Ampitheatre. (See Marin Shakespeare Company.) Call for production and ticket information for university offerings. **Website: www.dominican.edu**

Film Institute of Northern California
38 Miller Avenue, Mill Valley   383-5256

The Film Institute, in addition to producing the Mill Valley Film Festival and operating the Rafael Film Center, has a continuously evolving outreach and education program. In addition to promoting media literacy, its goals include reaching underserved groups in the community, such as senior citizens. The Institute works with local teachers and schools, often integrating film programs with existing curricula. Students also have an opportunity to meet with directors, animators and actors in special programs and presentations.
website: www.finc.org.

Marin Center   472-3500
Avenue of the Flags, San Rafael

The Marin Center consists of the 2,000-seat Marin Veterans' Auditorium, 22,500 square foot Exhibit Hall, 300-seat Showcase Theater, Fairgrounds and Meeting Rooms. Marin's premiere performing arts and convention center is home to the Marin Symphony, Marin Ballet, Marin Speaker's Series, Marin Dance Theatre, Italian Film Festival and Choral Singers of Marin.

Performing artists from all over the world appear on Marin Center's stages under the banner of Marin Center Presents. Recent guests have included Ray Charles, Willie Nelson, Tom Jones, John Lee Hooker, The Chieftains, Kodo (Japan's finest Taiko drummers), and the Vienna Boy's Choir.

Major consumer shows in the Exhibit Hall include the Antique Show and Sale (March and November), Sir Francis Drake Kennel Club Dog Show (September), Marin Quilt and Needle & Art Show (Labor Day Weekend), and the Antique American Indian Art Show (February.)

Marin Center is also home to the award-winning and innovative Marin County Fair held over the July Fourth weekend. This annual community celebration is the largest event in Marin, attracting over 100,000 fairgoers to the beautiful Frank Lloyd Wright designed fairgrounds.

402

For event and ticket information, call the Marin Center Box Office at **472-3500.** For booking information contact Jim Farley, **499-6400.** More information may be found on the following **websites: www.marincenter.org or www.marin-fair.org**

Marin Shakespeare Company   456-8104
Forest Meadows Amphitheatre, Grand Avenue, Dominican University, San Rafael

The Marin Shakespeare Company presents Shakespearean offerings outdoors, July through September, on Friday, Saturday and Sunday evenings, in addition to Sunday matinees. Bring your own picnic, or try their Theatre Cafe. They also have an extensive educational program which includes classes in the Young Company (ages eight to twelve), teen programs, professional actor training, and programs for school groups. For tickets and information call or order on-line at **www.marinShakespeare.org**

Marin Theater Company   388-5208
397 Miller Avenue at La Goma street, Mill Valley

This professional theater company specializes in contemporary and American classics. As a full-time performing arts conservatory, the participants educate 350 children and adults yearly. Their community out-reach program includes touring school shows and student matinees. The main stage season is September to June.

Mill Valley Film Festival   383-5256
38 Miller Avenue, Suite 6, Mill Valley
(Also see: Film Institute of Northern California)

This international film festival, produced by the Film Institute of Northern California, is highly acclaimed by both audiences and film professionals. Many thousands of tickets are sold each season. It features some 120 independent, U.S. and world cinema offerings, with works from up to 40 different countries represented. These works include full-length features, shorts, videos and documentaries. Among films that have premiered here are *On Golden Pond*, *The Piano, My Left Foot* and *Shine* . Each year a tribute is paid to someone in the film industry; past tributees include Robin Williams, Robert Altman, and Alan Arkin.

The ten-day festival uses several Marin venues, including the restored Rafael Film Center in San Rafael and the newly-renovated Sequoia Theater in Mill Valley. In addition to independent screenings, the Festival produces New-Media/VideoFest, filmmaker seminars, a children's festival, special musical presentations, and opening and closing galas. **website: www.finc.org.**

The Mountain Play   383-1100
177 East Blithedale Avenue, Mill Valley

Since around 1913 there have been outdoor summer performances near the summit of Mt. Tamalpais. Recently, 24,000 people attended the six mid-May to mid-June productions, many taking the free shuttle buses up the mountain and enjoying their picnic lunches before the overture of a Broadway musical. *West Side Story, Hello Dolly, and South Pacific* are among the recent offerings. The mountain amphitheater, in the style of a Greek theater, has 3750 stone seats—be sure to bring a pillow! In addition to the performance itself, there are magnificent vistas beyond the stage to San Francisco Bay. Visit their website at **www.marinweb.com/mtnplay/** for more

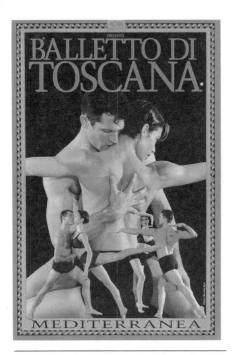

The Italian dance company, Balletto di Toscana, made its only Bay Area appearance at the Marin Center.

information, which includes an excellent section on services for persons with disabilities. (A park policy which limits seating to 3750, also limits major events of 500 people or more to no more than six such events in May and June. In effect, this means only the Mountain Play can be staged at the Mountain Theater.)

Novato Community Players   892-3005
Corner of Machin and DeLong Avenues, Novato

The origins of the Novato Community Players go back to 1919, when they were a section of the Novato Improvement Club. Since then, they have given hun-

dreds of productions financed through community support, membership volunteerism, and ticket sales. The group presents four shows a year, including a major musical. They welcome all people interested in live theater in a variety of areas, from actors to makeup artists.

The Osher Marin   479-2000
Jewish Community Center
200 North San Pedro Road, San Rafael

For the past ten years, CenterStage, the cultural arts division of the Osher Marin Jewish Community Center, has presented a variety of offerings in the performing and literary arts. These include internationally-known authors, artists in conversation with guest interviewers, solo theater artists, comedians, chamber ensembles, dance performances, and singers and musicians in a casual cabaret setting. The summer outdoor concerts, which include jazz, pop and world music, are always well-attended. The Center also sponsors an annual film festival and a children's Buddy Club, often with magicians, clowns and ventriloquists. Cafe fare is usually available before most performances. The theater has 432 seats, all within 75 feet of the stage, and half-price student tickets are available for all performances. Reservations can be made through Bass Ticket Centers at 478-2277. **website: www.marinjcc.org/centerstage**

The Playhouse in San Anselmo   456-8555
27 Kensington Road, San Anselmo

This is a non-profit theater rental facility. Community groups in Marin sponsor a variety of musical and dramatic productions, dance performances and musical events.

Entertainment at the Marin County Fair by the Port City Jazz Band. Trombone, Bob Mielke; trumpet, Ev Farey; Bass, Jim Mainack; banjo, Ken Keeler. On the right is Jim Farley, Director of the Marin County Fair and the Marin Center, which consists of the Marin Veterans Memorial Auditorium, Exhibit Hall, and Showcase Theatre.

The Rafael Film Center   454-1222
1118 4th St., San Rafael
(Also see: Film Institute of Northern California)

The beautifully renovated Rafael Film Center complex, owned and operated by The Film Institute of Northern California, showcases independent, foreign and retrospective films and videos from all over the world. It also offers special screenings with filmmakers, seminars, tributes and mini-festivals. Calendar information on **website: www.finc.org.**

Ross Valley Players   456-9555
The Barn, Marin Art & Garden Center
30 Sir Francis Drake Boulevard, Ross

Celebrating its 70th anniversary in 1999, the Ross Valley Players is the oldest continually operating community theater organization west of the Rockies. They present a regular season of six full productions, running a total of 36 weeks throughout the year. The offerings range from mystery comedies to classical drama, and they often have outstanding guest directors. The Summer Cabaret shows are always popular. For information and/or tickets, call 456-9555.

Shakespeare at Stinson   868-1115
Highway 1 & Calle del Mar, Stinson Beach

This dramatic company has a 155- seat outdoor theater located in the heart of Stinson Beach. They offer three full productions each season, May through October, Fridays at 7:00 p.m. and Saturdays and Sundays at 6:00 p.m. Picnicking is encouraged; wear warm clothing. (Outdoor heaters are provided.) They offer Kids Free Nights, Family Nights, and student matinees. Reservations may be made by calling the above number. **website:**

www.shakespeareatstinson.org

The schools in Marin County have long had a reputation for excellence. The following information has been excerpted from the publication *Marin County Public Schools, Services, Programs and School Information, 1999-2000,* compiled by the Marin County Office of Education in collaboration with Marin County School Districts and with the permission of Mary Jane Burke, Marin County Superintendent of Schools. The Marin County Office of Education is located at 1111 Las Gallinas Avenue/P.O. Box 4925, San Rafael, CA 94913. Telephone: 472-4110. **Website: http://marin. k12.ca.us.** Fax: (415) 491-6625. TDD: (415) 491-6611.

The following data was compiled by the county office staff or obtained from the California Basic Educational Data System (CBEDS) and the California Department of Education.

STUDENT ACHIEVEMENT

For the 1998-99 school year, all California school districts administered the Stanford 9 Achievement Tests (SAT-9), published by Harcourt Brace, to all students in grades 2 through 8. The National Median is 50 percentile.

2000 Scholastic Aptitude Test (SAT) Scores

	MARIN COUNTY	CALIFORNIA	NATION
Verbal:	551	497	505
Math:	556	518	514

There are 19 public school districts in Marin County. Each district is governed by its own elected board of trustees, is supported by both local and state funds, and is responsible for the policies and operations of the schools within its boundaries.

Among the several special programs offered by the Marin County Office of Education are the following three samples.

REGIONAL OCCUPATIONAL PROGRAM (ROP)

The Regional Occupational Program provides career and vocational training to enable students to succeed in a complex, rapidly changing, global economy. ROP serves high school students and adults with programs ranging from automotive repair to video production.

SPECIAL EDUCATION

Specialists in visual impairment, psychology, hearing impairment, speech and language, occupational therapy and other learning specialists work with students having all levels of disabilities and specialized needs.

SCHOOL TO CAREER (415) 491-6631

School to Career is a public school reform movement focusing on preparing students for the world of work through redesigning curriculum, teaching strate-

◀ *Tamalpais High School in Mill Valley.*

gies and building a working relationship with non-education agencies.

All of the school districts with high schools have School to Career initiatives underway. Many of the K-8 districts are moving to define School to Career activities. Districts have asked the Marin County Office of Education to provide leadership in coordinating district efforts through forming a countywide plan, making School to Career a top priority in the work of staff, and providing resources. Inherent in the design is collaboration among business, education, government, parents, students, and community groups. Following goal setting, implementation is to reach all students and provide them with two options at the high school, community college, and university levels. Those options are continued education or immediate entry into the world of work. School to Career emphasizes life-long learning with citizens entering and exiting education and work as the career paths require.

All times noted for the districts below are daytime hours.

BOLINAS-STINSON UNION SCHOOL DISTRICT

All times noted are daylight hours.
Star Route, Bolinas, CA 94924
(415) 868-1603 Fax: (415) 868-9406

The Bolinas-Stinson Union School District is an elementary district serving the West Marin community of Bolinas. The District has only one school, Bolinas-Stinson School, for kindergarten through 8th grade. Class sizes average 20.4 students. Bolinas-Stinson Union School Dis-

trict students also reside in the Tamalpais Union High School District. The office of the Bolinas-Stinson Union School District is open Monday through Friday from 8:00 a.m. to 4:00 p.m.

SUPPORT SERVICES

The Bolinas-Stinson Union School District has a resource specialist and part-time aide, librarian, and special support aide for grades kindergarten through eight. The Marin County Office of Education provides a part-time speech therapist, a psychologist, and a nurse. In addition, West Marin Health and Human Services provides a counselor one day a week.

BOLINAS-STINSON SCHOOL

Grades: Kindergarten–8
Star Route, Bolinas, CA 94924
(415) 868-1603

214 students

School hours:
Bolinas campus: 8:25 to 2:45 (Grades 1 - 8)
Stinson campus: 8:45 to 1:00 (Kindergarten); 8:45 to 2:30 (Grades 1 - 3)
Library hours: 8:00 to 2:45

Bolinas-Stinson School is located on two sites. The Bolinas campus serves grades 1 - 8.

The Stinson site, situated a mile north of Stinson Beach, offers elementary education for kindergarten through grade 2.

The sites share a common literature-based curriculum that includes language arts/reading, mathematics, science, health, history/social studies, physical education, art, crafts, music, and computer education. The staff includes 10 certificated teachers and 5 part-time classroom aides. Classes average 21 students for 1998-99 but ranged from 16 to 26 students.

DIXIE SCHOOL DISTRICT

380 Nova Albion Way
San Rafael, CA 94903
(415) 492-3700 Fax: (415) 492-3707

The Dixie School District is an elementary district serving the northern San Rafael communities of Terra Linda, Marinwood, Lucas Valley, and a portion of Contempo Marin. It was founded in 1864, making it one of the oldest school districts in Marin County. Dixie School District includes three elementary schools for kindergarten through fifth grades: Dixie School, Vallecito School, and Mary E. Silveira School. Sixth through eighth graders attend Miller Creek Middle School. District enrollment is 1,935. Class sizes average 20 students in kindergarten through third grade, 23 students in grades four and five, and 25 students in grades six through eight. Dixie School District is within the San Rafael High School District, and most Miller Creek graduates attend Terra Linda High School. The Dixie School District Office is open Monday through Friday, 8:00 a.m. to 4:30 p.m.

DIXIE SCHOOL

Grades: Kindergarten - 5
1175 Idylberry Road
San Rafael, CA 94903
(415) 492-3730

427 students

School hours:
8:15 to 11:50 (Kindergarten)
8:15 to 2:35 (Grades 1 - 5)
Library hours: 7:45 to 2:45

Dixie School is located in the Lucas Valley area of San Rafael. The school facility includes a library and turfed play field. A new multi-purpose room was completed in 1997.

MARY E. SILVEIRA SCHOOL

Grades: Kindergarten - 5
375 Blackstone Drive
San Rafael, CA 94903
(415) 492-3741

431 students

School hours:
8:15 to 1:20 (Kindergarten)
8:15 to 2:35 (Grades 1 - 5)
Library hours: 8:00 to 3:00

Mary E. Silveira School, situated in San Rafael's Marinwood area, has a library, multi-purpose room, and a turfed play field.

VALLECITO SCHOOL

Grades: Kindergarten - 5
50 Nova Albion Way
San Rafael, CA 94903
(415) 492-3750

434 students

School hours:
8:15 to 11:50 (Kindergarten)
8:15 to 2:35 (Grades 1 - 5)
Library hours: 8:00 to 3:00

Vallecito School, selected as a California Distinguished School, is located in the Terra Linda area of San Rafael. The school facility includes a library, multi-purpose room, kitchen, and play field.

MILLER CREEK MIDDLE SCHOOL

Grades 6 - 8
2255 Las Gallinas Avenue
San Rafael, CA 94903
(415) 492-3760

641 students

School hours: 8:00 to 2:55
Library hours: 7:30 to 3:30

Miller Creek Middle School, selected as a California Distinguished School, is situated in the Lucas Valley area of San Rafael.

KENTFIELD SCHOOL DISTRICT

699 Sir Francis Drake Boulevard,
Kentfield, CA 94904
(415) 925-2230 Fax: (415) 925-2238

The Kentfield School District serves the
central Marin Communities of Greenbrae
and Kentfield. The District includes two
schools: Anthony G. Bacich Elementary
School (K - 4) and Adaline E. Kent Middle
School (5 - 8). District enrollment is 1,096
students, with class sizes from 18 - 25.
Kentfield School District graduates attend
Redwood High School in the Tamalpais
Union High School District. The District
Office is open Monday through Friday
from 8:00 a.m. to 5:00 p.m.

ANTHONY C. BACICH ELEMENTARY SCHOOL

Grades: Kindergarten - 4
25 McAllister Avenue
Kentfield, CA 94904
(415) 925-2220

591 students

School hours:
8:00 to 11:45 or
12:00 to 3:45 (Kindergarten)
8:15 to 2:15 (Grades 1 and 2)
8:15 to 2:45 (Grades 3 and 4)
Library hours: 8:15 to 3:15

Bacich Elementary School is located in
Kentfield, adjacent to a tidal creek and
fronting a creekside marsh. A ten-year
restoration project of the marsh, managed
by The Environmental Forum of Marin,
provides an outside learning environment
for Bacich students. Teachers are supported by teacher aides and supplemen-
tary instructors in music, Spanish, physical education, and computers.

Bacich has been named a California
Distinguished School in recognition of
the students' outstanding academic
performance

A. E. KENT MIDDLE SCHOOL

Grades: 5 - 8
250 Stadium Way
Kentfield, CA 94904
(415) 458-5970

520 students

School hours: 8:15 to 3:00
Library hours: Mon., Fri. and Minimum
Days: 8:15 to 3:40; Tues., Wed., Thurs.:
8:15 to 5:00

Kent Middle School is situated near
the business center of Kentfield and
across from the College of Marin campus.
A challenging academic program provides the basic foundation for a curriculum that also offers Spanish at all grades
and extensive enrichment instruction.

Kent Middle School is recognized as a
California Distinguished School, the
state's highest honor for overall academic excellence.

LAGUNITAS SCHOOL DISTRICT

P.O. Box 308
San Geronimo, CA 94963
(415) 488-4118 Fax: (415) 488-9617

The Lagunitas School District is a kindergarten through 8th grade district on two
adjoining campuses: Lagunitas Elementary School and San Geronimo Valley
Elementary School. Both sites are located
in the center of the San Geronimo Valley,
which includes the towns of Forest
Knolls, Lagunitas, San Geronimo, and
Woodacre. District enrollment is 423 students. Class sizes average 20 students
per teacher in grades K-3, and 25 or less
in grades 4-8. Lagunitas School District

students also reside in the Tamalpais Union High School District. The Lagunitas School District Office is open Monday to Friday from 7:00 a.m. to 4:30 p.m.

LAGUNITAS SCHOOL

Grades: Kindergarten - 8
P. O. Box 308
San Geromino, CA 94963
(415) 488-9437

252 students

School hours: The hours vary for each program and grade level
Library hours: Arranged by classroom teachers

Lagunitas School houses the Public Montessori Program (K-5) and the middle school for the District.

SAN GERONIMO VALLEY SCHOOL

Grades: Kindergarten - 6
P.O. Box 308
San Geronimo, CA 94963
(415) 488-9421

171 students

School hours: The hours vary for each program and grade level
Library hours: Arranged by classroom teachers.

San Geronimo Valley School houses the Academics and Enrichment (AandE) program (K-6) and the Open Classroom (K-6).

LARKSPUR SCHOOL DISTRICT

230 Doherty Drive
Larkspur, CA 94939
(415) 927-6960 Fax: (415) 927-6964

The Larkspur School District serves the communities of Larkspur and Corte Madera. The District has two schools: Neil Cummins Elementary School, for kindergarten through 5th grade students, and Henry Hall Middle School for grades 6-8. District enrollment is 960 students. Classes average 25 students per teacher, with grades K-3 averaging 20 or fewer. Larkspur School District students also reside in the Tamalpais Union High School District. The Larkspur School District Office is open Monday through Friday from 8:00 a.m. to 4:30 p.m.

NEIL CUMMINS SCHOOL

Grades: Kindergarten - 5
58 Mohawk Avenue
Corte Madera, CA 94925
(415) 927-6965

630 students

School hours:
8:15 to 11:45 or 12:00 to 3:30 (Kindergarten)
8:30 to 2:40 (Grades 1 - 3)
8:30 to 3:00 (Grades 4 and 5)
Library hours: 8:30 to 3:30

Neil Cummins School is located in Corte Madera adjacent to the town park. The school has an enrichment program that includes music, art, science lab, library, technology lab, and motor skills. The average class size is 24 students, with grades K-3 averaging 20 or fewer.

Neil Cummins School was honored in 1989 and 1997 as a California Distinguished School, the state's highest honor for overall program excellence.

HALL MIDDLE SCHOOL

Grades: 6 - 8
200 Doherty Drive
Larkspur, CA 94939
(415) 927-6978

330 students

School hours: 8:40 to 3:10
Library hours: 8:30 to 3:30

Hall Middle School offers a transitional program from a self-contained core of instruction in the 6th grade to a fully departmentalized program in the 8th grade. The academic curriculum includes language arts, social studies, mathematics, science, Spanish, health and physical education. Elective courses are offered in computers, drama, art, woodshop, band and other subjects. The average class size is 20.3 students.

Hall Middle School was recognized in 1986, 1990, 1992, and 1996 as a California Distinguished School, the state's highest honor for overall program excellence. In 1998, Hall Middle School was designated a National Blue Ribbon School.

MILL VALLEY SCHOOL DISTRICT

411 Sycamore Avenue
Mill Valley, CA 94941
(415) 389-7700 Fax: (415) 389-7773

The Mill Valley School District is an elementary district serving Mill Valley and the unincorporated areas of Alto, Strawberry Point, Tamalpais Valley, Muir Beach, Panoramic Ridge and Homestead Valley. The District includes four elementary schools for kindergarten through fifth grade: Edna Maguire, Old Mill, Park, and Tamalpais Valley. Sixth through eighth graders attend Mill Valley Middle School. All of these schools have achieved status as California Distinguished Schools. District enrollment is 2,360 students. Class Size Reduction has been implemented in Grades K-3, with class size average under 20 students. Mill Valley School District students also reside in the Tamalpais Union High School District. For a nominal fee, the District provides bus service to transport students from Strawberry and

Muir Beach. The Mill Valley School District Office is open Monday through Friday from 8:00 a.m. to 4:00 p.m.

EDNA MAGUIRE SCHOOL

Grade: Kindergarten - 5
80 Lomita Drive
Mill Valley, CA 94941
(415) 389-7733

550 students

School hours:
8:30 to 11:50 or 11:30 to 3:00(Kindergarten)
8:30 to 2:50 (Grades 1 - 5)
Library hours: 8:30 to 2:50

Edna Maguire School, a 1998 California Distinguished School, is the largest elementary school in the District. It is situated in a residential area on 11 acres of land at the foot of surrounding hills. It features "The Children's Garden," a one-third acre fenced plot of land with individual classroom garden beds, an orchard and a pumpkin patch.

The school offers additional assistance to students who speak English as a second language. Part-time instructional assistants work with small groups of students in order to individualize instruction.

On-site day care is available before and after school.

OLD MILL SCHOOL

Grades: Kindergarten - 5
352 Throckmorton Avenue
Mill Valley, CA 94941
(415) 389-7727

310 students

School hours:
8:40 to 12:00 or 11:30 to 3:00 (Kindergarten)
8:30 to 2:50 (Grades 1 - 5)
Library hours: 8:30 to 2:50

Old Mill School, the District's oldest elementary school building, is a 1998

California Distinguished School. This modern facility incorporates computer technology and internet access in all of its classrooms and the library/media center. The school is three blocks from Mill Valley's business district and across from Old Mill Park and the Mill Valley Public Library. The facility has a large auditorium and 14 classrooms.

On-site child care is available before and after school.

PARK SCHOOL

Grades: Kindergarten - 5
360 E. Blithedale Avenue
Mill Valley, CA 94941
(415) 389-7735

300 students

School hours:
8:30 to 11:50 or 10:00 to 1:30 (Kindergarten)
8:30 to 2:50 (Grades 1 - 5)
Library hours: 8:30 to 2:50

Park School is the second oldest school building in the Mill Valley School District. It is located in the geographic center of Mill Valley across from Boyle Park and the municipal tennis court. The school has 15 classrooms and a large auditorium that is used most evenings and weekends for community events.

Before and after school day care is provided on site.

TAMALPAIS VALLEY SCHOOL

Grades: Kindergarten - 5
350 Bell Lane
Mill Valley, CA 94941
(415) 389-7731

440 students

School hours:
8:30 to 11:50 or noon to 3:20 (Kindergarten)
8:30 to 2:50 (Grades 1 - 5)
Library hours: 8:30 to 2:50

Tamalpais Valley School is situated in the southernmost boundary of Mill Valley on eight acres of land. It is located at the edge of the Golden Gate National Recreation Area, which provides a natural setting for environmental studies by classroom teachers and students. Part-time instructional assistants work in classrooms in the morning hours.

A large community field serves as a playground for physical education activities. Modular classrooms have been added to the school facility to house the expanding school enrollment.

Before and after school childcare is available on site.

MILL VALLEY MIDDLE SCHOOL

Grades: 6, 7 and 8
425 Sycamore Avenue
Mill Valley, CA 94941
(415) 389-7711

760 students

School hours:
8:00 to 2:50 (Grades 7 and 8)
8:50 to 2:50 (Grade 6)
Library hours: Mon. - Thurs. 7:30 to 4:30
Friday 7:30 to 3:30

Mill Valley Middle School is adjacent to Bay Front Park and the Mill Valley Recreation Center. Each grade level is housed in a separate wing of the building. Its large library serves as the school's central core.

Mill Valley Middle School offers an academic program that includes English, mathematics, social studies and science. Additionally, art, technology, and physical education classes taught by credentialed teachers round out the program. Foreign language is offered to all 7th and 8th grade students.

NOVATO UNIFIED SCHOOL DISTRICT

1015 Seventh Street
Novato, CA 94945
(415) 897-4201 Fax: (415) 898-5790
www.novato.ca.us/nusd

The Novato Unified School District serves students in kindergarten through grade 12 in north Marin. The District includes eight elementary schools, three middle schools, two high schools, one continuation high school, an independent study program for K - 12 (NOVA), and a charter school for grades K - 8. June 1999 district enrollment is 7,739 students. The Novato Unified School District Education Center is open Monday through Friday from 8:00 a.m. to 4:30 p.m.

SUPPORT SERVICES

The Novato Unified School District has 811 certificated teachers and classified personnel. Schools share the services of speech therapists, library media specialists, psychologists, and nurses. Counselors are on staff at each secondary school. All schools offer assistance to non-English speaking students. Classes for gifted and talented students are offered in grades 4 to 8, and the high schools offer honors and Advanced Placement classes. Every elementary school has privately operated on-site childcare. School bus transportation is available for a fee.

HAMILTON SCHOOL

Grades: Kindergarten - 5
1 Main Gate Road
Novato, CA 94949
(415) 883-4691

254 students
School hours:
8:30 to 11:50 or 11:40 to 3:00 (Kindergarten)
9:30 to 3:00 (Grades 1 - 3)
8:30 to 3:00 (Grades 4 - 5)
Library hours: 8:30 to 12:00 and 12:30 to 3:00

Hamilton Elementary School includes two campuses - the former Meadow Park School and Hamilton School. The combined campus occupies 18 acres. There are two libraries, a multi-use room and turfed playing fields.

LOMA VERDE SCHOOL

Grades: Kindergarten - 5
399 Alameda de la Loma
Novato, CA 94949
(415) 883-4681

435 students
School hours:
8:30 to 11:51 or 11:25 to 2:45 (Kindergarten)
9:30 to 2:55 (Grades 1 - 3)
8:30 to 3:00 (Grades 4 - 5)
Library hours: 8:30 to 12:00 and 12:30 to 3:00

Loma Verde Elementary School is located on 12 acres. It has a multi-use room, computer/science lab, library and turfed playing field.

Loma Verde is a California Distinguished School.

LU SUTTON SCHOOL

Grades: Kindergarten - 5
1800 Center Road
Novato, CA 94947
(415) 897-3196

462 students
School hours:
8:15 to 11:35 or 11:45 to 3:05 (Kindergarten)
9:30 to 2:55 (Grades 1 - 3)
8:30 to 2:55 (Grades 4 - 5)
Library hours: 8:30 to 12:00 and 12:30 to 3:00

Lu Sutton Elementary School, located on 10 acres, has a multi-use room, library, and turfed playing fields. It was named after a former principal.

Students participate in a broad-based program with an instructional focus on language, math, and science.

LYNWOOD SCHOOL

Grades: Kindergarten - 5
1320 Lynwood Drive
Novato, CA 94947
(415) 897-4161

418 students

School hours:
8:30 to 11:40 (Kindergarten)
9:30 to 2:50 (Grades 1 - 3)
8:30 to 3:00 (Grades 4 - 5)
Library hours: 8:30 to 12:00 and 12:30 to 3:00

Lynwood Elementary School is situated on 10 acres. Lynwood has a multi-use room, library, computer lab, and turfed playing fields.

Lynwood is a California Distinguished School.

OLIVE SCHOOL

Grades: Kindergarten - 5
629 Plum Street
Novato, CA 94945
(415) 897-2131

398 students

School Hours:
8:30 to 11:50 or 10:00 to 1:50 (Kindergarten)
9:30 to 2:55 (Grades 1 - 3)
8:30 to 2:55 (Grades 4 - 5)
Library hours: 8:30 to 12:00 and 12:30 to 3:00

Olive School is located on 13 acres. It has a multi-use room, computer room, library, and turfed playing fields.

Olive is the only school in Marin County to offer parents the choice of an alternate school calendar. This calendar, which began in August 1993, provides shorter academic terms and more frequent vacations.

PLEASANT VALLEY SCHOOL

Grades: Kindergarten - 5
755 Sutro Avenue
Novato, CA 94947
(415) 897-5104

526 students

School hours:
8:15 to 11:35 or 11:45 to 3:05 (Kindergarten)
9:30 to 2:55 (Grades 1 - 3)
8:30 to 3:00 (Grades 4 - 5)
Library hours: 8:30 to 12:00 and 12:30 to 3:00

Pleasant Valley School is located on 12 acres. It has a library, community center, and turfed playing fields. The community center provides for many uses, from basketball to rooms for science, music, and computer lab. Every classroom has a computer, in addition to the computer lab where classes are scheduled weekly.

Pleasant Valley is a California Distinguished School.

RANCHO ESSENTIALIST SCHOOL

Grades: Kindergarten - 5
1430 Johnson Street
Novato, CA 94947
(415) 897-3101

505 students

School hours:
8:20 to 11:40 or 11:50 to 3:10 (Kindergarten)
9:30 to 3:00 (Grades 1 - 3)
8:30 to 3:00 (Grades 4 - 5)
Library hours: 8:30 to 12:00 and 12:30 to 3:00

Rancho School is located on 11 acres. It has a library, multi-use room, computer lab, and turfed playing fields.

415

Rancho School is the home of the Essentialist Program, a more structured approach to education, with an emphasis on basic academic skills and subjects and establishment of good study habits. Rancho Essentialist School serves students from throughout the Novato Unified School District.

Rancho is a California Distinguished School.

SAN RAMON SCHOOL

Grades: Kindergarten - 5
45 San Ramon Way
Novato, CA 94945
(415) 897-1196

510 students

School hours:
8:20 to 11:40 or 11:40 to 3:00 (Kindergarten)
9:40 to 2:55 (Grades 1 - 3)
8:30 to 3:00 (Grades 4 - 5)
Library hours: 8:30 to 12:00 and 12:30 to 3:00

San Ramon Elementary School is located on 11 acres. It consists of three buildings clustered around a library. Kindergarten classes are held in a separate cluster. The school is surrounded by turfed playing fields.

San Ramon is a California Distinguished School.

HILL MIDDLE SCHOOL

Grades: 6 - 8
720 Diablo Avenue
Novato, CA 94947
(415) 893-1557

543 students

School hours: 8:00 to 2:10
Library hours: 8:30 to 12:00 and 12:30 to 4:00

Hill Middle School is a remodeled school, reopened in 1991. In separate quarters, the campus also is home to

NOVA, the District's independent study program, North Marin High School, a continuation high school, and the Margaret Todd Senior Center. The school facilities include a multi-use room, library, computer and science labs, art room, a new media center and several turfed playing fields.

The visual, performing and practical arts, foreign languages and computer education are an integral part of the curriculum.

Hill is a California Distinguished School.

SAN JOSE MIDDLE SCHOOL

Grades: 6 - 8
1000 Sunset Parkway
Novato, CA 94949
(415) 883-7831

474 students

School hours: 8:00 to 2:10
Library hours: 8:30 to 12:00 and 12:30 to 4:00

San Jose Middle School is located on 18 acres. Special facilities include a gymnasium, library, two computer labs, wood shop, and several large turfed playing fields.

A common core curriculum is taken by all students in English/language arts, history, social science, science, and physical education. Math is offered in heterogeneous groups. Elective exploratory courses allow students to pursue areas of interest. Band, Chorus, and Creating Writing/Arts/Crafts and Drama are the electives in Grades 7 and 8. Spanish is offered in Grade 8.

San Jose is a California Distinguished School and is the first recipient of a Hewlett/Annenburg Grant in Marin County.

SINALOA MIDDLE SCHOOL

Grades: 6 - 8
2045 Vineyard Road
Novato, CA 94947
(415) 897-2111

774 students

School hours: 8:20 to 2:30
Library hours: 8:30 to 12:00 and 12:30 to 4:00

Sinaloa Middle School is located on a 25-acre wooded site. Its facilities include a gymnasium, library, computer lab, wood and metal shops, art and home-making room, and several large turfed playing fields.

NORTH MARIN HIGH SCHOOL

Grades 9 - 12
720 Diablo Avenue
Novato CA 94947
(415) 892-8733

69 students

School hours: 8:20 to 2:30

North Marin High School is the District's continuation high school. It is located on the Hill Middle School campus and shares facilities with the NOVA Education Center.

NOVA EDUCATION CENTER

Grades: Kindergarten - 12
720 Diablo Avenue
Novato, CA 94947
(415) 897-7653

154 students

Center hours: 8:00 to 4:00

NOVA Education Center is located at the Hill Middle School site on 6.2 acres and shares facilities with North Marin High School.

NOVA is an independent study program offering self-directed and individualized learning experiences for elemen-tary, secondary, adult education and co-enrollment students.

The adult program offers the general education diploma as well as some fee classes. Co-enrolled students are able to complete credits to graduate with their regular school classes. NOVA requires the same number of credits for promotion.

NOVATO HIGH SCHOOL

Grades: 9 - 12
625 Arthur Street
Novato, CA 94947
(415) 898-2125

1,024 students

School hours: 8:15 to 2:25
Optional period: 7:20
Library hours: 7:30 to 3:00, plus 1.5 additional hours one day a week

Novato High School is situated on 38 acres. It has 56 classrooms and labs, a lecture hall, career center, library, music room, two computer labs and two gyms. Outdoor facilities include tennis and basketball courts, softball and baseball diamonds, a football stadium, and a swimming pool.

The academic program covers college preparatory courses (including honors and advanced placement classes), vocational and general education, art, music, home economics, business, and industrial arts.

Novato High has won the Marin County Academic Decathlon three years in a row.

SAN MARIN HIGH SCHOOL

Grades 9 - 12
15 San Marin Drive
Novato, CA 94945
(415) 898-2121

996 students

School hours: 8:20 to 2:30
Optional period: 7:25
Library hours: 7:30 to 3:00, plus 1.5 additional hours one day a week.

San Marin High School is located on 39.6 acres. It has a gymnasium, student center, career center, science lecture room, and language, computer and photo labs. Its athletic facilities include tennis and basketball courts, baseball diamonds, and a football stadium.

San Marin has an award-winning band and choir and an assortment of clubs to meet the wide range of student interests. Community service is a graduation requirement to promote student involvement in the community.

NOVATO CHARTER SCHOOL

Grades Kindergarten - 8
601 Bolling Drive
Novato, CA 94949
(415) 883-4254

225 students

School hours:
8:45 to 12:45 (Kindergarten)
8:45 to 3:00 (Grades 1 - 5)
8:30 to 3:00 (Grades 6 - 8)
Library hours: Classroom libraries are open during school hours

Novato Charter School is an alternative public school which offers a Waldorf-inspired educational community in which teachers nurture the imagination in the early years, building a foundation for abstract thinking, gradually and appropriately challenging the intellect throughout the grades. The philosophy places equal emphasis on a solid academic program, artistic expression, social development and attention to the inner life and natural rhythms of the child.

Novato Charter School offers visual and performing arts, foreign language, music programs, handwork, woodworking, gardening and environmental education, games and celebration of seasonal festivities.

REED UNION SCHOOL DISTRICT

105A Avenida Miraflores
Tiburon, CA 94920
(415) 435-7848 Fax: (415) 435-7843

The Reed Union School District (RUSD) is an elementary district serving the southern Marin communities of Belvedere, Tiburon, and a portion of East Corte Madera. Its three school sites are located in Tiburon: Reed School for kindergarten through second grade; Bel Aire School for grades 3, 4 and 5; and Del Mar Middle School for grades 6, 7 and 8. District enrollment is around 1,050 students. Last year's average class size was 20.5. RUSD students are also in the Tamalpais Union High School District and usually attend Redwood High School. The District Office is open Monday through Friday from 8:00 a.m. to 5:00 p.m.

REED SCHOOL

Grades: Kindergarten, 1 and 2
1199 Tiburon Boulevard
Tiburon, CA 94920
(415) 435-7840

354 students

School hours:
8:15 to 11:45 or 12:00 to 3:30 (Kindergarten)
8:30 to 2:30 (Grades 1 and 2)
Library hours: 8:30 to 3:00

Reed School offers a nurturing and challenging climate for the primary age student. In addition to a full academic program, there is a school-wide focus on developmentally appropriate programs, positive reinforcement, integration of art into the curriculum, Spanish and culture, beginning computer education, and a special motor development program. The school facilities include a multi-purpose room, library, music room and turfed athletic field. Average class size is 18.

A childcare center adjacent to Reed School is available for parent-paid before and after school care.

BEL AIRE SCHOOL

Grades: 3, 4 and 5
277-A Karen Way
Tiburon, CA 94920
(415) 388-7100

366 students

School hours: 8:20 to 2:40
Library hours: 8:30 to 3:00

Bel Aire offers an academic curriculum in language arts, math, history/social studies, and science. The school facility includes a multi-purpose room, library, computer laboratory, music room, and turfed athletic field. Average class size is 18 in 3rd grade and 25 in 4th and 5th grades.

Parent-paid, on-site childcare is available before and after school.

DEL MAR SCHOOL

Grades: 6, 7 and 8
105 Avenida Miraflores
Tiburon, CA 94920
(415) 435-1468

330 students

School hours: 8:30 to 3:00
Library hours: 8:15 to 3:15

Del Mar provides a daily academic program in language arts, math, science, history/social studies, and physical education, with electives in art, music,

journalism, yearbook and computer technology. Students take Spanish daily in the 7th and 8th grades for a semester or full year and twice a week in 6th grade. Class size in academic subjects ranges from 20 to 23.

The school facility includes a gymnasium, library, computer laboratory, music/drama room, snack bar, and turfed athletic field.

Del Mar has been named a California Distinguished Middle School in recognition of its academic excellence, peer-counseling, and leadership programs.

ROSS SCHOOL DISTRICT

P.O. Box 1058
Ross, CA 94957
(415) 457-2705 Fax: (415) 457-6724

The Ross School District serves the central Marin community of Ross and sections of Kentfield. The District has only one school, Ross School, which provides education for students —kindergarten through eighth grade. Class size averages 18-20. Ross School students also reside in the Tamalpais Union High School District. The school office is open Monday through Friday from 8:00 a.m. to 4:00 p.m.

In partnership with Apple Computer, Inc., Ross School is a model for training teachers to integrate technology to enhance teaching and learning within the classroom setting. Ross School has also been a partner with the Exploratorium to support the development of teaching resources for science in the classroom.

ROSS SCHOOL

Grades: Kindergarten - 8
Lagunitas Road and Allen Avenue
P.O. Box 1058
Ross CA 94957
(415) 457-2705

418 students

School hours:
8:30 to 12:30 (Kindergarten)
8:30 to 2:30 (Grades 1 - 3)
8:30 to 3:00 (Grades 4 - 8)
Library hours: 8:00 to 3:30 daily

Ross School has been recognized twice as a California Distinguished School, the state's highest honor for overall academic excellence. *Child Magazine* also nominated Ross School as one of the top ten schools in the nation.

ROSS VALLEY SCHOOL DISTRICT

46 Green Valley Court
San Anselmo, CA 94960
(415) 454-2162 Fax: (415) 454-6840

The Ross Valley School District is an elementary district serving the central Marin communities of San Anselmo and Fairfax. Ross Valley graduates attend high school in the Tamalpais Union High School District. The District includes four schools: Brookside Elementary School, Manor Elementary School and Wade Thomas School for kindergarten through fifth grade; and White Hill School for sixth, seventh and eighth grade students. District enrollment is 1,801 students, with class sizes averaging 23.2 at K-5 for the 1999-2000 school year. The District Office is open Monday through Friday from 7:00 a.m. to 4:00 p.m.

BROOKSIDE ELEMENTARY SCHOOL

Grades: Kindergarten - 5
Upper Campus: 46 Green Valley Court
(415) 454-7409
Lower Campus: 116 Butterfield Road
(415) 453-2948

526 students

School hours:
8:35 to 11:55 or 9:35 to 12:55 (Kindergarten)
8:20 to 1:50 or 9:20 to 3:05 (Grades 1 - 2)
8:20 to 2:55 (Grades 3 - 5)
Library hours: 8:30 to 3:00

Brookside School, a 1995-96 California Distinguished School and recipient of the Golden Bell Award, is housed on two separate sites in suburban San Anselmo. The facilities include music rooms, art rooms, and computer labs. The Upper Campus (3rd-5th grades) has 258 students; the Lower Campus (K - 2nd grades) has 244.

Brookside has partnerships with the Marin Community Foundation and the Autodesk Foundation to provide resources for project-based learning and ongoing curriculum and instructional improvement.

Private, parent-paid childcare is available on site.

MANOR SCHOOL

Grades: Kindergarten- 5
150 Oak Manor Drive
Fairfax, CA 94930
(415) 453-1544

336 students

School hours:
8:30 to 11:55 (Kindergarten)
8:30 to 1:55 or 9:30 to 3:05 (Grades 1, 2, 3)
8:30 to 3:05 (Grades 4 - 5)
Library hours: 8:30 to 3:00

Manor School is situated in the Oak Manor neighborhood of Fairfax. The facility has a library, art room, computer lab, and multi-purpose room for school-wide events. It also has two playing fields, a nature trail, and a school garden.

Manor School has partnerships with Marin Community Foundation, Autodesk and Youth in Arts.

WADE THOMAS SCHOOL

Grades: Kindergarten - 5
150 Ross Avenue
San Anselmo, CA 94960
(415) 454-4603

342 students

School hours:
8:30 to 12:00 (Kindergarten)
8:30 to 1:55 or 9:30 to 3:05 (Grades 1 - 3)
8:30 to 3:05 (Grades 4 - 5)
Library hours: 8:30 to 3:00

Wade Thomas School, a 1996-97 California Distinguished School recipient, is located in one of San Anselmo's oldest residential neighborhoods and is built on the site of the very first school in San Anselmo. The school facility includes a multi-use room and playground, which are used extensively by the community during non-school hours.

Wade Thomas has partnerships with the Marin Community Foundation and the Autodesk Foundation to provide resources for project-based learning and the use of technology as an integral part of students' education as well as a partnership with Youth-In-Arts.

WHITE HILL MIDDLE SCHOOL

Grades: 6, 7 and 8
101 Glen Drive
Fairfax, CA 94930
(415) 454-8390

597 students

School hours: 8:50 to 3:15
Library hours: 8:30 to 3:00

White Hill Middle School is located at the base of White's Hill on a 22-acre site in Fairfax. It is the only middle school in the Ross Valley School District.

White Hill offers academic challenge and breadth of opportunity. Modern technology is integrated into the core class curricula. The elective program includes visual and performing arts, foreign language and computers, taught by specialized, credentialed teachers. Band, chorus, foreign language classes, and other enrichment programs meet in the 45-minute period before normal school hours. More than one-third of the students have elected to take a 7-period day.

White Hill has a partnership with the Marin Community Foundation and the Autodesk Foundation to provide resources to support project-based learning.

NICASIO SCHOOL DISTRICT

The Nicasio School District has four combination classrooms and provides an education program for kindergarten through eighth grade. These students reside in the Tamalpais Union High School District.

NICASIO SCHOOL AND DISTRICT

Grades: Kindergarten - 8
Nicasio Valley Road
Nicasio, CA 94946
(415) 662-2184

65 students

School hours:
9:00 to 12:00 (Kindergarten)
9:00 to 3:00 (Grades 1 - 8)
Library hours: 9:00 to 3:00

Nicasio School has four certificated teachers with combined classes for grades K-1, 2-3, 4-5, 6-8. Classroom teachers are also assisted by a full-time certificated math-computer teacher. Students also receive Spanish and music instruction and

421

Nicasio School, Nicasio.

two teacher's aides work closely with all the teachers.

SAN RAFAEL ELEMENTARY SCHOOL DISTRICT

310 Nova Albion Way
San Rafael, CA 94903
(415) 492-3200 Fax: (415) 492-3245

The San Rafael Elementary School District serves neighborhoods within the central Marin community of San Rafael. The District has six elementary schools, one K-7 school, and one middle school. The schools for kindergarten through fifth grade are: Bahia Vista, Coleman, Gallinas, Glenwood, Laurel Dell, San Pedro and Sun Valley Elementary Schools. Gallinas, now serving grades K-7, is in the process of converting to a K-8 school. J. B. Davidson Middle School serves students in grades 6-8. District enrollment is 3,592 students. Students of the San Rafael Elementary School District are also in the San Rafael High School District. The District

Office is open Monday through Friday from 8:00 a.m. to 5:00 p.m.

BAHIA VISTA SCHOOL

Grades: Kindergarten - 5
125 Bahia Way
San Rafael, CA 94901
(415) 485-2415

443 students

School hours:
8:00 to 11:35 or 11:00 to 12:30 (Kindergarten)
8:00 to 2:20 (Grades 1 - 5)

Bahia Vista School serves the communities east of Highway 101 and south of the San Rafael Canal, including Larkspur Landing.

The school has a strong focus on literacy and recently adopted "Success for All," a phonics-based reading program developed at Johns Hopkins University.

English learning students also receive daily structured, systematic instruction in English Language Development.

The school facility includes a multi-purpose room, kitchen, and library. There are computers in every classroom. The Bahia Vista Family Center is a Healthy Start Program.

COLEMAN SCHOOL

Grades: Kindergarten - 5
140 Rafael Drive
San Rafael, CA 94901
(415) 485-2420

364 students

School hours:
8:30 to11:50 or 11:15 to 2:36 (Kindergarten)
8:30 to 2:36 (Grades 1 - 5)

Coleman School, located east of Highway 101 near Central San Rafael, serves the Dominican neighborhood and downtown San Rafael. Because Coleman School is adjacent to Dominican College, it shares resources with the college and serves as a professional development school for the Dominican School of Education.

The school has a library, computer lab, and two play areas. Technology supports learning across the curriculum. Every classroom has access to state of the art technology. In addition to the core curriculum, Coleman offers music, PE, creative arts instruction, and an after school tutorial.

Parent-paid after school day care is available on site.

DAVIDSON MIDDLE SCHOOL

Grades 6 - 8
280 Woodland Avenue
San Rafael, CA 94901
(415) 485-2400

871 students

School hours: 8:00 to 2:11

Davidson Middle School is a culturally diverse 6th - 8th grade school offering a comprehensive core curriculum with elective classes in foreign language, music, industrial arts, drama, art, and computer literacy. Also available are advanced classes in mathematics, English, support classes in special education, and English Language Development. Davidson offers programs for gifted and talented students and countywide competitive sports.

Various forms of technology exist in all the classrooms. The campus has two multimedia computer labs and a science technology lab.

Davidson is a California Distinguished School, a National Blue Ribbon School, and a National Excellence in Education Award recipient.

GALLINAS SCHOOL

Grades: Kindergarten - 7
177 North San Pedro Road
San Rafael, CA 94903
(415) 492-3150

565 students

School hours:
8:50 to 12:10 Kindergarten+
9:00 to 12:20 Kindergarten
11:45 to 3:08 Kindergarten
Early Childhood Campus:
1:50 to 12:10 Kindergarten+
11:35 to 2:55 Kindergarten

Gallinas School emphasizes a curriculum that challenges each child to excel in reading, writing, mathematics, and science. The school is expanding classroom technology to enhance student learning. Art, music and special physical education programs provide enrichment to all students. Students may opt to participate in a Spanish/English Literacy Program that develops student literacy in both languages by grade 5. The school's access to wetlands fosters specialized environmental science projects. The school has a library, computer labs, gym, kindergarten wing and several playgrounds.

Gallinas Early Childhood Center has Kindergarten classes and a Kindergarten Plus Program. The K Plus Program is an early intervention program for Kindergarten students not ready for 1st grade.

Day care is available before and after school.

GLENWOOD SCHOOL

Grades: Kindergarten - 5
25 Castlewood Drive
San Rafael, CA 94901
(415) 485-2430

400 students

School hours:

9:00 to 12:20 or 11:45 to 3:06 (Kindergarten)
9:00 to 3:06 (Grades 1 - 5)

Glenwood School, a National Blue Ribbon School, located east of Central San Rafael, serves the area from Bayside Acres east to Peacock Gap. Glenwood School has a multi-use room, state of the art computer lab, a large library and baseball diamond and soccer fields. The school's access to a marsh provides for a seasonal life studies program.

The school community is culturally diverse, representing many countries. Education workshops help parents integrate learning into family life.

Day care is available before and after school.

LAUREL DELL SCHOOL

Grades: Kindergarten - 4
225 Woodland Avenue
San Rafael, CA 94901
(415) 485-2317

140 students

School hours:

8:30 to 12:05 (Kindergarten)
8:30 to 2:36 (1 - 4)

Laurel Dell School, the District's newest school, opened its doors September 4, 1996. Laurel Dell serves students both in the Bret Harte neighborhood and throughout the district. The school offers students a multi-age classroom experience. The program will expand each year to include new multi-age classes, ultimately serving students through grade five. Laurel Dell has a large playground area with a brand new play structure.

Off-site day care is available after school with available transportation.

SAN PEDRO SCHOOL

Grades: Kindergarten - 5
498 Point San Pedro Road
San Rafael, CA 94901
(415) 485-2450

406 students

School hours:

9:00 to 12:30 or 11:30 to 3:06 (Kindergarten)
9:00 to 3:06 (Grades 1 - 5)

San Pedro School is located east of downtown San Rafael. It serves the communities east of Highway 101 and the area south of the San Rafael Canal. The school has 19 classrooms, 2 special day classrooms, a multi-use room, and a library. Computers are used in all subject areas, with 3 to 7 computers in every classroom.

San Pedro School utilizes a special grant for "Success for All," an intensive, phonics-based reading program.

Off-site day care is available after school with available transportation.

SUN VALLEY SCHOOL

Grades: Kindergarten - 5
75 Happy Lane
San Rafael, CA 94901
(415) 485-2440

370 students

School hours:
8:30 to 11:50 or 11:15 to 2:36 (Kindergarten)
8:30 to 2:36 (Grades 1 - 5)

Sun Valley School is located at the western end of San Rafael adjacent to rolling hills and acres of open space. The school serves the western portion of San Rafael including the Gerstle Park and Spring Grove areas. Sun Valley School has a library, soccer field and school garden.

Kindergarten classes are held in split sessions. Team teaching is offered whenever possible. Sun Valley's multi-age classes (K-1, 1-2, 1-2-3, 3-4, 4-5) provide a valuable alternative for children.

Off-site day care is available after school with available transportation.

SAN RAFAEL HIGH SCHOOL DISTRICT

310 Nova Albion Way
San Rafael, CA 94903
(415) 492-3233 Fax: (415) 492-3245

The San Rafael High School District provides secondary education to students residing in two elementary districts of central Marin: Dixie School District and San Rafael Elementary School District. The San Rafael High School District has two high schools, an alternative school, and an adult education campus for those wishing to complete their high school requirements. District enrollment is 1,905 students. San Rafael High School District students also reside in the Marin Community College District. The District Office is open Monday through Friday from 7:45 a.m. to 4:45 p.m.

STUDENT ACHIEVEMENT

The SAT results for both San Rafael High School and Terra Linda High School are consistently above the state and national averages.

SAN RAFAEL HIGH SCHOOL

Grades: 9 - 12
185 Mission Avenue
San Rafael, CA 94901
(415) 485-2330

874 students

School hours: 8:00 to 3:15 M - F
Library hours: 7:30 to 3:30

San Rafael High School is a 111-year-old institution occupying 33 acres in central San Rafael. The school has an auditorium, theater, wood and metal shops, five computer labs, a swimming pool, two gyms, six tennis courts, a radio station, and an all-weather track and lighted athletic field.

San Rafael High offers college preparatory instruction and 21 honors/advancement placement courses in math, English, foreign language, social studies, fine arts and science. In May 1999, 87 Advanced Placement exams were taken with a passing rate of over 80%. In addition to challenging academic courses, San Rafael High offers courses in technology, business, industrial arts, computer networking and other vocations. Along with the award winning music program, courses are also offered in theatre and fine arts.

Approximately 80 % of the students enter college each year.

TERRA LINDA HIGH SCHOOL

Grades: 9 - 12
320 Nova Albion Way
San Rafael, CA 94903
(415) 492-3100

1033 students

School hours: 8:00 to 3:10 M - F
Library hours: 7:45 to 3:15

Terra Linda High School provides comprehensive ninth through twelfth grade education on a 33-acre campus in northern San Rafael. TLHS has two computer labs, a journalism lab, a Computer Assisted Design lab, and a physics lab. Athletic facilities include a gymnasium, pool, football, soccer and baseball fields.

TLHS offers more than 20 honors/advanced placement courses in English, math, science, social studies, and foreign language. Terra Linda also provides technical preparation in business, design/construction, and auto mechanics as well as a hospitality/tourism academy. Quality drama, music and athletic programs are also offered.

More than 90% of the graduates enter post-secondary educational institutions.

SAUSALITO SCHOOL DISTRICT

630 Nevada Street, Sausalito, CA 94965
(415) 332-3190 Fax: (415) 332-9643

The Sausalito School District is an elementary (K-8) district drawing its student population from Sausalito and Marin City. The District has two schools: Bayside/Martin Luther King School and North Bay School. District enrollment is 285 students. Class size averages 15 students. Sausalito School District students attend high school in the Tamalpais Union High School District. School office hours are 8:00 a.m. to 4:00 p.m. Monday through Friday.

BAYSIDE/MARTIN LUTHER KING SCHOOL

Grades: Preschool Montessori - 8
630 Nevada Street
Sausalito, CA 94965
(415) 332-1024 Fax: (415) 332-7816

232 students

School hours: 8:20 to 2:50
Library hours: Classroom libraries are open during school hours

Bayside/Martin Luther King School is located on a wooded 13-acre site in Sausalito. Facilities include a computer laboratory and visual arts room, and a two-story library.

In addition to language arts, mathematics, science, social studies and physical education core curriculum, elective classes are offered in art, computer science, instrumental music, Spanish, PASS (Promoting Achievements in Schools through Sports), visual and performing arts, student growth and Montessori programs. A competitive sports program is provided for students in grades 6 - 8.

Bayside/MLK School was honored in 1989 as a California Distinguished School in recognition of its program excellence.

Private, on-site day care is available before and after school.

NORTH BAY SCHOOL

Grades: Kindergarten - 8
610 Drake Avenue
Sausalito, CA 94965
(415) 332-3573 Fax: (415) 332-2492

53 students

School hours: 8:20 to 2:50
Library hours: Classroom libraries are open during school hours

North Bay School is located on a sunny, 11-acre site in Marin City. North Bay is a multi-age grouping school alternative. This program has been designed to serve children who can benefit from a small multi-age setting.

The school has three classroom groups: grades K - 2, grades 3 - 5, and grades 6 - 8. Each group has a teacher and teacher's aide as well as assistance from parent volunteers.

SHORELINE UNIFIED SCHOOL DISTRICT

10 John Street
Tomales, CA 94971
(707) 878-2266 Fax: (707) 878-2554

The Shoreline Unified School District is a K-12 school district serving the West Marin communities along Bodega Bay and Tomales Bay. The District includes four elementary schools (Bodega Bay Elementary School, Inverness Elementary School, Tomales Elementary School, West Marin Elementary School), a high school (Tomales High School), an independent study school (Shoreline Independent Study School) and a continuation high school (Shoreline Continuation High School). District enrollment is 855 students. The average class size is 20 students per teacher. The Shoreline Unified School District Office is open Monday through Friday from 8:00 a.m. to 4:30 p.m.

INVERNESS ELEMENTARY SCHOOL

Grades: Kindergarten - 1
Bayview and Mesa Street
Point Reyes Station, CA 94956
(415) 669-1018

55 students

School hours:
8:45 to 12:00 (Kindergarten)
8:45 to 2:45 (Grade 1)
Library hours: 90 minutes per day

Inverness Elementary School offers developmentally appropriate education for primary age children.

The school has three K-1 classrooms. Average class size is 20 students.

TOMALES ELEMENTARY SCHOOL

Grades Kindergarten - 8
40 John Street
Tomales, CA 94971
(707) 878-2214

250 students

School hours:
8:30 to 12:00 (Kindergarten)
8:30 to 2:50 (Grades 1 - 8)
Library hours: 8:30 to 3:00

Bilingual education, literacy technology, and assessment are the focus of curriculum development at Tomales Elementary School. The average class size is 19 students.

Parcel tax funds provide programs in music, drama, library, art, computer, counseling, and provide instructional assistants.

The school has a Bilingual Advisory Council to address the needs of bilingual learners.

WEST MARIN ELEMENTARY SCHOOL

Grades: Kindergarten - 8
11550 Highway 1
Point Reyes Station, CA 94956
(415) 663-1014

180 students

School hours: 8:45 to 3:00
Library hours: 8:30 to 3:00

Reading, language arts, English as a Second Language, and physical education are the focus of curriculum improvement at West Marin Elementary School. 2nd and 3rd grade classes average 20 students per teacher. Classes in 4th through 8th grade average 25 students.

TOMALES HIGH SCHOOL

Grades 9 - 12
Irvin Lane
Tomales, CA 94971
(707) 878-2286

295 students

School hours: 8:40 to 3:10
Library hours: 8:30 to 3:00

Curriculum improvement is an ongoing part of the daily academic program at Tomales High School. The average class size is 17.2 students per teacher.

Funds from the parcel assessment are allocated to expanding library resources and instructional programs for art, science, computers, and music.

TAMALPAIS UNION HIGH SCHOOL DISTRICT

P.O. Box 605
Larkspur, CA 94977
(415) 945-3720 Fax: (415) 945-3719

The Tamalpais Union High School District provides secondary school education to students residing in ten elementary districts in central and southern Marin: Bolinas-Stinson Union, Kentfield, Lagunitas, Larkspur, Mill Valley, Nicasio, Reed Union, Ross, Ross Valley, and Sausalito School Districts. The Tamalpais Union High School District includes three comprehensive high schools: Redwood, Sir Francis Drake, Tamalpais, all of which are California Distinguished Schools, and two alternative schools, San Andreas

Continuation and Tamiscal Independent Study. District enrollment is 3,363 students. Tamalpais Union High School District students also reside in the Marin Community College District. The Tamalpais Union High School District office is open Monday through Friday from 7:30 a.m. to noon and 1:00 p.m. to 4:30 p.m.

In 1997-1998, 64% of the District's seniors took the SAT exams (compared to 43% nationally), and the District's mean verbal and math scores were 557 and 562 respectively; well above the national mean scores of 505 and 512.

REDWOOD HIGH SCHOOL

Grades: 9 - 12
395 Doherty Drive
Larkspur, CA 94939
(415) 924-6200

1,300 students

School hours: 8:00 to 3:10
Library hours: 7:30 to 4:00

Redwood High School occupies 57 acres in a residential area of Larkspur. As one of northern California's top academic high schools, Redwood offers an outstanding college preparatory curriculum which includes Honors and Advanced Placement classes, as well as the opportunity for individual study and research through a Senior Project program.

SIR FRANCIS DRAKE HIGH SCHOOL

Grades 9 - 12
1327 Sir Francis Drake Boulevard
San Anselmo, CA 94960
(415) 453-8770

1,013 students

School hours: 8:00 to 3:20
Library hours: 7:30 to 4:00

Sir Francis Drake High School is located in a residential section of San

Sir Francis Drake High School, San Anselmo.

Anselmo in the Ross Valley. The facilities consist of a series of one-story buildings, a large gymnasium, pool, tennis courts, playing fields, and art studios in a nicely landscaped environment.

Drake High School has a mix of renowned integrated curricula and rigorous traditional and honors programs that focus on preparing students for college and life in a rapidly changing world.

In November 1999, Drake was honored by The United States Department of Education as a "NEW AMERICAN HIGH SCHOOL," an award that reflects "Dramatic improvement in the quality of education for students."

TAMALPAIS HIGH SCHOOL

Grades: 9 - 12
Miller Avenue and Camino Alto
Mill Valley, CA 94941
(415) 388-3292

950 students
School hours: 8:00 to 4:00

Library hours: Mon., Tues., Thurs. and Fri.: 7:30 to 4:00 ; Wed.: 7:30 to 4:30

Tamalpais High School, founded in 1908, is the oldest school in the Tamalpais Union High School District. The school is renowned for the beauty of its college-style campus featuring clusters of classroom buildings surrounded by landscaped grounds, art studios, computer labs, a media center in the library, two pools, two gymnasiums, and expansive athletic fields.

With 85% of graduates entering college, Tam offers a strong college preparatory program, including Honors and Advanced Placement, and features unique programs integrating English and social studies, the sciences, and a project-based Interactive College Prep Math class.

Mary Jane Burke became the Marin County Superintendent of Schools in January of 1995. She was reelected without opposition to her second term in June of 1998. She is an enthusiastic spokesperson for public education and has presided over an unprecedented surge in public interest and involvement in the 19 school districts of Main County. She has enlisted business, government, nonprofit agencies and community members in supporting public schools. The result has been test scores that lead the state in every academic area and a majority of high school graduates enrolling in college or university.

Under Ms. Burke's leadership, the Marin County Office of Education offers a variety of special programs on behalf of all students in the county—Special Education, Alternative Education, the Regional Occupational Program and leadership in the School to Career effort. In Alternative Education, the Marin County Office of Education operates Sobriety High School—a charter school for students in recovery from alcohol and drug use. In the Regional Occupational Program, courses are offered for high school students and adults in auto repair, hairstyling, business technology, health service professions, electronics, entrepreneurship and marketing, radio broadcasting, television production, welding and word processing. Special Education serves students from those who need some special help to those who are severely challenged. School to Career relates the world of work to the academic experience.

During Ms. Burke's tenure as Marin County Superintendent of Schools, all schools in Marin County have been brought into the new electronic era. Instruction in computers, the Internet and e-mail are a part of all classrooms. Teachers have been trained and students have been challenged to master the computer skills needed for them to acquire the basic knowledge, skills and attitudes required to be self-fulfilled productive citizens. In addition, Ms. Burke has offered extensive professional training to teachers and provided programs for parents and students. Working with law enforcement, county agencies, school districts and nonprofit groups, a School/Law Enforcement Partnership was formed to work on the issues of school safety.

Born and raised in Stockton, California, Mary Jane Burke is the oldest of eight children. She is a graduate of Dominican University of California in San Rafael, where she earned her Bachelor of Arts and Master of Arts degrees. She holds credentials as a teacher in regular and special education and as an administrator.

Ms. Burke began her work at the Marin County Office of Education as a volunteer and instructional assistant in special education. She then became a teacher in special education. She served as a Principal, Program Manager for Due Process, Director of the Special Education Local Plan Area, Director of Employer/Employee Relations, Assistant Superintendent for Education Services and Personnel and Deputy Superintendent. She is active in many civic organizations.

A mother of two children who are both graduates of Marin County public schools and now in college, Mary Jane Burke understands the importance of education from the parent's point of view. Her late husband, Dr. Larry Lyon, was superintendent of the Dixie School District for 15 years. Ms. Burke always asks one question about anything that her office does —"Is it good for kids?" She believes that everyone should be involved in our schools because it is in the classrooms where differences are made for children and families. Making those differences, Ms. Burke believes, is the most important work in the world.

The Author

Patricia Arrigoni has written about Marin County since 1965 when she joined the staff of the *Ross Valley Reporter,* contributing feature articles, photographs, and a weekly column. A graduate of Dominican University of California in San Rafael, she was also employed there as Director of Public Information.

As a free-lance writer, Arrigoni has traveled extensively in Europe, Africa, the Far East, Central and South America, the United States and Canada. She worked as travel editor of the five Marin Scope Newspapers for ten years and published in many Bay Area newspapers and magazines. She was also syndicated weekly with Gannett News Service of Arlington, Virginia, for four years, writing travel articles and supplying photographs. She has had a one-woman photography show at the Marin County Civic Center, primarily of African and Galapagos wildlife. This same photo exhibit showed in several business offices and banks in Marin and San Francisco.

She currently writes a travel column and contributes features and photographs to the *Marin Independent Journal* in Marin County. Her articles are also syndicated by Copley News Service (San Diego), on a free-lance basis. She is Senior Editor of the magazine *International Travel News* (Sacramento), to which she contributes a column, photographs and feature articles.

Arrigoni has written a popular book for children titled *Harpo, the Baby Harp Seal,* based on four trips to the ice floes in the Gulf of St. Lawrence, Canada, where she witnessed the birth of these seals.

In June, 1999, an original two hour Movie-of-the-Week, *Silent Predators,* based on a novel written by Arrigoni and Fred Brown, was shown on the Turner Television Superstation. Von Zerneck/Sertner Films produced the movie for Ted Turner and it has continued to air regularly in 2000.

Patricia Arrigoni is past president of the Travel Journalists Guild, a national group based in Chicago. She is a member of the Bay Area Travel Writers in San Francisco, Wednesday Morning Dialogue (a Marin women's business group), and the Bay Area Independent Publishers Association as well as several local historical societies.

Patricia is married to Peter Arrigoni, and they have two children, James and Robert. James and his wife Trudy are parents of granddaughter Samantha Rose Arrigoni.

ACKNOWLEDGEMENTS

Acknowledgments from previous editions.

As I compiled the facts for this book, hundreds of people helped me by answering questions, reading portions of the manuscript for accuracy, and making intelligent suggestions. I should particularly like to thank:

Sarah Allen, field researcher on marine mammals; Bill Allen, President, Fairfax Historical Society; Ron Angier, Mt. Tamalpais State Park; Adele Anthony, San Francisco Theological Seminary; Frank Archibald, San Geronimo Valley Water Treatment Plant; Bob Armstrong, park technician, Corps of Engineers Bay Model, Sausalito; Peter R. Arrigoni, former Marin County supervisor.

Lynn Bagley, aide to Congressman John Burton; William T. Bagley, former Marin assemblyman; Thomas J. Barfield, Marin historian and writer; Beverly Bastian, The Landmarks Society of Belvedere and Tiburon; Peter Behr, former state senator; Sheila Berg, Dixie Schoolhouse Foundation; Connie Berto, consultant on horses and trail maps; Woody Binford, founder of first Marin airport; Pat Briggs, Bay Conference Center; Don Brittson, Marin County Farm Advisor; Le Roy Brock, chief ranger, Point Reyes National Seashore; Mary Bruce, typist and Slide Ranch; Charmaine Burdell, Marin historian; Cassie Burke, ranger at Angel Island State Park.

Carney Campion, Golden Gate Bridge, Highway and Transportation District; Gordon L. Chan, biology department, College of Marin; Margaret Coady, Novato historian; Katherine Coddington, San Anselmo Historical Museum; Nancy Curley, Larkspur Heritage Committee; Carol Dahlman, Larkspur Recreation Department; Robert E. David, Golden Gate Bridge District photographer; Mary Case Dekker, curator of Falkirk Community Cultural Center; Don Dimitratos, Marin County Parks and Recreation Department; Peter Dreyfus, Mill Valley Library.

Carla Ehat, Marin Oral History Program; James Farley, Manager, Marin Center; Fred Faude; Roy Flatt, ranger at Mt. Tamalpais State Park; Al Fleming, Marin City Development Corp.; Francis T. Fogarty, manager, Marin County Chamber of Commerce and Visitor's Bureau; Glen Fuller, Muir Woods National Monument; Alan Freeland, lawyer.

Betty Gardner, West Marin historian; Gary Giacomini, Marin County supervisor; Dan Goltz, former San Anselmo planning commissioner; Charles Grasso, Fairfax historian and police chief; Carl Harrington, Golden Gate Ferries; Harry Hearfield, Golden Gate Bridge, Highway and Transportation District; Burr Heneman, executive director, Point Reyes Bird Observatory; Marvin Hershey, site manager, Muir Woods National Monument; Jean Hitchcock, Mill Valley Public Library; Dave Hodgson, Sausalito Historical Society; Ken Hough, Golden Gate Bridge, Highway and Transportation District; Don Hunter, director of parks and recreation for Mill Valley; Brian Hubbard, Richardson Bay Audubon Center and Sanctuary.

Pierre Joske, director, Marin Parks and Recreation Department; Robert Kane, publisher, Presidio Press; Alice C. Katzung, executive director, Marin Wildlife Center; Anne T. Kent, Marin Oral History Program; Martye Kent; Betty Krause, Larkspur historian; Helen Lamb, Marin Art and Garden Center; Emma M. Lawson; Dewey Livingston, Pt Reyes National Seashore; Bunny Lucheta, aide to Senator Barry Keene; William S. Mailliard, former Marin congressman; Paul S. Marcucii, historian for San Francisco Yacht Club; Adrianne Marcus; Marin Builders Exchange; Jack Mason, historian and writer; Charles Mastin, College of Marin Reference Room; Paul Maxwell, director, Yosemite Institute; Elsie P. Mazzini, president, Marin County Historical Society; William McCluskey, Marin Academy; Don McCune, ranger, Tomales Bay State Park; Ulla McLean, executive secretary, Coastal Parks Association; Barbara Melville, Humane Society of Marin; Ralph Moreno, Reference Room, Mill Valley Public Library; Alison Murphy, Bay Area Discovery Museum; Gayle Murphy, San Domenico Riding School; Phil Murphy, St. Vincent's School; Doug Nadeau, Golden Gate National Recreation Area.

James Neider, California State Parks; Beth Olivier, Marin County Chamber of Commerce; Steve Olsen, district ranger, Marin Headlands; Larry Perkins, ranger, China Camp; David Plant; Kristy S. Powell, manager, Corinthian Yacht Club; Tom Price, former Marin County supervisor; Inez Purser; Earl Reink, Mill Valley Library volunteer; Mark Reisenfeld, Marin County Planning Department; Leonard Richardson, headmaster Katharine Branson/Mt. Tamalpais School; Patrick L. Robards, ranger, China Camp; Liz Robertson, Sausalito Historical Soci-

433

ety; Robert Roumiguiere, Marin County supervisor.

Alice Sagar, Fairfax historian; Phil Schaeffer, former director, Western Education Center, Richardson Bay Wildlife Sanctuary; Vera Schultz, former Marin County supervisor; Darrell Scott, general manager, Vindar Aviation; Ruth Scott; Dick Shaler; Susan Shea; Nancy Skinner, College of Marin hiking instructor; Mark Smith, Golden Gate Baptist Theological Seminary; Marion Spillman; Carol Staley, assistant Marin County clerk; Sally Stanford, life-time vice-mayor, Sausalito; Boyd Steward; Madeline Stiver, Miwok Archeological Preserve.

Louise Teather, writer and historian; Elizabeth Terwilliger, naturalist and writer; Silvia Thalman, Miwok Archeological Preserve; Bill Thomas, Golden Gate National Recreation Area; Thompson family, Marin French Cheese Company; Jane Toops, historical photos; Jack Tracy, founder, Sausalito Historical Society; Ron Treleven, publicist, College of Marin; Diane Van Renselaar, editor; Claire Villa, San Anselmo Historical Commission and Historical Society; Ken Watts, Marin Rod and Gun Club; Barbara Weitz, horse information; Lt. White, San Quentin; Ranger Mike Whitehead, Angel Island State Park; Brian Wittenkeller, Marin County Parks and Recreation Department; Maureen Woods, National Marine Fisheries Service; Michael Wornum, former Marin assemblyman and Larkspur city councilman; Mel Zell, Marin Rod and Gun Club; Clerin Zumwalt, Audubon Society.

Thank you to the following people who generously helped update the 2001 edition of *Making the Most of Marin*.

Jim Arrigoni, fishing information; Peter Arrigoni, political history; Marge Bartolini, the Jerry Russom Open Space Area; Beverly Bastian, Belvedere-Tiburon Landmarks Society; Dave Bernardi, Department of Public Works, San Rafael; Bob Berner, Marin Agricultural Land Trust; Connie Berto, horse information and map; and Barbara Blum, Marin County Convention and Visitors Bureau.

Renata Brillinger, Slide Ranch; Mary Jane Burke, Marin County Schools; Matt Cerkel, Marin Municipal Water District lakes; Lynn Chandler, WildCare; Pennell Chapin, Marin Art and Garden Center; Ellen Cohen, Point Reyes Bird Observatory; Mary Currie, Golden Gate Bridge, Highway and Transportation District; Aida Dearteaga, San Quentin Prison; John Dell'Osso, Point Reyes National Sheashore; and Larry Dito, Parks and Recreation, Novato.

Deborah Dollinger, Audubon Canyon Ranch; Chris Edgerton, Marin Historical Society; Carla Ehat, Ross Historical Society; Jim Farley, Marin Center; Mimi Farina, Bread and Roses; Michael Feinstein, Golden Gate National Recreation Area; Nick Franco, Angel Island; Nancy and Larry Gapinski, golf; Eva Ghilotti, horses; Shirley Gremmels, City of Novato; Dr. L. Martin Griffin, Audubon Canyon Ranch and Audubon Cypress Grove, Tomales Bay; Ed Hulme, Chief Park Ranger, Marin County.

Erik Johansson, tennis; Rick Johnson, Marin Humane Society and dog parks; Jane Lange, Falkirk Cultural Center; Brita Larsson, Romberg Tiburon Center; Lawson's General Store, Dillon Beach; Gail Lester, Marin Headlands; Fred Lew, Olompali State Historic Park; Joan Lisetor, College of Marin; and Casey May, Marin Municipal Water District.

Carlene McCart, San Rafael Parks; Dan McNear, McNear's Brickyard; Ron Miska, City of San Rafael Open Space; Mia Monroe, Muir Woods; Dolly Nave, bocce ball courts, Albert Park and Marin Community Fields; Lois Parks, Tomales Regional History Center; Carlos Parrata, Tomales Bay State Park; Tom Peters, Marin Community Foundation, and Cathy Petrick, GGNRA camping.

Elaine and Bill Petrocelli, Book Passage; Steve Petterle, Open Space and Park Planner for the County of Marin; Carol Pott-Berry, San Francisco Theological Seminary; John Reese, Marin Humane Society; Dolores Richards, Bolinas Museum; Pat Robard, China Camp; Ken Robbins, Marin Airport; Bob Roumiguiere, political history; and Shirley Schaufel, Marin Museum of the American Indian.

Nancy Skinner, Mt. Tamalpais and historical photos; Lori Stokes, Dominican University of California; Don Streeper, San Rafael Parks; Laura Williams, Point Reyes Bird Observatory; and Maryann Woodruff, transcription and proofing.

434

Index

E

F

G

I

J

Jack London, 33, 34
Jack Mason Library, 322
Jack Mason Museum, 330, 332
Jackson, George, 211
Jackson, Jonathan, 211
James Guthrie Associates, 48
Jean, Eleanor McArdle, 165
Jensen, Donald A., 206
Jepson Memorial Grove, 323
Jerry Russom Open Space Area, 218
Jewell, Ellen Dolliver, 125
Joe Pedrolli and Son, 194
Johannson, Erik, **363**
John F. McInnis County Park, 220, 368
John Reed's mill, **49**, 58
John Thomas Howell Botanical Garden, 67
Johnson's Oyster Farm, 314
Johnson, Huey, 147
Johnstone Trail, 323
Jones, George, 205
Jones, Henry, 241
Jones, Tom, 402
Jordan, Leland, 206
Jose Moya del Pino Library, **151**, 152, 176
Juan B.R. Cooper, 145
Juan Manuel de Ayala Vista Point, 8
Junction, The, 119, 155
Justin Morgan, 308

K

Kaiser Hospital, 217
Kashow, Israel, 75
    Island, 75
    house, 76
    and yacht club, 76
Keanograph Factory, 164
Keeler, Ken, **405**
Keener, Robert "Bunkie", 74
Kehoe Beach, 326
Kelley Brothers, 76
Kenneth C. Patrick Information Center, 305, 319
Kent Dam, 268
Kent family, 142
    Kent, Adaline, 139, 141
    Kent, Albert, 139
    Kent, Anne, 141, 142
    Kent, Elizabeth Thacher, 141
    Kent, Martye, 141
    Kent, Roger, 142, 147
    Kent, Sherman, 142

Kent, Thomas, 141
Kent, William, 100, 102, 104, 108, 139, 141
    and Muir Woods Inn, 100
    and Redwood Canyon, 100, 102
Kent Island, 290, 324
Kent Lake, 169, 371
Kent, A.E., Middle School, 410
Kent Woodlands, 119, 142, 324
Kentfield, 110, 119, 124, 132, 133, 137, 139
    School District, 410
    Stadium, 141
Kettenhofen, Ernest "Kett", 147
Keys Creek, 337
Keys Creek/Walker Creek Delta Saltwater
    Wildlife Sanctuary, 336
Keys Embarcadero, 337
Keys Estero, 337
Keys, John, 337
Kilham Farm, 348, 352
Kilham, Lumpy, 348
King Ranch, 124
King, B. B., 56, 57
King, Patrick, 124
Kingston Trio, 57
Kirby Cove, 17
Kittle, A. J., 151
Konatich, Anton, 334
Korean War, 79
Krause, Betty, 124, 127, 128
Kritzberg, Fred, 129
Kule Loklo, 305, 307, 308

L

Lagoon Courts, 368
Laguna Ranch, 311
Lagunitas, 263, 268
    School, 411
    School District, 410
Lagunitas Creek, 259, 333
Lagunitas Development Company, 262
Lagunitas Lake, 110, 111, 169, 352-353, 371
Lake Alpine, 111
Lake Ewok, 276
Land grant, 174
    Lucas Valley, 174
    Marinwood, 174
    San Pedro Point, 174
    San Pedro, Santa Margarita, y Las
        Gallinas, 174
    Terra Linda, 174
Land Investors Research, 335
Landmark Associates, 242
Landmarks Society, 64, 67, 73, 76

M

MacKenzie, Alister, 366
MacPhail, Bruce, 129
Madrone Group, 271
Madrone Picnic Area, 269
Maggiora and Ghilotti Contractors, 129, 194
    Ghilotti, Gary, 129
    Ghilotti, Glen, 129
    Ghilotti, Greg, 129
    Ghilotti, H.J. Babe, 129
    Ghilotti, Jim, 129
    Lehman, Ted, 129
Mahoney, Jim, 129
Mailliard, Adolph, 261, 266
    and Bonaparte, Joseph, 261
Mailliard, William Somers, 261
Mainack, Jim, **405**
Major General John Fulton Reynolds, 86
Maloney, Douglas, 113, 249, 252
Mangus, Ashley, **351**
Manka's, 313
Manor Hill, 163, 164
Manor School, 420
Mansion Row, **172**, 176, 178, **179, 184, 185**
Maple Lawn, 178, **179**, 180
Mar-Ghi Arabians, 348
Marconi Conference Center, 113, 334
Marconi Wireless Company, 333
Maria B. Freitas Park, 217, 368
Mariani, Eugene, 36
Marilli, Elizabeth, 126
Marilli, Serefino, 126, **128**
Marin 4-H Club, 355
Marin Academy, 179, 184, **185**
Marin Agricultural Land Trust (MALT), 113,
    264, 275, 330
Marin Airporter, 228, 401
Marin Art and Garden Center, **151**-152, 176
Marin Arts Council, 181, 183
Marin Audubon Society, 90
Marin Ballet, 402
Marin Beach and Tennis Club, 197, 369
Marin Boys School, 163
Marin Builders Exchange, 146, 149, **247**
Marin Catholic High School, 132, 265
Marin Center Box Office, 402
Marin Charter and Tours, 401
Marin Chinese Cultural Group, 202
Marin City Community Development
    Corporation, 47
Marin City Community Services District, 47
Marin City Redevelopment Agency, 47
Marin City, USA, 47, 48
Marin Community College District, 144, 233

Marin Community Fields, 129, **130**
Marin Community Foundation, 23, 47, 146,
    181, 182, 184, 193, 249, 250, 251, 263,
    264, 284
Marin Conservation Corps, 113
Marin Conservation League, 112, 147, 152, 192,
    335
Marin Council of Agencies, 113, 265
Marin Council of Boy Scouts of America, 167,
    214
Marin Country Club, 366
Marin Country Day School, 79
Marin County,
    Airport, 246
    Board of Supervisors, 25, 48, 73, 113, 147,
        162, 192, 212, 259, 271, 275, 300, 320
    Chamber of Commerce, 113
    Civic Center, 152, 171, 196, 198, 203, **205,
        206, 207,** 208, **210,** 215, 220, 360
        Auditorium, **209**
        Lagoon, **211,** 216
        Volunteer Office, 208
    Conservation League, 271
    Dog Park Groups, 360
    Fair, 152, 278, 402, **405**
    Library, 142
        Anne Kent California Room, 143
    Marin Center, 399, 402, **404, 405**
    Nature Preserve, 289
    Office of Education, 407
    Open Space District, 253, 263, 343, 356, 357,
        360
    Parks Department, 245
    Pony Club, 350, 355
    Public Schools, 407
    Sheriff, 356
    Shootout, 216
    Superintendent of Schools, 407
    Superior Court Judge Harold Haley, 211
Marin Countywide Plan, 148
Marin Dance Theatre, 402
Marin Forum, 4
Marin French Cheese Company, 279
Marin Fruit and Grocery, 36
Marin Garden Club, 152
Marin General Hospital, 131
Marin Golf and Country Club, 233
Marin Grand Jury, 162
Marin Headlands, xi, 7, 9, 11, 19, 47, 147, 345
    Hostel, 20, **21**
    Visitor Center, 361
Marin Heritage, 181
Marin Historical Society, 172, 176, 178, 179,
    180, 186
Marin Horse Council, 356
Marin Humane Society, 233, 359, 360

O

R

S

Photographs on previous pages:

Page 459   Looking down an estero into Drake's Bay in the Point Reyes National Seashore.

Page 460   Drake's Beach, Point Reyes National Seashore.

Page 461   Ten Mile Beach, Point Reyes National Seashore.

ORDER FORM

For **MAKING THE MOST OF MARIN** $24.95

By mail from the publisher:

Travel Publishers International
P.O. Box 1030, Fairfax, CA 94978

Name:_____

Address:_____

City:_____ State:_____Zip:_____

Telephone: _____

eMail _____

Please make checks payable to: Travel Publishers International

	Qty.	Cost	Total
Making the Most of Marin	1	$24.95	$24.95

Sales Tax:
(In CA. add 7 % (0.07) per book
or $1.75 per book) $ 1.75

Shipping:
Book Rate: Add $4.00 for the first
book and $1.75 for each additional book $ 4.00

                Total for one book: $30.70

For each additional book, add $28.40   _____

            TOTAL ENCLOSED: _____

Telephone orders:
Book Passage, (415) 927-0960. Open until 10:00 p.m. daily.

MAP:
Horse Trails of Marin